THE GROTESQUE IN PHOTOGRAPHY

THE GROTESQUE

IN PHOTOGRAPHY

designed by ALBERT SQUILLACE

...SQUE

by A.D. COLEMAN

A RIDGE PRESS BOOK

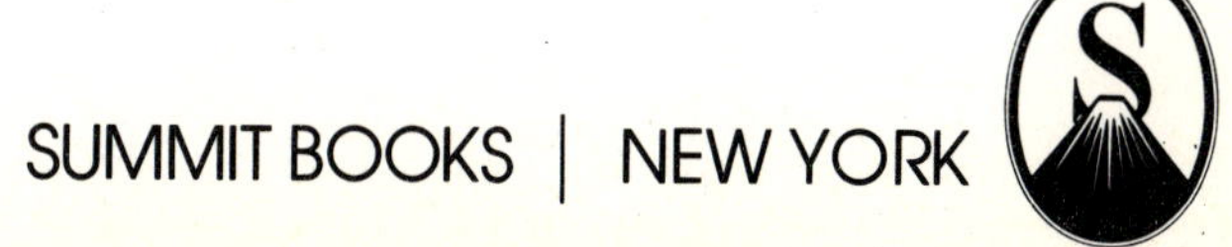

SUMMIT BOOKS | NEW YORK

To T., my partner, for seeing me through another.

Completion of this project was made possible in part
by an Art Critic's Fellowship from the National Endowment
for the Arts in Washington, D.C., for which
I wish to thank my fellow citizens. I hope it reflects
something of their awesome diversity.
   I am grateful to the various sources — mostly
the photographers themselves — who have made these
images available for reproduction,
as well as to all those photographers, whether included
or not, whose work has led to this study.
   I'd also like to express my appreciation
to Adie Suehsdorf, Al Squillace, and Jerry Mason,
for tenacity (or faith) above and beyond the call of duty;
and also to Ruth Birnkrant and Ronne Peltzman for
their assistance, advice, and encouragement.
         A.D.C.

Editor-in-Chief: Jerry Mason
Editor: Adolph Suehsdorf
Art Director: Albert Squillace
Associate Editor: Ronne Peltzman
Associate Editor: Joan Fisher
Art Associate: Liney Li
Art Production: Doris Mullane

Coleman, Allan D
  The grotesque in photography.

  "A Ridge Press book."
  1. Photography of the grotesque.   I. Title.
TR686.C64   779   77-22678
ISBN 0-671-40014-2
ISBN 0-671-40016-9 pbk.

Printed and bound in Italy by Mondadori Editore, Verona.

CONTENTS

INTRODUCTION

By the end of the 1960's it must have been apparent to any alert observer that a generation of photographers was actively engaged in stretching the boundaries of their medium by overriding externally imposed limitations and violating all prohibitions in regard to technique, form, style, subject matter, and content.

Given the spirit of that decade, which embraced flux, experiment, innovation, and iconoclasm in all the arts, that was hardly surprising. In responding to their imagery in my role as a critic, I found myself provoked and stimulated in a variety of ways by much of it. Moreover, I found myself disturbed and left uneasy by encounters with certain photographs—not because they were unpleasant on a purely sensory level, but because some relationship between style, technique, form, subject matter, content, cultural context, and the medium itself generated emotional and intellectual stress. These images aroused discomfiture, anxiety, anger—feelings I did not associate with what was generally called "creative" photography.

It rapidly became clear that this was not the accidental effect of occasional images. Certain kinds of photographs—and, significantly, many photographs by certain photographers—evoked these responses consistently, not only from me but from others. There was no value judgment involved (at least not on my part), merely the fact of my reactions. The work simply existed; my problem was coming to terms with my response to it. Habitually, my solution to that problem is to seek the right questions. In this case, the questions that confronted me critically were: Why did this imagery have this effect? How could this phenomenon be described and defined?

In searching for a means of describing, interpreting, evaluating, and explaining these images, I came finally to the concept of *the grotesque*. Of all the terms I considered (and eventually discarded), it was the only one that effectively encompassed the diverse but related pictures that are discussed and in many cases reproduced in this volume.

The grotesque is a loaded term, one that carries a great deal of emotional and even cultural weight. That became evident not only during the course of my research into its origin and evolution but also in correspondence with the photographers whose work I believe exemplifies it. Many of those who are included in this collection were disturbed by the term, even when they themselves employed all its synonyms in referring to their work. Of the others who are mentioned here but not represented by images, a considerable number are absent as a result of their own refusal (or that of their representatives) to accept the application of that term to their imagery.

Yet the power inherent in the word is not inappropriate to the charged nature of these photographs. And of all the common synonyms for works of this sort, *the grotesque* is the only one with an extensive history of critical usage in the visual arts. Additionally, it has been utilized not only as a descriptive adjective but as a modality—a distinctive conceptual framework, inclusion within which involves characteristic cognitive and performative operations. That is, works within the grotesque mode—at least those deliberately created to evoke the particular response — embody certain specific attitudes and understandings communicated by way of certain specific methods.

My intent in anthologizing and grouping these images has been to establish a groundwork for consideration of the grotesque as a mode of photography. I believe it is particularly pertinent to contemporary photography. In the next chapter I have attempted to indicate its historical antecedents within the medium itself. I have refrained from tracing its origins back into the history of the other graphic arts on the assumption that such connections can be easily made by the reader. To be sure, the images in this book have parallels elsewhere in the other visual arts, whether in ancient Greek frescoes, illuminated manuscripts, medieval bestiaries, or the works of such masters as Bosch, Breughel, Goya, Tchelitchew, Orozco, and countless others. The impulse from which the grotesque springs is ancient and deep. But rather than establishing "credentials" for such work in photography by belaboring its analogues in other media, I have been concerned with exploring its photographic evolution, variety, and volume.

This book, therefore, should not be considered a definitive study. For various reasons, a considerable amount of imagery central to this mode was unavailable for inclusion in this volume—enough so that I hesitate even to call it comprehensive. Moreover, I have no doubt that there is much relevant work that has been overlooked. Certainly one consequence of this publication will be to acquaint me with the extent of my own ignorance of the field.

From my standpoint, this book is a critical survey—a foundation, a beginning. Certain lines of inquiry merit much further investigation. For example, why have so few women worked extensively in this mode? Why has it been so persistently slighted by critics and historians? What impact is it having on its culture? What are the connections between and influences on these particular artists?

The issues raised by this body of imagery are not only crucial to photography and to contemporary art generally, but reach into psychology, sociology, and history. It is my hope that this initial survey will stimulate others to add their own perceptions and questions to mine.

In exploring the concept of the grotesque as it applies to photography and as it manifests itself in various forms of photographic imagery, a dilemma that is essentially semantic must be acknowledged.

The term *grotesque* has several established meanings and an even larger number of accepted vernacular usages.* Unlike much of the descriptive and analytical vocabulary applied to the visual arts, the word *grotesque* actually originated as a description of a particular form of visual art. Its source is Italian: *La grottesca* (noun) and *grottesco* (adjective) are both derived from *grotta*, meaning "cave." They were "coined to designate a certain ornamental style which came to light during the late fifteenth-

century excavations, first in Rome and then in other parts of Italy as well, and which turned out to constitute a hitherto unknown ancient form of ornamental painting."† That style of painting was distinguished by its emphasis on unnatural, biomorphic mergings of plant, animal, and human features.

At its birth, then, the word had a quite narrow and specific meaning, restricted to a certain genre of graphic art. Over time, however, its meanings multiplied and expanded. Other forms of visual art were grouped under its aegis. Applied to music, it was utilized to denote certain melodic and harmonic structures. In literature, it was employed as a classification for several sorts of language, setting, action, and protagonist.

Even within the comparatively narrow confines of the creative media, therefore, the word was gradually put to serve diverse tasks. In those contexts *the grotesque* implied, among other things, dissonance; exaggeration (usually beyond the point of caricature, which was generally seen as a separate though related category); anomalousness or incongruity; and major spiritual deformity. Consistently, too, whether implicitly or explicitly, the term carried metaphysical and philosophical connotations, suggesting that the proverbially beneficial natural order of things had been subverted or had even had the lie given to it.

Webster's Seventh New Collegiate Dictionary gives the following definitions.

grotesque: n.
  1. a piece of decorative art characterized by fanciful human and animal forms often interwoven with foliage or similar figures that may distort the natural into absurdity, ugliness, or caricature.
grotesque: adj.
  of, relating to, or having the characteristics of grotesque: as (a): fanciful, bizarre (b): absurdly incongruous (c): departing markedly from the natural, the expected, or the typical. Syn.: see *fantastic*.
grotto:
  1: cave. 2: an artificial recess or structure made to resemble a natural cave.

†This quotation is from *The Grotesque in Art and Literature* (1957) by the late Wolfgang Kayser. I have drawn extensively on this classic study, as references to it in the text will indicate. Kayser's propositions have been invaluable to my understanding of the mode. His analyses of the grotesque—particularly its metaphysical implications—were grounded in a modernist sensibility; he was highly sympathetic to the philosophical issues underlying this "comprehensive structural principle of works of art."

7

As the word came into the vernacular its meanings were broadened even further, to such an extent that it now covers not only severe physical abnormality but even inappropriate though not particularly uncommon human behavior. Thus diluted and defused, it is not surprising that the word entered into British adolescent slang during the 1960's in a tolerantly diminutive form—"grotty"—as a synonym for the merely peculiar, unpleasant, and unhip.

Yet these distinct and considerable shifts in the meanings of this word are more than simply those inevitable changes which all language undergoes in popular usage. I would suggest that something more significant is represented thereby: a gradual but profound alteration of Western culture's world view, a major revision of its perception of "normality." And I would further suggest that much of that alteration can be traced to the impact of photography on that culture.

Consider the word's evolution. Originally it is used exclusively to denote imagistic fantasies whose impact on their viewers is due in large part to that audience's recognition of the biological impossibility of those forms. The effect of that art is therefore largely attributable to an awareness of the artist's intentional violation of natural laws in conceiving those visions. Though that meaning remains operative, another comes to join it, seemingly its antithesis: those demonstrably possible and even documentable natural phenomena and forms of human behavior that are only divergent from the norm.

Is this simply coincidental—that a word should come to mean such different things? Or have the attitudes behind the definitions shifted? And if so, why?

The descriptive verisimilitude of photography—its capacity for arresting permanently the light reflected off the surface of small segments of reality—had no precedent among the graphic arts or in any form of visual communication. Camera optics continually reaffirm, in a most reassuring manner, the Renaissance perspective in which we have been trained to see. In a culture addicted to "reason" as exemplified by the scientific method, photography's technological and mechanistic premises are sufficient proof of the unimpeachability of photographic images as accurate and trustworthy documents.

Most early writings on photography encapsulate those responses. The enchantment of the medium was its credibility, which in turn was based on its automatic verification of the highly arbitrary strategies of Renaissance perspective, which are deeply ingrained in Western culture. The uncanny accuracy and exquisite detail of photographic imagery was cited repeatedly in those writings. The camera (a construction of wood, metal, cloth, and glass) was frequently referred to as a "witness," while the photographer tended to be relegated to the position of "operator," as though he or she were not actually the maker of the images but only the impersonal servant of the machine that made them.

Western culture's first and strongest commitment to photography, then, was to its ostensibly accurate, impartial function as a visual recording system. The reasons for this are complex and beyond the scope of this study. But this commitment was (and still is) widespread—indeed, almost unanimous—within that culture. It was also profound and not at all limited to the visually naïve. As recently as 1953, for example, so sophisticated a theorist of the visual arts as William M. Ivins, Jr., then Curator of Prints and Drawings of the Metropolitan Museum of Art, called photography the first visual medium "without syntax." By that he meant that under normal operating conditions there supposedly was no human interference between the event in front of the lens and the image that resulted.

With a belief in the photograph's objectivity so prevalent, it is hardly surprising that one of the first applications of photography was the visual exploration of the external world, particularly its more remote and exotic aspects. Thus employed, one of the medium's earliest effects was to amplify the truth of Hamlet's admonition to

Horatio: "There are more things in heaven and earth . . . than are dreamt of in your philosophy." This has been one of photography's continuing contributions to the perception of the world. Presenting as it does a reasonable two-dimensional replication of its subjects, photography opened up to members of a photographic culture a variety of vicarious experience whose range and quantity was inconceivable prior to the medium's invention. Suddenly it became possible to observe objects, creatures, people, and events from all parts of the globe, in all the astonishing and unimaginable diversity of the real world—far more than any single human being could encounter in person in the course of a lifetime.

Photography, then, can be said to have generated a major alteration of world view. In doing so, it led to an inescapable conclusion. There was little the creative imagination could conceive, no matter how apparently absurd or extreme, that did not have its parallel somewhere in the natural world or in the panorama of human behavior. And there was much in reality beside which the most seemingly exaggerated imaginative projections paled by comparison. In this new context the concept of *the grotesque* required revision. Within a homogeneous society whose world view is restricted, abnormality can be a fixed and even absolute idea. In a fluid society able to see beyond its own perimeters, abnormality becomes relative. People who pierce their noses with pieces of bone are grotesque only among those who do not.

Consequently, in coming to some definition of the grotesque in photography, two often contradictory sets of guidelines must be considered simultaneously. One of those circumscribes the traditional meaning of the word as applied to the visual arts, aimed here at its specifically photographic manifestations: certain kinds of hallucinatory, visionary images that violate common knowledge of the workings of the natural world. Because that meaning is comparatively exact, it is relatively simple to determine what imagery is appropriately categorized thereby.

But another set of guidelines must also be taken into account. They outline the newer meanings of the term as a synonym for nonfictional phenomena (and images thereof) that exist at or beyond the edges of cultural and psychological norms—violations of the social order rather than the natural order of things. Those are not one and the same, and descriptions of real events that force the recognition of the arbitrariness of beliefs, standards, and value systems reassert that distinction.

The latter is a much looser gauge than the former, for those norms are constantly changing. The commonplace events and behavior of one culture, social stratum, or era may become the grotesqueries of another. As far as possible, I have attempted to compensate for my own subjectiveness and biases by including in that second category images whose grotesqueness is not solely a matter of my own opinion. In most cases, either the general subject matter or the images themselves have been elsewhere defined as grotesque.

This does not mean that I find all the images that follow to be grotesque. Nor should the reader feel constrained to do so. Ever since the term entered into the critical vocabulary its application has been the subject of debate, no doubt because its connotations have been so varied and wide-ranging. In defining a work as grotesque, the response is as essential as the structure. Ideally, this broad cross section will enable readers to pinpoint its meaning for themselves.

In concluding his study, Wolfgang Kayser offers three hallmarks of the grotesque. "The grotesque is the estranged world. . . . The grotesque is a play with the absurd. . . . The grotesque is an attempt to invoke and subdue the demonic aspects of the world." Keeping those in mind, an examination of the images that follow may lead to some clearer and more precise understanding of *the grotesque*—and may also reveal something about the enormous shaping influence of photography on the perception of the world and the lives lived within it.

1 THE ROOTS OF

To begin with, a truism: The history of photography encompasses all photographs ever made. This might seem self-evident. Yet much of what is generally defined as "the history of photography" has been restricted quite narrowly (and often politically) to certain branches of what is variously called "serious," "creative," or "art" photography. That those branches are significant and influential is undeniable. Yet the origins of much contemporary photography of all kinds—including the above—can be traced to other sources. Some of these could be called the vernacular usages of photography, the diverse practical functions for which the medium has proved suitable.

The pervasiveness and multiplicity of such functions is well known. Yet in many cases they are familiar to the general public only by name, not by direct experience. Thus, for instance, while medical, anthropological, and police crime-lab photographs are produced by the millions, their intended audience is specific and extremely limited. Composed of specialists interested primarily in the informational content of these images, that audience is inured or oblivious to their potential emotional impact and does not demand any esthetic resolution or justification.

Presented in a radically different context—that of "serious / creative / art" photography, say—such images might evoke another set of responses. Certainly it would have been possible to assemble a book-length group of them so bizarre and repellent as to alienate most viewers and affect them as grotesque in essence. But that is not the purpose of this survey. My concern in this study is to map tentatively the evolution of the grotesque as a mode of conscious photographic expression, not simply to anthologize informationally intended images whose subject matter alone might predictably shock the reader.

At the same time, such images are unquestionably a part of the tradition of the grotesque in photography and must be accounted for in its history. Many of the contemporary photographers represented here are directly aware of these comparatively obscure and/or naïve grotesqueries. Whether they have deliberately searched them out, accidentally come across them, or encountered them during some overlap of professional activity and personal expression, photographers have come in contact naturally with this imagery. Surely, therefore, it can be said to have exerted an influence on photographers themselves.

As for the general public, the existence of such imagery is a well-established fact even for those who have never seen a single example. Yet such innocence is increasingly rare. This means that the imagery has become part of the visual environment in which other kinds of photographs also operate. Additionally, more and more undeniably grotesque vernacular images have transcended the restrictions of professional applications to become public, or have even been made specifically for public presentation (as with many news and war photographs). Deposited thus in the image banks of mass consciousness, they too contribute to the context in which all photographic imagery must stand for interpretation and evaluation.

Much of the imagery that constitutes the roots of the grotesque in photography can without exaggeration be called unprecedented. Among the many purposes to which photography was applied early on were some that no medium had ever previously performed; they depended entirely on unique characteristics of photography and could even be said to have been invented expressly for it.

Much of that same imagery could also be termed naïve in that there often was no intent to evoke the sense of the grotesque on the part of the photographer, nor any response to the image as grotesque on the part of its original audience. The grotesqueness of many of these pictures is retroactive, the product of the gap between nineteenth-century sensibilities and those of the present.

One clear example of this shift in attitude can be seen in the contrast between the two images of hunters with their kill on page 18. The first is an anonymous postcard made sometime around the turn of the century, evidently intended for distribution by mail to friends in celebration of this achievement. The second, from a recent series by Les Krims titled *The Deerslayers*, takes a decidedly more jaundiced and ambivalent view of the event, although Krims himself is quick to point out that deer hunting is necessary to keep the species from mass starvation through overpopulating available habitat.

For another instance of such change in social mores and its manifestation in photographs, consider the post-mortem daguerreotypes on pages 14–15. Such images began to be commissioned not long after the medium of photography made its public debut in 1839. That was an age in which infant mortality rates were extraordinarily high. Because photography had not yet been simplified enough to be widely accessible as a hobby, most photographs were made by professionals. Few parents had the opportunity—which we take for granted today—of making photographs of their own children. Consequently, if a child died in infancy it was quite likely that no image of it had been made during its lifetime. So it became customary to have dead children photographed on their death beds or in

THE GROTESQUE

their coffins. Sometimes the children's bodies were even brought to the photographer's studio and posed for a portrait in death. (This was also a not-infrequent practice with deceased adults.)

Needless to say, the intent on the part of all concerned was ceremonial, commemorative, solemn, and loving. The act sprang from a poignant, painful cherishing of the subjects, with no suspicion that the resulting images would ever be considered grotesque.

Yet alterations in cultural attitudes toward death have been so drastic—at least in the United States—that by the latter part of the nineteenth century the actual body was photographed far less frequently. As the cabinet photograph by C. E. Dickerman on page 14 indicates, the body itself was replaced by symbols of the deceased and of his/her mourners, in this case a funeral wreath and a photograph of the deceased while still alive. Photographs of cadavers ceased to be made for commemoration and display, and began to be taken principally for the record, as was the case with Charles Heinrichs's morgue photo of a murder victim (page 26). Today in the United States it is highly uncommon for commemorative post-mortem or coffin photographs to be made of anyone other than public figures lying in state. The custom has, however, remained strong in many parts of Europe.

It may not be entirely coincidental that as the evolution of social customs led to a decline in popularity of this form of death imagery another rose to replace it. As though by cultural consensus, certain forms of death were tacitly agreed upon as "public" and therefore worthy of increasingly widespread dissemination by way of the photographic image. War, crime, and disaster (natural or man-made) rapidly became mainstays of such reportage.

In each of these areas, photography provided the public with mounting numbers of images which, by their very nature, offered an involvement with the events depicted on a higher order of magnitude than any of the other existing visual communication systems. The photograph particularized by encoding a specific instant in time and space. Purely manual graphic techniques could not equal that effect. Additionally, the information provided by the photographic image was quite unlike—and often contradictory to—portrayals of the same subjects in the other visual media. For example, the standard approach to military subjects had always been to concentrate on heroics —charging horses, assaults on the barricades, and the like. Owing to technical limitations in equipment and materials, early photographs could not render fast action. So the first photographs of war portrayed the aftermath of battle— demolished buildings, shattered landscapes, and broken bodies. Where painting had directed its attention to the intangible glories of war, photography focused on its ghastly effects.

In different forms, these images reached an ever-growing audience. The photographs made during the Civil War by the "Brady team"—such as the one by Alexander Gardner on page 23—sometimes were converted into several forms of line illustration for reproduction in periodicals. (The halftone process was not invented until the 1880's.) Original prints were sold, singly as well as in sets and bound volumes. Some were stereographic images, made to be viewed through a stereoscope, which far from being a mere parlor fad was in fact the first successful means devised for mass communication by photographic image. For decades it was a rare household that was without a stereoscope; and the images — usually original prints of good quality — provided an effective illusion of three-dimensionality.

The Civil War was perhaps the first major war to be thoroughly documented photographically. Virtually everything that did not fall outside the medium's technical limitations was photographed, including the war's continuing effect on its casualties (page 22). As the medium advanced technically, war photography became an area of specialization with its own bizarre subgenres; aerial photographs of bombing missions, infrared studies of enemy troop movements, and reportage are only a few. Experts in the latter have brought us ever closer to the instant of death. Robert Capa's famous image of the falling Spanish Loyalist comes to mind, as does Eddie Adams's picture of a summary execution in Vietnam (page 28).

Indeed, the photographic history of the Vietnamese conflict—if it is ever assembled—will embody most aspects of the grotesque. In addition to the already published images of death, disfigurement, suffering, and torture, there are voluminous amounts of photographs in private hands that make the published images look tame. It must be remembered that the images that have been published—Nick Ut's picture of the napalmed children running down the road, the many images of flaming Buddhist monks, the color photographs of the My Lai massacre—are those that in one way or another made it past the censors. Many did not and many more were smuggled out. The world is in for a revelation when they eventually surface, as they must.

Unlike painters, photographers had a difficult

time avoiding the realistic details of war's effect on all those it rolled over. The visual accounts they provided in turn affected other artists. It is hardly coincidental that fictional accounts of battle became more grimly realistic in the second half of the nineteenth century, subsequent to the invention of photography. (Stephen Crane's *The Red Badge of Courage*, published in 1895, is a case in point.) Doubtless, these changes reshaped the public's perception of war.

Prior to photography, illustrations of crime stories in tabloids — whether woodcut, line drawing, or engraving — usually depicted the actual criminal acts involved, as reconstructed by the artists. Obviously it was impossible to photograph most crimes when they occurred. So forensic photography and photoreportage of violent crime were devoted initially to consequences: the fate of the victims and, whenever possible, the doom of the culprits. As public execution fell out of legal and social fashion it was replaced by photographic documentation of executions. Alexander Gardner's series on the hanging of the Lincoln conspirators (pages 24–25) includes the ascent to the scaffold, the final rituals, and the twisting bodies among its selected highlights.

One function of such images is to provide graphic evidence that the wages of sin is death. Everything from legal execution to vigilante "justice" (page 24) has been documented photographically — even informal lynching. In our century, faster film and lighter equipment have made possible such astonishing and unique images as Tim Howard's unauthorized photograph of the electrocution of convicted murderer Ruth Snyder (page 29). Taken with a hidden camera on January 13, 1928, it captures the instant of her high-voltage end. The New York *Daily News* filled its front page with this picture. By the 1960's, inevitably, it was no longer surprising to be barraged with photographs illustrating the explosion of an assassinated president's skull or the ad-hoc extermination of his alleged killer. Nor was it startling to find a Latin-American dictatorship providing the world with visual proof of the elimination of one of its archenemies (page 27). That practice was already almost a century old by the time of Che Guevara's death. This can be seen in the stereo card of Jesse James's body by A. A. Hughes on the same page, the photograph of Cole Younger's corpse with the bullet holes neatly marked (page 26), and the postcard—one of many from a souvenir set— showing the mass burning of bodies of defeated Mexican rebels (page 26). These events may have shocked viewers of the pictures, but the existence of the images themselves was taken for granted.

Much the same could be said for photographs of disasters. Fires, floods, train wrecks, airplane crashes, earthquakes—such images provide evidence ad infinitum of either the random violence of a chaotic universe or the wrath of a vengeful god. What has it meant in terms of this culture's world view to have such visual proof dropped at the doorstep for close to a century, to be absorbed with the morning coffee?

Certainly, on the level of individual experience it has its frightening aspects. There is nourishment aplenty for paranoia in endless visual accounts of madness, violence, pain, and mortality. But it brings with it the vicarious thrill of being eyewitness to carnage, balanced by the protection of the photograph's ultimate artificiality. Each such image tacitly exempts its viewers from the specific moment of doom it describes, leaving them free to say, as the British put it, "I'm all right, Jack."

That sequence of responses is similarly evoked by photographs of human oddities. All those shown here were made for comparatively wide distribution and public consumption. Some were made for sale as objects of interest in and of themselves. Mathew Brady's stereograph of Tom Thumb's wedding; the cartes-de-visites of the Siamese twins, the armless lady, and the male dwarf; and the postcard of Margaret Anderson, "World's Smallest Lady" (pages 19–20)—these are all mass-produced photographic prints sold as souvenirs to the general public. Others were made as illustrations for somewhat specialized audiences. O. J. Rejlander's "Fear" (page 22) is one of a series of images made during experiments that led to Charles Darwin's book *The Expression of the Emotions in Man and Animals*, first published in 1872. And Eadweard Muybridge's sequential images (page 21) are from his monumental project, *Animal Locomotion*. Published in 1887, this enormous compendium of human and animal movement was intended for the use of scholars, doctors, scientists, and artists. (The British painter Francis Bacon, whose work contains many grotesque elements, has incorporated a number of Muybridge's images into his canvases, among them this one of a deformed boy walking on all fours.)

With very few exceptions, the work discussed so far was created by photographers who, by their own lights, were not creating grotesqueries or even addressing the theme, but were simply documenting their realities. But the first hundred years of photographic history also contain a variety of grotesqueries in other than strictly documentary form.

Louis Ducos du Hauron, a Frenchman who made the world's first color photographs, also experimented with special lenses and created a series of remarkable self-portraits in the grotesque mode (pages 16–17) in 1888. During the same period it was a hobby of the upper class, particularly in England, to make collages incorporating hand-painted elements, bits of magazine illustrations, and fragments of photographs. Some unusual and distinctly grotesque imagery resulted, notably from the hands of a British financier, Sir Edward Blount. Equally strange cartes-de-visites like those from the firm of C. D. Fredericks (page 20) were also not uncommon. These photomontages may have been commissioned by their subjects as comic "calling cards."

But images such as these were not taken seriously as expressive photography. Considered (if at all) only as curiosities, they did not enter the mainstream of art photography in their time. When they were made, photography had already undergone the first of its major branchings. One group of practitioners devoted itself to a documentary (or, as it was sometimes called, "naturalistic") approach. The other was committed to the pictorialist mode, which permitted any and every kind of technical manipulation of the image but was conceptually limited to the tepid pictorial conventions of genre painting. To the naturalists the articulation of personal fantasies was irrelevant; to the pictorialists the deliberate crafting of a truly ugly or frightening image was unthinkable.

Subsequent developments in the morphology of "creative" photography precluded much involvement with the grotesque, outside of its appearance in documentary imagery. The "straight" or "purist" school of photography, whose ascendance began in the late 1920's, disdained many of the techniques vital to the grotesque mode and ignored its themes entirely. Photographers working with those techniques and exploring those themes were disparaged by their peers, disregarded by critics and historians, and thus never reached a wide popular audience.

The techniques discarded by the "straight" photographers—staged events, symbolically arranged still lifes, the manipulation of negatives and prints—were put to use in various genres of commercial photography, particularly advertising and fashion.

Because one function of fashion photography is to titillate the jaded sensibilities of the wealthy, images with grotesque overtones are not uncommon in this genre. Some fashion photographers have restricted their attraction to the grotesque mode to their noncommercial work. Sometimes the dividing lines are less clearly drawn. George Platt Lynes, Erwin Blumenfeld, Nikolas Muray, Irving Penn, Paul Outerbridge, and more recently Helmut Newton, Guy Bourdin, Deborah Turbeville, and Chris von Wangenheim have all entered the territory of the grotesque.

The main tributaries of the river of the grotesque in photography, then, have been these:

(1) the widely disseminated documentary or photojournalistic imagery of violence, social aberration, suffering, and death;

(2) the equally omnipresent commercial imagery—advertising, fashion, illustration, even postcard—in which fantasy was permissible;

(3) the vernacular imagery made for medical/anthropological/forensic/military purposes, which created an enormous body of unintentionally grotesque images though the audience for same was limited; and

(4) work by those few photographers who disregarded the fashion for "purism" and pursued the grotesque aspects of their own personal visions despite pressure to the contrary: William Mortensen, Clarence John Laughlin, Francis Brugiere, and sundry others.

These separate streams first came together in the early 1960's. A dramatic increase in the quantity and quality of photographic education in America released a generation of highly trained, expressive photographers who had an extensive background in the history of their medium. They began their careers as professional artists in a decade of ferment and experimentation in all the arts. Inevitably, they brought the same energies to photography, along with a certain attitude — literary critics dubbed it "black humor"—that was striking a responsive chord in a surprisingly broad audience.

By most previous standards it was a negativistic attitude, even a decadent one. It seemed joyless (though it was often deeply sensual and ferociously comic); pessimistic (though its central theme was survival under stress); and without redemption (though it was profoundly moral). Madness, paranoia, hallucination, ugliness—these were the givens of this form.

Yet it was an attitude absolutely harmonious with its time, not because it was imposed on its epoch, but because it sprang naturally from it. The significance of that phenomenon is just beginning to be recognized and explored; it is impossible to analyze it in this context. I am not implying that black humor in literature was the inspiration for increased activity in the grotesque mode of photography. I am only analogizing to point out a parallel. The rise of black humor in literature was not only the manifestation of the *Zeitgeist* at that point in history. It had its equivalent in contemporary photography as well. The chapters that follow show the many directions in which this impulse has flowed over the past half century.

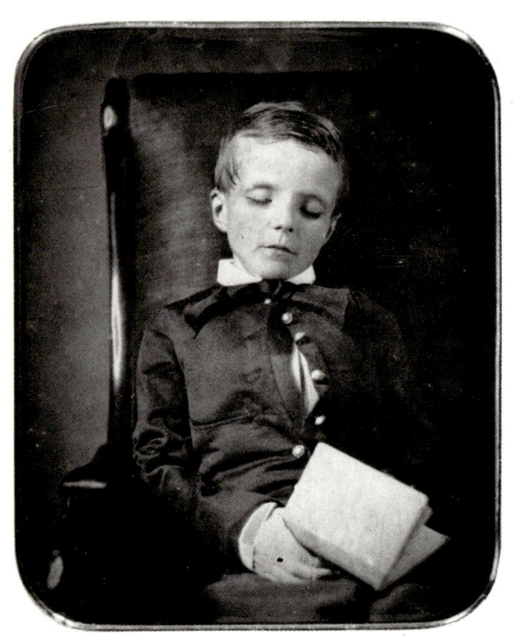

Collection: IMP/GEH

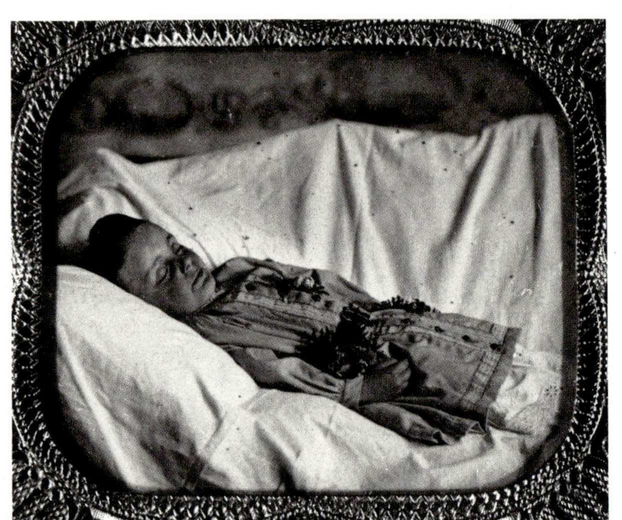

Collection: IMP/GEH

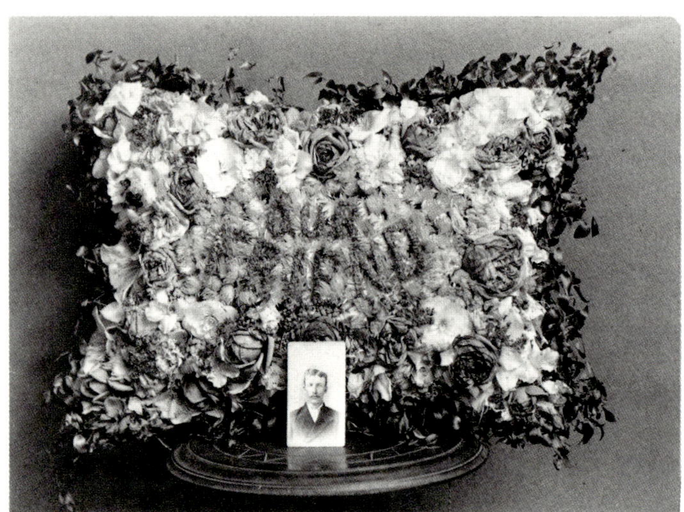

Collection of A. D. Coleman

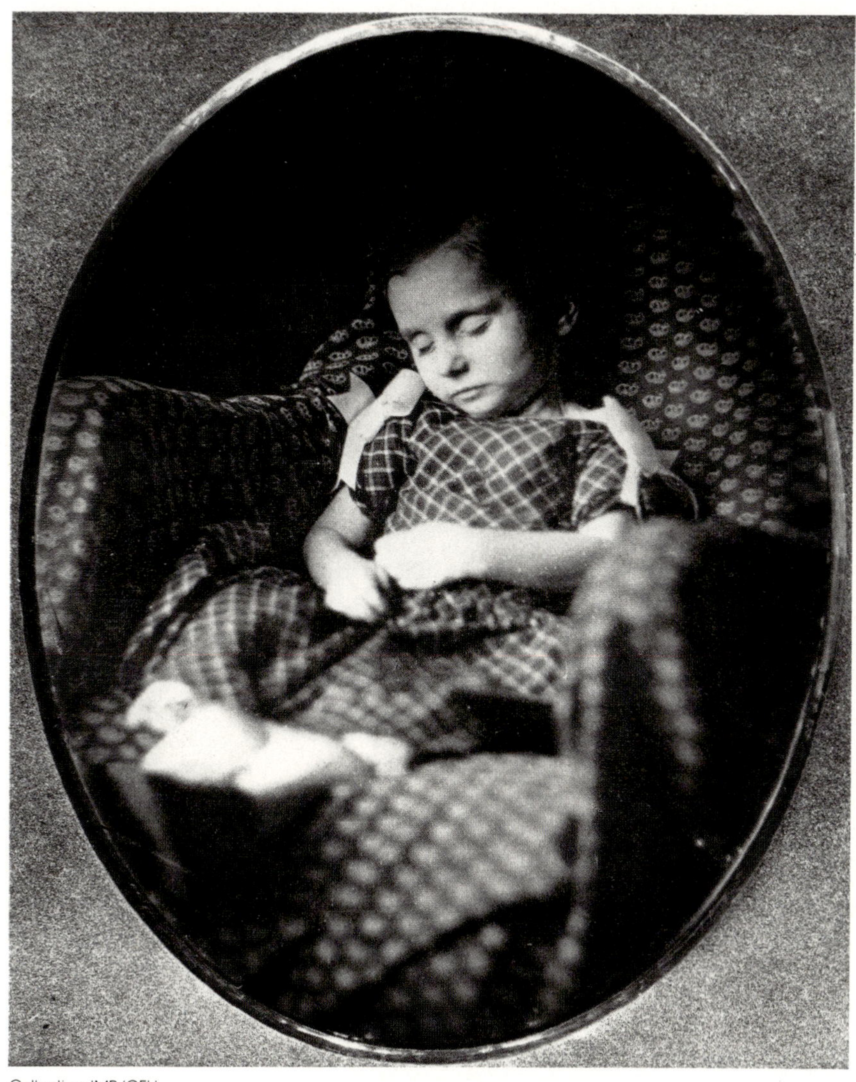

Collection: IMP/GEH

Above and opposite (top right and left): Anonymous
post-mortem daguerreotypes of children, ca. 1850. Bottom left:
Cabinet photograph by C. E. Dickerman, St. Johnsbury,
Vermont, ca. 1880.

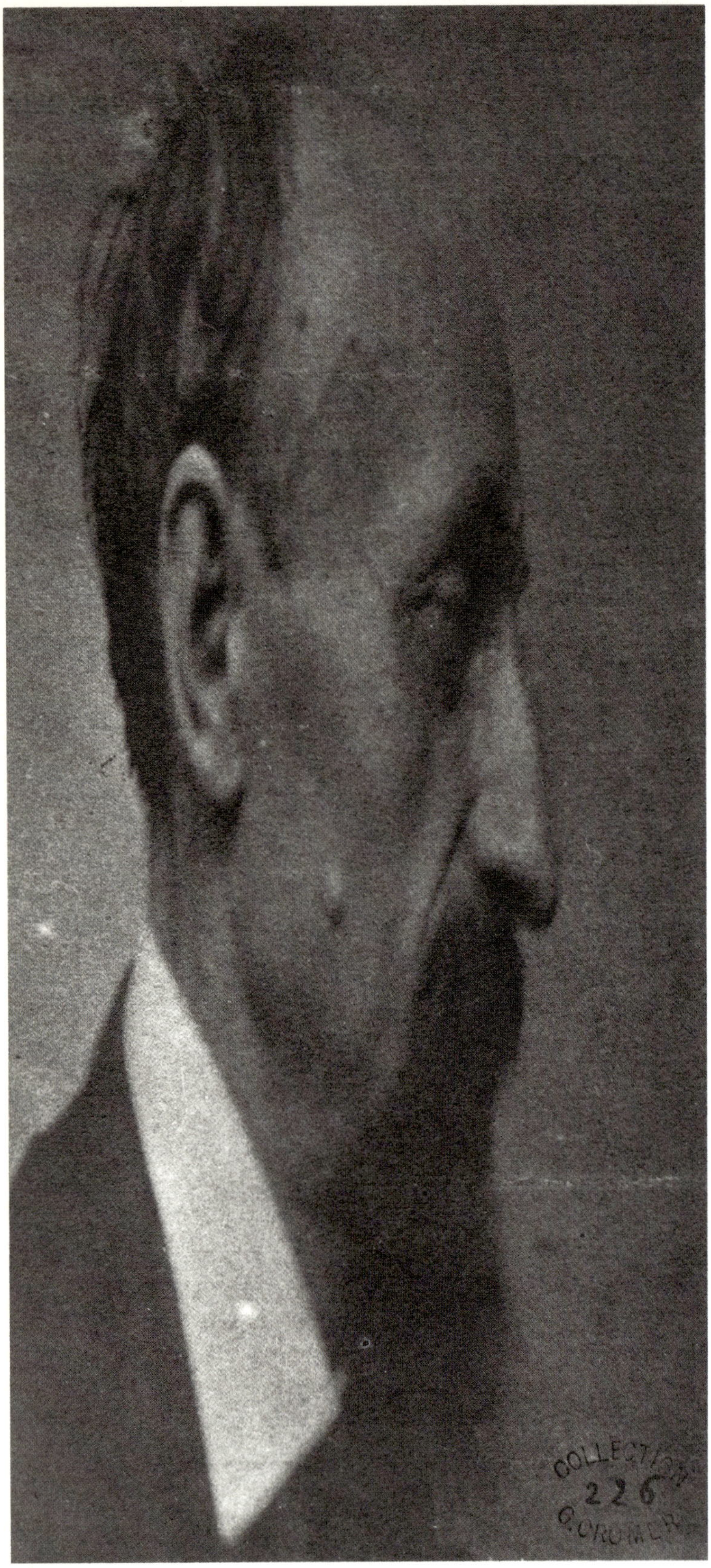

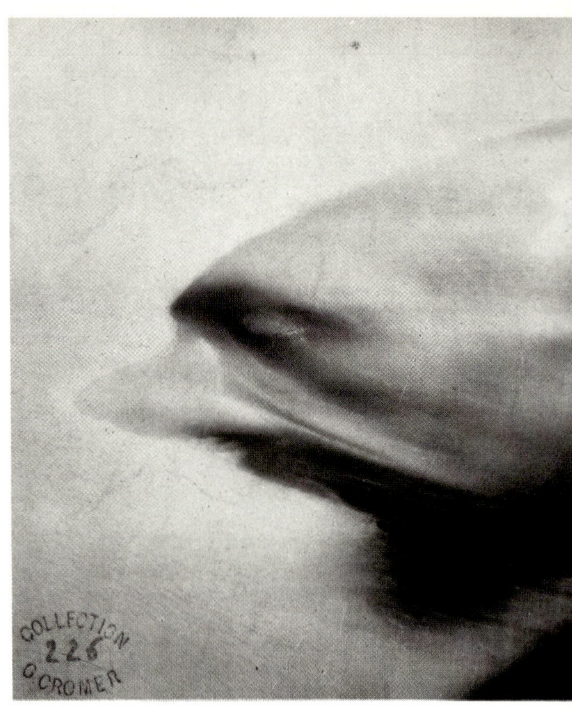

Collection: IMP/GEH

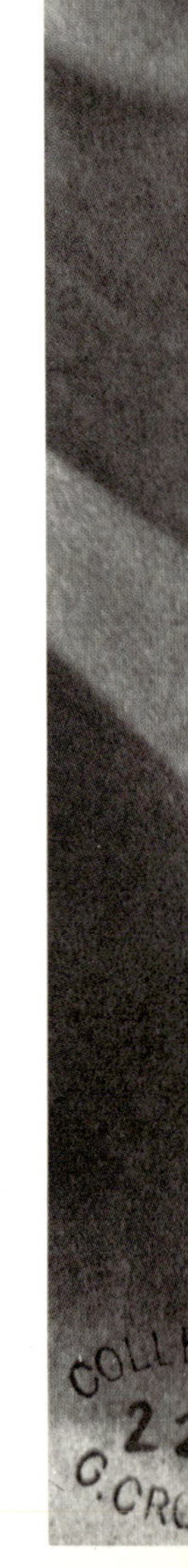

Self-portraits by Louis Ducos du Hauron, made in 1888

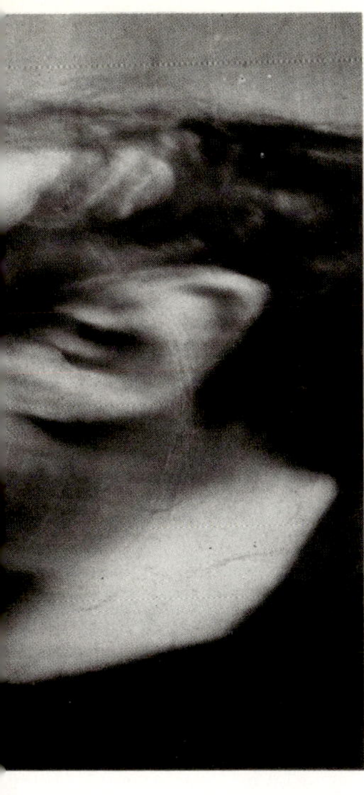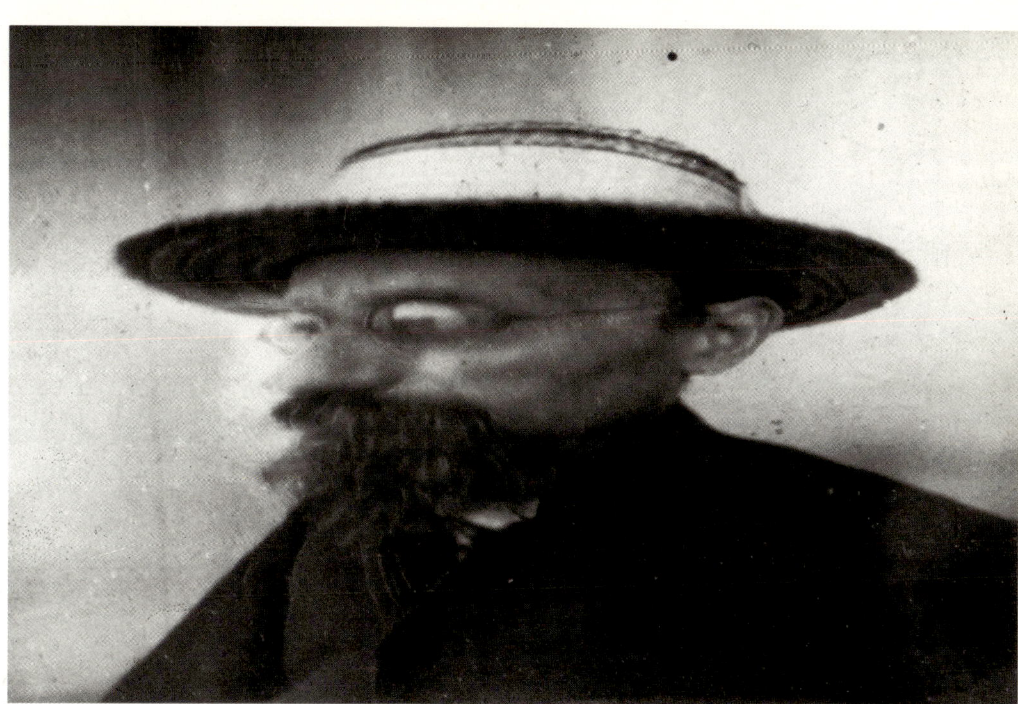

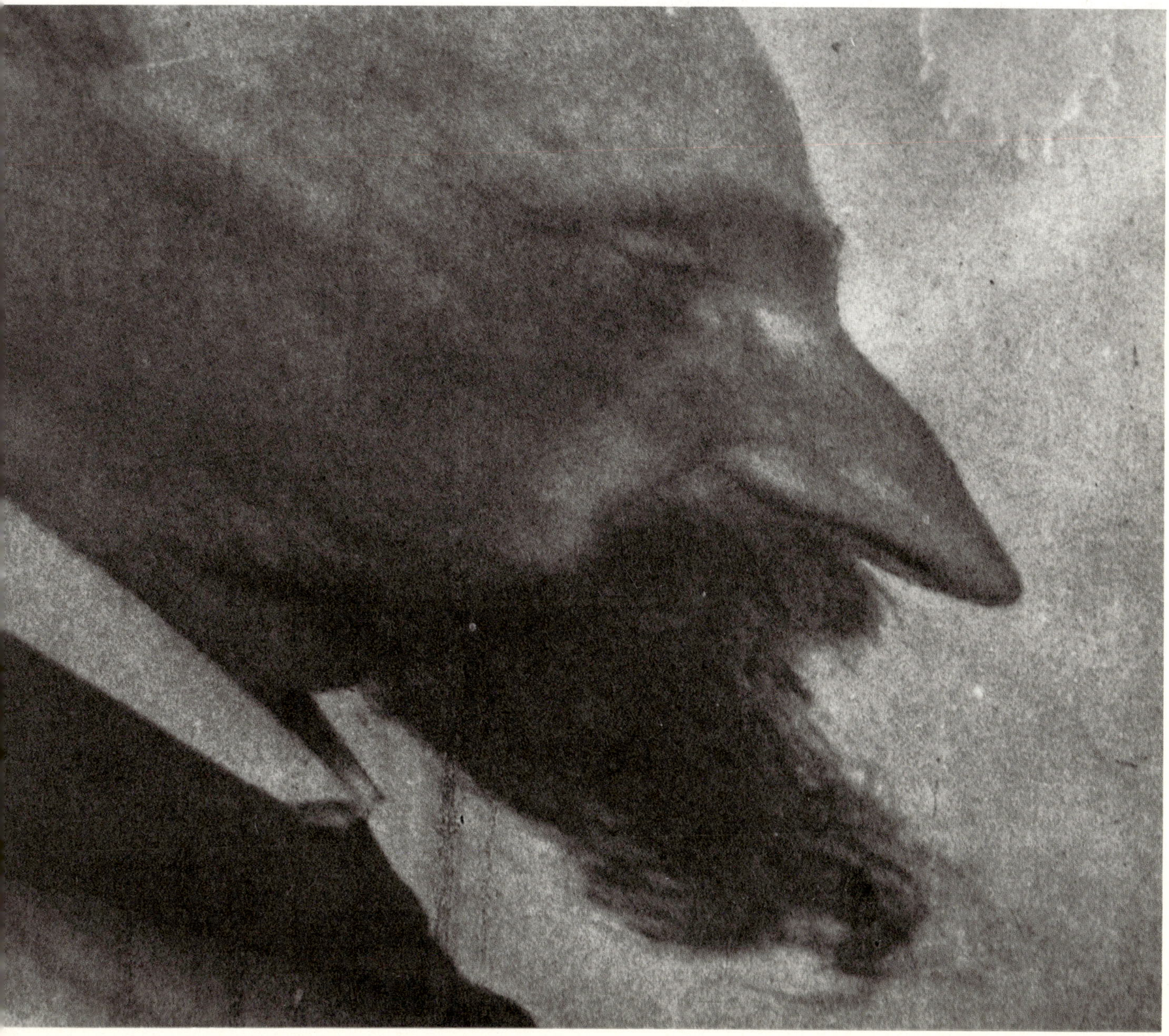

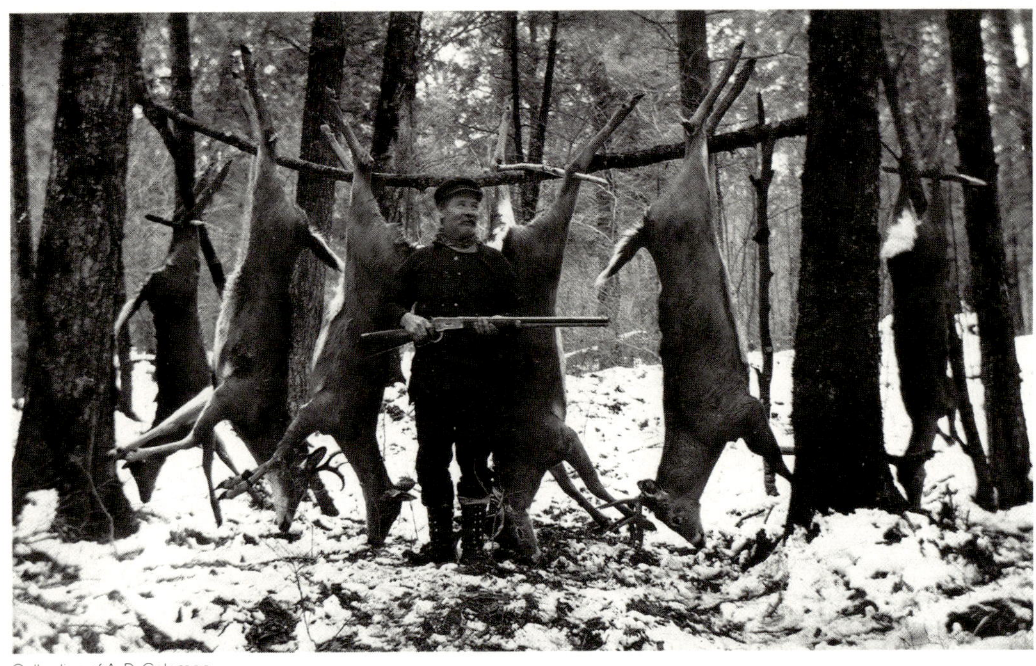

Collection of A. D. Coleman

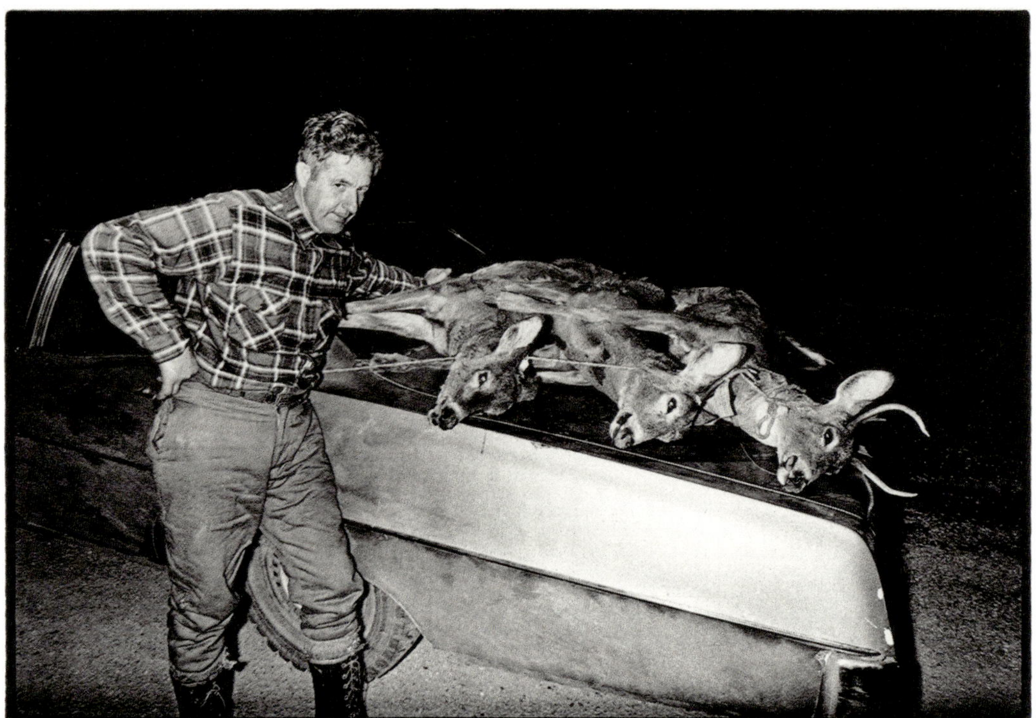

© 1971 Les Krims

Top: Anonymous postcard, ca. 1910,
inscribed on back, "Ike is standing by the deer Gene shot.
The one with its head on the ground."
Bottom: A contemporary version of the same subject,
from The Deerslayers, 1971, by Les Krims.

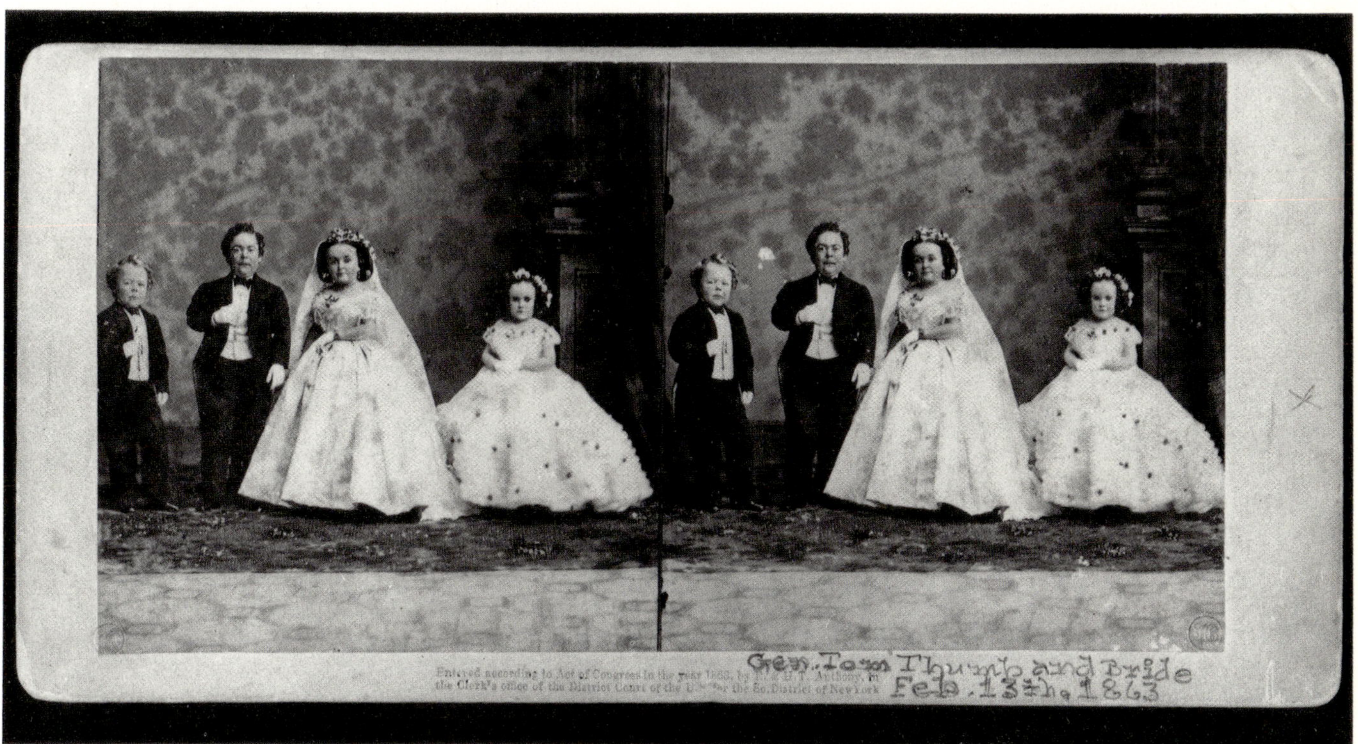

Collection: IMP/GEH

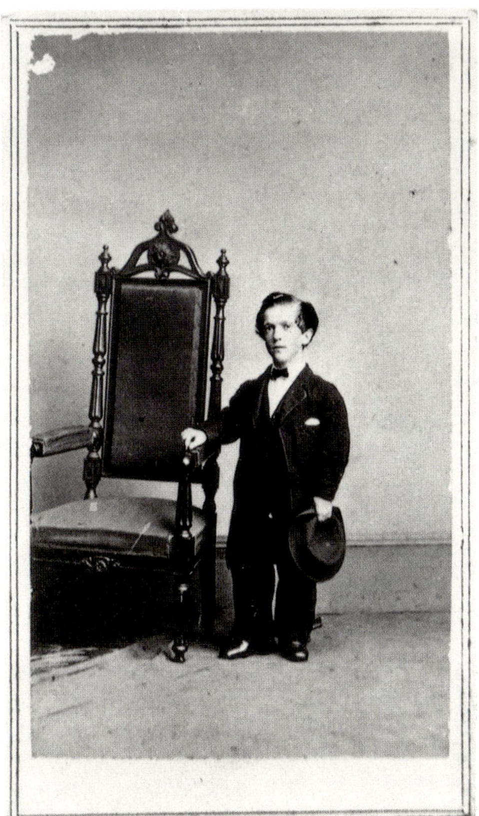

Collection: Visual Studies Workshop

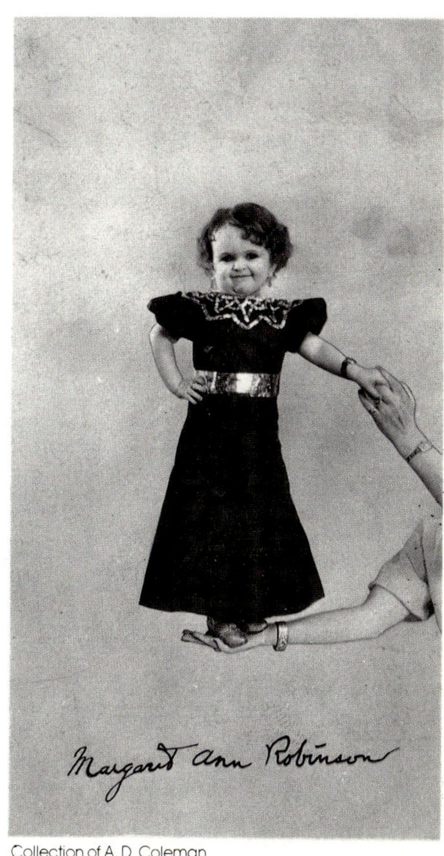

Collection of A. D. Coleman

Top: "The Fairy Wedding Party," stereograph by Mathew Brady;
Tom Thumb's wedding day, February 13, 1863 (left to right:
Commodore Nutt, Mr. and Mrs. General Tom Thumb,
Miss Minnie Warren). Bottom left: Carte-de-visite by
C. D. Fredericks & Co., New York. Bottom right: Anonymous
souvenir postcard of "The World's Smallest Lady," 1935.

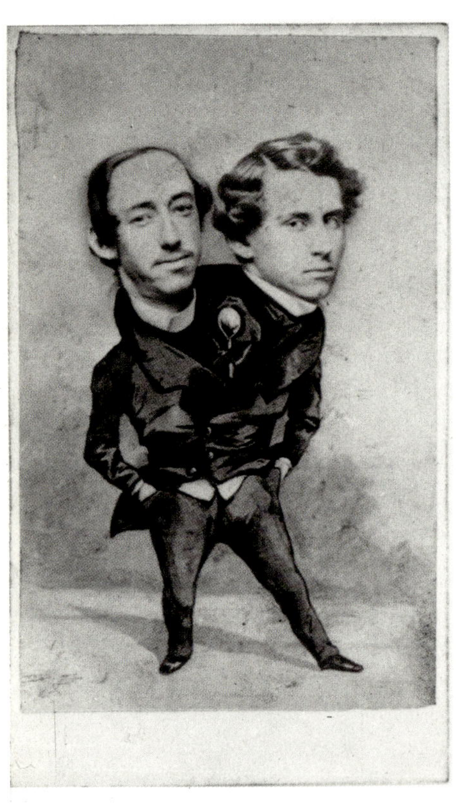

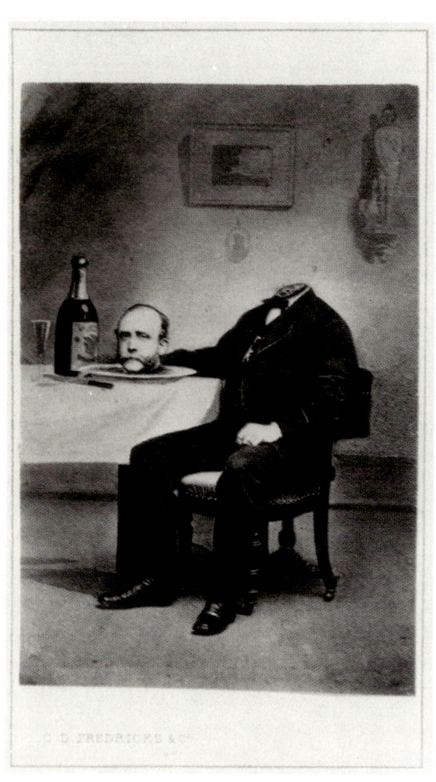

Collection: Visual Studies Workshop

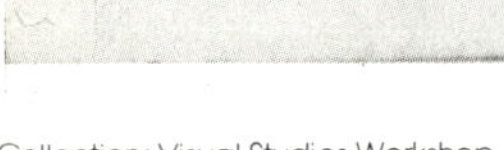

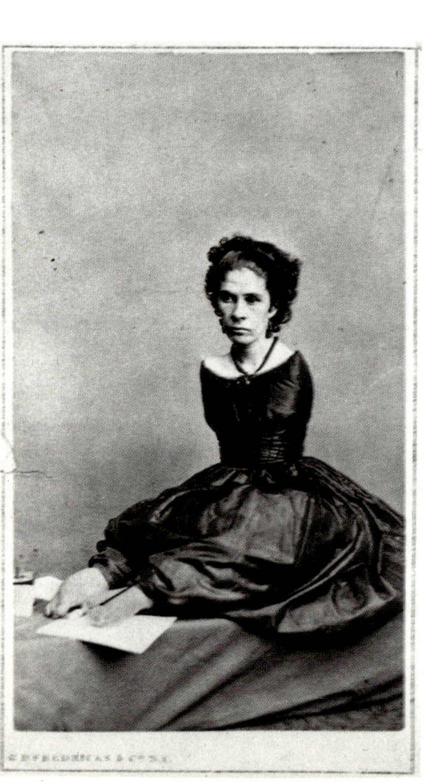

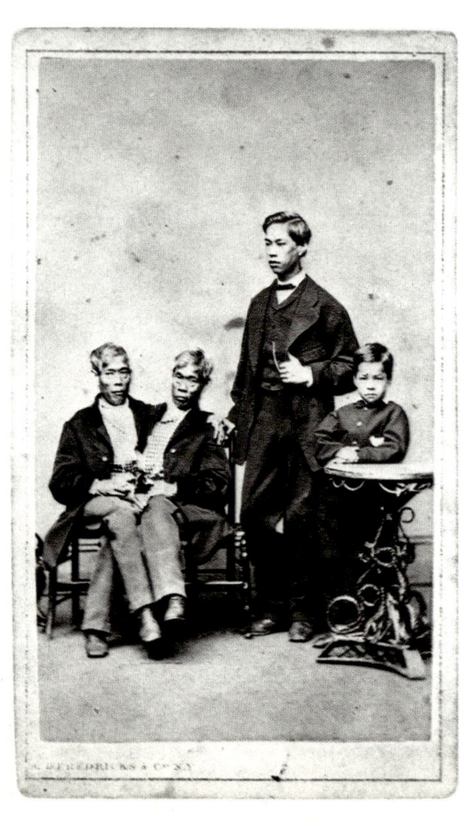

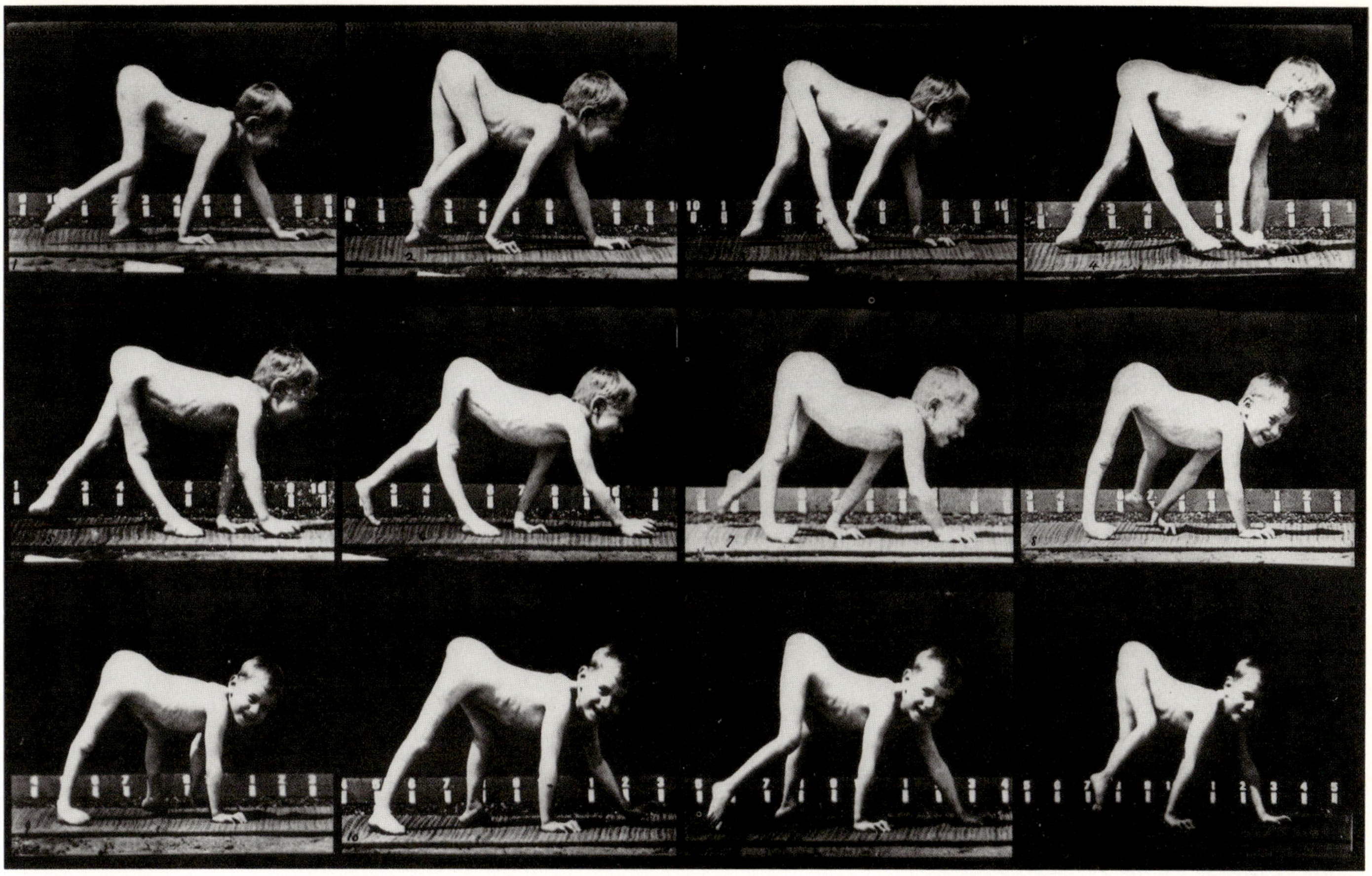

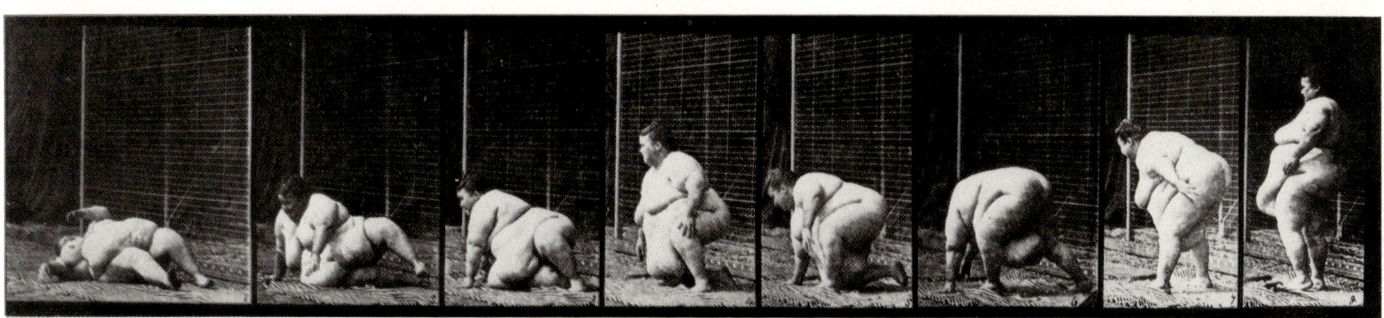

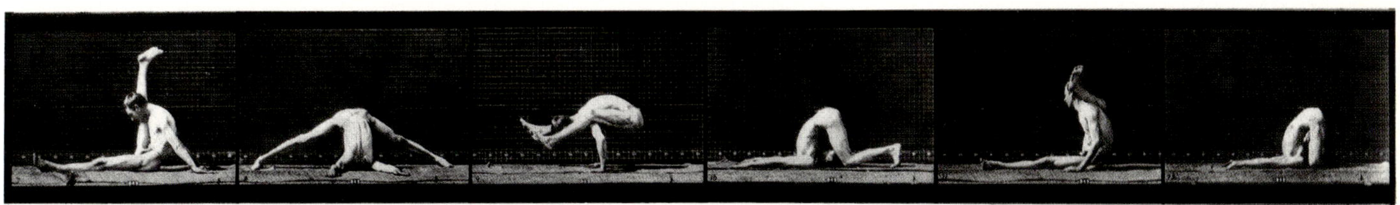

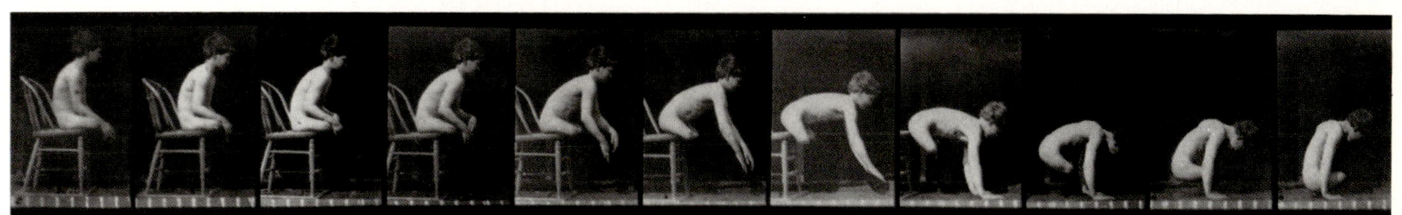

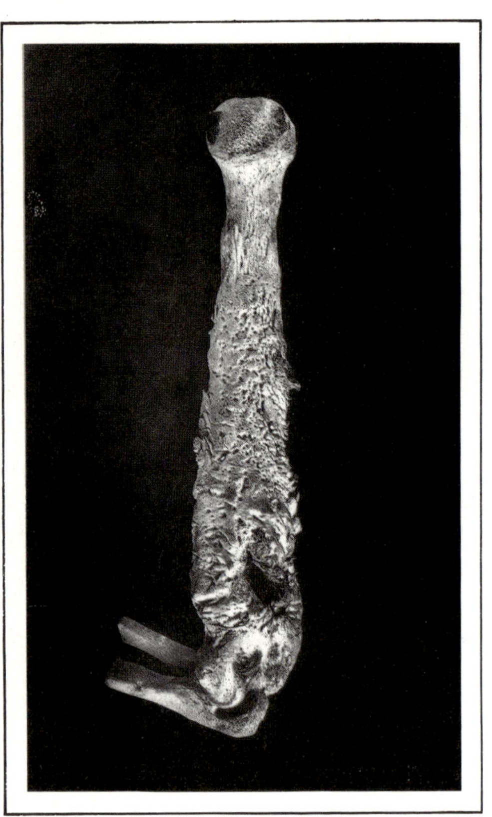

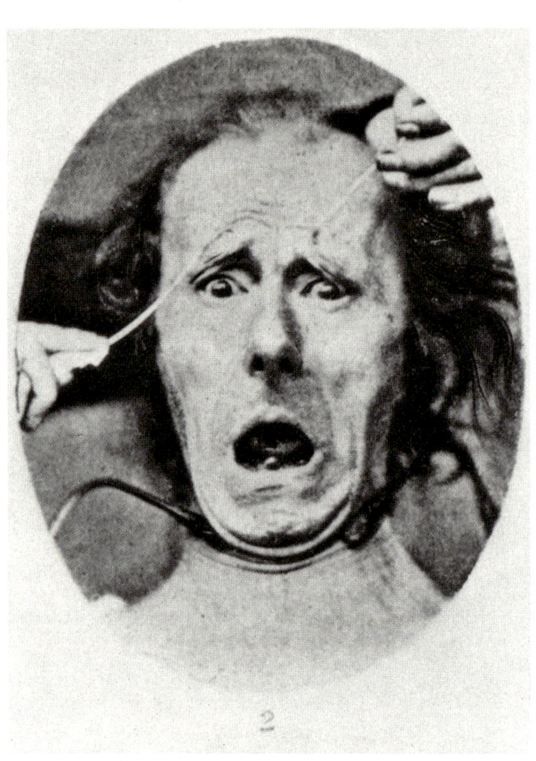

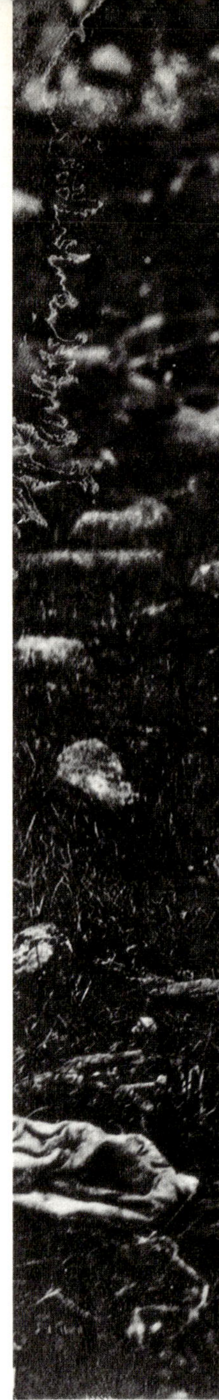

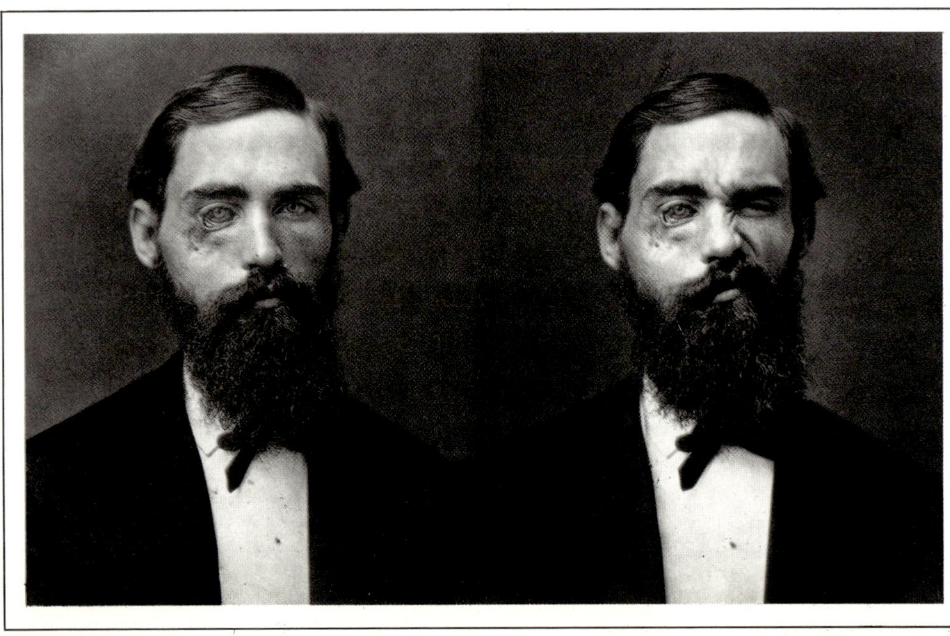

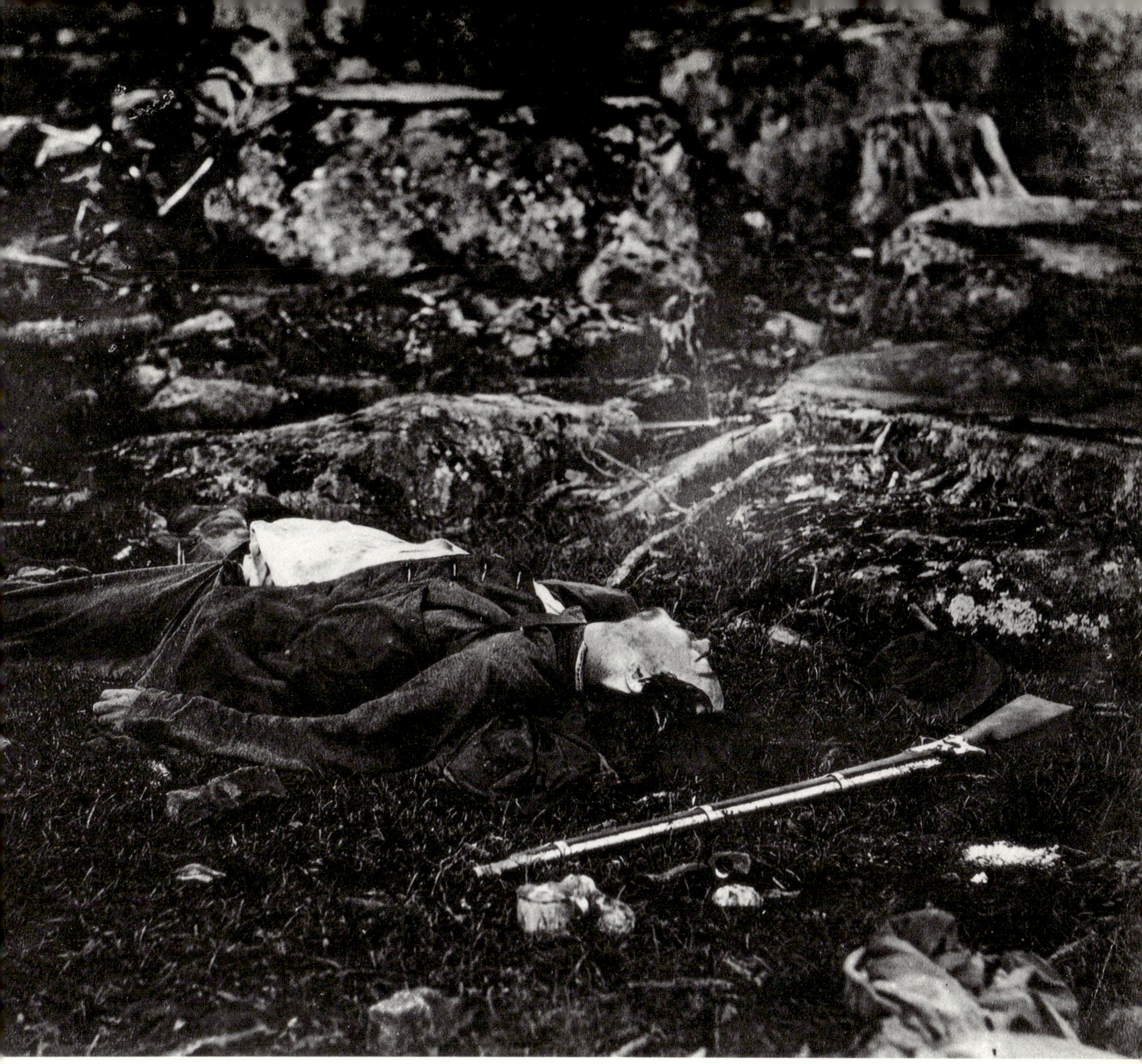

Opposite: Plates by Ward (top left)
and W. Bell (bottom) from
*The Medical and Surgical History of
the War of the Rebellion*, 1877. Opposite,
top right: "Fear," by O. J. Rejlander,
an illustration from Charles Darwin's
*The Expression of the Emotions in Man and
Animals*, 1872. This page: "Body of a Confederate
Sharpshooter among the Rocks of Little Round Top,
Gettysburg, Pa., July 1863," by Alexander Gardner.

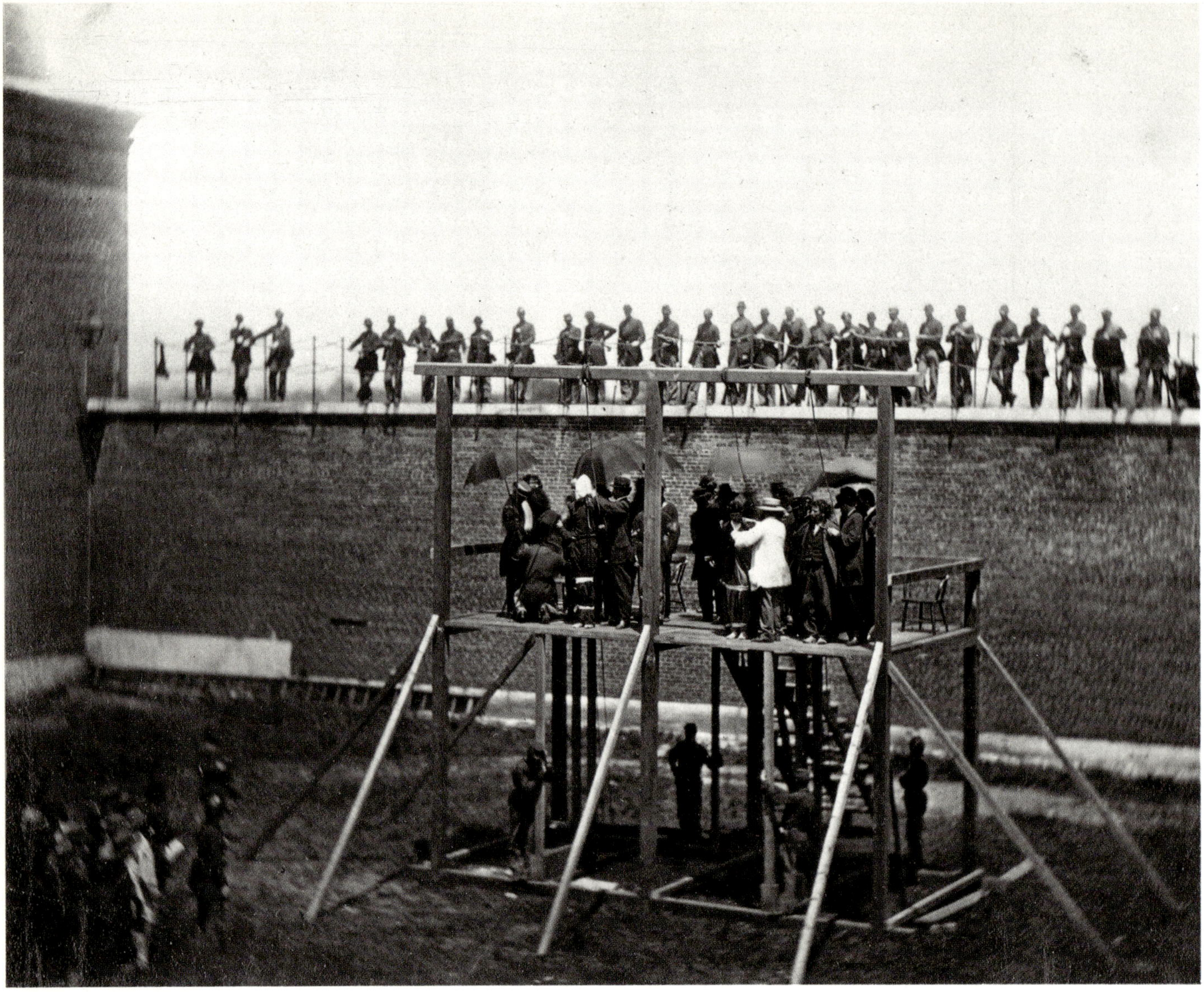

Collection: Visual Studies Workshop

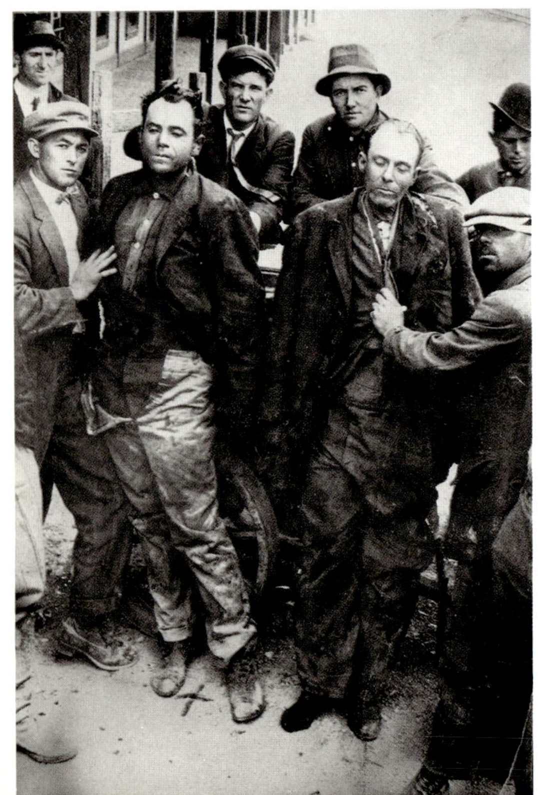

Culver Pictures

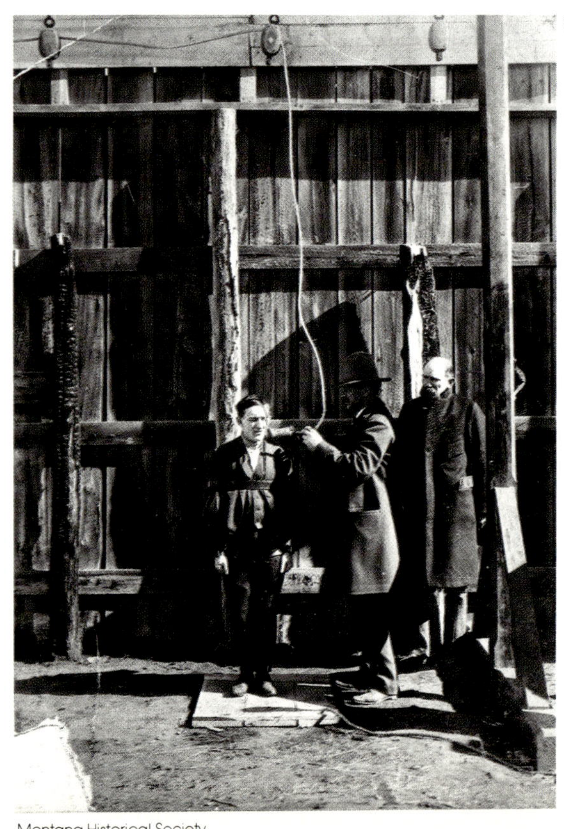

Montana Historical Society

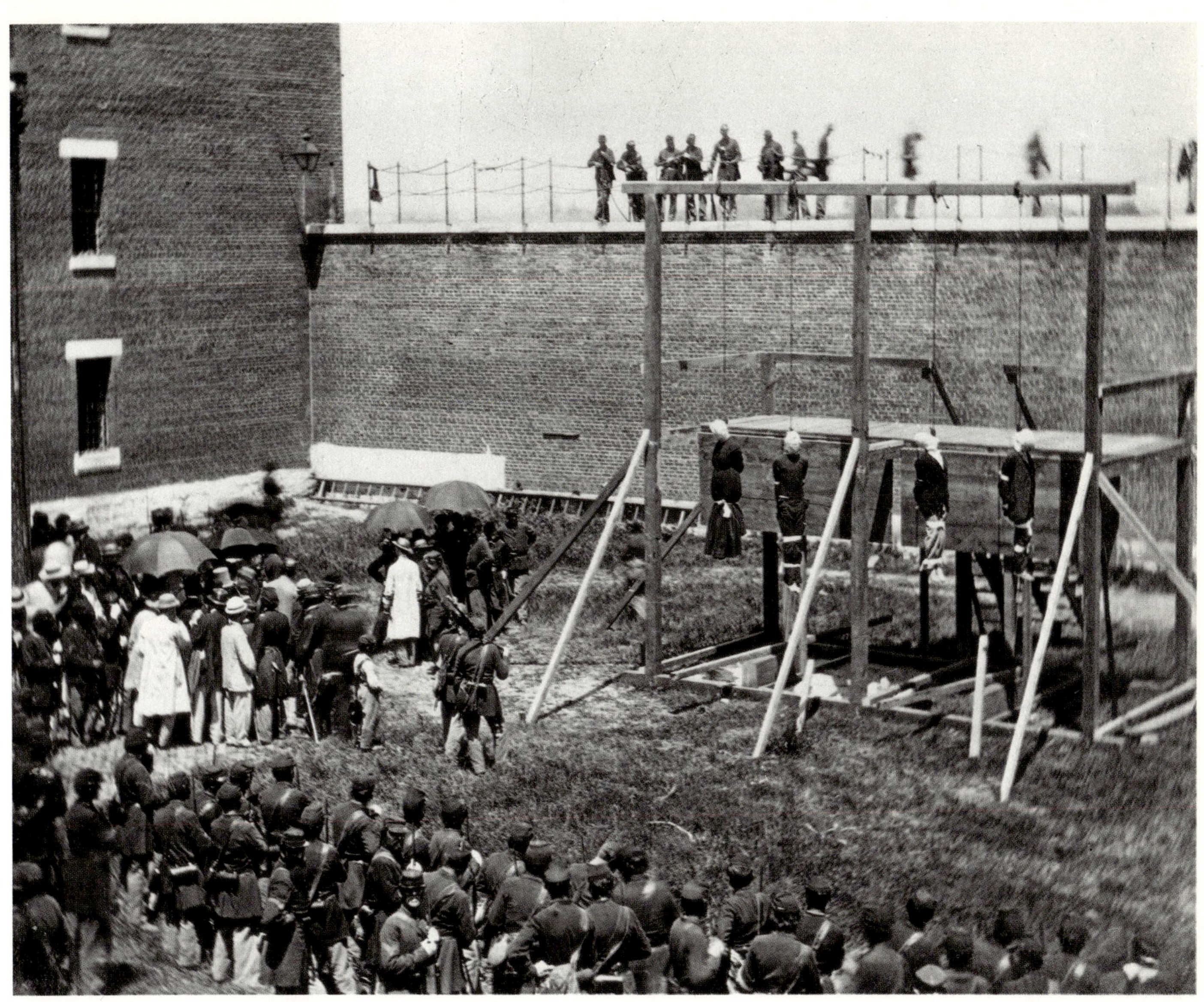

Above and opposite, top: Two images from Alexander
Gardner's series, "Execution of the Presidential Conspirators,
July 7, 1865." Left, "Adjusting the Ropes"; right, "The Trap
Sprung." Opposite, bottom left: Anonymous photograph
of bodies of outlaws Ben Kilpatrick and "his accomplice,
Ed Welch," 1911. Bottom right: Anonymous photograph of
"Billie Calder, hanged Mar. 16, 1900, in Lewistown, Montana."

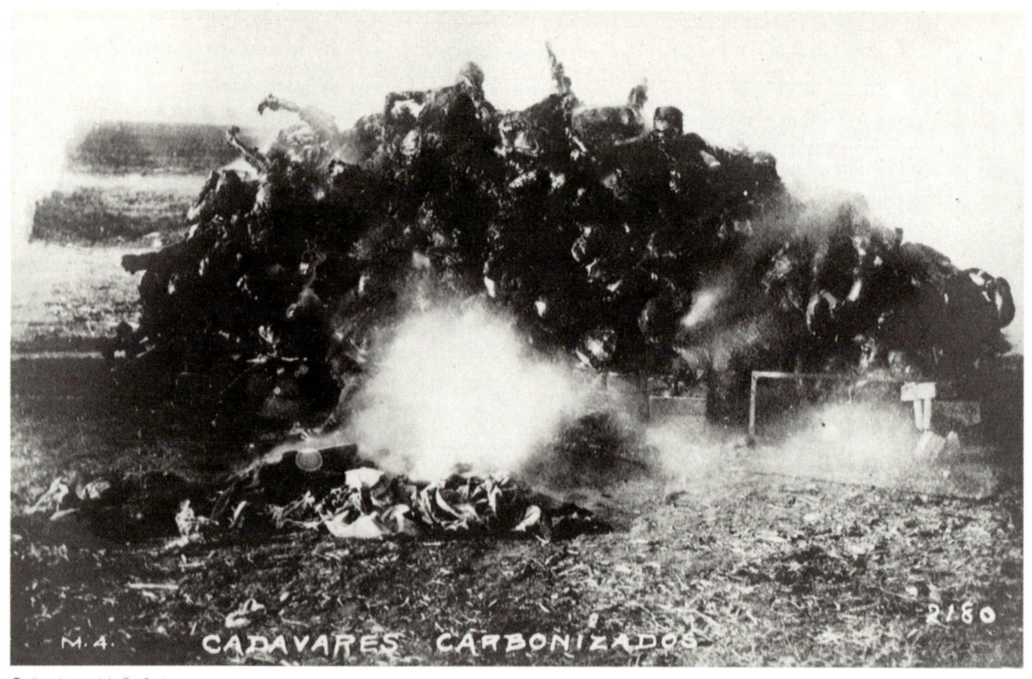

Collection of A. D. Coleman

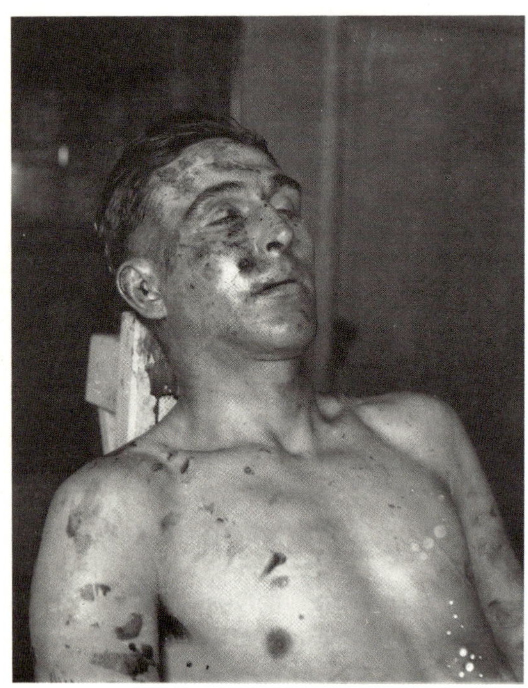

This page, top: Anonymous postcard from a series on
the Mexican revolution, this one showing the mass burning
of bodies of dead rebels. Above: Morgue photograph
of unidentified murder victim, February 17, 1926, by
Charles Heinrichs of Paterson, New Jersey. Right:
Cole Younger dead in a railroad car —
photographer possibly Bay of Albuquerque.
Opposite, top: Jesse James in his coffin,
stereograph by A. A. Hughes and Bro., 1882.
Bottom: Bolivian air force officials in morgue
with body of Che Guevara, Valle Grande, Bolivia,
October 12, 1967.

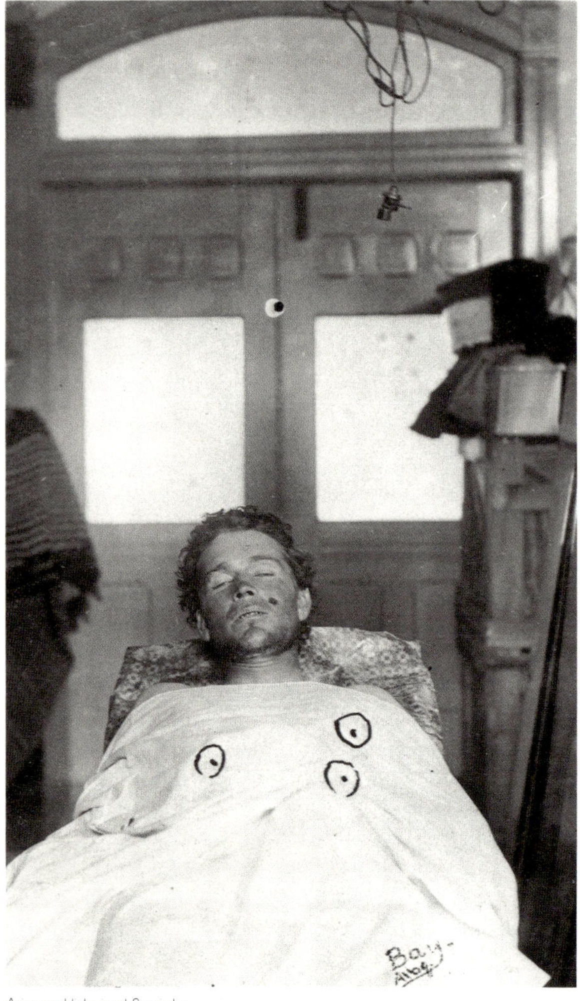

Arizona Historical Society

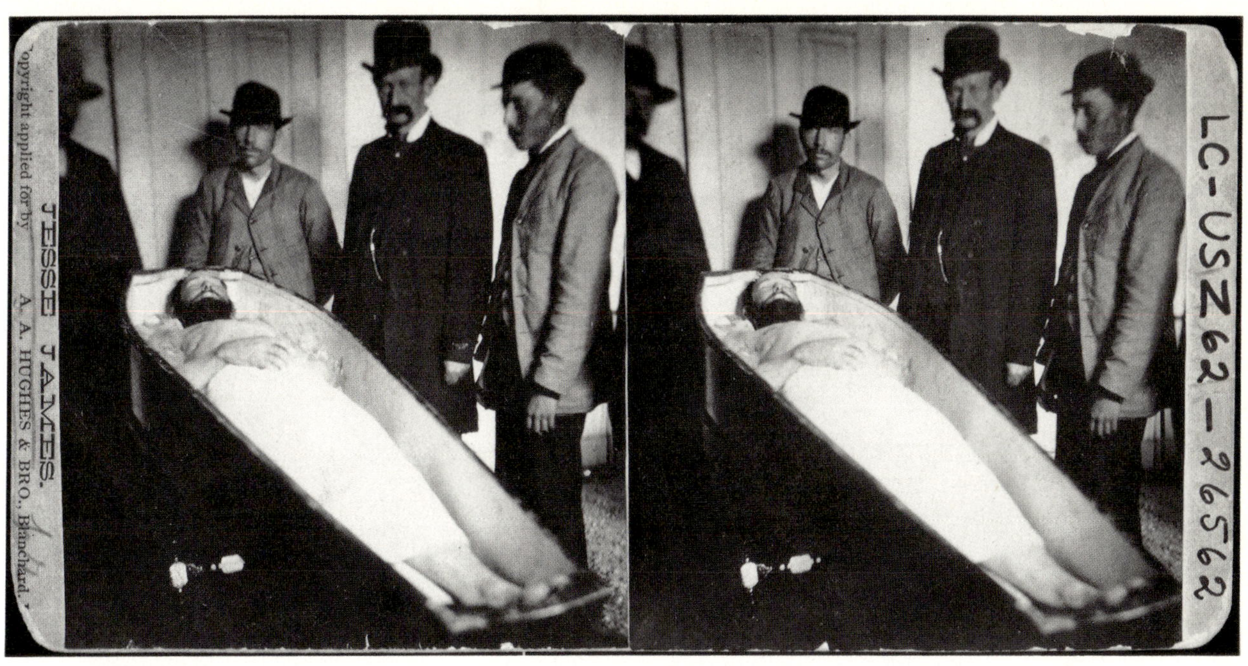

Library of Congress

UPI

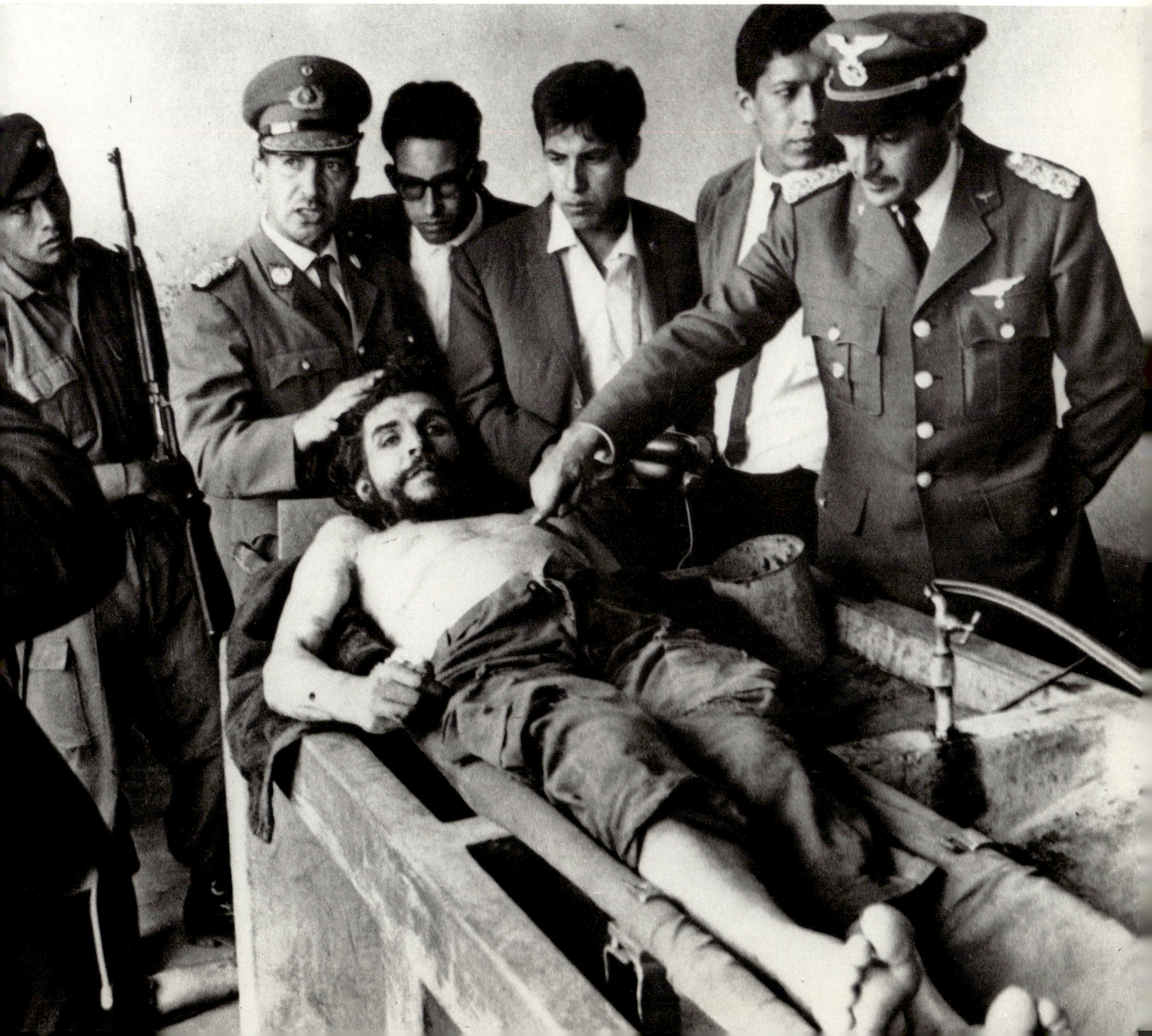

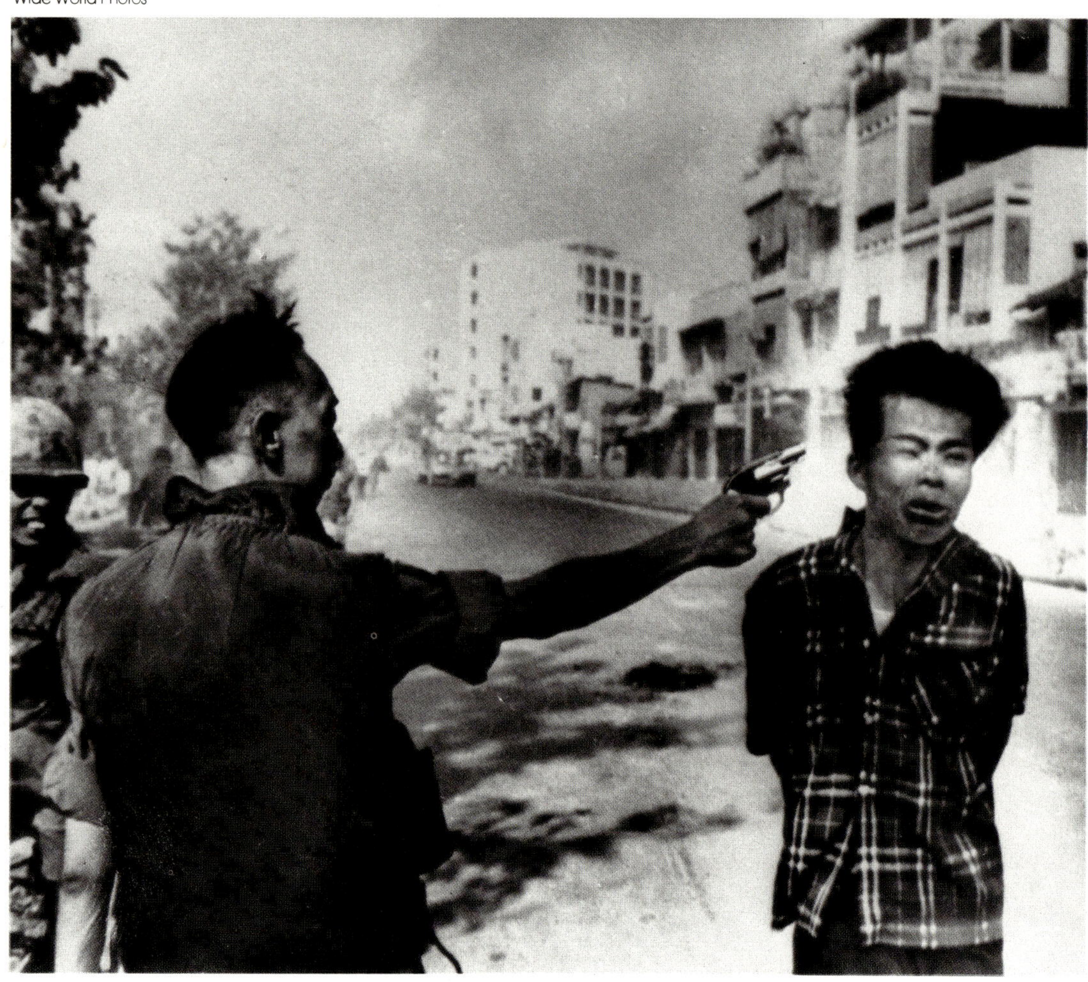

Above: Summary execution of Viet Cong suspect
by National Police Chief of South Vietnam, February
1, 1968; photograph by Eddie Adams. Right:
Electrocution of convicted murderer Ruth Snyder,
January 13, 1928 — an unauthorized photograph
made with a hidden camera strapped to the
ankle of reporter Tim Howard.

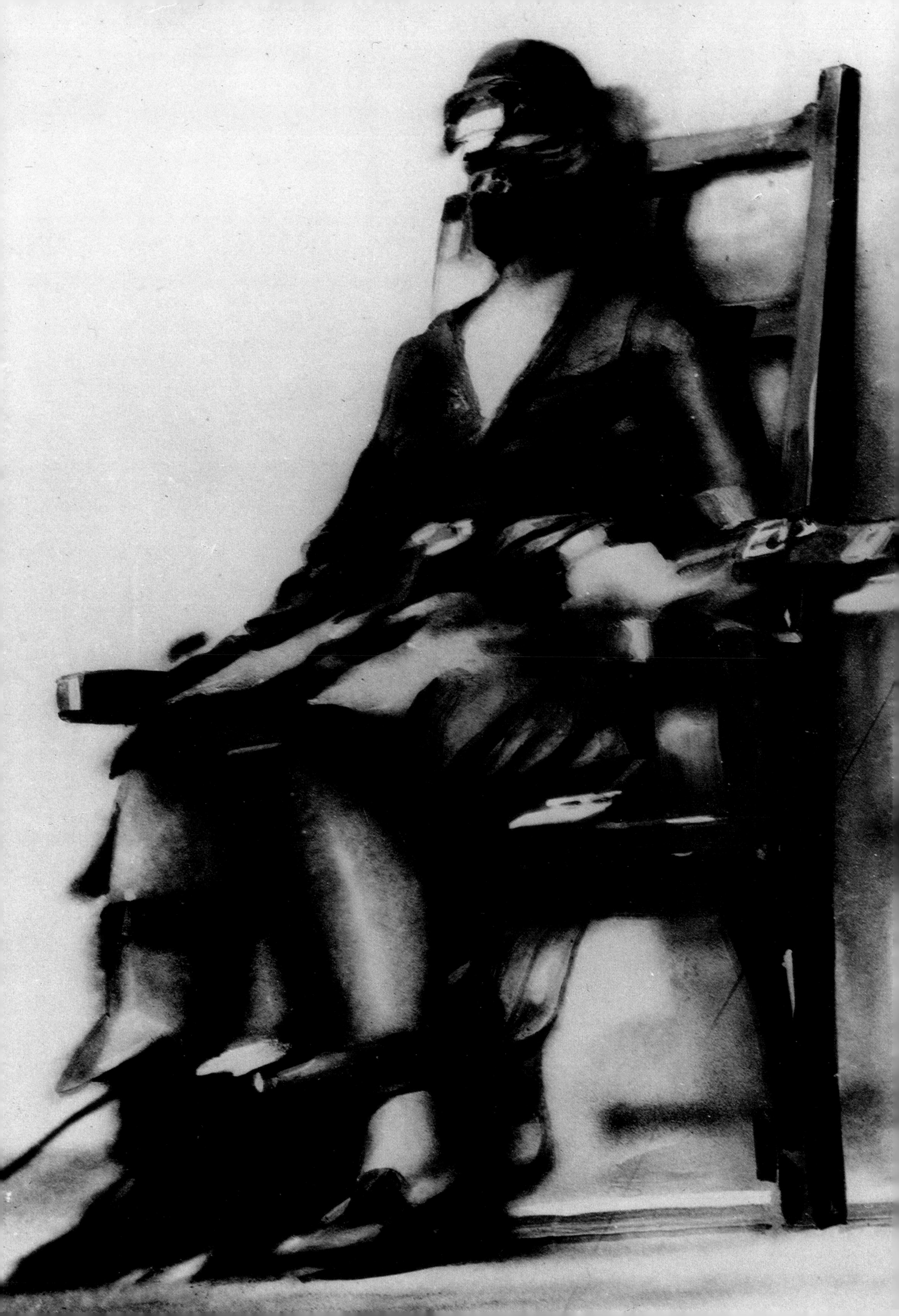

2 REALITIES

When it comes to visual description, photography remains the only game in town. Its earliest function as a witnessing process has not yet been superseded. The print media — newspapers, magazines, and books — continue to rely on photographs for visual documentation. Videotape is gradually supplanting still imagery in television reportage, although video equipment itself is still quite primitive: expensive, bulky, undependable, and intrusive enough so that there are many situations that remain accessible only to the still camera.

Predominantly as a result of exposure to photography, we are becoming visually sophisticated enough as a culture to realize that photography is not a transcriptive process but a descriptive one. We are beginning to develop our awareness of the extent to which people inevitably shape the photographs they take casually, as well as the ones they make deliberately, whether they do that shaping knowingly or unconsciously. We are even learning the dimensions of the gap that lies between any event and any photograph of it.

Yet, for better or worse, the photograph has become an acceptable surrogate for direct experience on many levels. And some impulse in human beings—curiosity, a thirst for knowledge, a lust for vicarious thrills, whatever it may be—pushes many people to see everything they can lay their eyes on. Consequently, photography has been used consistently to examine the abnormal as well as the commonplace and the banal. From the sheer volume and diversity of the resulting images we are learning that we live in a world so bizarre that "normalcy" itself may be the most remarkable aberration of all.

For some photographers who work within the informational/representational modes (which are usually referred to as "straight" or "documentary"), disturbing subject matter is not necessarily a predilection. It simply comes with the territory.

Thus we could point to such grisly images as Margaret Bourke-White's 1945 portrayals of German concentration-camp victims (those from Buchenwald, for example), or her "Vultures of Calcutta, India, 1946," in which carrion-eating birds tear at corpses, as representative of a kind of imagery whose grotesqueness resides in the subject matter, not in the photographer's attitude toward it. Such has been the case with a number of photographers.

Lewis Hine made a powerful series, *Morons in Institutions*, in the eastern United States in the early 1920's, but these images seem linked more directly to his crusade against the exploitation and mistreatment of the underprivileged than to any psychological or esthetic attraction to the visual potential of the mentally defective.

Because deformity and/or the destruction of the physical self is a central theme in the grotesque mode, photographs depicting such actualities evoke its impact. Some of W. Eugene Smith's images of the mercury-poisoning victims of Minamata, or his "Iwo Jima, 1945," showing the rotting corpse of a soldier; the Vietnam reportage of Philip Jones Griffiths, Larry Burrows, and many others; Mark Edwards's images of cadavers being gnawed by scavenger dogs behind the Taj Mahal; Donald McCullin's visual accounts of human suffering around the globe—these are additional examples of what might be thought of as an adjunct to the grotesque mode. They are not made accidentally or naïvely. Yet I think it is safe to say that most if not all of the photographers mentioned so far would have preferred never to encounter the events they've portrayed.

Other photographers deliberately seek out such subjects as vehicles for the exploration of more personal concerns. It is not possible to generalize about their reasons, and speculation in that regard is rarely fruitful. It is not unreasonable, however, to discuss the effects of their imagery, or to suggest that differences in motivation and intent may be reflected in differences of style and content.

Weegee—Arthur Fellig—consistently addressed the theme of the grotesque in several styles (see also Chapter 4), particularly its manifestation in violent, messy, public death. "As a free-lance newspaper photographer I covered a murder a night," he wrote. To assist him in this task he had a police radio installed in his car. He was the first photojournalist to do so.

Weegee's appetite for both the excesses and the nuances of American urban life was enormous. He relished the sprawled corpses of assassinated mobsters as thoroughly as he enjoyed teenagers swooning over Frank Sinatra. His photographs of crimes of violence (pages 54–59) epitomize the variety of tabloid imagery that has helped to make "grotesque" a household word of sorts—a branch of entertainment for the whole family, a spectator sport for children and adults alike.

Yet, more than any press photographer before

him or since, Weegee also made himself a star in these events. Calling himself "Weegee the Famous," he became a folk hero and a legend in his role as a self-appointed roving public eye. Not content to be an anonymous reporter, he transformed himself into a picturesque personality whose presence at such events was an event in itself, which converted those incidents from statistics into spectacles. His raw slices of city life were collected in several books, most notably *Naked City*, which inspired a long-running television series.

Such younger contemporary photographers as Charles Gatewood and Paul Diamond are Weegee's lineal descendants. In some significant ways they differ radically from him. They tend to work independently rather than on assignment, and their imagery is usually presented in galleries and books, not newspapers or magazines. Yet their subject matter is essentially the same: the extremes of public behavior and the overall weirdness of urban life.

As can be seen from their images (pages 48–53, 64–69), both work extensively in public situations. Gatewood is particularly fond of the Mardi Gras festivities in New Orleans, to which he has returned year after year to photograph the revelers. He has also recently completed a project on tattooing as an art form. Diamond spends much of his working time simply exploring whatever locale he finds himself in, equipment in hand; sometimes his subjects are strangers, sometimes friends and relatives.

With their role as photographers clearly stated, through the visibility of their equipment, Gatewood and Diamond enter into and become part of the events they photograph. To some extent they even use their medium as a goad. The presence of the camera frequently entices their subjects into outrageous performances.

Here is a paradox: While some people will never do in front of a camera those things they do freely in their private lives, others will under certain conditions display for the camera aspects of themselves which they might never exhibit in everyday circumstances (the photographic demonstration of Heisenberg's uncertainty principle that observation automatically alters that which is observed). Living as we do in a photographic culture, we have become aware of photographs as, among other things, potential stages on which to act out and verify our inner lives and fantasies. There is a cathartic aspect to such self-revelation, a confessional element. There is also a streak of

exhibitionism in many people that is specifically activated by the presence of a camera, corresponding to the undeniable streak of voyeurism manifested in our attraction to such images. Gatewood and Diamond are certainly aware of these factors and employ them effectively in their work.

The late Diane Arbus frequently expressed her feeling of empathy with the work of Weegee. It is Arbus's name that in recent years has been linked most closely to the theme of the grotesque in photography—to such an extent that although her images were not available for reproduction in this survey it seems necessary to discuss her work in connection with this theme.

In part, her linkage to the grotesque in the minds of critics and viewers is no doubt due to factors extraneous to her imagery—her suicide and the publicity surrounding it, for example, and the public's attitude toward members of sexual minorities, circus and side-show performers, and the other unusual individuals who were among her subjects. However, Arbus's vision was more complex than such oversimplifications acknowledge and the totality of her work is much more than a study of "freaks."

Her central inquiry was directed toward locating that line in contemporary American society which divides the normal from the abnormal. To some extent her determination of that location was unavoidably affected by aspects of her own personal history—her age, race, sex, and class, for instance. Yet even with all those built-in biases her instincts enabled her to pinpoint that position for herself with remarkable and consistent accuracy. Standing there, she photographed those who stood on both sides of that line. The result was a group of images that require the individual viewer to decide on which side each of her subjects belongs, and thus to examine the basis for those determinations.

The linked themes in the work of Diane Arbus, then, were the normality of so-called "freaks" and the freakishness of supposedly normal people. Part of the power of her work as a whole can be traced to the resonances between these images.

Much of the impact of individual images springs from her intentionally confrontational approach. She faced her subjects head-on, usually at a close distance, and always asked their permission before photographing. Thus these are not "candid" snapshots but transactional portraits, reflecting the conscious relationship between photographer, camera, and subject.

Arbus in turn confronts the viewer with her subjects: by bringing him/her face to face with them, for one thing, and also by making her prints so large (sixteen by twenty inches in most cases) that the miniaturizing effect of photography is lessened considerably. In those portraits in which the head of the subject fills the frame, the viewer encounters it virtually life-size. That violates many deeply inbred social norms. Cultural patterns of spatial distancing usually eliminate the possibility of such close proximity to strangers making eye contact with us, especially unusual strangers such as dwarves, tattooed men, and ferocious women. Through these stylistic decisions Arbus was pointing out our protective barriers by calculatedly violating them.

It is evident that there are structural properties to the grotesque as a mode—that the grotesque does not depend solely on subject matter or on audience response for its definition, but usually involves certain creative requirements as well. An entirely different example of this is the simple dislocation of habitual seeing which creates the fantastic profile in Clarence John Laughlin's "Head of Oceanus" (page 40). This same understanding of how things will appear when translated into photographic form resulted in Laughlin's "The Insect-Headed Tombstone" (page 41).

As this indicates, even within the sphere of common, everyday experience events occur which have (or can take on) a dark and even nightmarish quality. In the brooding images of Michael Martone (pages 70–71), for example, objects become frighteningly hallucinatory, glowing strangely in a gloomy darkness or an even more ominous light. Much the same could be said for Bill Brandt's study of statuary on page 109.

In both German and Japanese art the grotesque has long been recognized as a distinct mode. Perhaps that is why the work of Les Krims has met with such enthusiastic response in both these countries. Of all the younger American photographers, it is Krims who has involved himself most consistently and prolifically with the grotesque.

His work has taken two directions, which seem deliberately chosen to amplify each other. In one, as illustrated in the next chapter, he stages dramatic tableaux which he photographs. In the other, as can be seen here, he addresses unusual but actual events: a convention of dwarves and midgets, members of the Little People of America, for example (pages 42–47). Krims, who was for a time the official photographer for the L.P.A., refers to them as "the ultimate minority." He has also photographed such real-life phenomena as American deer hunters displaying their kill (page 18). These images function as the objective correlative to his projective fantasies. An interplay is set up between these two facets of his work: the straightforward, representational series provide glimpses of a world peculiar enough for the staged scenarios to seem quite at home therein.

Death—an aspect of the decay and destruction of the physical self—has been a frequent subject for photographers, even those who are neither war- nor news-oriented. Most often the death portrayed is animal rather than human, and the most recurrent creature is the dead bird.

This is more than coincidental. For American photographers, at least, the animals most often encountered, whether living or dead, are household pets and birds. As free beings the latter carry a symbolic connotation of their own which cats and dogs do not share. This adds an element of poignant irony to their being brought down by death. (There is also a connection with traditional still-life painting which often incorporates dead game birds.)

In any case, the dead bird is by now a photographic cliché, a predictable image in the portfolio of every advanced student. Manuel Alvarez Bravo, David Batchelder, and Edward Weston are among the few who have lifted such images above the ordinary. Weston's "Pelican on Sand" (page 39) is one of several major images he made of this subject.

Other dead creatures have also become the subjects of photographs, if less frequently. Frederick Sommer, who has lived for years in the dry regions of Arizona, has photographed the desiccated, virtually mummified remains of wild animals—rabbits, coyotes, and frogs among them—that have perished in the desert. In striking contrast, he has also photographed the liquid, viscous fetuses and other parts of unborn fowl.

Les Krims, Jeffrey Silverthorne, Manuel Alvarez Bravo, Marion Faller, Emmet Gowin, and Paul Diamond have also photographed the carcasses of animals. Diamond's ferocious close-up of a set of snarling dog teeth bared in a rictus of death (page 69) is such a "found" event, as is Gowin's "Butchering, Near Chatham, Va." (pages 34–35).

Of all deaths, those of human beings are most powerfully affecting. Richard Avedon's portraits of his dying father, showing the man's progressive deterioration; Avedon's "portrait" of Andy Warhol, which studies the horribly scarred torso that resulted from an attempt on Warhol's life; Frederick Sommer's "Detail," a still life involving the severed foot of a hobo, cut off by a railroad train—all these images force us to face the inevitability of death and the fragility of flesh.

The responses of photographers to these and even more terminal manifestations of our mortality are as diverse as their sensibilities. Alvarez Bravo, who has photographed death in many forms, sometimes explores it matter-of-factly, sometimes poetically. Weegee, as noted, had a taste for the extravagant sensationalism of violent death. Edward Weston, by contrast, approached the dead man he came across during a photographic tour through the Southwestern desert in much the same formal fashion as he did so many of his other subjects, treating it as a still life. Indeed, without the caption's information we would be hard pressed to know whether the man was dead or only sleeping (pages 38–39).

Emmet Gowin's images of Rennie Booher in her coffin (pages 36–37) are similarly understated, but within the context of his work they have other ramifications. Gowin's photography, though very deliberate and formally conscious, incorporates many elements of vernacular imagery, especially from the snapshot/family-album matrix. Thus these images refer tacitly to the coffin photographs of the nineteenth century.

At the same time, Gowin has structured one ongoing channel as a family album, centered around his relatives: his wife Edith, their children, and the larger circle of family members. Rennie Booher was one of these, and photographs of her alive have appeared in exhibits and publications of Gowin's imagery over the past decade. For anyone familiar with Gowin's work, therefore, these images of her corpse have reverberations. They are not simply anonymous images of a disconnected death, but symbols of the termination of a life with which the viewer has become intimately involved through Gowin's photography. They are part of a larger metaphor concerning the cycles of living and dying. (In the second version of the same image, Gowin has combined two negatives in the same print, creating a

vision of the earth swallowing the body.)

A not-dissimilar effect was achieved by August Sander's "My Wife in Joy and Sorrow," which shows his spouse holding their twin infants, one of whom is dead.

The transition from life to death, from flesh to meat, has its rituals in society. One of these is the autopsy. Alwyn Scott Turner, Wolf von dem Bussche, and Jeffrey Silverthorne are among those who have photographed this activity. But death has been ritualized in other ways in other times. Peter Hujar's "portraits" (pages 60–63), made circa 1963, are of the mummified cadavers of monks, members of the clergy, and wealthy patrons of the Capuchin monastery in Palermo, Italy. What Nadar in the nineteenth century saw merely as a collection of random bones, and Elliott Erwitt once used as a humorous counterpoint to the arguments of the living, Hujar sees as a group of living gestures arrested by death.

There is no simple summation to be made of such diverse and unsettling images. They are not only consciously made artifacts but also descriptions of demonstrably real aspects of the world. Thomas Mann has written, "The grotesque is that which is excessively true and excessively real, not that which is arbitrary, false, irreal, and absurd." Could any images fit that definition better?

Even though we might define all photographs as "fictions," insofar as they are all no more than partial and highly subjective descriptions of individual perceptions, these more than any other kind of photograph within the grotesque mode embody ambiguous questions for the viewer to confront. As Kayser points out, "As long as the ornamental and pictorial grotesques were regarded merely as something alien to nature and arising from the artist's 'subjective' imagination, they could justly be rejected by those who held that art is based on the principle of imitation." But if all these things exist to be seen, are they not natural? If so, where does their grotesqueness lie—in the events depicted, in the depiction, or in our response? If not, then what is normality—a statistic, a specifiable quality, or merely an attitude?

Unlike grotesque works in other graphic media, these are not fabrications, not illustrations of fantasies or visions or dreams. They are representations of things as they are. As such they provide cruel evidence to buttress Goethe's words: "Looked at from the height of reason, life as a whole seems like a grave disease, and the world like a madhouse."

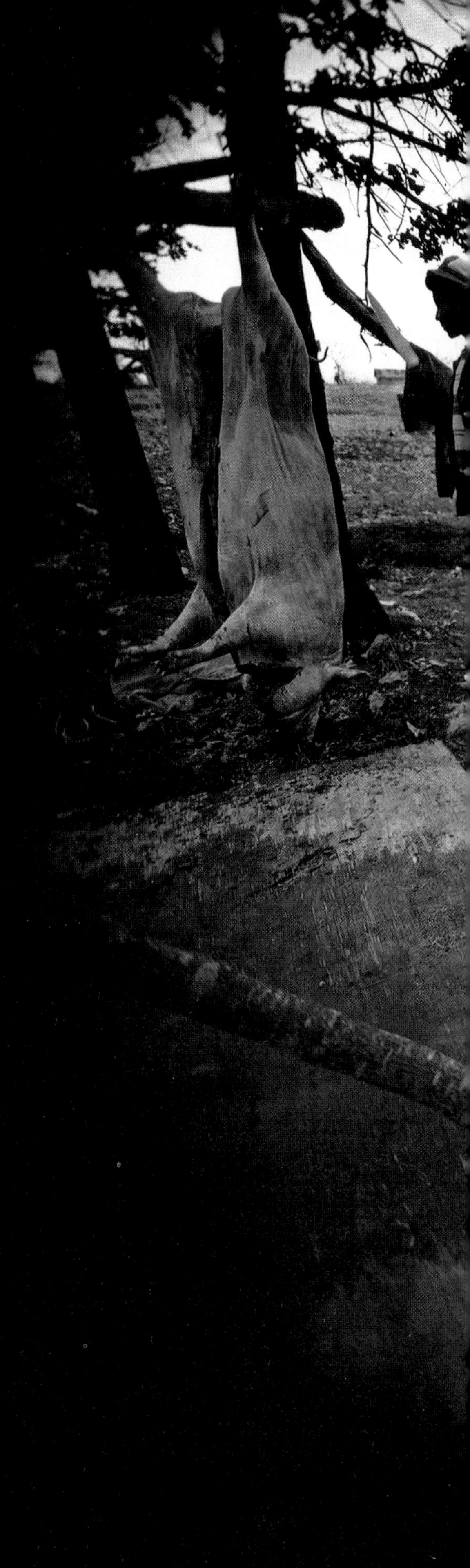

Butchering, Near Chatham, Va., 1970

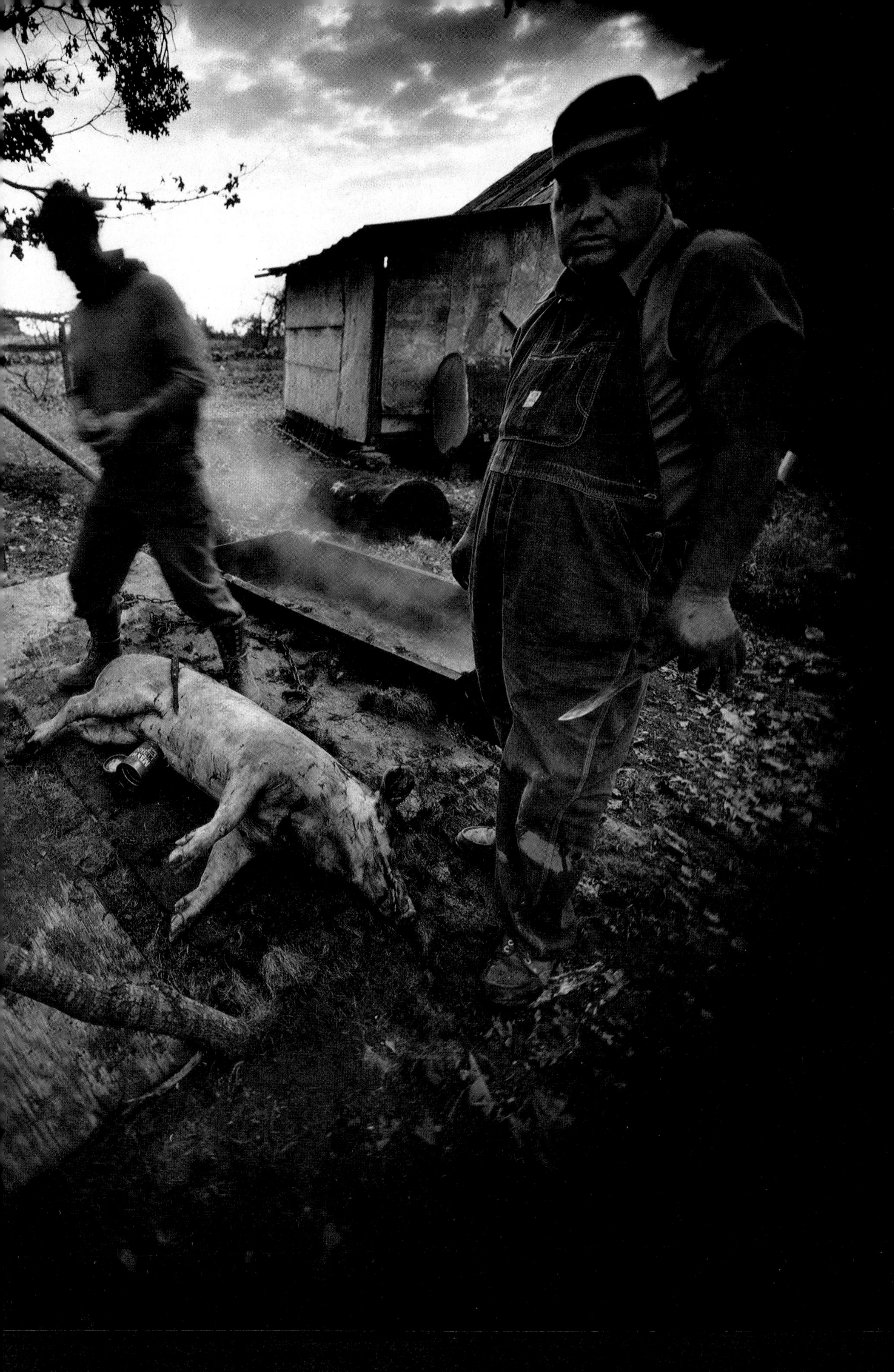

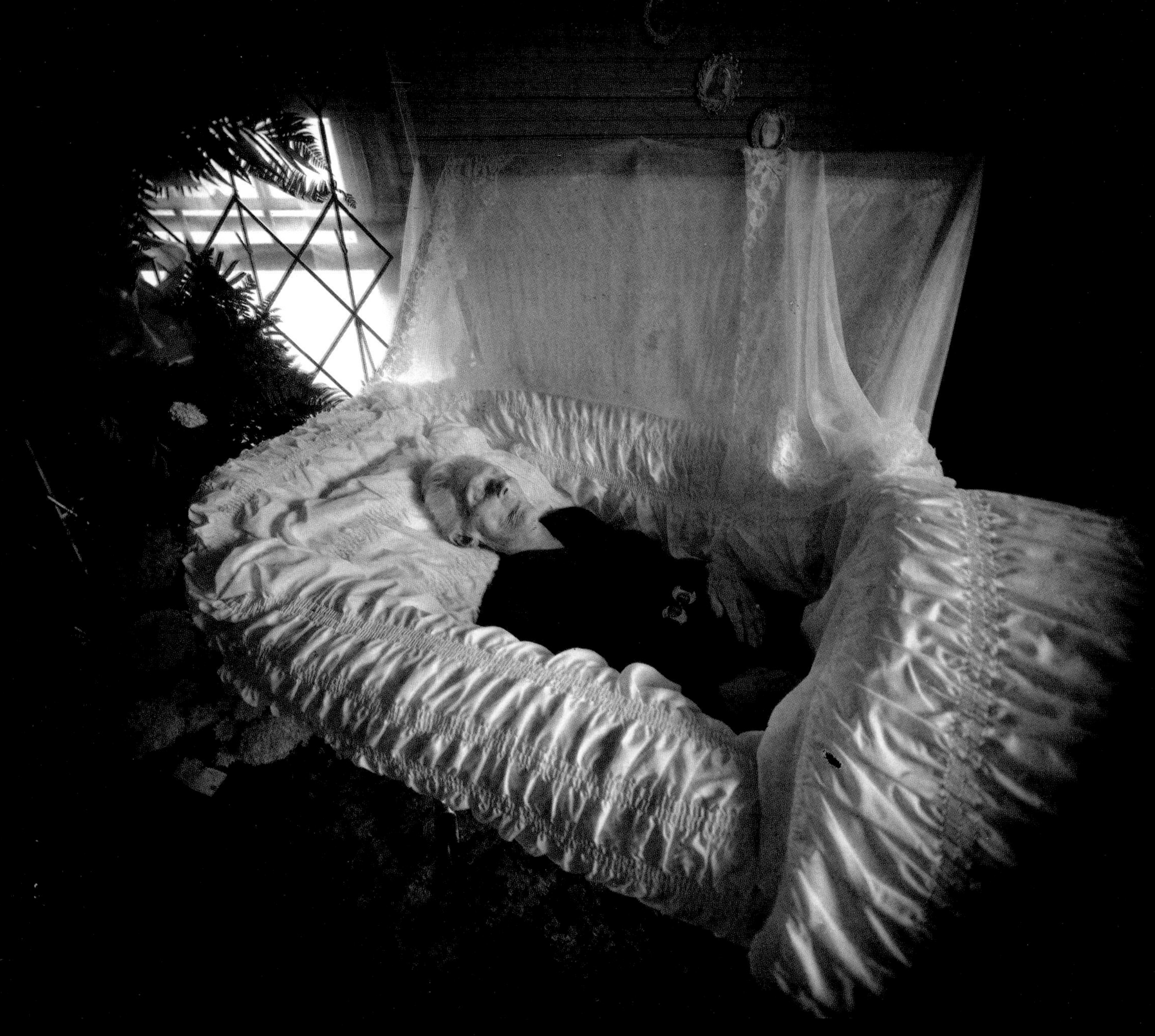

Rennie Booher, Danville, Va., 1972

EMMET GOWIN

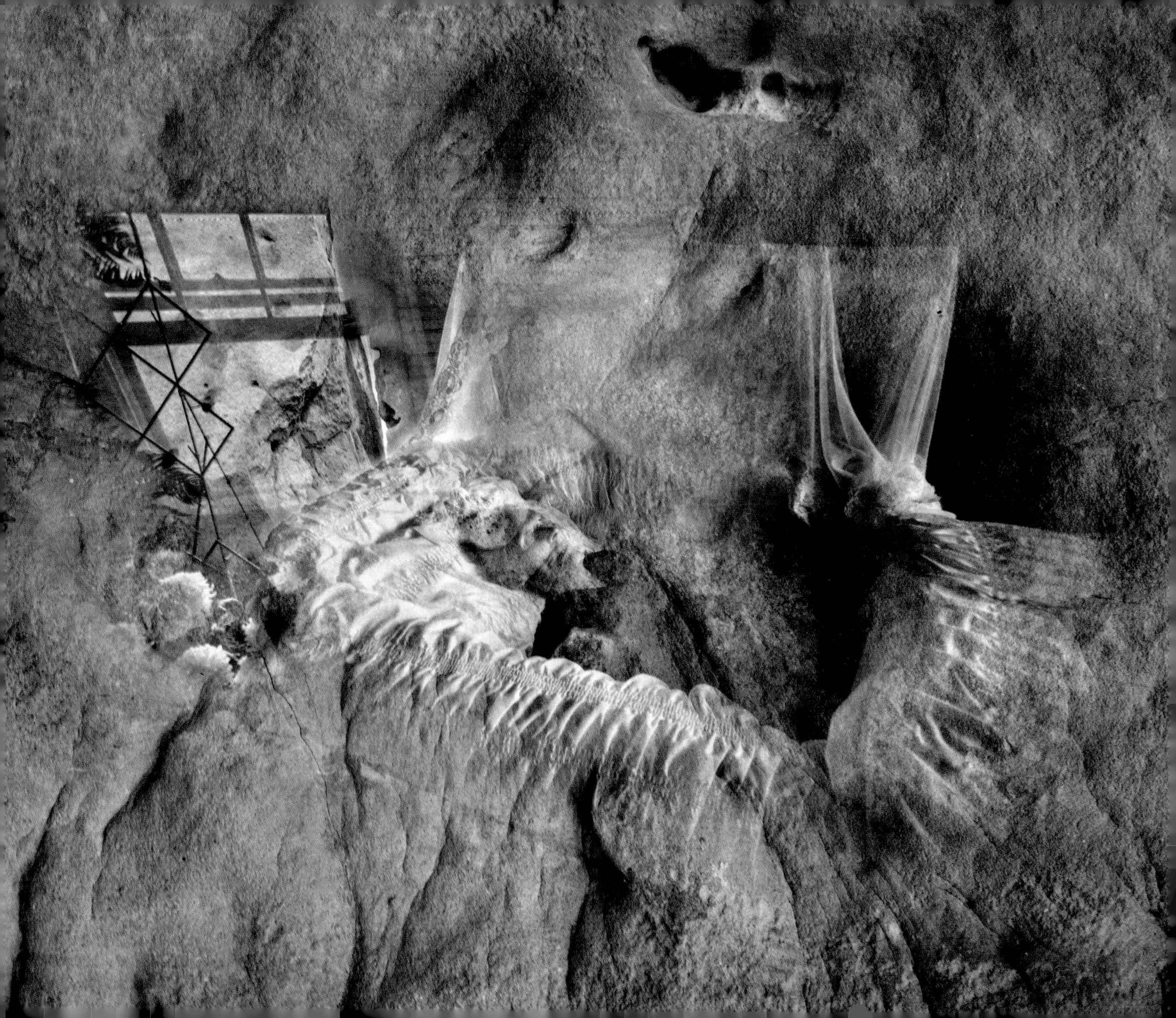

EDWARD WESTON

Dead Man, Colorado Desert, 1938

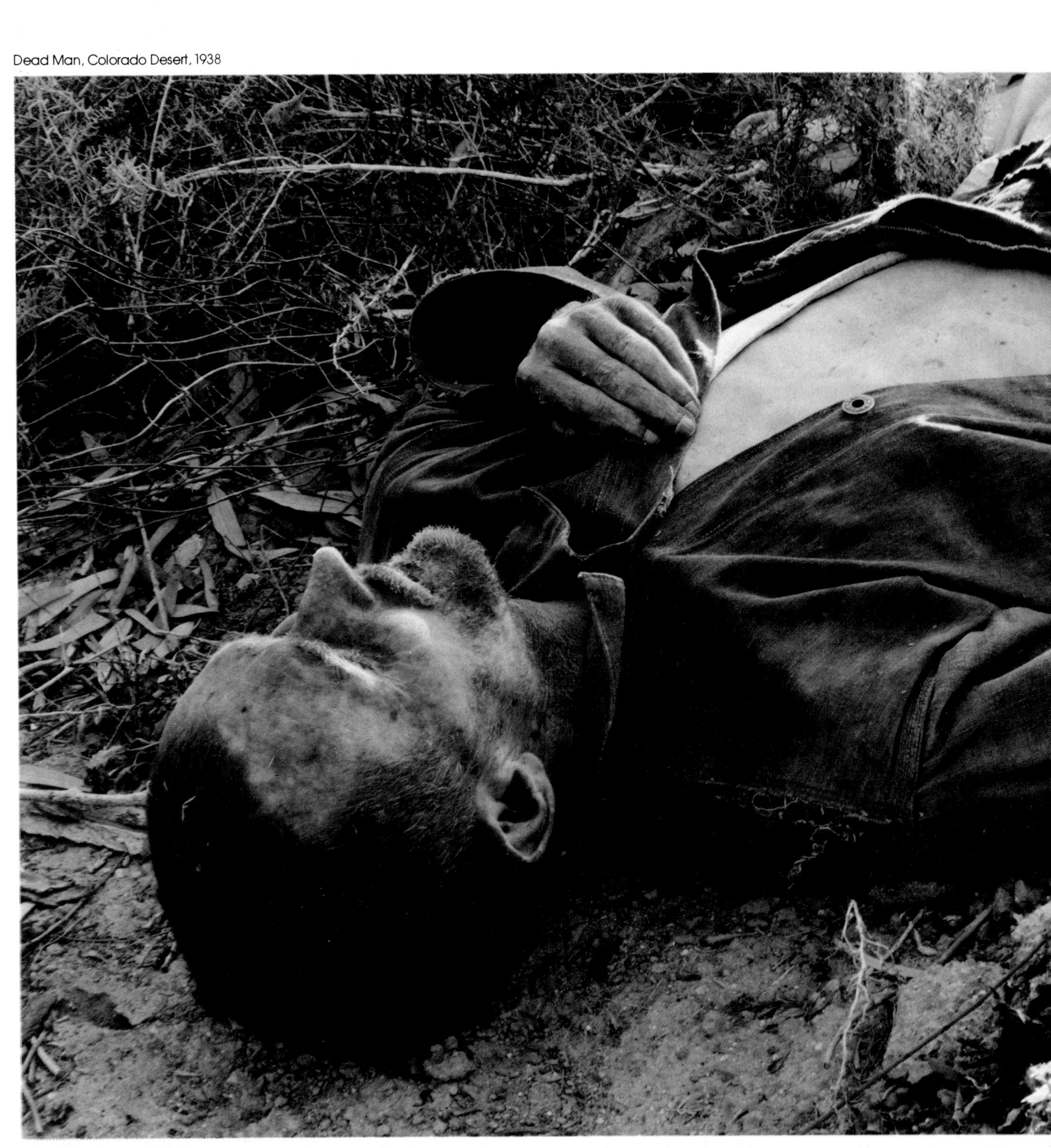

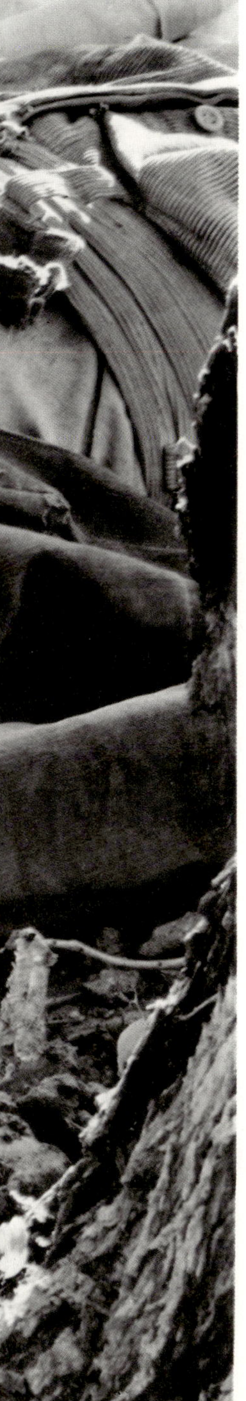

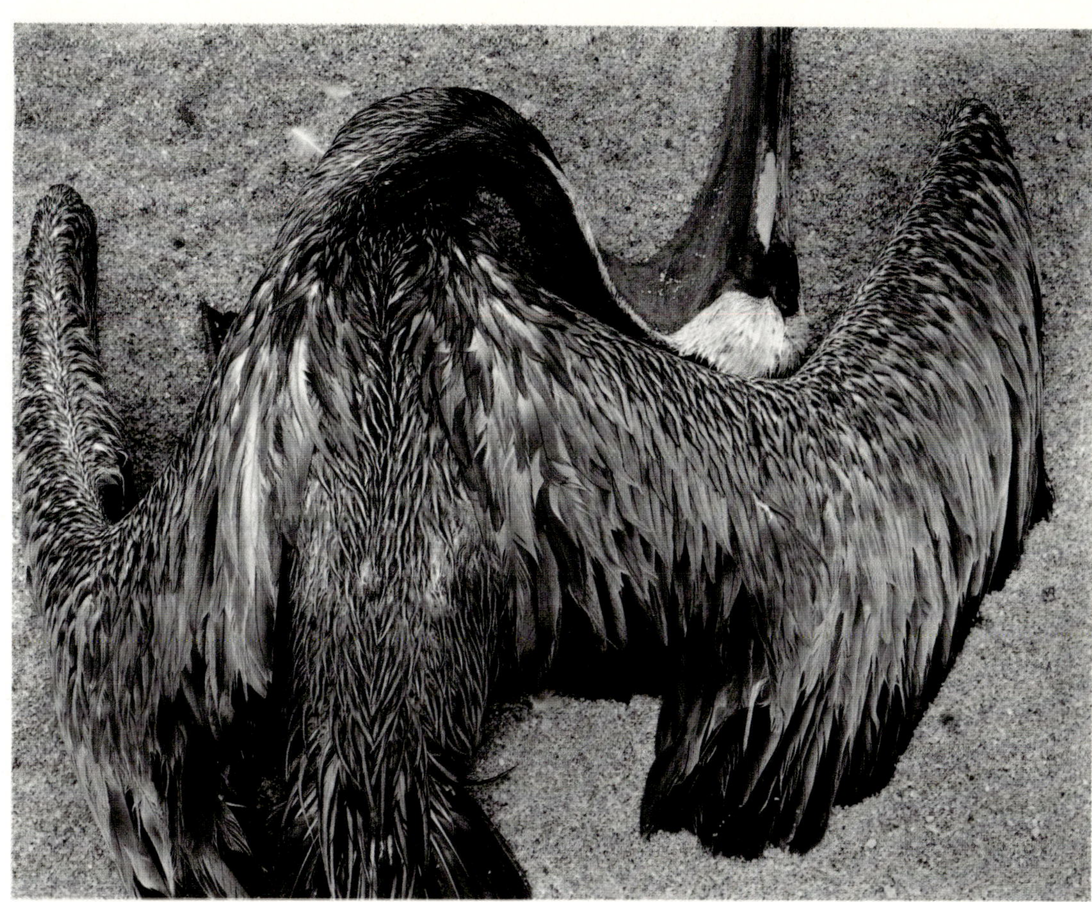

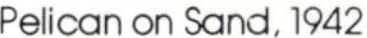
Pelican on Sand, 1942

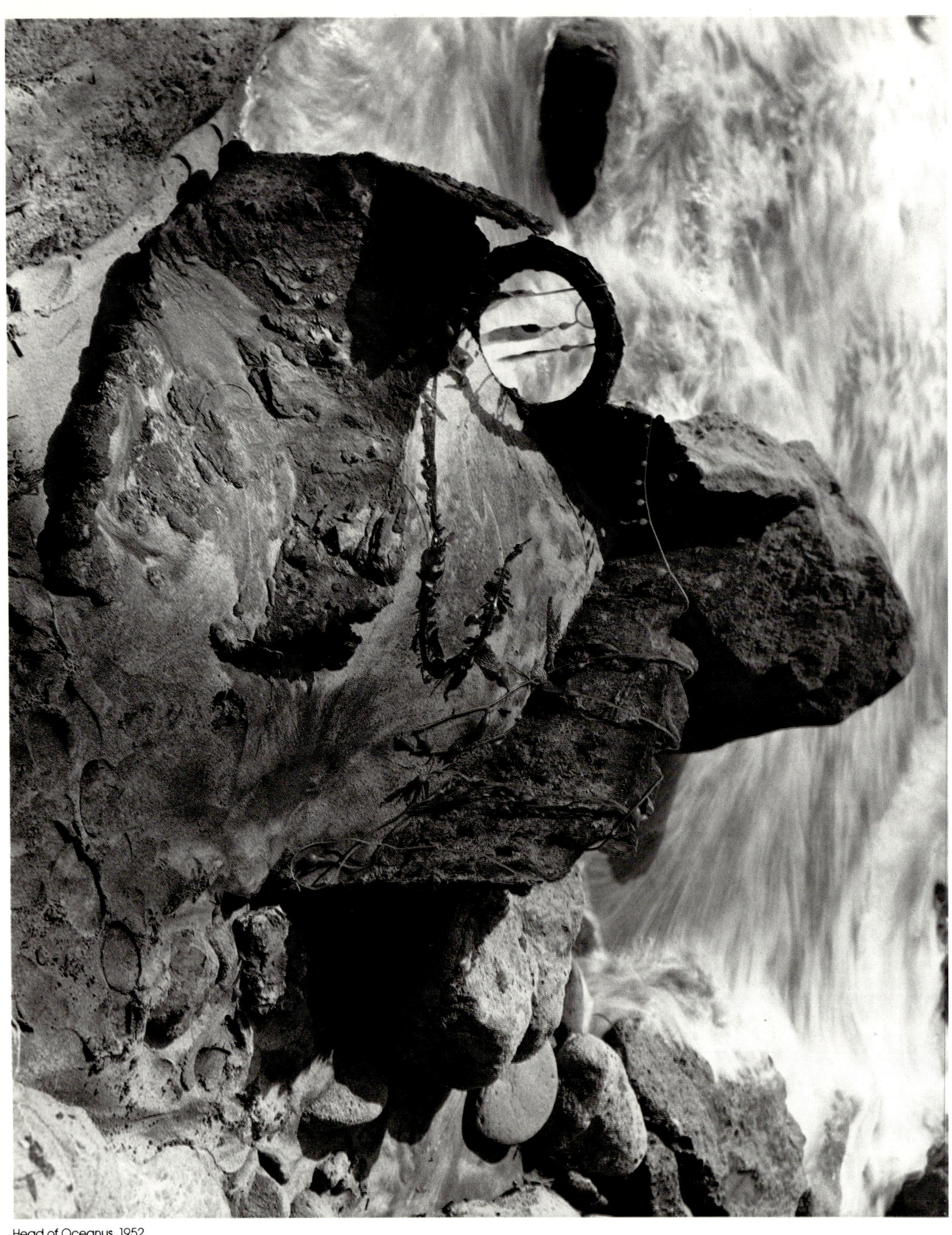

Head of Oceanus, 1952
(From Group B: Marine Forms)
Here are the remains of a truck which had fallen onto a California beach, from a cliff, and was then invaded by sand, and corroded by sea water…
Seen as a horizontal picture, the "naturalistic" meaning only is
apparent. But when seen vertically (as here), a completely different meaning emerges — and
the wreck becomes the powerful and disturbing head of a sea monster, or
perhaps of the sea god, Oceanus, whose nose is a rock, and whose eye has a pupil
of sea weed. This is the grotesque created by wind and water,
and aided by the human imagination. — C.J.L.
Copyright 1952 by Clarence John Laughlin.

CLARENCE JOHN LAUGHLIN

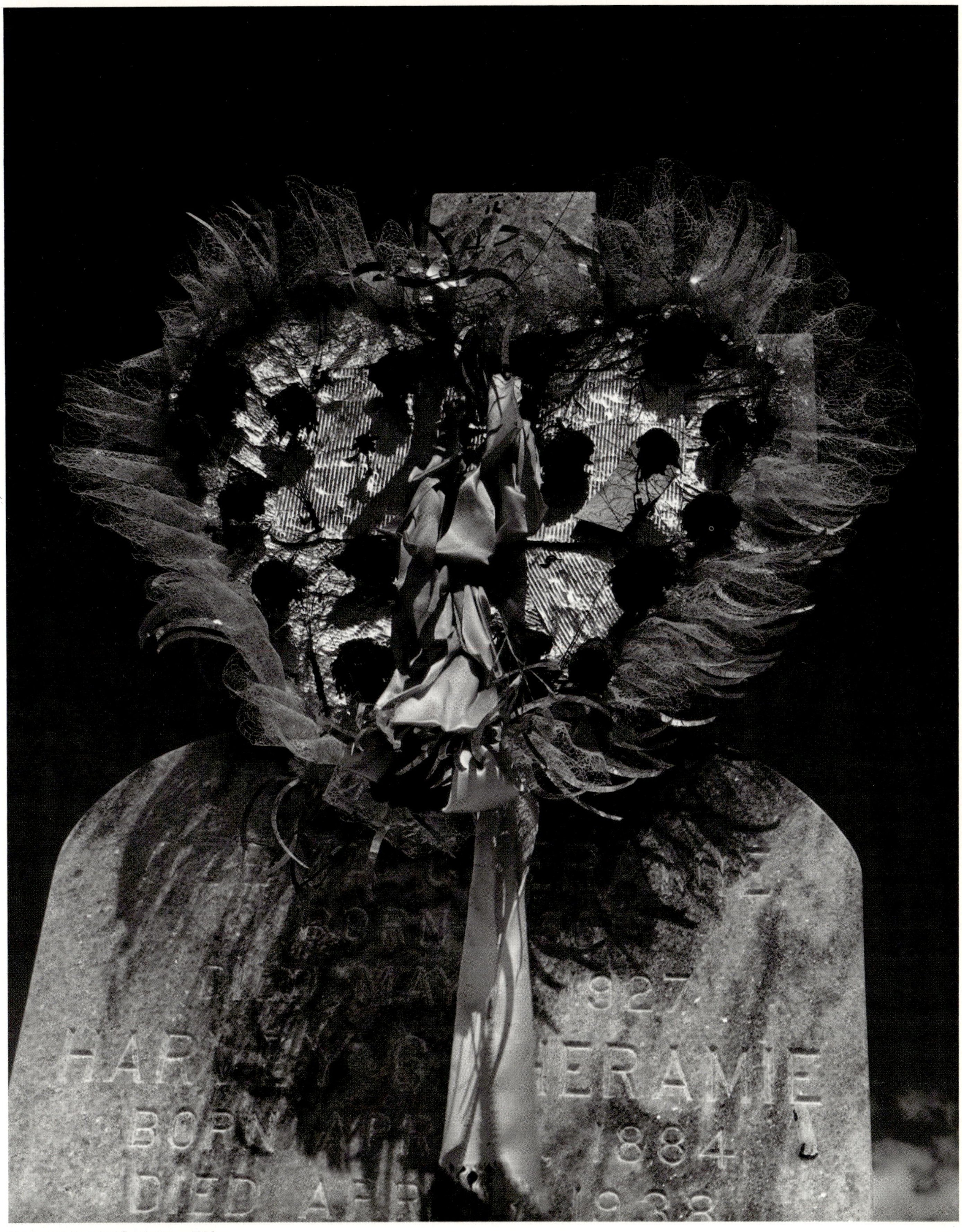

The Insect-Headed Tombstone, 1953
(From Group M: The Louisiana Plantations)
A memorial wreath in one of the strange south Louisiana swamp cemeteries — which, till
not long ago, contained some extraordinary American folk art.
This wreath is made of aluminum foil, lace, ribbons, and carnations, and
was created by hand. It has a remarkably fantastic
quality (probably because the subconscious mind is highly active
in much of this rural folk art), and suggests the head of a huge multi-eyed insect.
It is out of a world where hope and memory, magnified by
powerful emotion, transcend the world of reason. — C.J.L.
Copyright 1953 by Clarence John Laughlin.

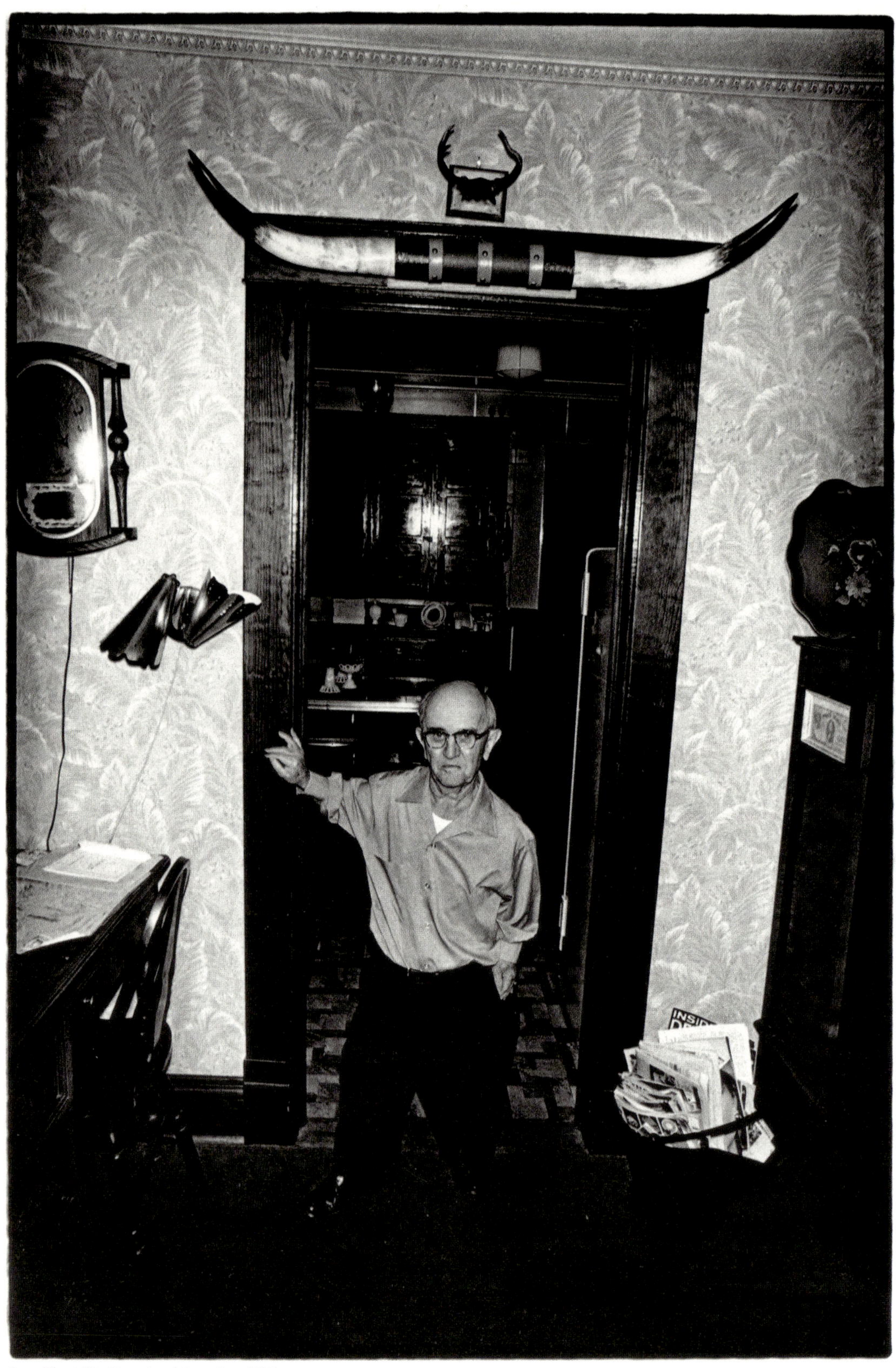

from The Little People of America, 1971

Photographs pp. 42-47 © 1971 Les Krims

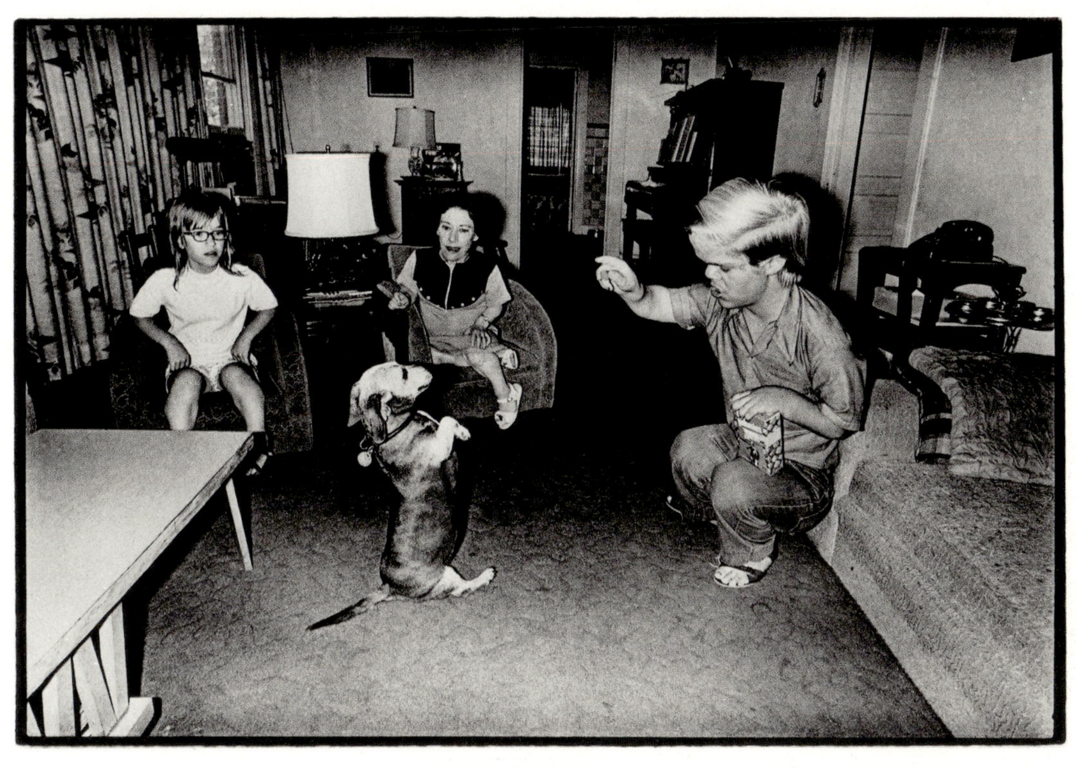

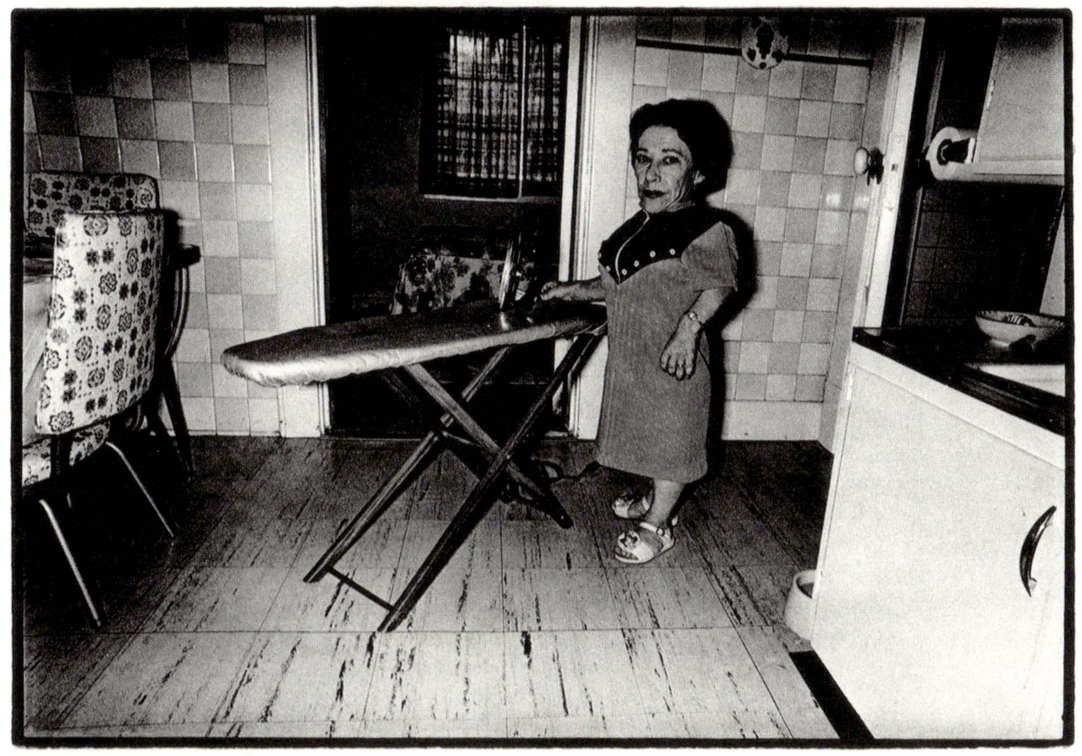

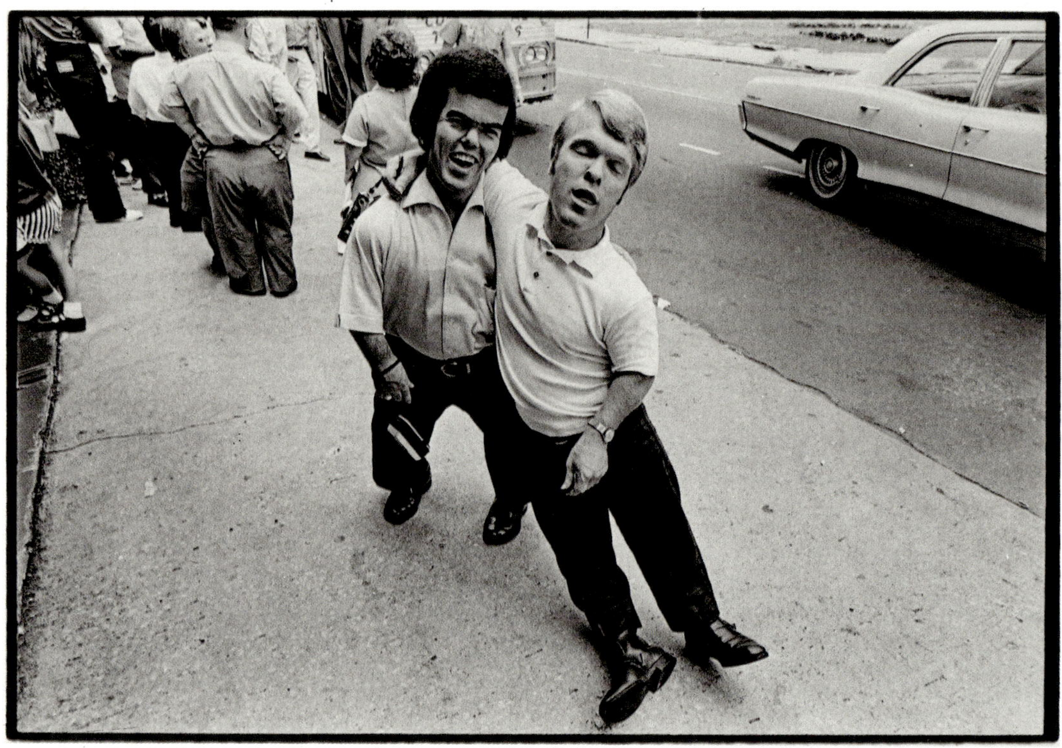

from The Little People of America, 1971

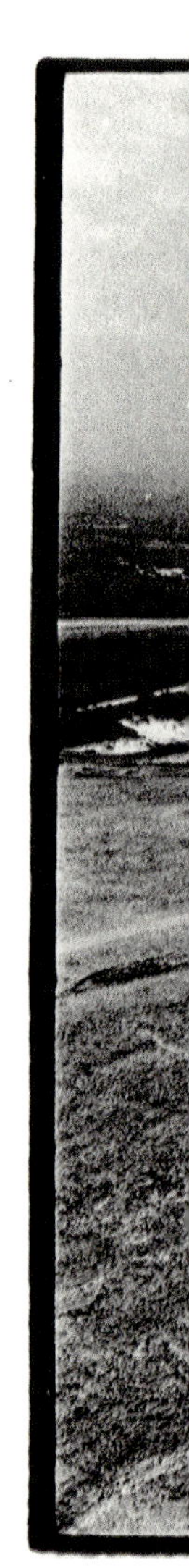

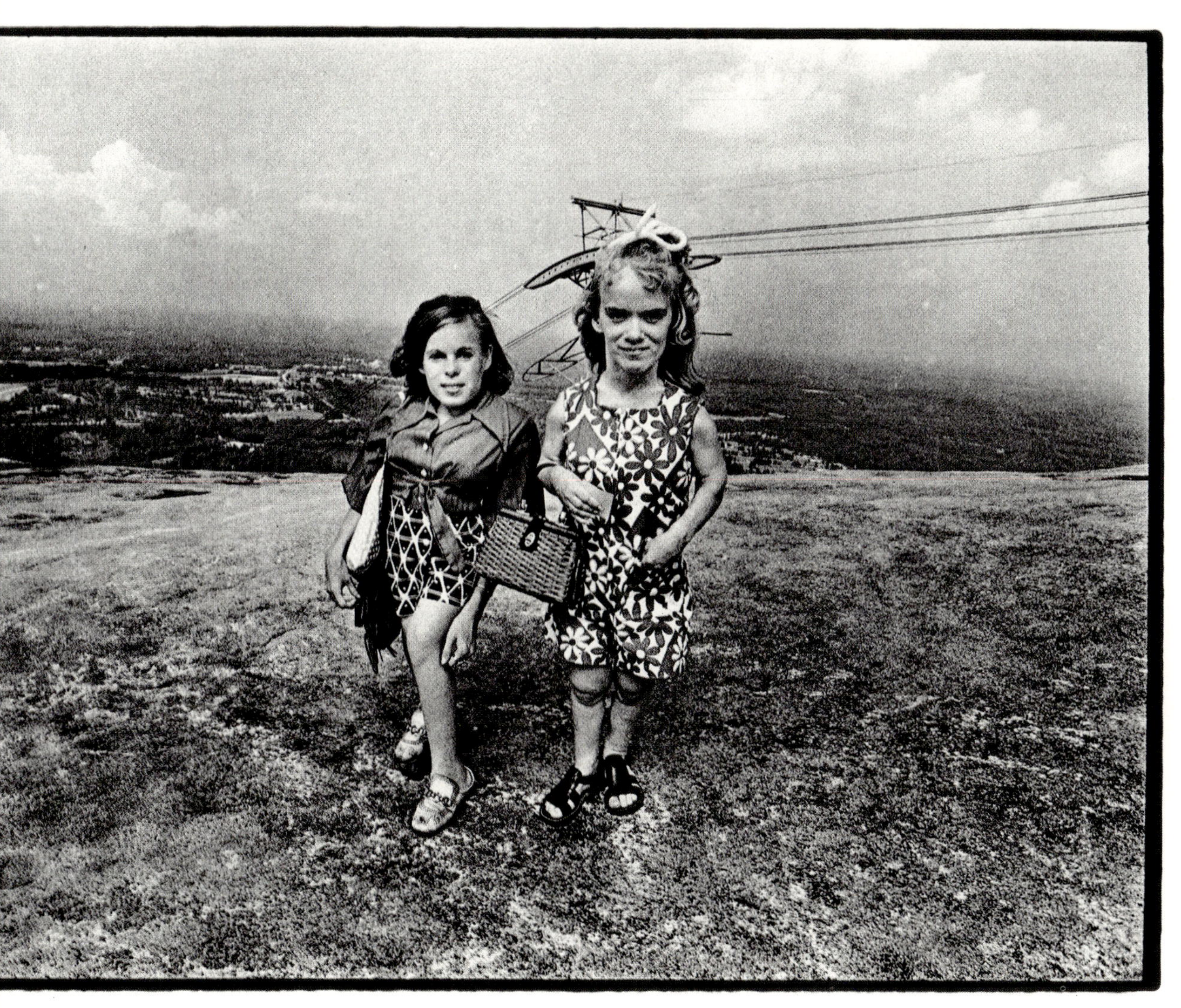

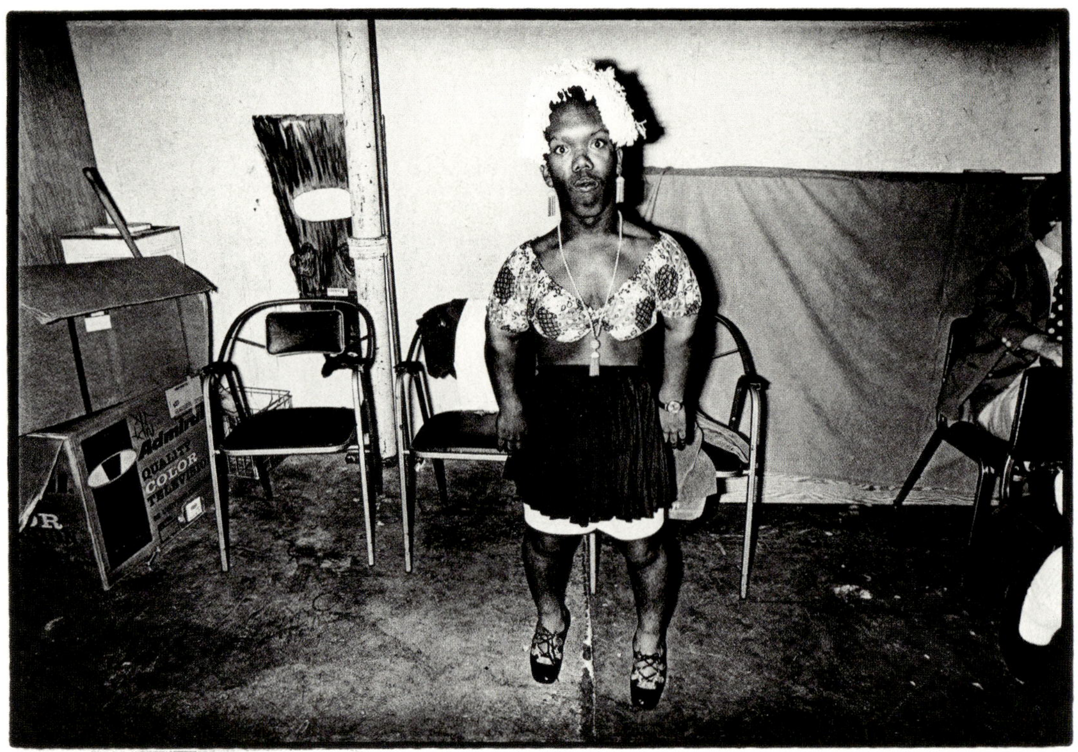

from The Little People of America, 1971

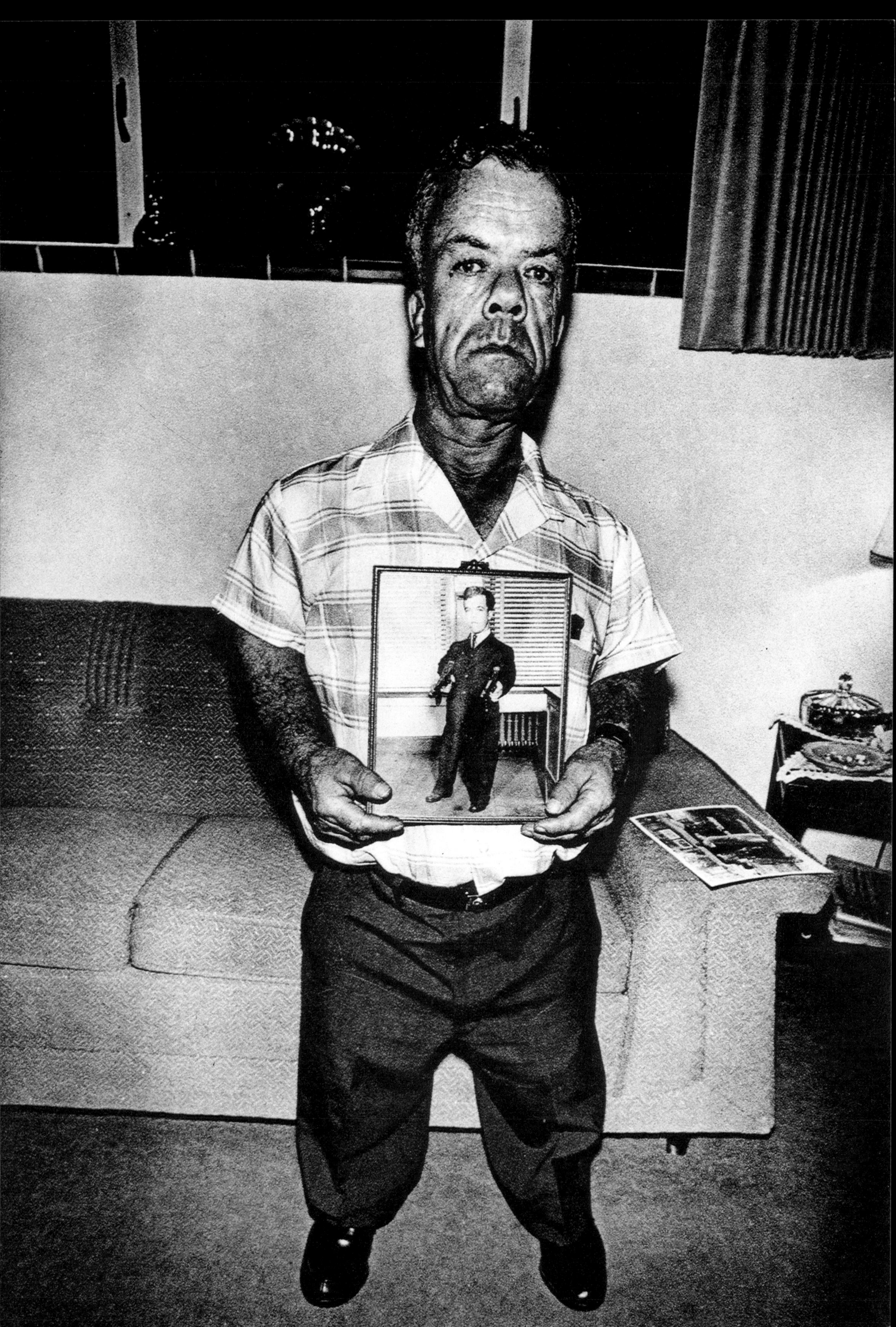

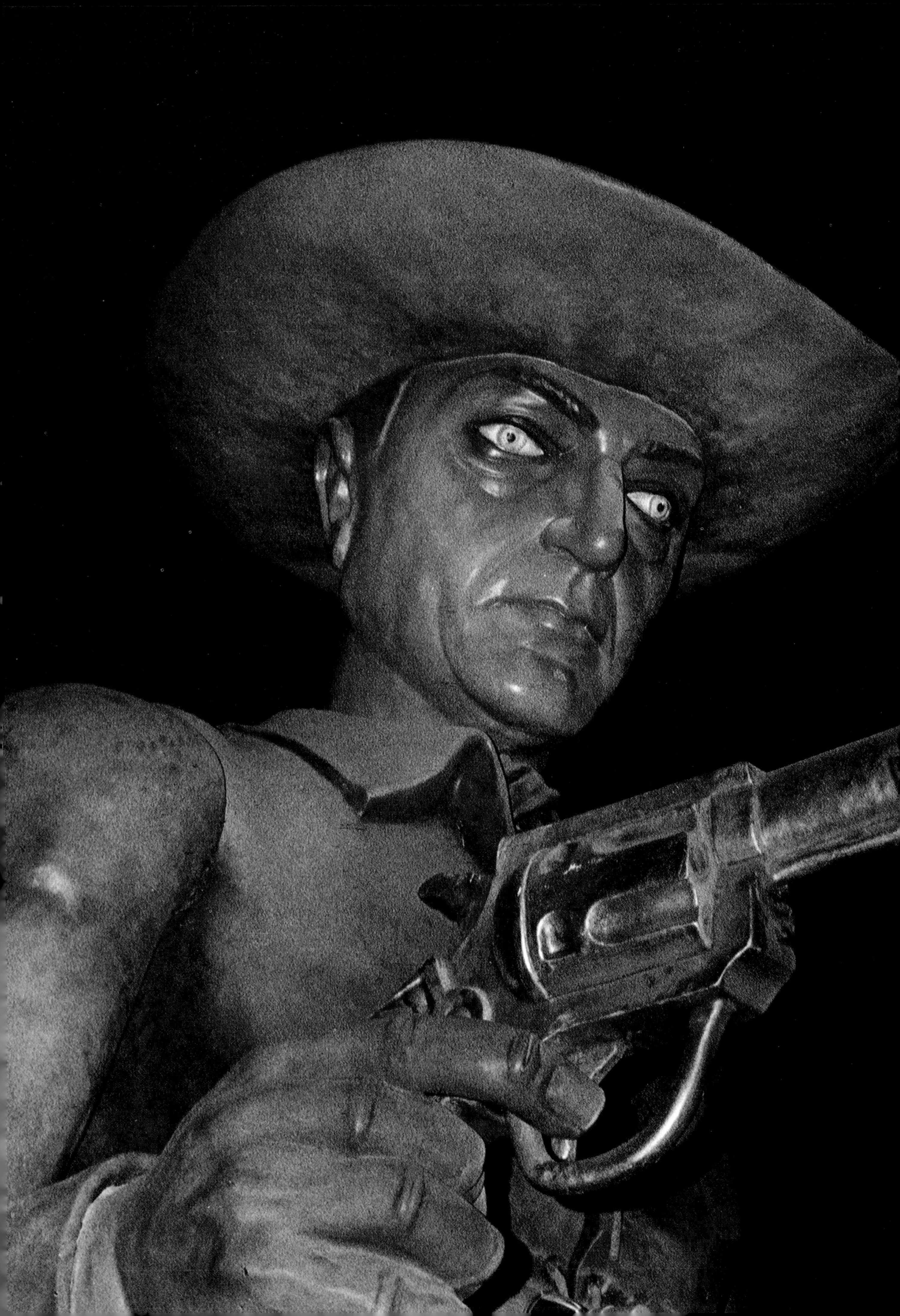

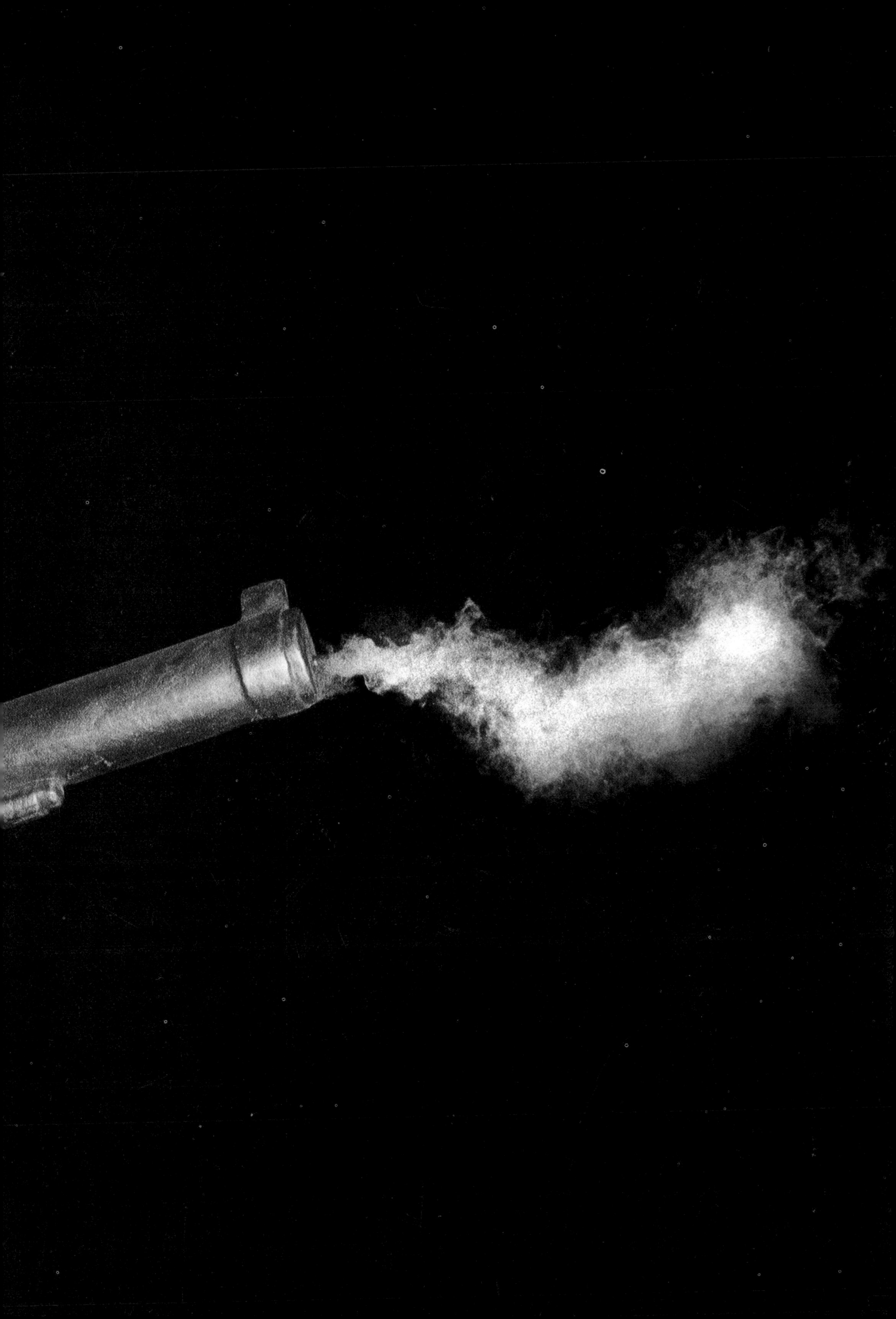

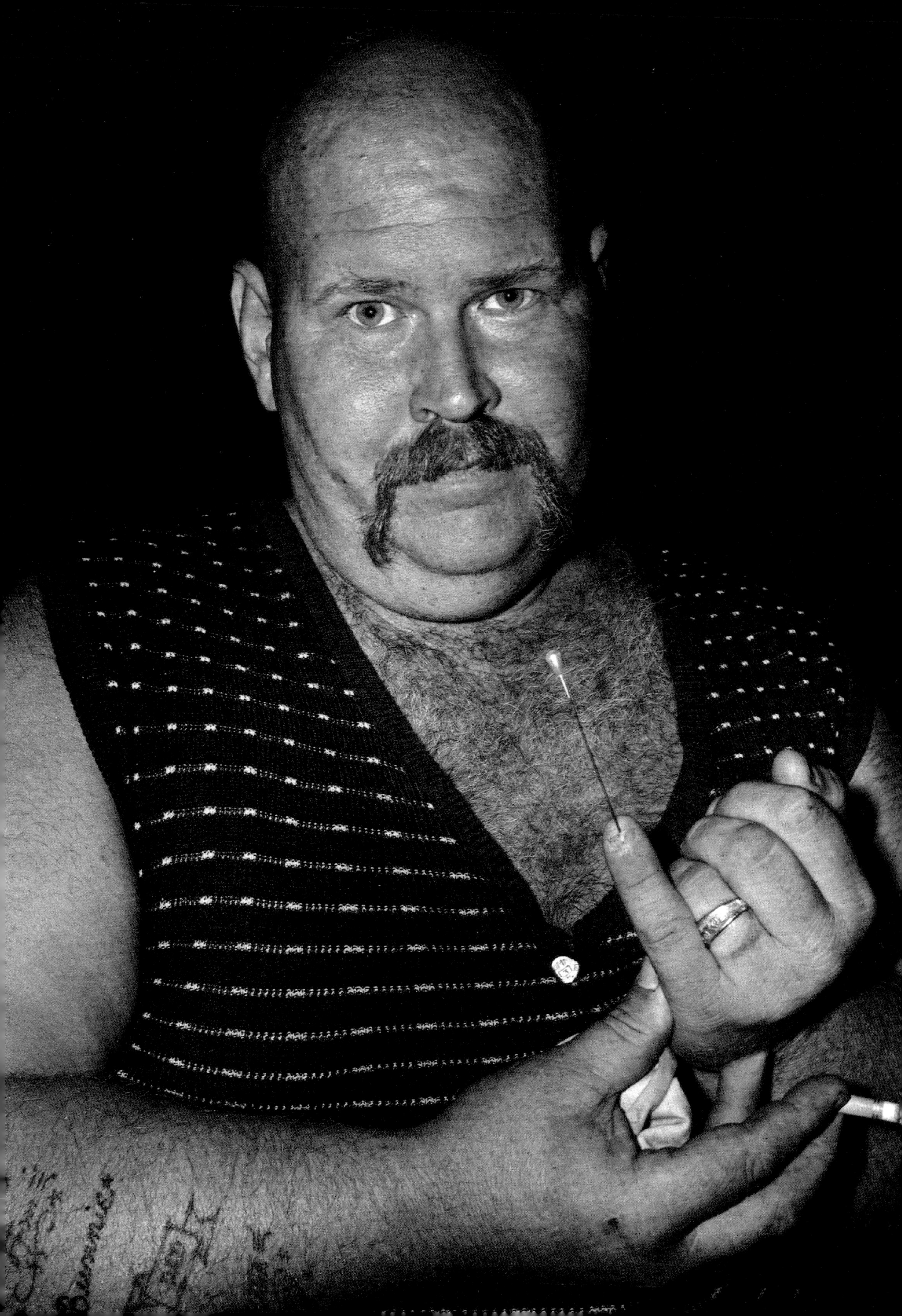

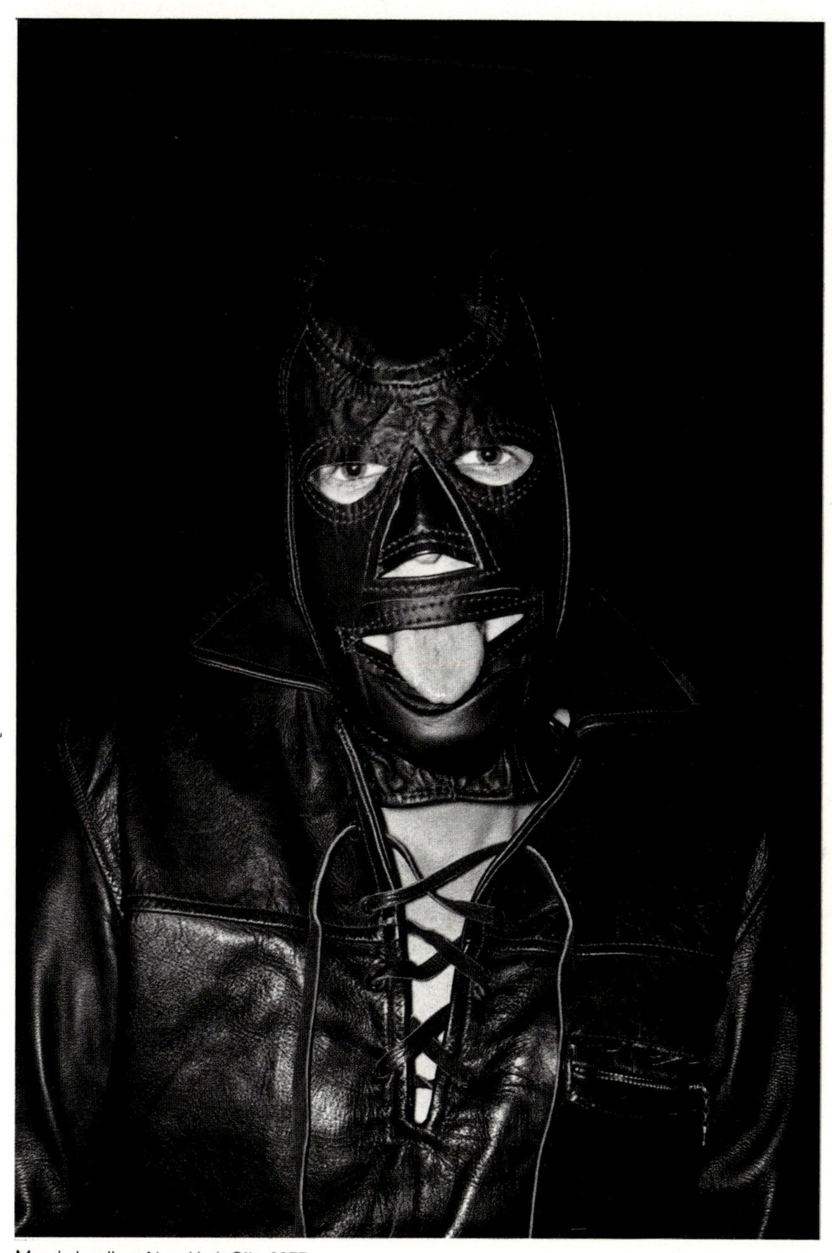

Man in Leather, New York City, 1977

Human Pincushion, New York State Fair, Syracuse, 1976

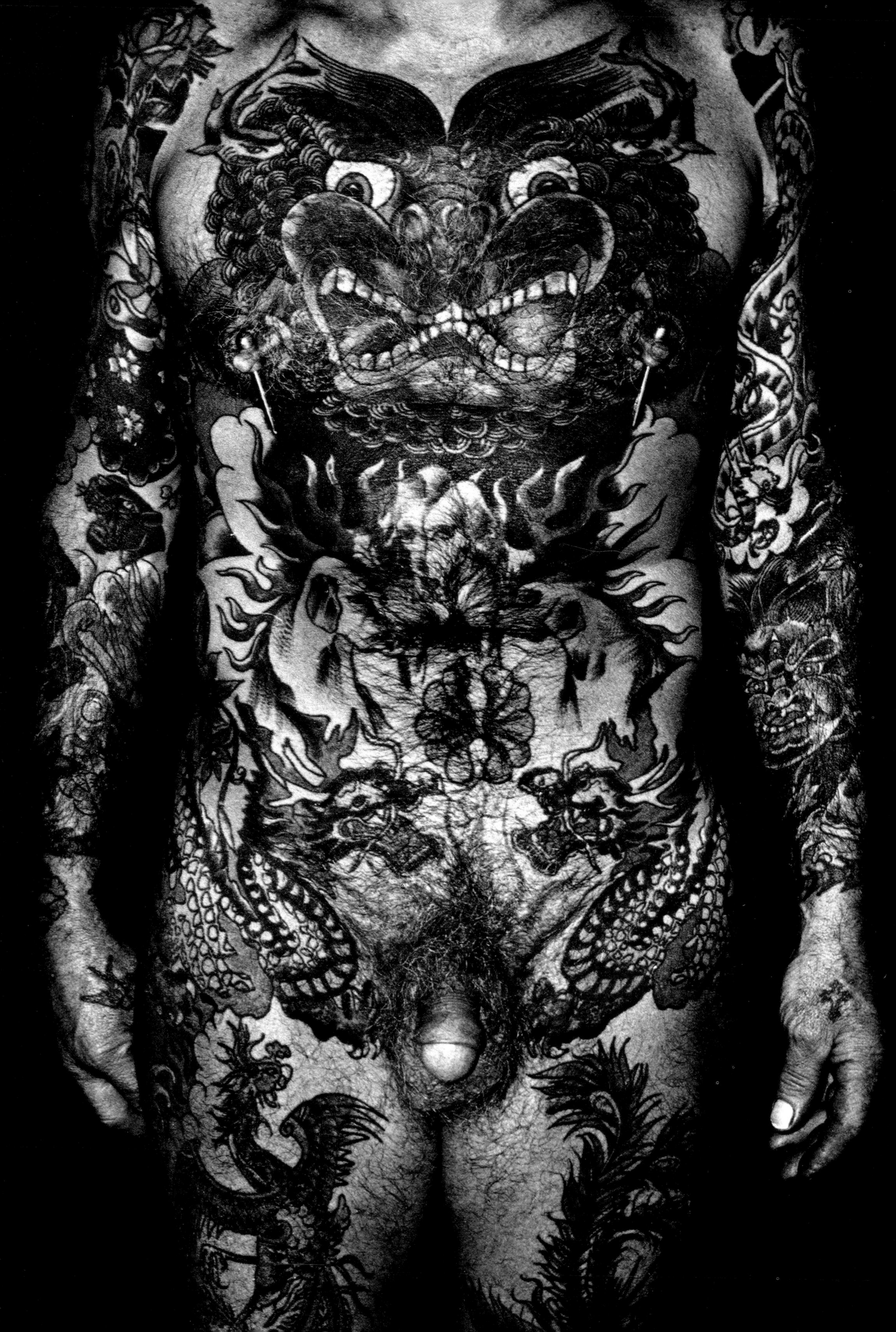

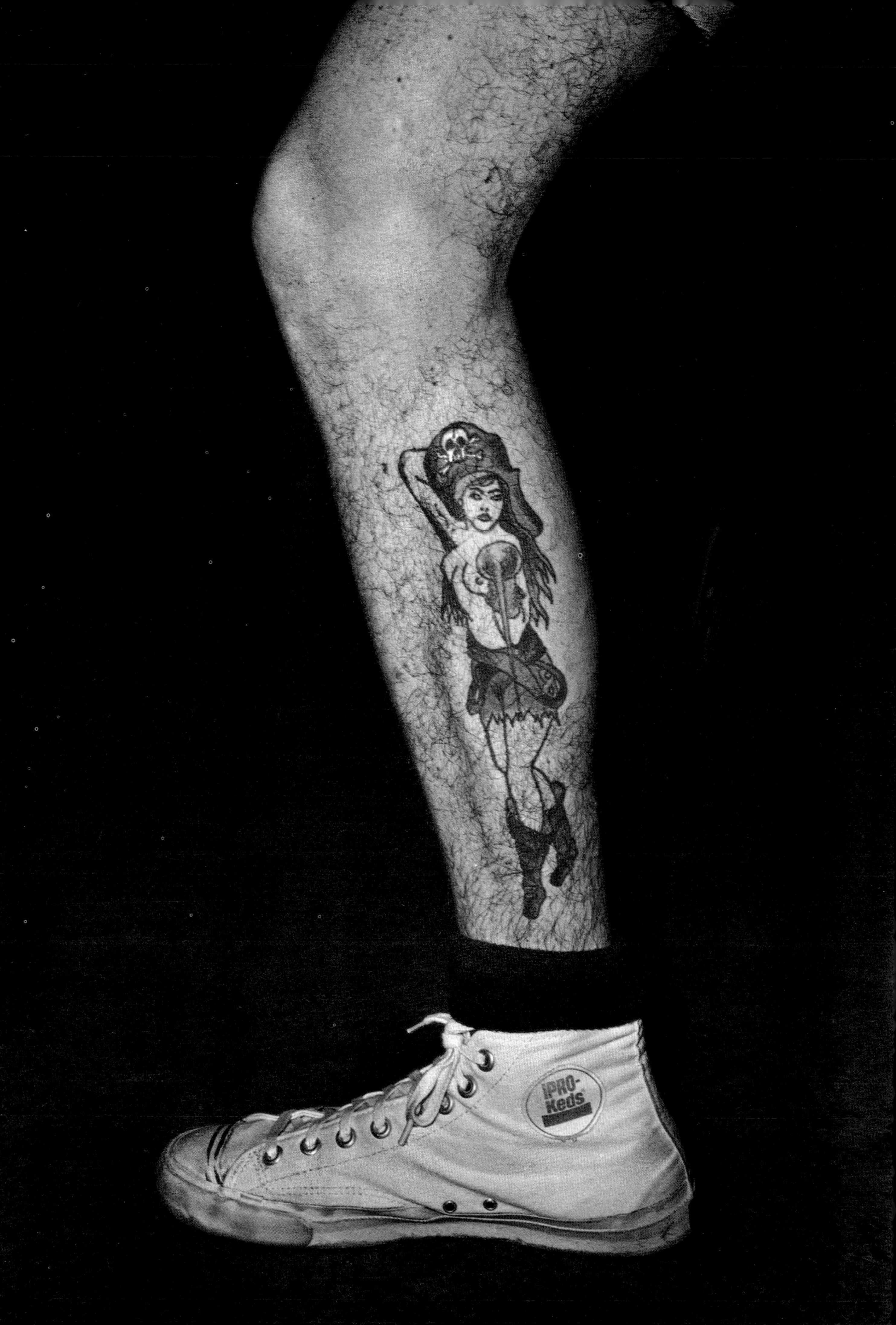

PRO-
Keds

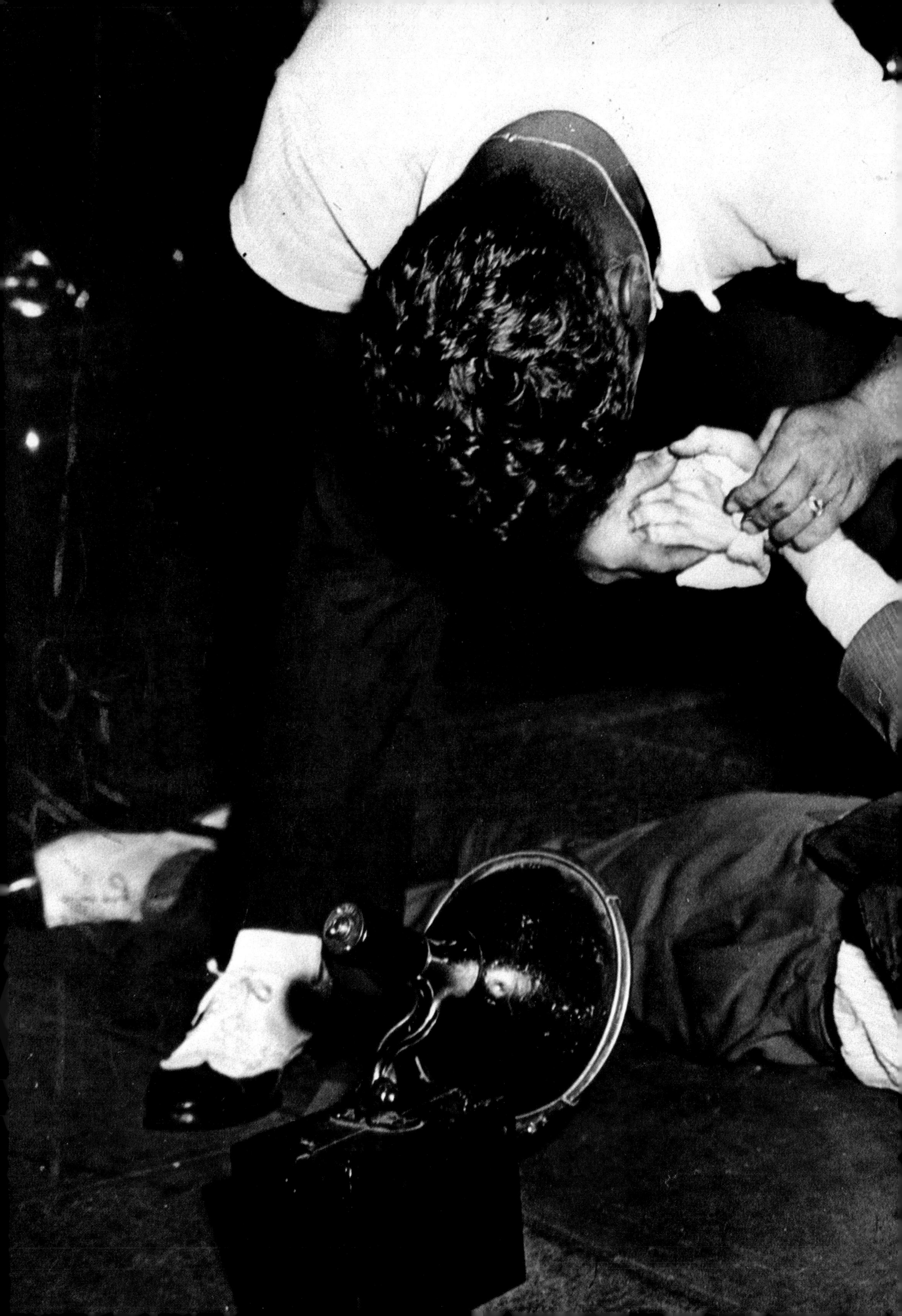

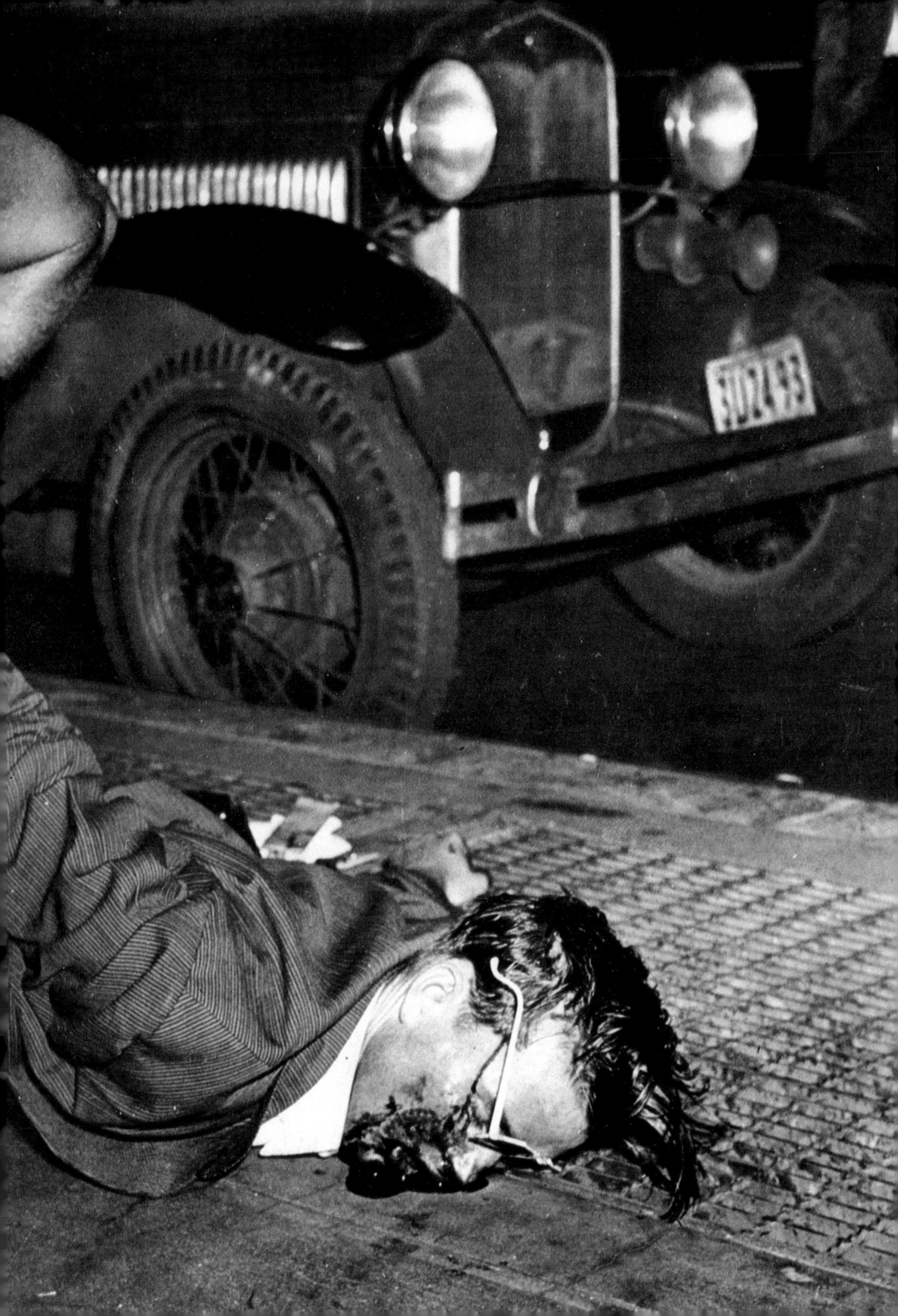

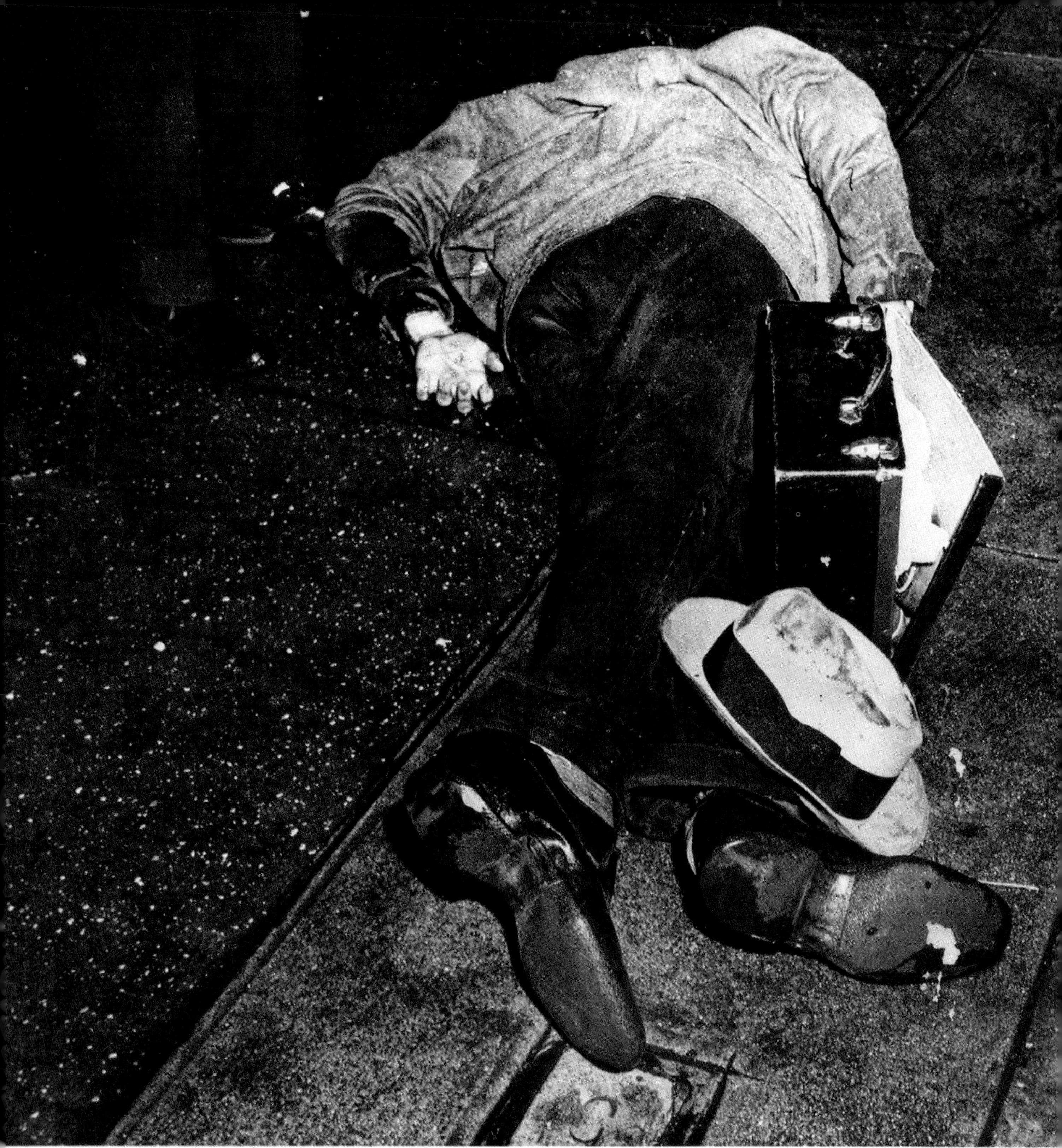

Murder in Hell's Kitchen. This longshoreman
was going to the laundry with a suitcase, was
shot and killed.

WEEGEE (ARTHUR FELLIG) preceding pages : Fingerprinting the Victim

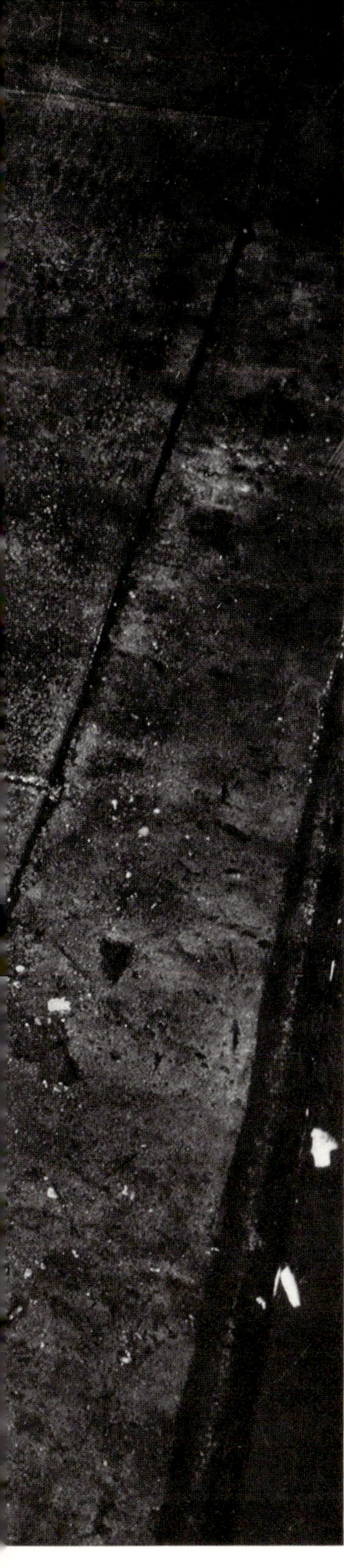

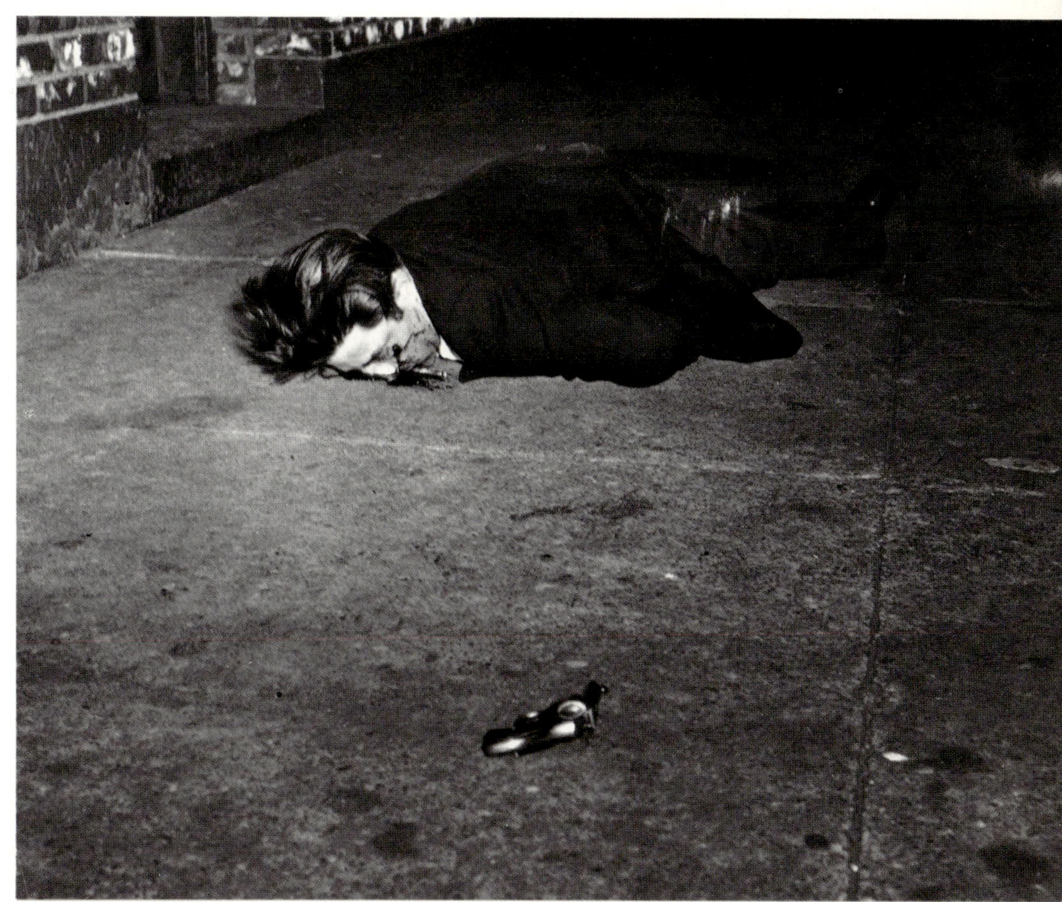

Man Murdered on Street

Close-Up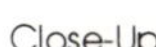

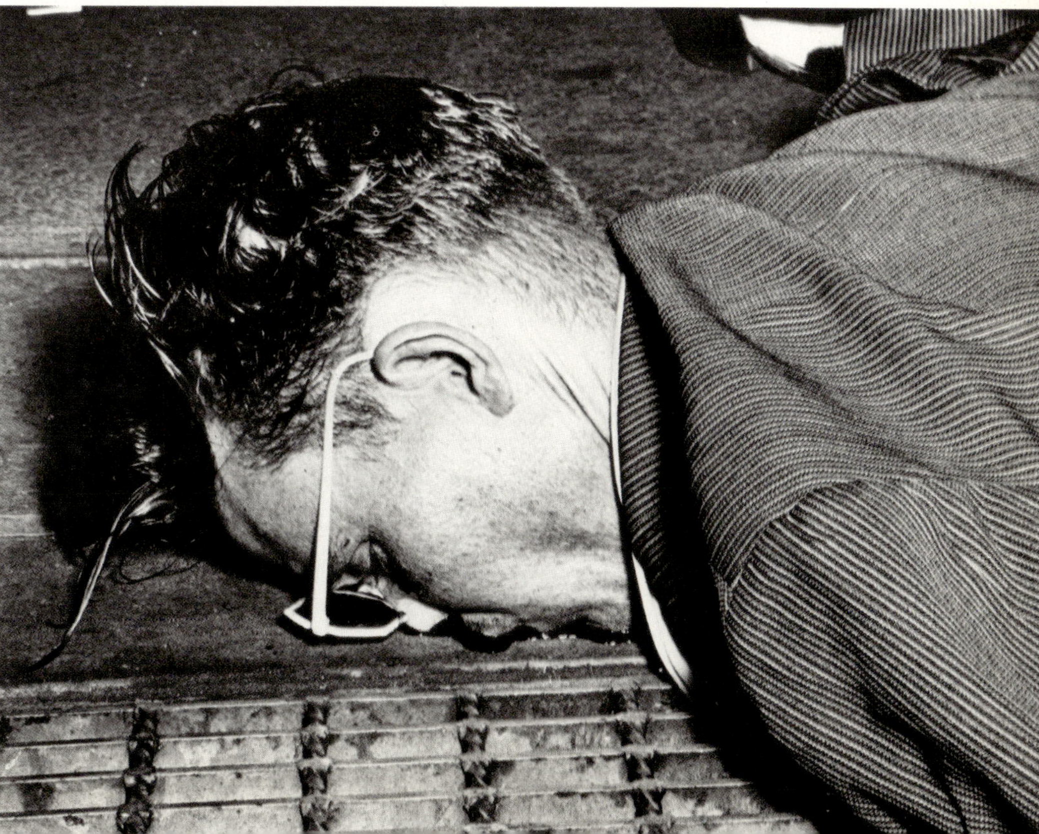

WEEGEE (ARTHUR FELLIG)

Curious bystander lights a match and bends
over to see if murdered man is still alive. Man
died while Weegee was taking picture. He had
met another sailor, with whom he'd had
an argument in Argentina. Police caught the other man.

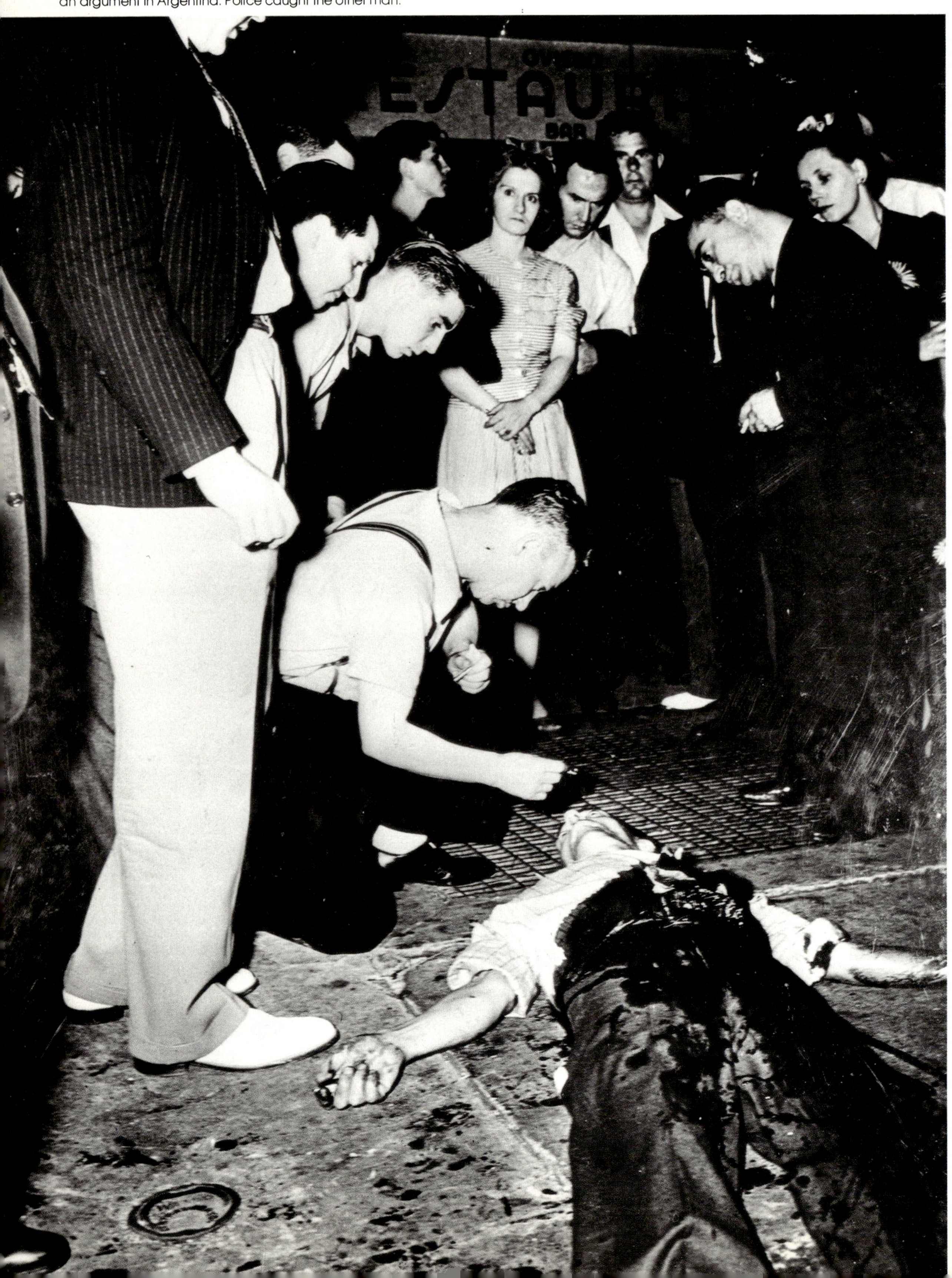

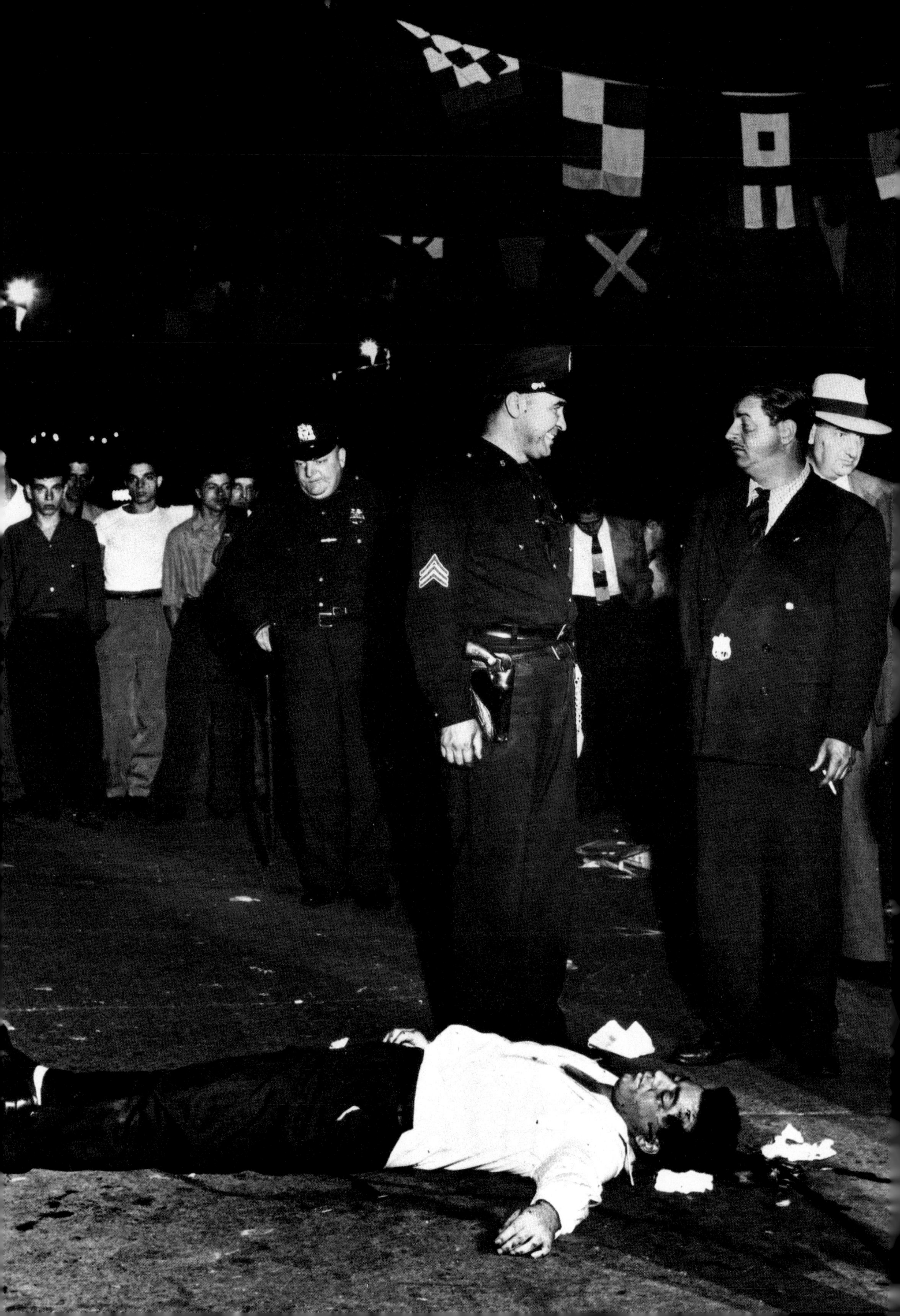

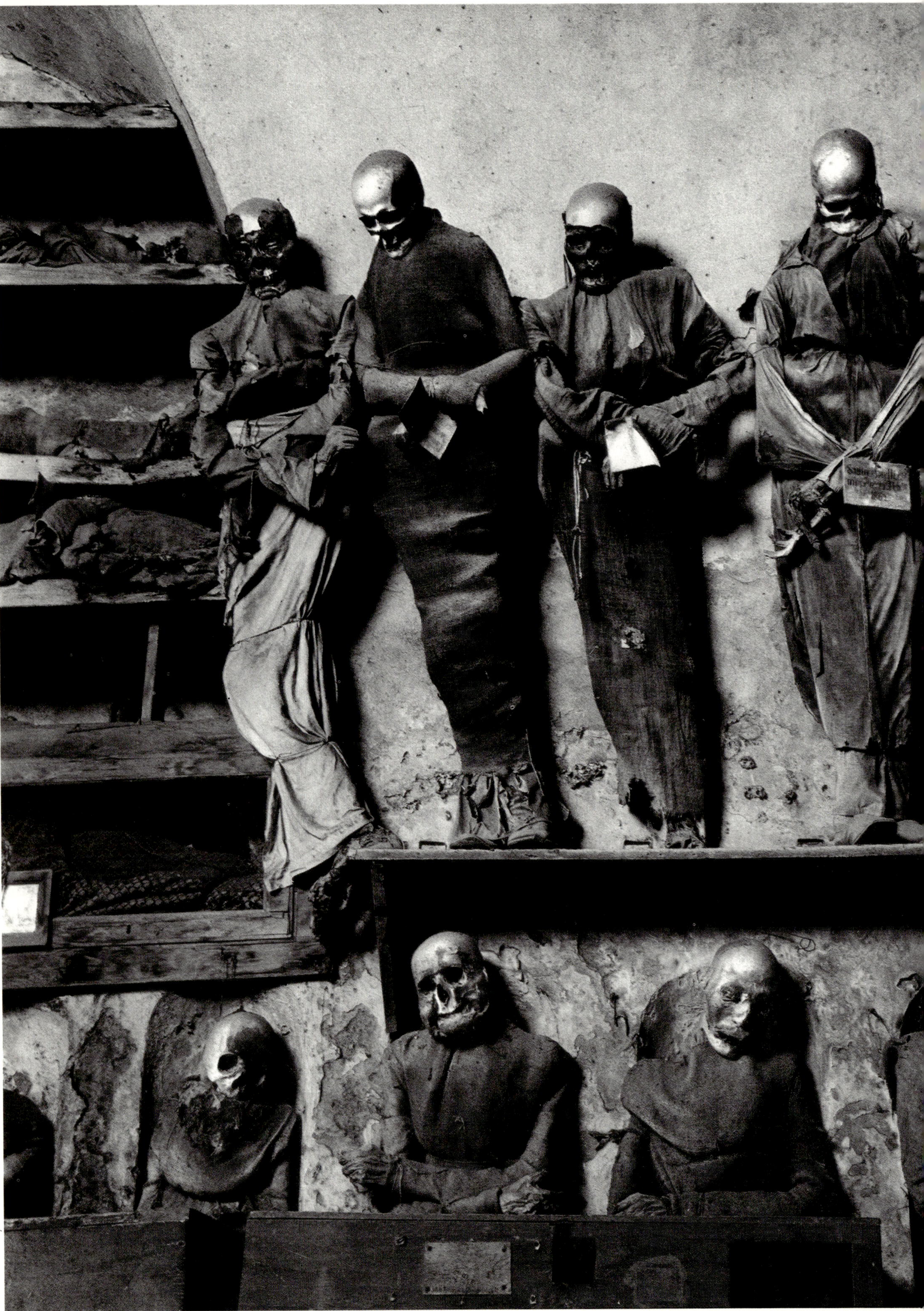

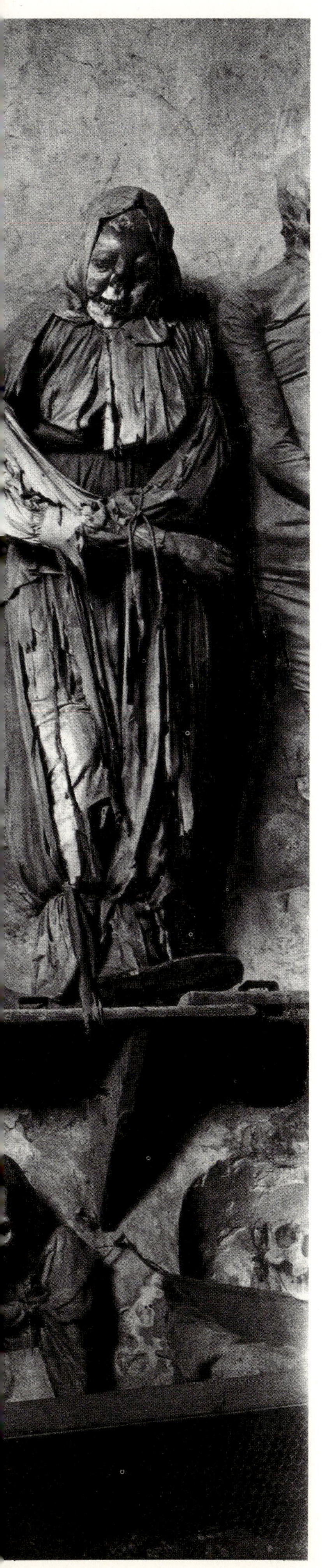

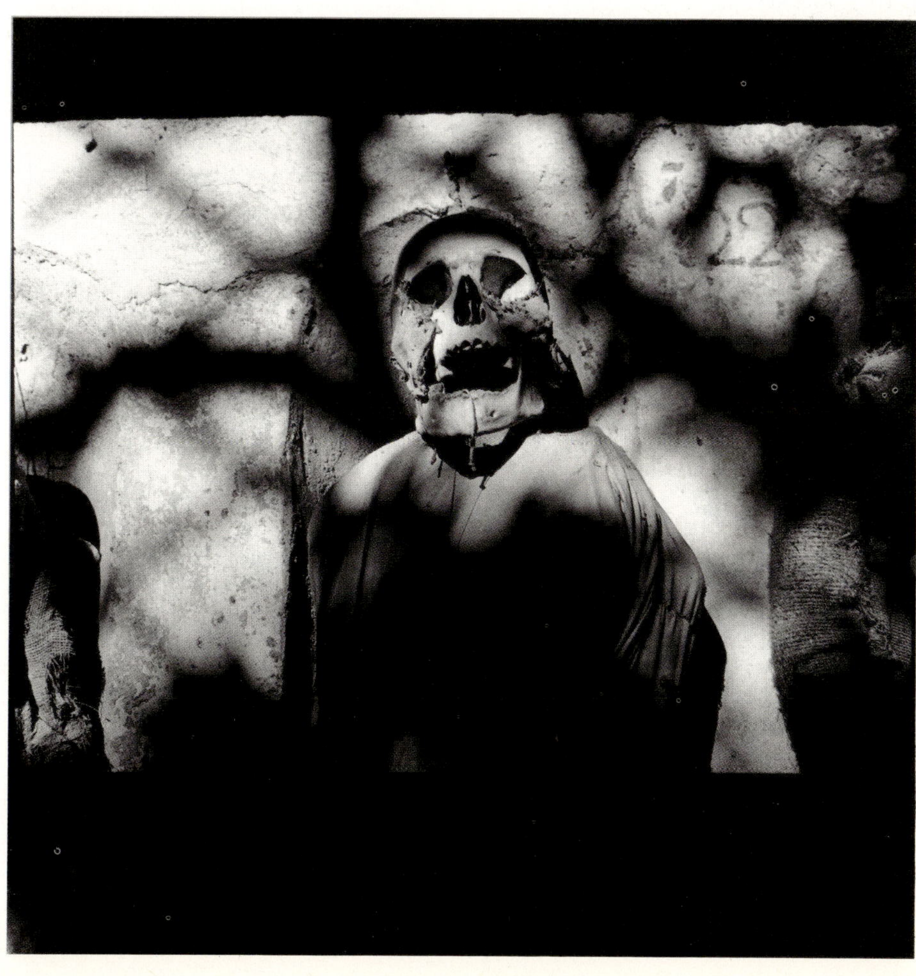

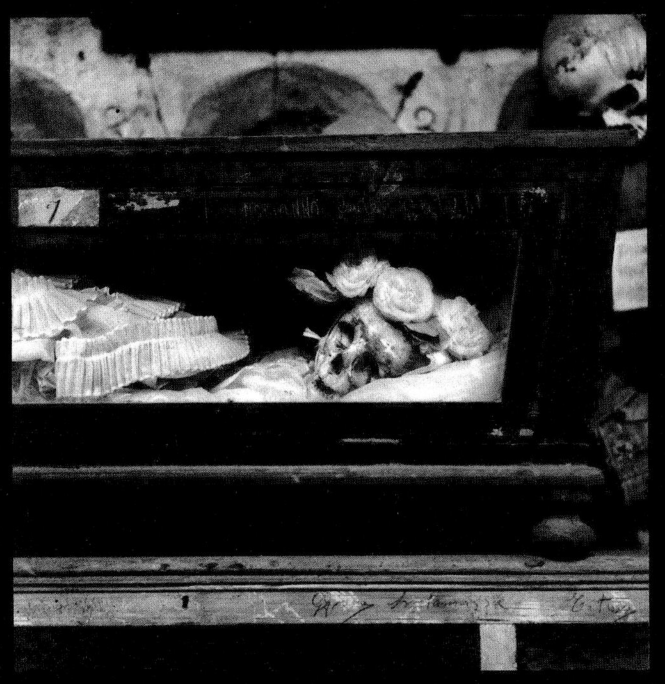

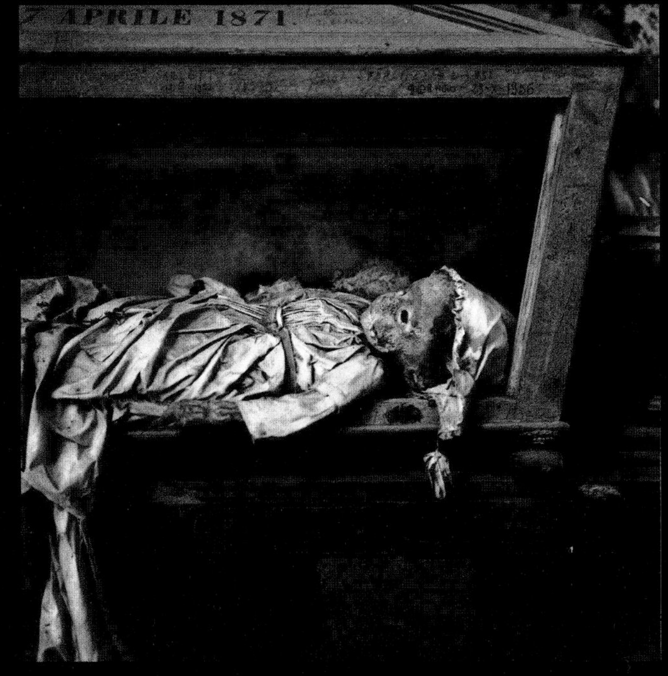

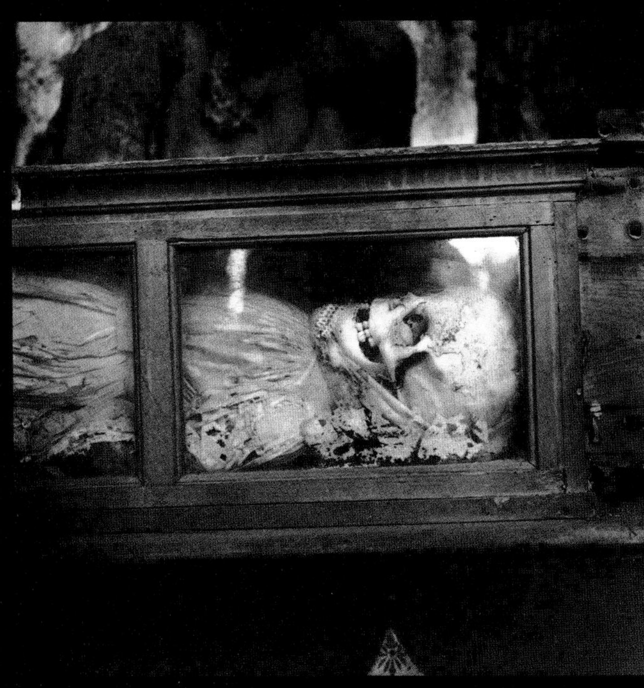

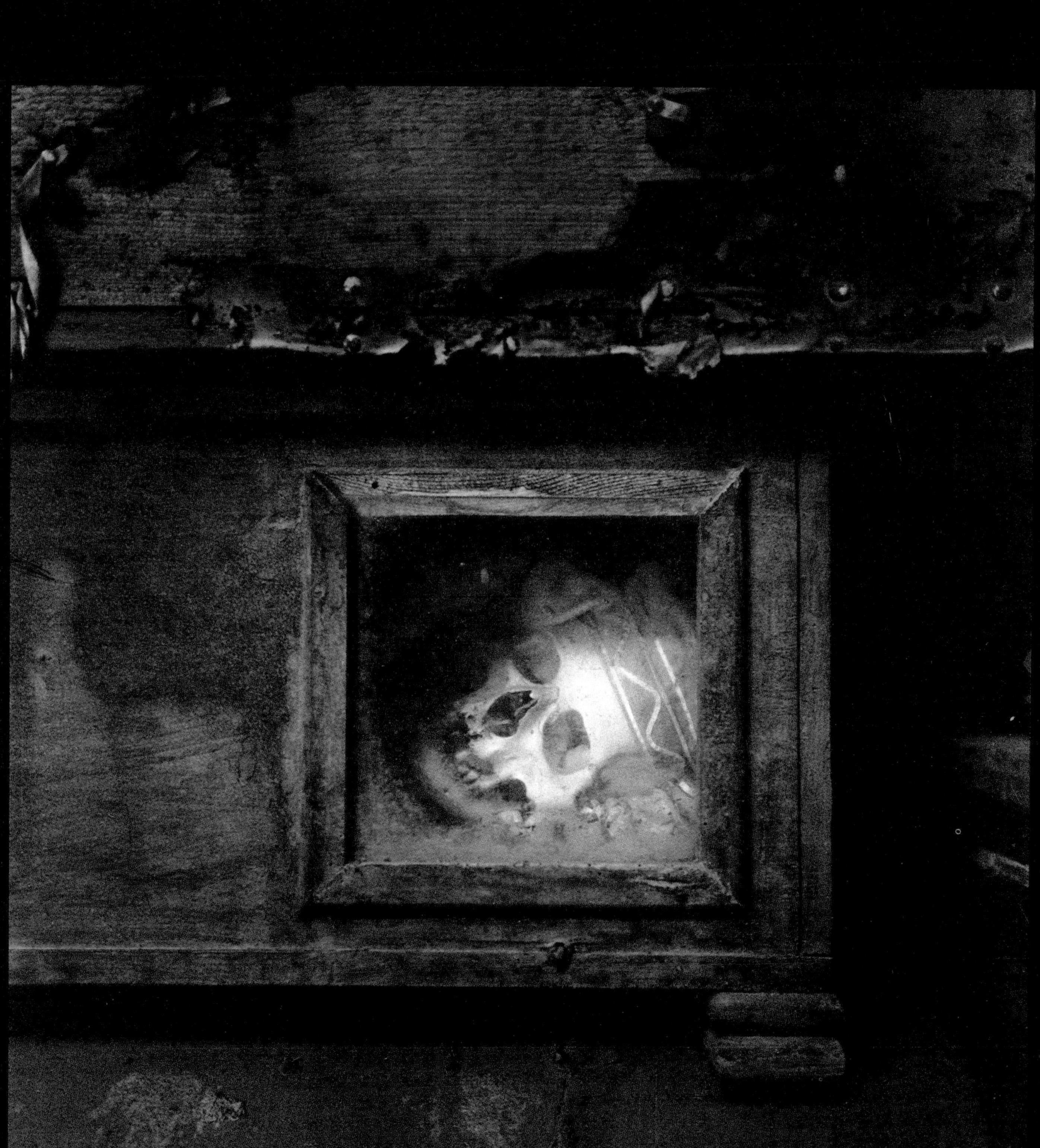

PAUL DIAMOND

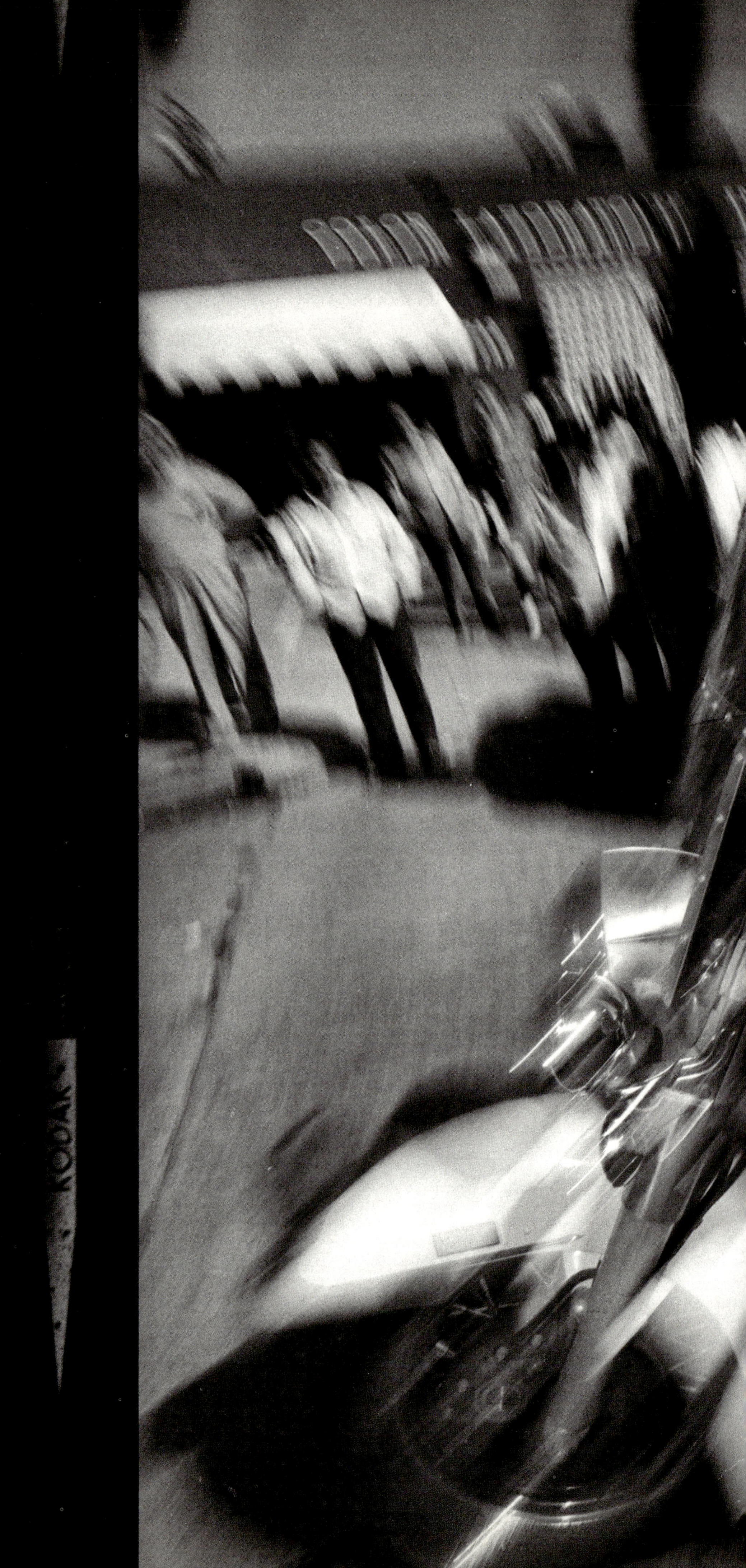

   This Softer than Harder, LA, 1976

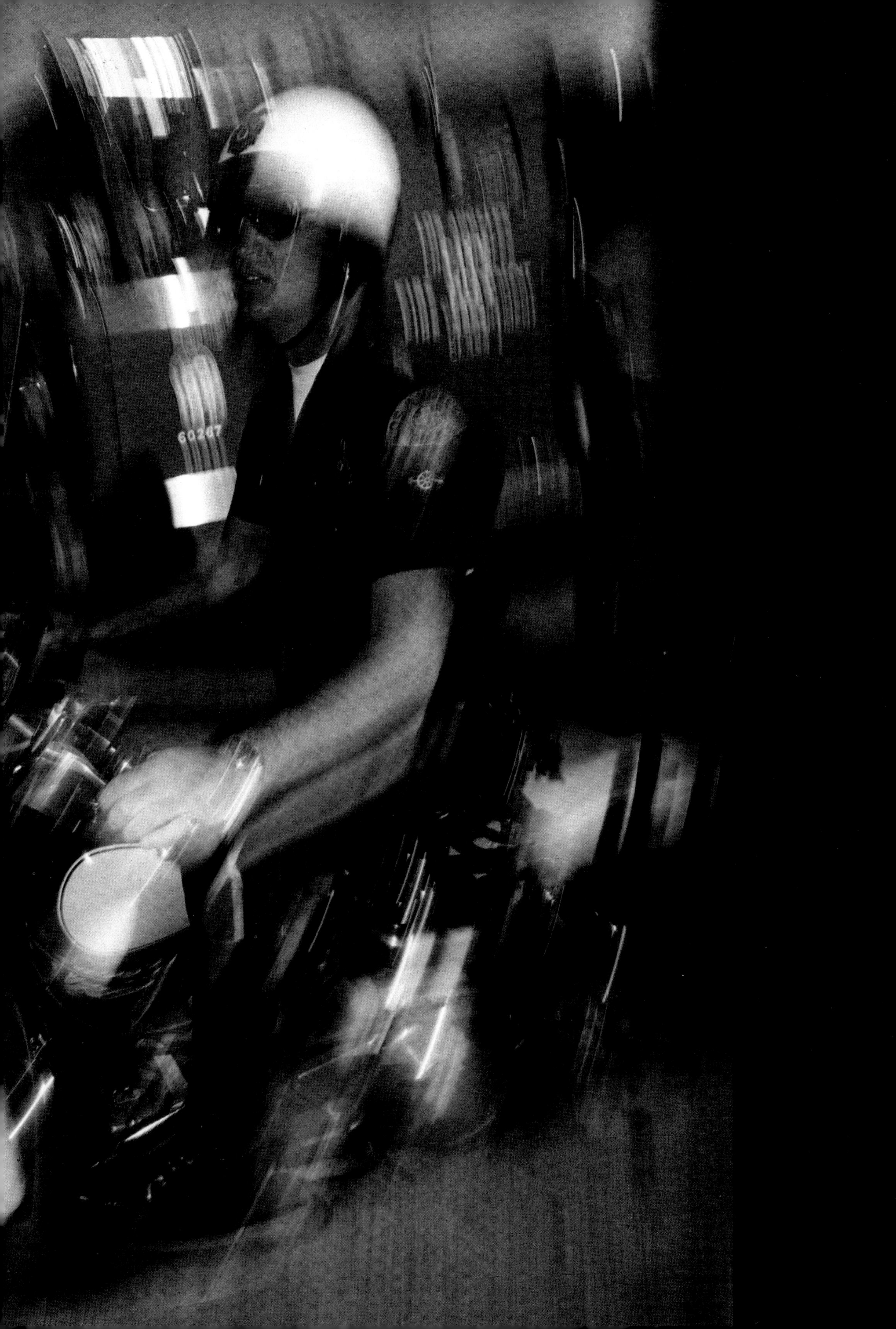

Street Game, NYC, 1974

Hopi Bridgework, SF, 1975

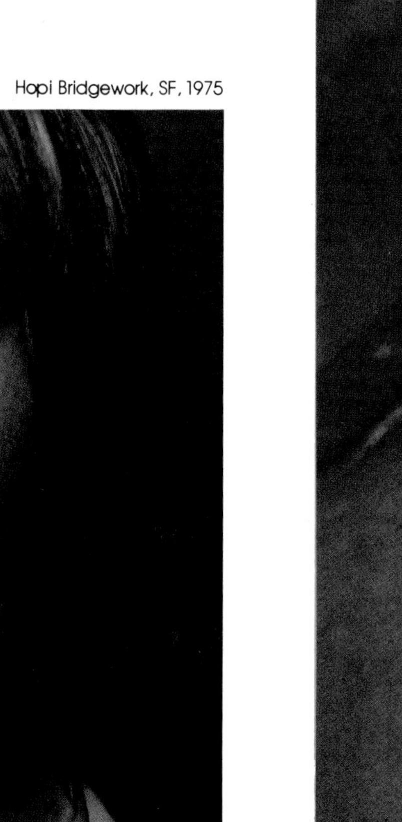

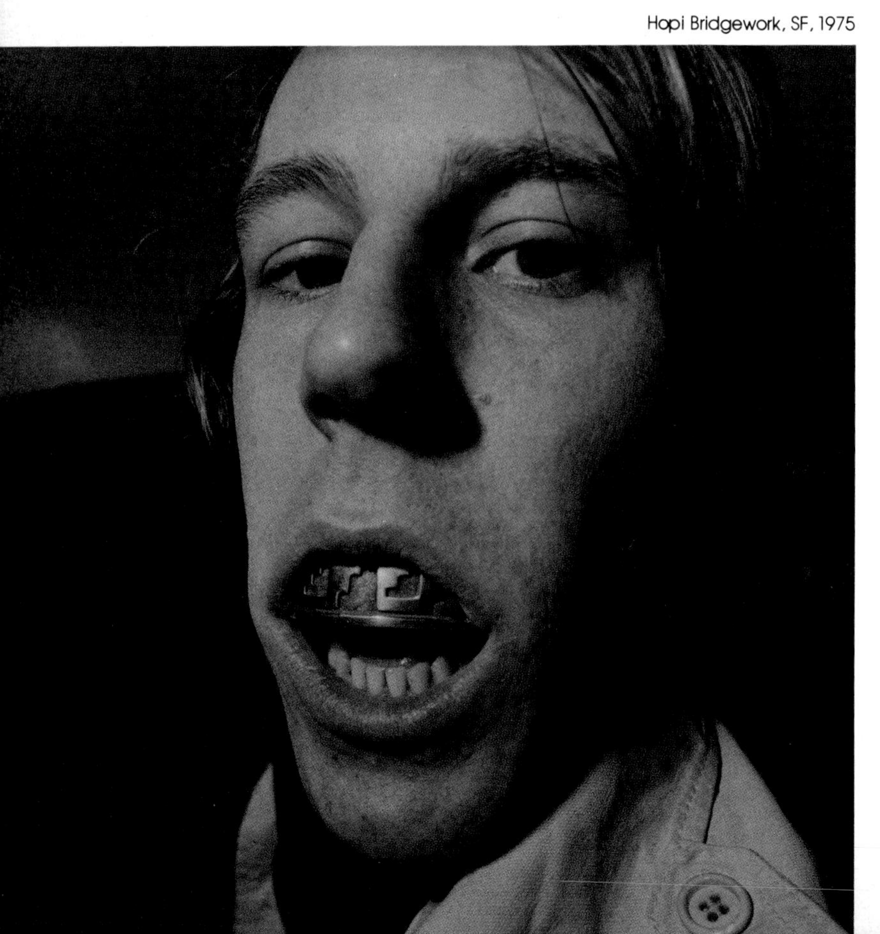

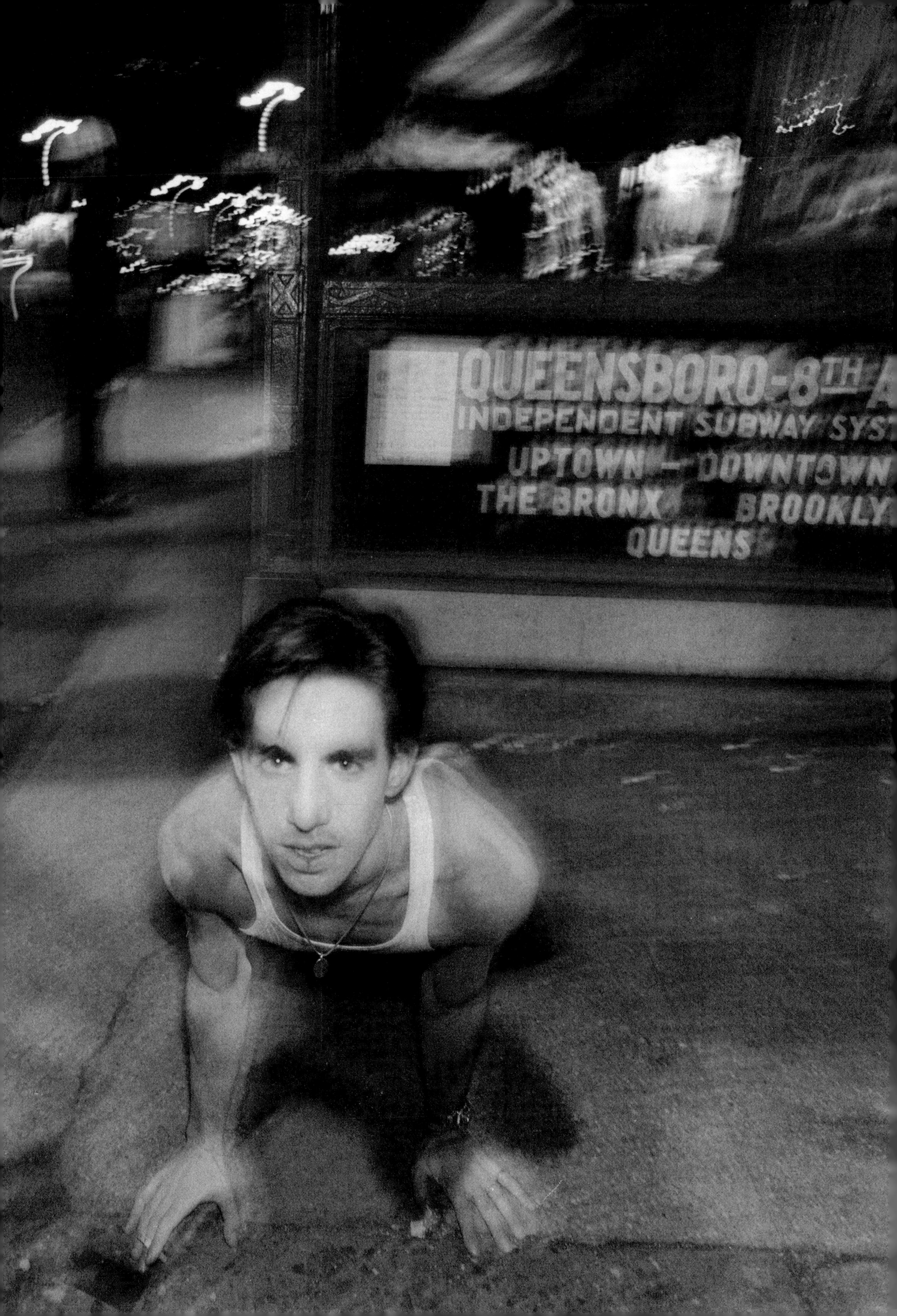

QUEENSBORO-8TH A
INDEPENDENT SUBWAY SYST
UPTOWN — DOWNTOWN
THE BRONX   BROOKLY
QUEENS

PAUL DIAMOND

Canine Experience, SF, 1975

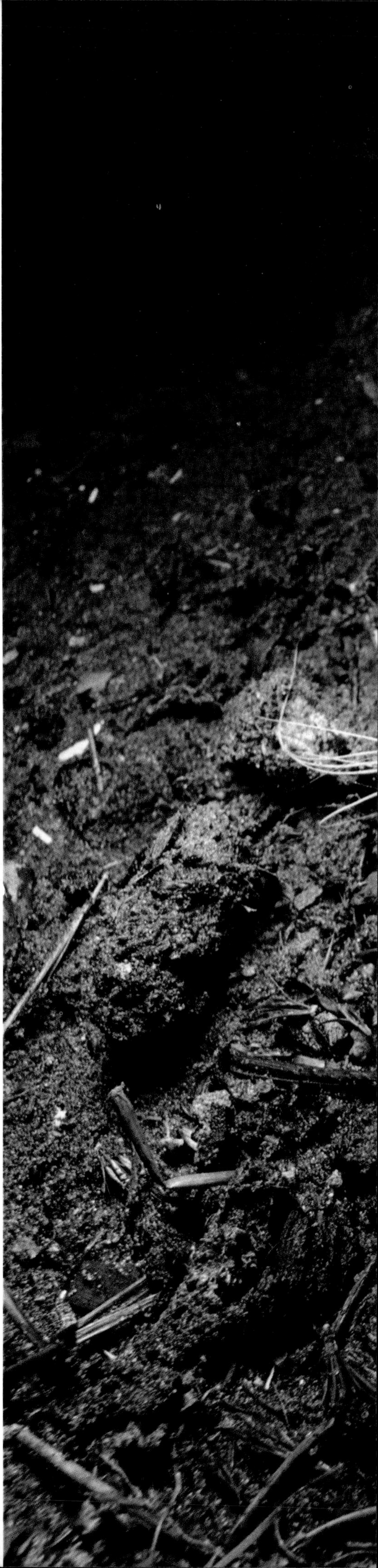

Dessert, SF, 1974

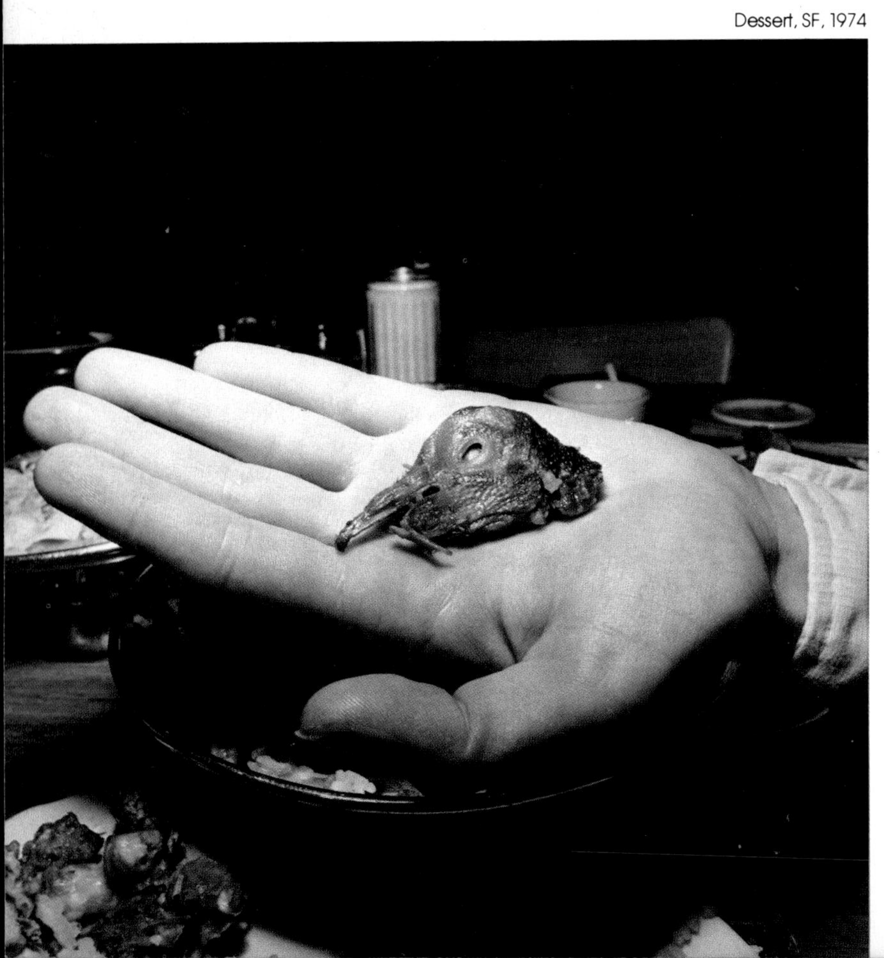

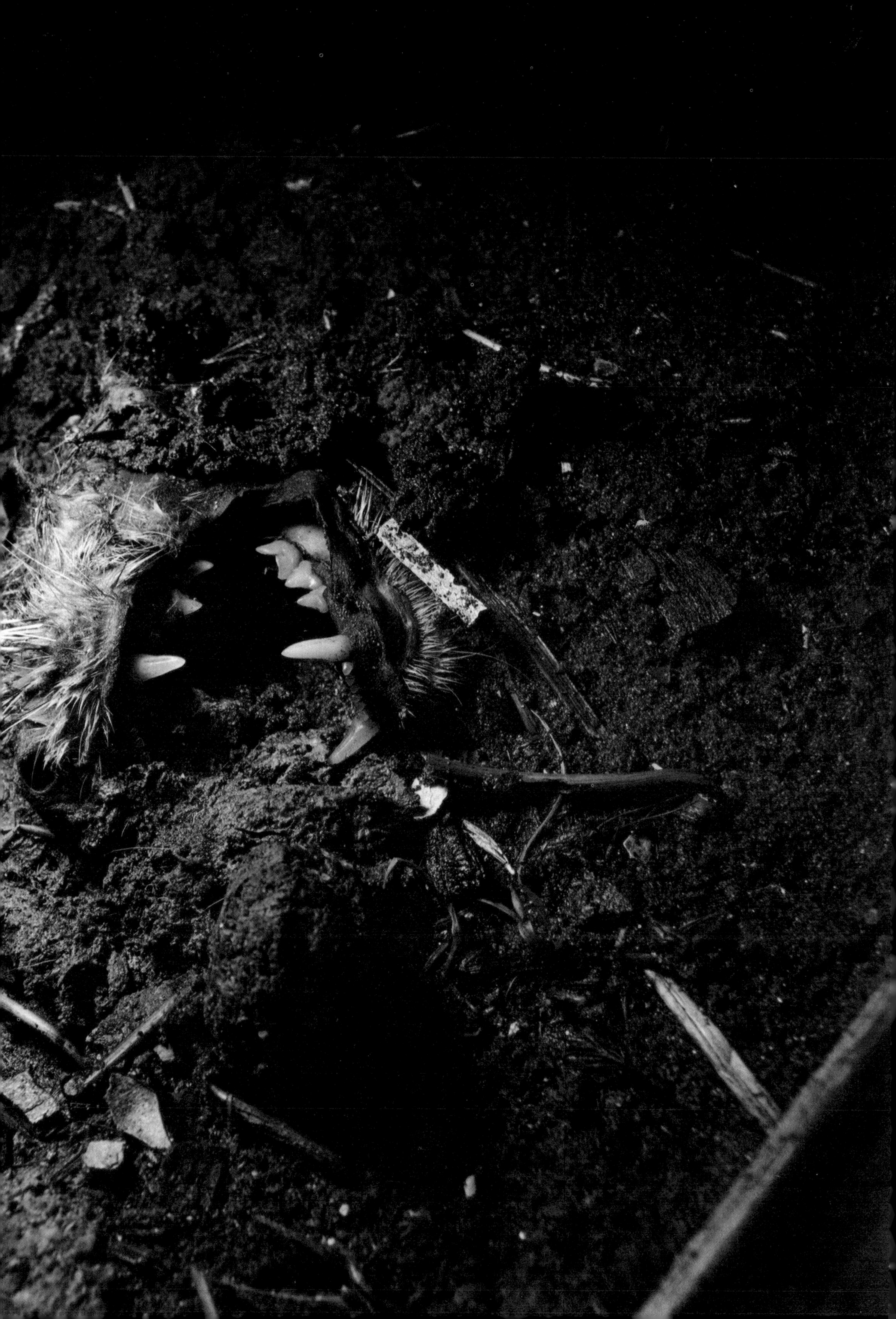

MICHAEL MARTONE

Untitled, New York City, 1973

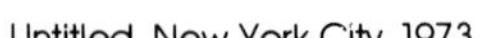

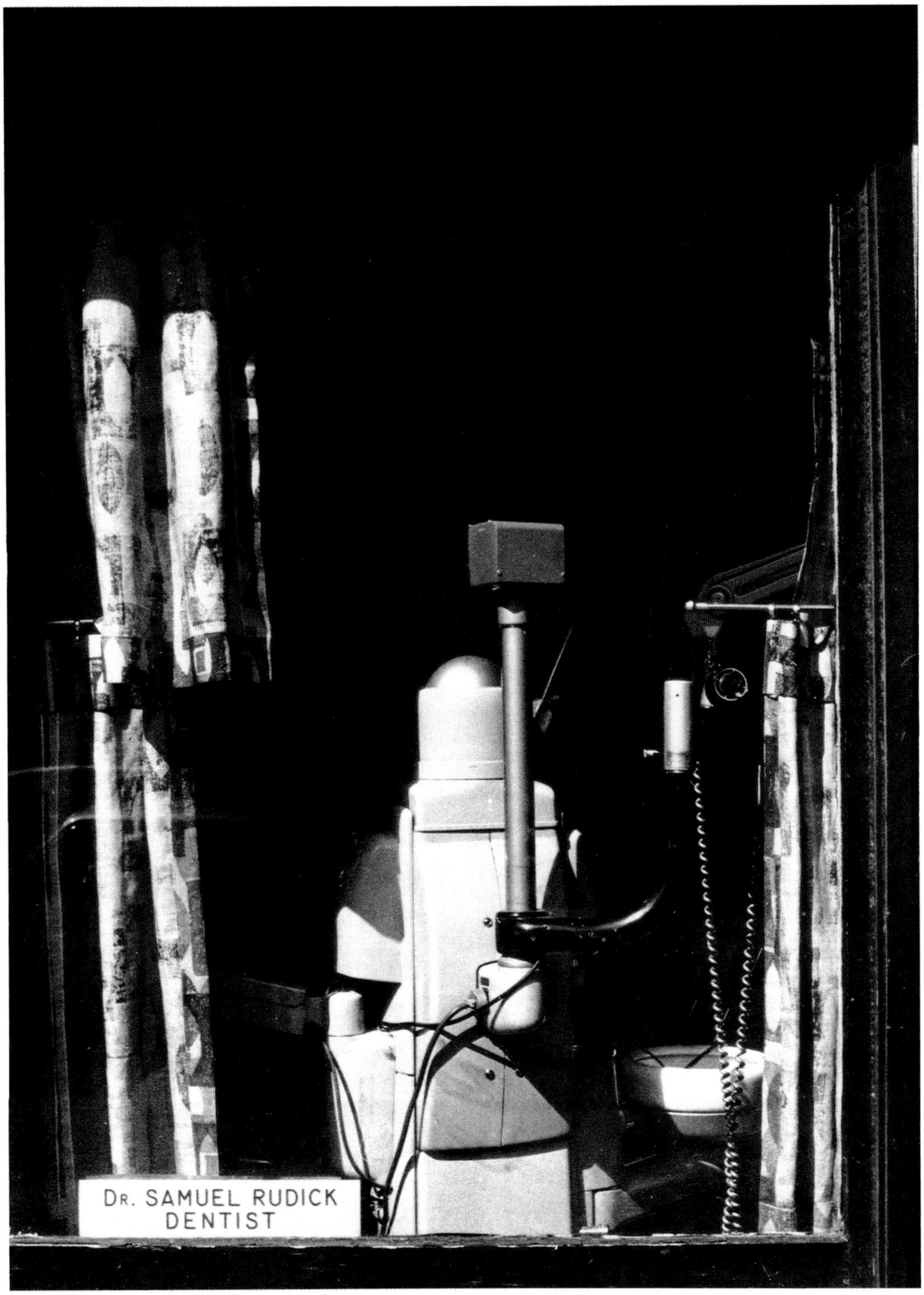

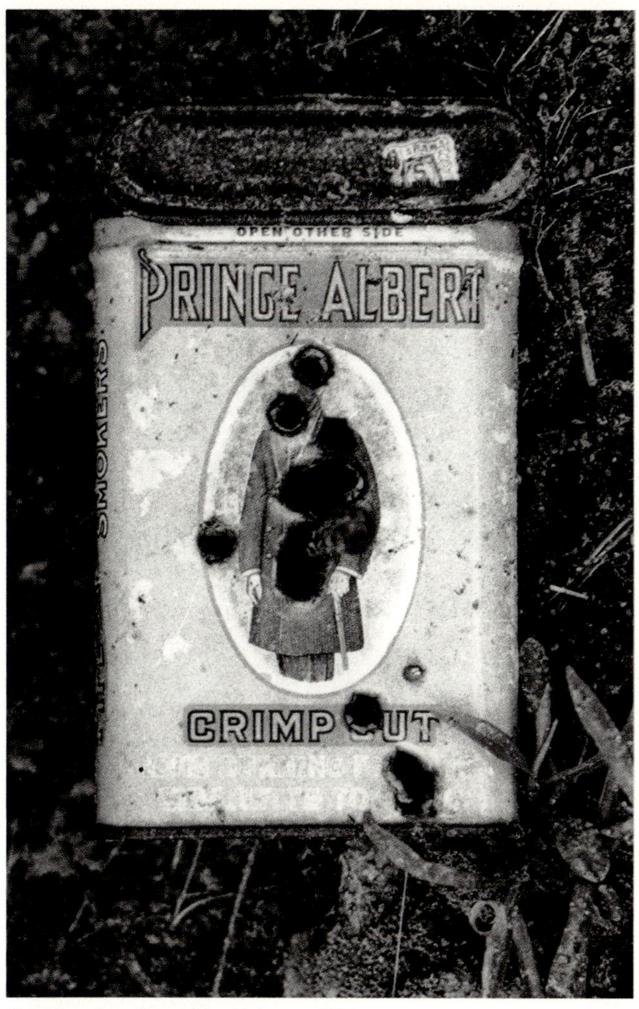

Pistol Practice, Greenville, Alabama, 1966

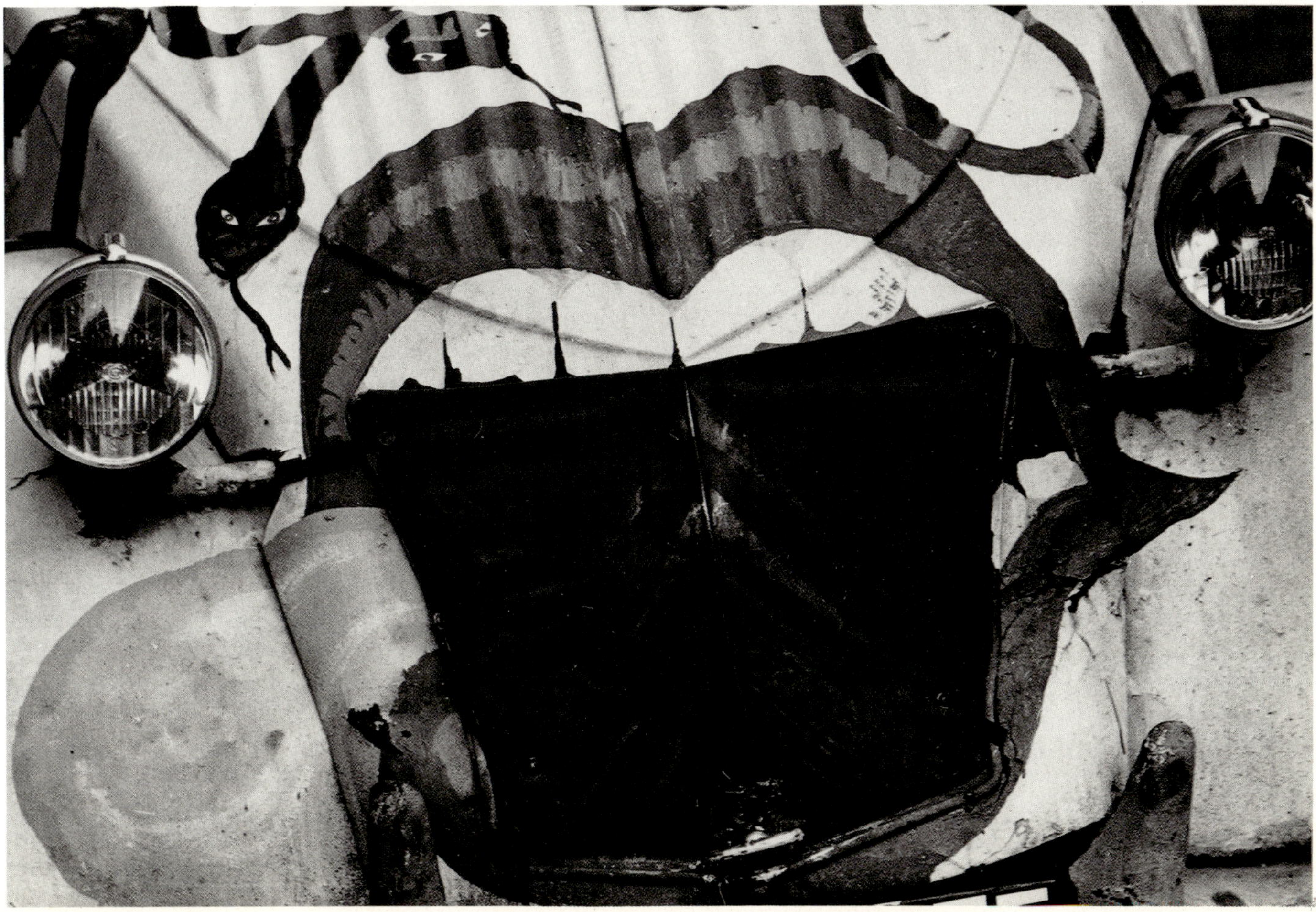

Automobile, Paris, France, 1976

3 CONSTRUCTED

Our faith in the accuracy and credibility of photographs is still so strong that it can easily be used against us. More than any other medium, photography depends for its impact on the viewer's acceptance of the axiom that seeing is believing. It is because that acceptance is virtually automatic that Buckminster Fuller has written, "Seeing-is-believing is a blind spot in man's vision."

The exploitation of that blind spot is the theme of this section. The photographs brought together here show things that actually exist and events that actually happened. But these things and events didn't exist or happen independently of the images. In fact, it is doubtful that they would have existed or happened at all if it hadn't been for the photographers who created, generated, or instigated them in one fashion or another.

These photographers are working within what I have elsewhere defined as the *directorial mode.* In most of its familiar usages, photography treats the external world as a given to be altered only through strictly photographic means (point of view, framing, printing, etc.) en route to the final image. In the directorial mode, by contrast, the external world is viewed as raw material and is manipulated as much as desired prior to the exposure of the negative. I have applied the word *directorial* to works of this kind because their makers are approaching the presentation of their visions in an essentially theatrical way, creating (like the director of a play) a *mise en scène,* employing objects as props and people as actors, often working within a scenario. They have simply substituted the credence with which photographs are normally approached for the suspension of disbelief which effective theater wins from its audience.

Such images lead a double life of sorts. On one level—that of their "authenticity"—they are false documents, intentional fictions. That is to say, although they do contain those tenuous elements of real time and fact which all photographs encapsulate, they are not exercises in realism. These are not moments that the photographers simply excised from the flow of reality around them.

Yet, paradoxically, they do truly document something: the very process of creating false photographic documents. Thus, they stand in relation to the medium of photography much as the works of Pirandello and Beckett do to theater. All the assumptions, rituals, and roles in the spectator/actor/spectacle relationship are laid out in the open and the audience is left free to engage with the event on whichever level it finds most intriguing.

The methods these photographers have used to initiate these images, although they vary in elaborateness, are neither incomprehensibly arcane nor prohibitively expensive. Props, settings, and models by and large are commonplace: found objects, old dolls, Halloween masks; bedrooms, cemeteries, front yards. The human models are generally not physically extraordinary. The photographic equipment is not "hopelessly sophisticated" (to quote the late Minor White). And the printmaking covers the range from functional to virtuoso without differing significantly from that of photographers working in other directions.

What distinguishes these photographers from many of their fellows, even within the grotesque mode, has far less to do with any of the above than with such matters as attitude, sensibility, and intent. Certain choices must be made, and within the traditions of photography they are major ones. The photographic medium at birth was betrothed to the historical imperative of realism. To work in the directorial mode requires a photographer to violate more than a hundred years of trust in order to engage voluntarily in active deception. As a rule it involves an image-maker in a symbology that is not "found," but consciously chosen, imposed, and explored. The articulation of such a symbology is often impossible within the *snapshot* or *responsive* style. Consequently, random elements tend to be minimized. Only a few of these photographers court chance. The extent of their complicity in what takes place before the lens prior to the exposure is the extent to which they can be credited with—or held accountable for—all aspects of their imagery.

Sometimes that extent is purely visual—that is, primarily based on the understanding of optics. The images from André Kertész's *Distortions* series, made in 1932, and the one from Bill Brandt's classic *Perspective of Nudes,* made in Normandy in 1954, could be described this way. Kertesz created these images (pages 100–101) by photographing the reflections of his models in a carnival-style distorting mirror. Bill Brandt's fragmented, monumentalized nudes were made with an old Kodak camera whose wide-angle lens keeps in focus simultaneously everything it "sees." This enables Brandt to play with the spatial relationships between his models and their environment, creating images—such as the one on page 108—in which the human forms appear either monstrously disproportionate or misshapen. These originally aroused much controversy. A group of *Popular Photography's* editors responded to them

REALITIES

with "shock, repulsion, and disgust" as "bordering on the pornographic." Others commented favorably on the imagery's power and its deliberate grotesqueness. Fortunately, the work survived the antagonism to find a wide audience and to influence others, notably Karin Szekessy, Ralph Gibson, Larence Shustak, and Waclaw Nowak.

Many photographers have created still lifes, assemblages of inanimate objects, which they have then photographed. Often these have grotesque connotations. Frederick Sommer patiently organizes found objects into sculptures specifically for the camera. The same is true of Vilem Kriz, as can be seen in his surrealistic constructions (pages 136–137). Berenice Abbott (in her "Parabolic Mirror"), Josef Sudek, Ruth Bernhard (in her "Untitled, 1955," a luminescent cow skull draped with a rosary), and Jacqueline Livingston have all worked in this fashion. Another example is Erwin Blumenfeld's "Minotaure" (page 95).

Photographers committed to a "straight" or "purist" stance, which requires maintaining the appearance of neutrality and/or fidelity in relation to subject matter, often have difficulty working in a more active, initiatory relationship to the event taking place in front of the lens. Yet even Edward Weston was able to do so. Although he did not pursue the grotesque mode extensively, he did not ignore it either, and there are many directorial aspects to his nudes, portraits, and still lifes.

Though they stand at a relatively light-hearted end on the scale of grotesquery, his parodies of 1940's war-drive propaganda—such as "Civilian Defense" (pages 138–139)—are fully realized images that amplify the directorial tendencies of a large number of his images. They also reveal much about his humor, evidence of which is hard to come by in his other photographs and writings.

Ralph Eugene Meatyard (pages 110–115) was an optician in Lexington, Kentucky. His interest in visual perception led him to photography and to experimentation which probed the relationships between human seeing and camera vision. In many of his images motion has been only partially arrested by the camera, so that elements become blurred, translucent, and ghostly.

The camera's lens can only investigate surfaces. It is up to the photographer to find within that limitation ways of articulating what is perceived and intuited beneath those surfaces. Meatyard's metaphor for this was the dime-store Halloween mask, a recurrent presence in much of his work. The settings in which he introduced these masks were usually casual and mundane, which makes the vibrations they set off even more eerie.

The intimate, familial settings are normality itself. Finding them inhabited by these demonic presences dressed in otherwise ordinary street clothes is discomfiting. This is particularly true of the extended series he called *The Family Album of Lucybelle Crater*. In this group of images, the character represented by one cronelike mask, whom Meatyard named Lucybelle Crater (a variant of the name of a character in Flannery O'Connor's fiction), covers the faces of a number of the photographer's friends and family circle. Very much in the Southern Gothic tradition, this series was made during the last few years of Meatyard's life, when he knew he was dying of cancer. Its theme would seem to be the essential otherness and shifting personae of people, even those to whom one is closest.

Clarence John Laughlin's photographs (pages 40–41, 116–119) could also be described as Southern Gothic in essence. Laughlin, who lives and works in New Orleans, Louisiana, has based much of his work on the hag-ridden mythos of the Deep South: the moldering plantations, decrepit mansions, crumbling cemeteries, and dank, encroaching vegetation, which are emblematic of a past still haunting the present. His intent goes beyond that, however to—as he says—"the creation of a connected sequence of symbols dealing with the misery and madness of modern man . . . images of the fear, the hate, and the confusion which led to the two great World Wars."

A frequent apparition in Laughlin's imagery is a mysterious female figure, often veiled or faceless, who seems to represent (among other things) Southern womanhood in all its cultural and historical implications. She walks through Laughlin's settings and participates in his tableaux like an ambiguous specter, sometimes seductive, sometimes repellent, never neutral.

Elements of the grotesque have been present in Arthur Tress's work from the beginning, even though his first themes were such social ones as ecology and the quality of urban life. Like Laughlin and Meatyard, Tress uses human beings in his images (pages 120–129) not only as models but as actors. Usually the dramas they enact are their own, performed by them for the camera at the photographer's request. Thus most of them can be defined as collaborations between the photographer and the subject.

Another kind of collaboration resulted in Eikoh Hosoe's *Ordeal by Roses* (pages 102–107). This monumental work was the joint creation of Hosoe, one of Japan's finest photographers, and the late Yukio Mishima, the novelist and politician who committed suicide publicly in 1970.

Thematically recurrent in the work of both these artists is the cultural identity crisis set off by World War II, Hiroshima, and their aftermath. Though these images from the sequence are also powerful as individual statements, they interconnect in a multifaceted exploration of the traumas suffered from the war, the bomb, and Japan's Westernization. Mishima, who wrote the "script" for this sequence and played the central character, created in conjunction with Hosoe an autobiographical allegory of spiritual and cultural death and transformation.

As previously noted, there appears to be a particular affinity for the grotesque in Japanese art and culture. Thus it is not surprising that this quality has also flavored other of Hosoe's sequences, including his suite, *Man and Woman* (page 107), and his *Kamaitachi* sequence, a staged piece based on a Japanese folk tale.

Like Hosoe, both M. Richard Kirstel and Duane Michals tend to work in sequence form, as well as directorially. Stylistically, however, the differences among their images are apparent and considerable.

Of the three, Michals tends to be the most strictly narrative in approach. That is, his images are conceived, created, and arranged to convey a series of events so specifically that it is usually impossible to rearrange them at all. Narratively, they are so sparse and tightly edited that they lose their intended meaning if shuffled around. This is obviously the case with *Stefan Mihal's Suitcase*, (pages 96–99). According to Michals, Stefan Mihal is his alter ego.

The sequences of Hosoe and Kirstel, by contrast, are less specific in their narrative and thus open to a much wider range of interpretation. Whereas Michals often works with what appears to be autobiographical material, Kirstel, like Hosoe, probes cultural psychosis through the use of archetypal symbols. In Kirstel's case, one of the central symbols for almost a decade has been the doll.

As symbols of "the forsaking of childish things," abandoned dolls have become photographic clichés. Kirstel perceives and presents them quite differently. First, there is an obsessive overtone to his collecting, playing with, and photographing these artifacts as extensively as he does. This is part of the impact of the three sequences from which this sampling (pages 130–135) is drawn: *Karen's Party*, *Water Babies*, and *Projections*. Second,

Kirstel is not concerned with the potentially nostalgic connection between these dolls and their now-grown former owners. Wherever he finds his plastic friends originally, he places them in settings and configurations that transform them from discarded toys into totems. In these new contexts he photographs them in such a way as to make them look and feel lifelike, using them to create macabre epics. What is grotesque about these beings is not only the bizarreness of the events in which they are engaged but the almost imbecilic innocence with which they respond to these events.

It is surely not coincidental that, as Kayser indicates, "Among the most persistent motifs of the grotesque we find human bodies reduced to puppets, marionettes, and automata, and their faces frozen into masks." Kirstel has much more in common with such other devotees of this totem as Pierre Molinier and Hans Bellmer than with the camera crew in Vietnam that reportedly carried a broken doll along for all location shooting in order to film it in the rubble of napalmed villages as a sure-fire spot-news "grabber."

Some of the photographers already discussed share with Kirstel an awareness of the grotesque implications of nonliving humanoid artifacts: Meatyard, Tress, and Laughlin use such totems directly, while Michals insinuates in his sequence the conversion of a man into a disassembled object. To this group I would add Erich Hartmann, whose *Mannikin Factory* sequence is a grim metaphor of totalitarian society, and Inge Morath, who photographed people wearing masks designed by Saul Steinberg (the latter falling, like Weston's nude with gas mask, on the comic end of the scale of grotesquery).

Ellen Carey (pages 90–93) creates what might also be considered masks: additions to or substitutions for the usual facial appearance of her models. In some instances she achieves this by utilizing organic material such as spinach. In others she employs man-made objects like knitting needles. And in still others she literally "draws with light" in a darkened room, selectively illuminating portions of her subject's face.

Insanity is another theme essential to the grotesque. "The encounter with madness," according to Kayser, "is one of the basic experiences of the grotesque which life forces upon us." Certainly that is the force underlying Max Waldman's images (pages 140–147), although the emotional violence and hysteria they reflect are not real but theatrically generated. Waldman specializes in photographing performances—dance troupes, for example, and the casts of produced plays. This he does not simply for the record but in an attempt to re-create the feeling of the performance. In effect, he restages and redirects selected portions of these productions. This is necessary because, while it is obviously possible to convert the camera into a symbolic proscenium arch and utilize the photograph as a stage, the change in vehicle necessitates a change in vocabulary and point of view.

For his studies of the primal rituals of the Performance Group's *Dionysus in 69,* Waldman left the writhing knots of blood-smeared bodies in a gray, cavernous gloom. In his interpretation of the production of Peter Weiss's savage Marxist/Surrealist psychodrama, *The Persecution and Assassination of Jean-Paul Marat As Performed by the Inmates of the Asylum of Charenton Under the Direction of the Marquis de Sade,* Waldman spotlit the cast in harsh, brutal light, surrounding them with infinite, detailless darkness—a fit setting for paranoid lucidity. Even his grainy print style suits the occasion perfectly, evoking the grimy surfaces and fetid vapors of ancient dungeons.

The staged tableaux of many photographers whose imagery touches on the grotesque—including such other diverse figures as Angus McBean, Walter Chappell, and Christian Vogt—reach their audience only through the imagery. This is also true for the work of Les Krims. As indicated earlier, Krims has pursued his consistently grotesque vision along two main lines: the more peculiar manifestations of "real life," and the outpourings of his own fertile imagination. The images in this section (pages 76–89) are from the latter branch of his work. These are all preconceived scenarios—or, as Krims calls them, "fictions"—staged by the photographer more or less elaborately and acted out by various combinations of professional models, relatives, and friends.

These images refer intentionally to many vernacular and naïve forms of photographic grotesquery: medical photography, for example, in the *Macaroni Cures Cancer* series, and forensic imagery in *The Incredible Case of the Stack O' Wheats Murders.* They are often quite pointedly directed at aspects of our culture that are generally thought to be sacrosanct or taboo, yet they defy reduction to any single programmatic meaning. Frequently they manage to be simultaneously hideous and humorous.

Krims's work requires the viewer to clarify his or her own attitudes by presenting a steady flow of inexplicable, extremely abnormal but clearly articulated situations. These provoke, and indeed often demand, a response from the viewer. But since these are photographs, that response in its most appropriate form is an internal self-definition. One function of Krims's work for his rapidly growing audience is as a tool for testing the limits of one's own tolerance and locating one's sore spots.

These are difficult images to live with. No matter how unconventional one's attitudes may be, there are almost certainly images Krims has created that each viewer would consider excessive. Frequently his photographs arouse intense anger. Indeed, in 1971 a viewer in Tennessee kidnapped the child of a gallery volunteer during an exhibit that included Krims's work, and demanded the removal of Krims's pictures as ransom for the boy's safe return.

Relationship and context—from these sources come congruity and, of course, incongruity as well. The incongruous is an essential aspect of the perception of the grotesque. But the incongruities presented by the photographers represented in this section are not found, but rather *willed.* In perusing and considering them we must ask not only what we're looking at and what it means to the photographer, but also what the photographer means by it.

Some of these images generate their sense of the grotesque by presenting photographically accurate renderings of visual abnormalities whose nature is optical—those by Kertesz and Brandt, for example. Most, however, create that sense through the conscious juxtaposition of objects, people, settings, and actions in combinations that violate general assumptions as to their nature and purpose.

Sometimes the path taken is that of the mythmaker, whose objective is to extend or extrapolate from widely shared cultural definitions. This is achieved through the manipulation of a common symbology. Sometimes the stance is that of the diarist, the fantasist, or the dreamer, amplifying the voice of a more private experience.

In all cases we are being shown glimpses and visions of worlds that are hardly consonant with what most people consider to be their everyday perceptions. Yet the medium through which they are proffered records visually persuasive evidence that, if only for an instant and only by contrivance, those worlds did, and do, and can, exist. It would be well to remember that the subversion of expectations is one of the key tactics in all of contemporary art.

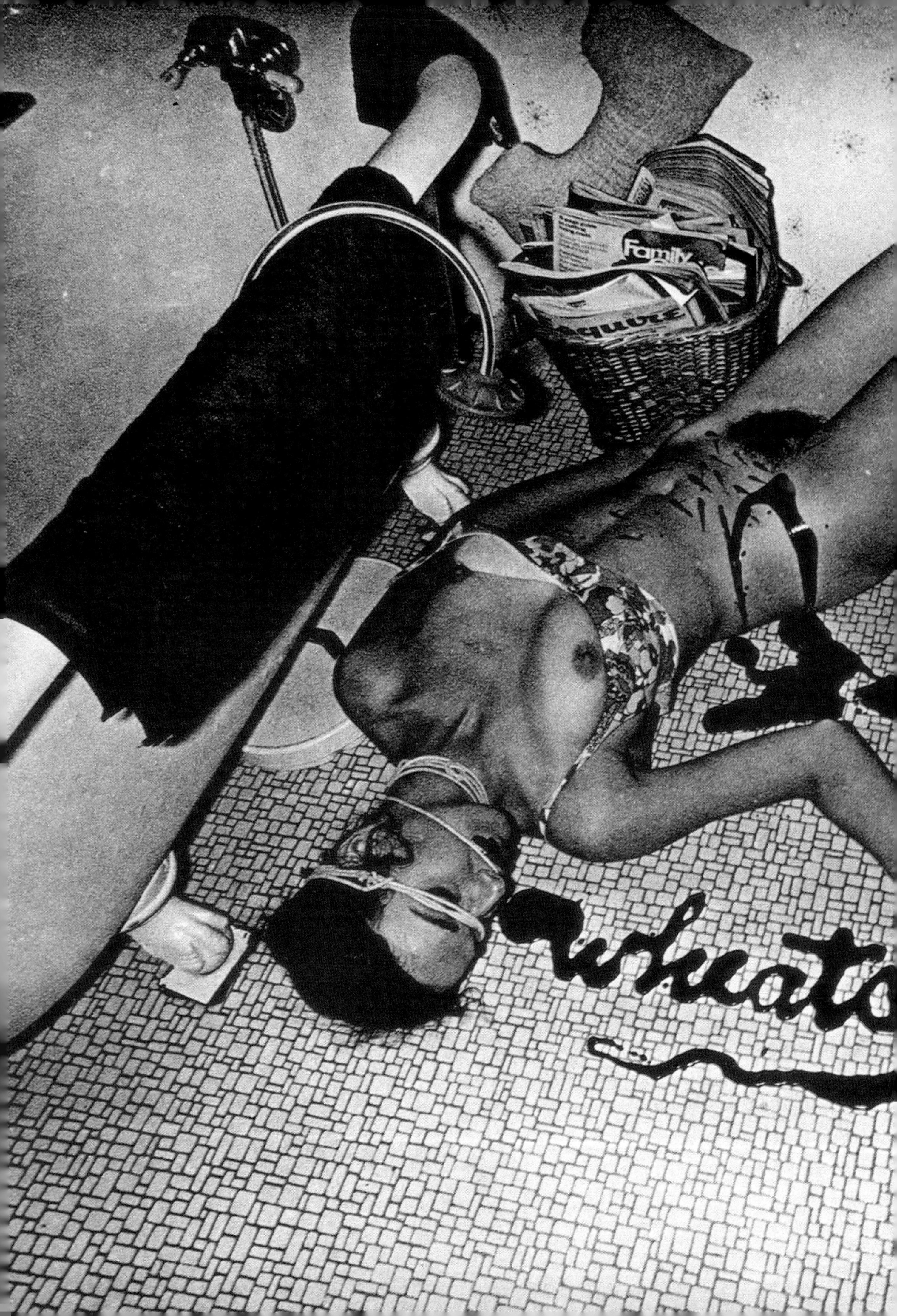

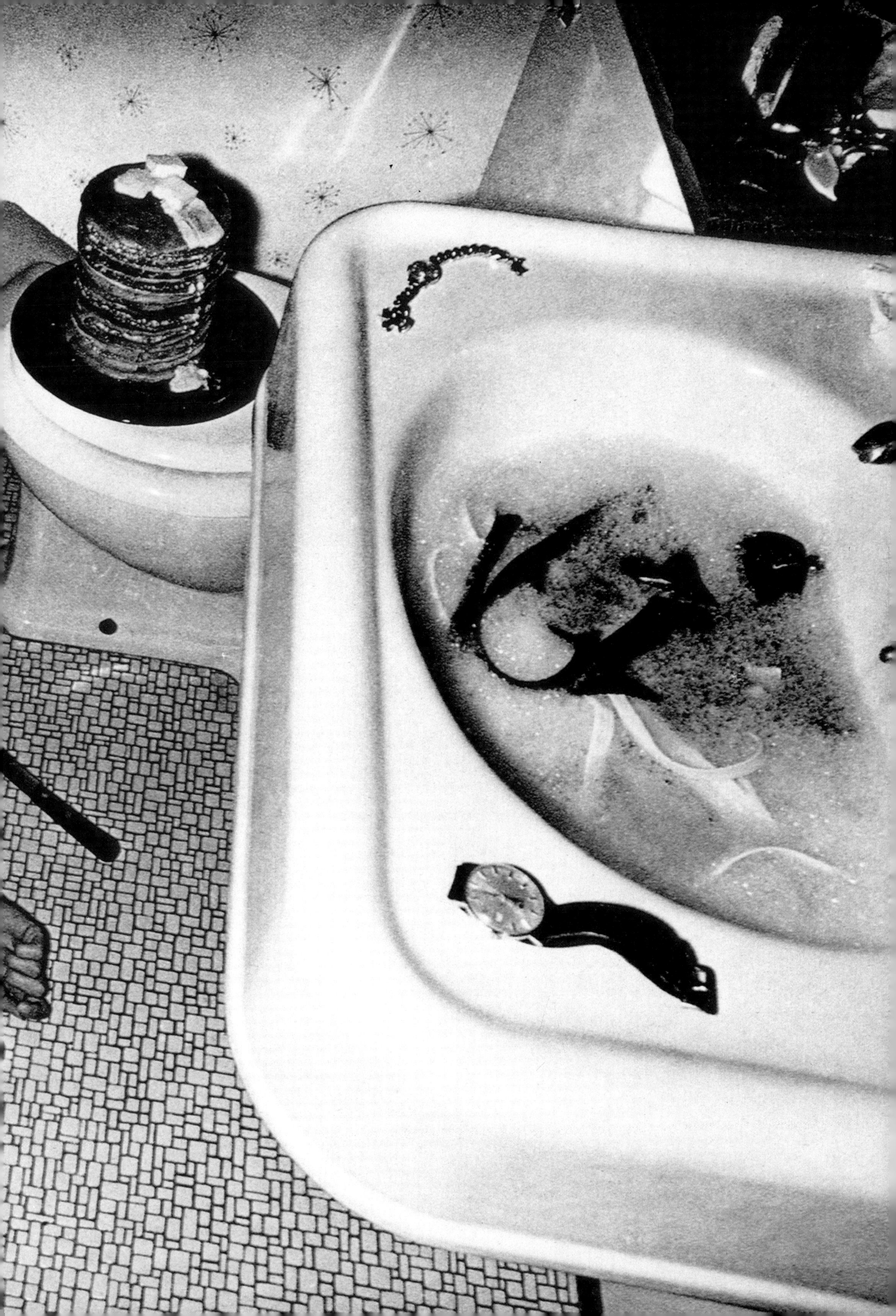

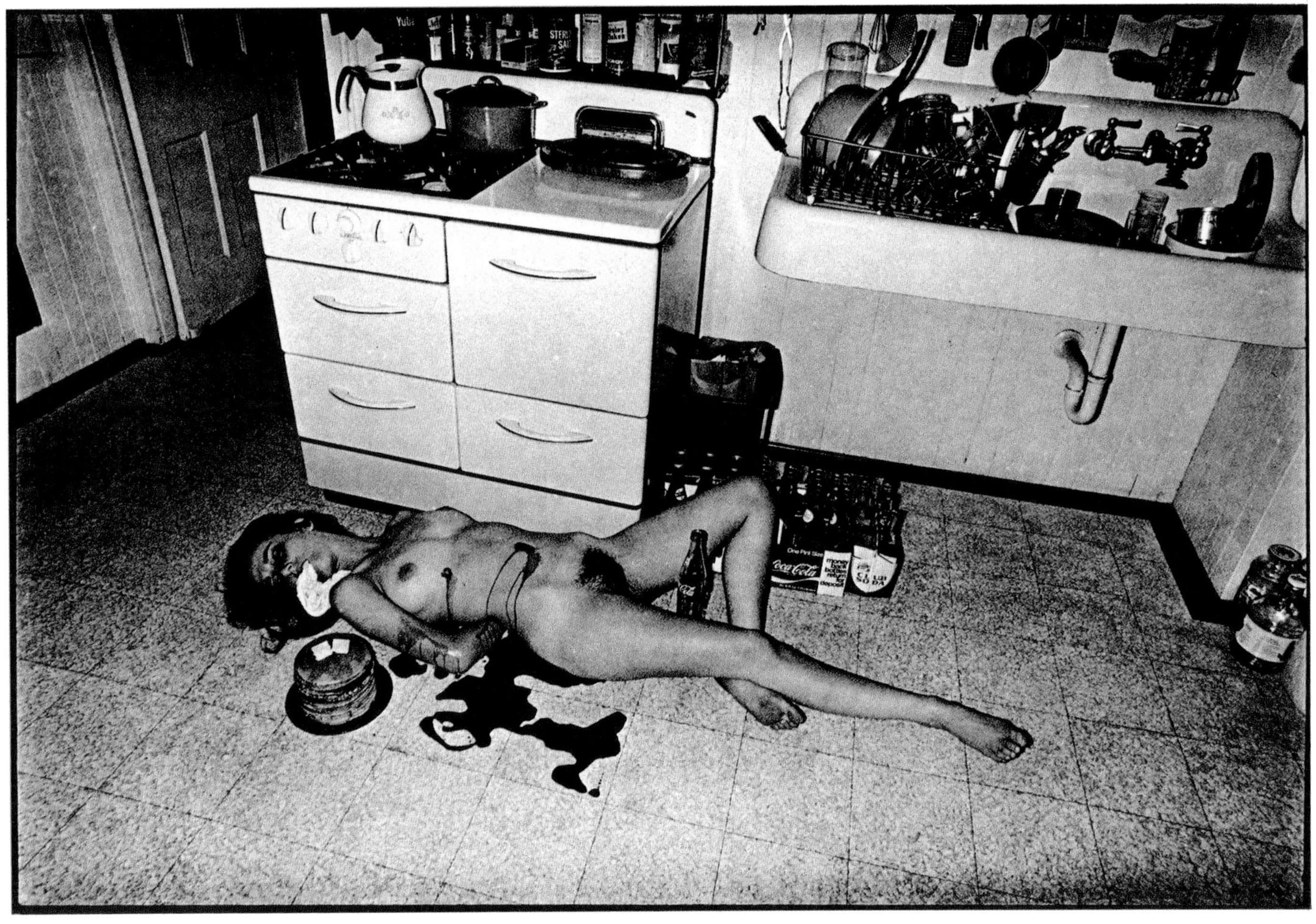

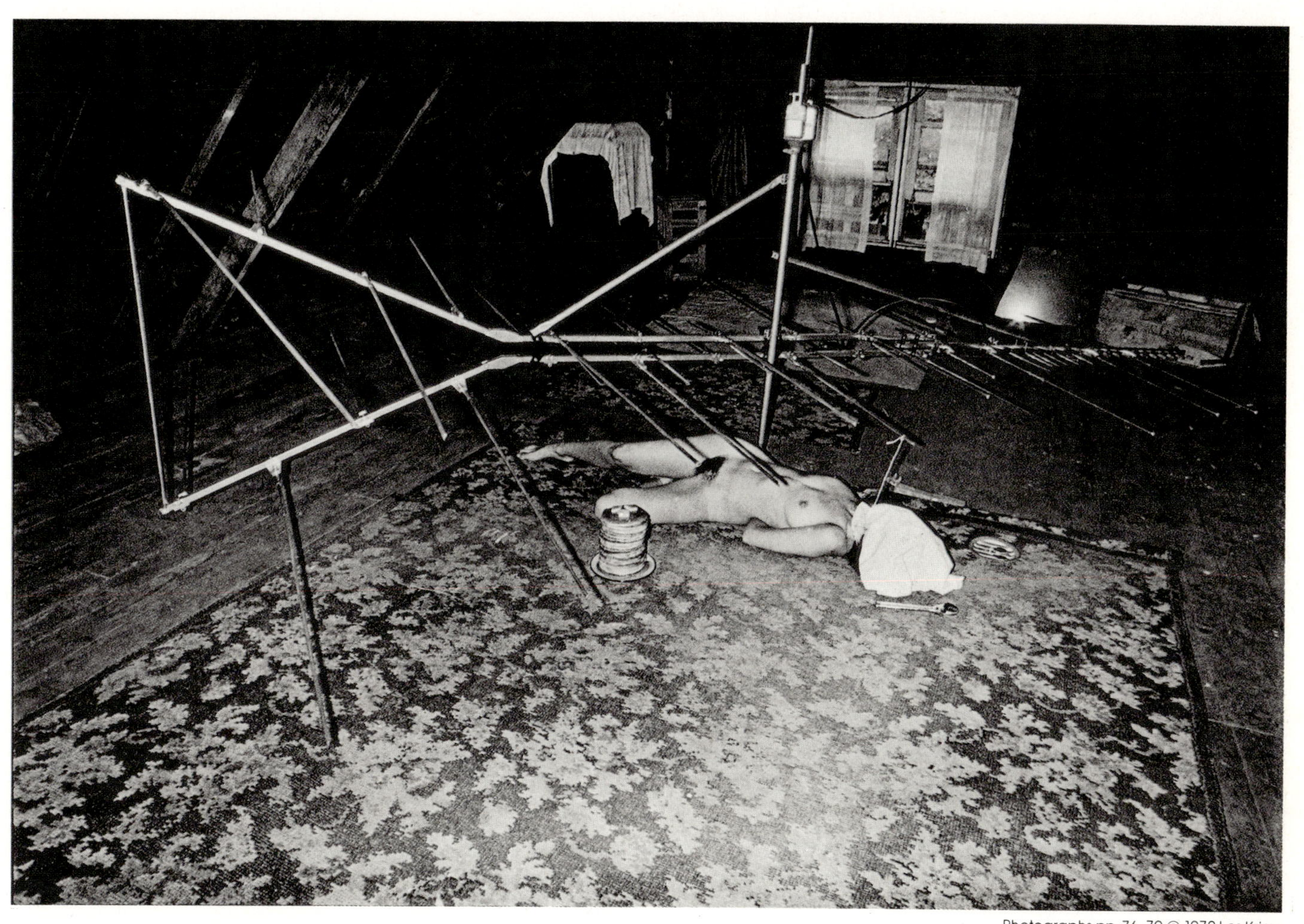

Photographs pp. 76-79 © 1972 Les Krims

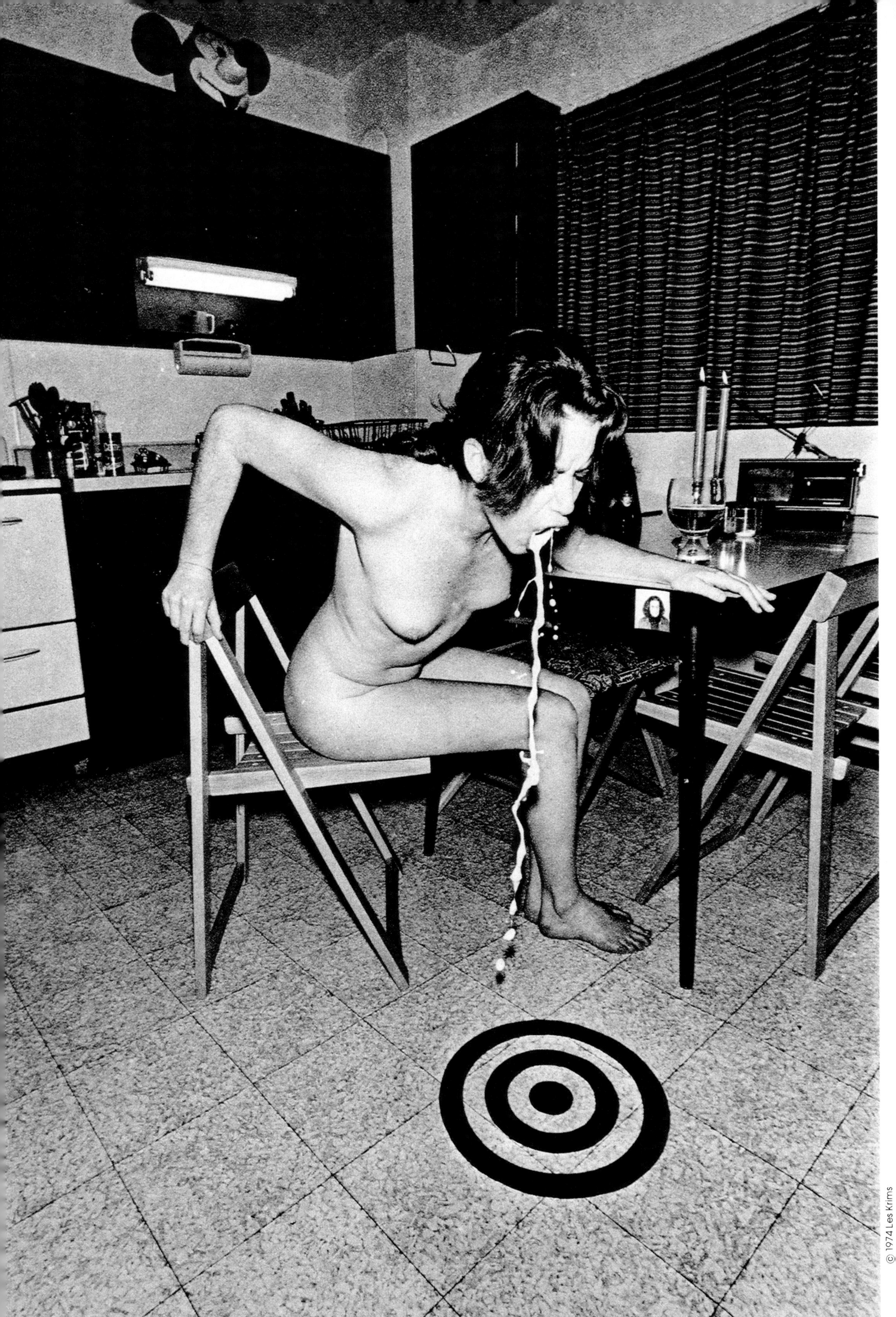

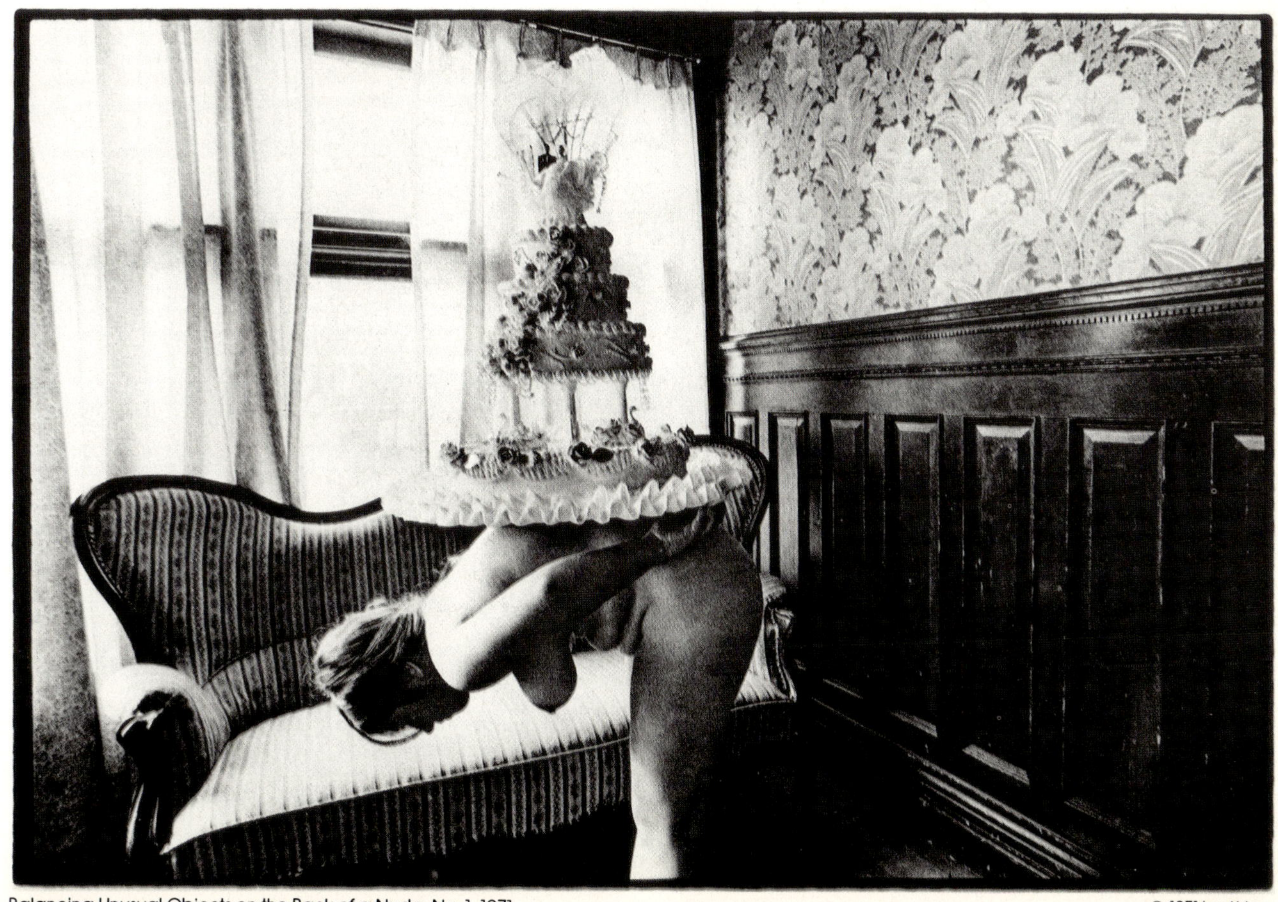

Balancing Unusual Objects on the Back of a Nude, No. 1, 1971

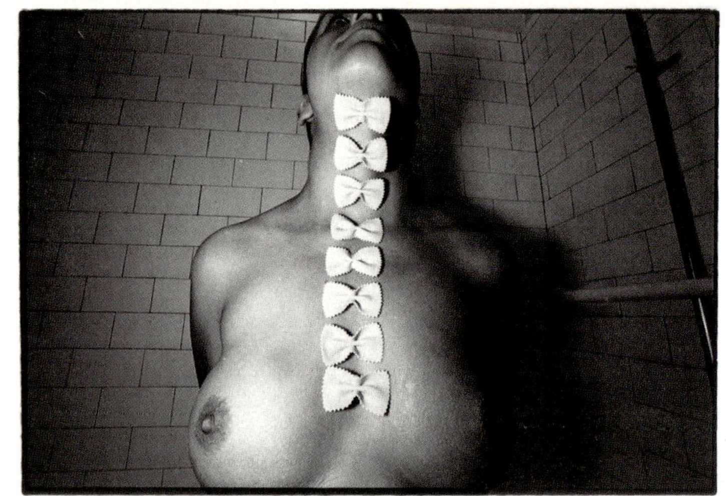

Undifferentiated Epidermoid
Carcinoma of the Larynx Responds
Miraculously to Enriched Egg
Macaroni Large Bows No. 60. Application
with Honey and Lemon Is Advised.
1976

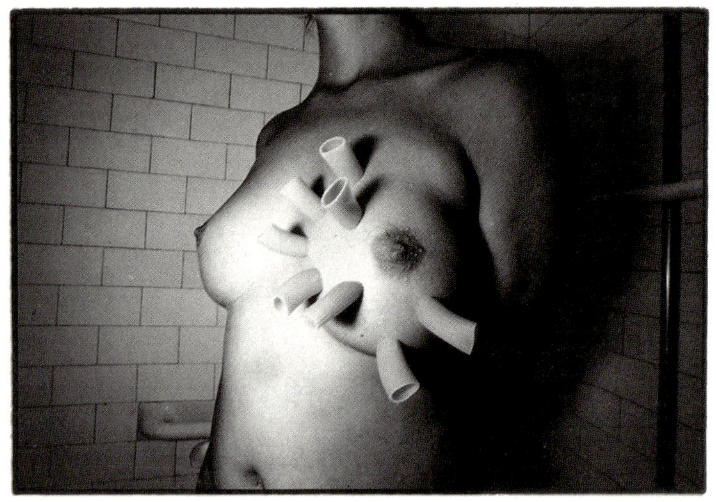

Inflammatory Carcinomas of the
Breast Have Been Cured When Treated with
Rigatoni Positioned to Accept Maximum
Energy Flow Around the Areolar Region.
An 89-Day Treatment Is Recommended.
1976

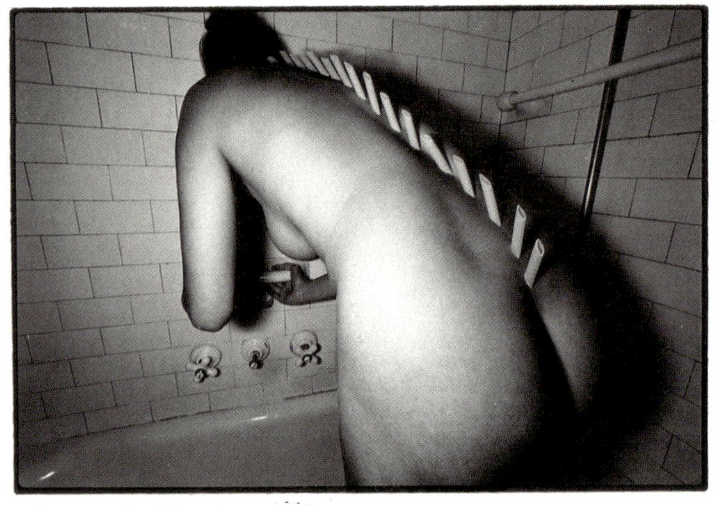

Osteogenic Sarcoma of the Spinal
Column Has Been Successfully Treated by
Application of Ribbed Spears No. 51.
After Application Elevating,
Depressing, and Flexing the Spine
37 Times Is Advised. 1976

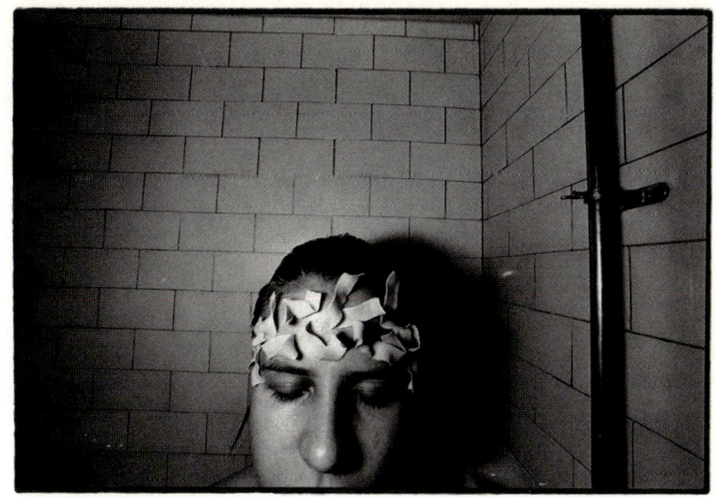

Astrocytoma, and Gliomablastoma of
the Brain, Can Be Cured with Golden Rich
Egg Noodles That Have Been Treated
with Concentrated Fish Protein. The
Letters ``H,'' ``E,'' ``A,'' ``L,'' from .
Enriched Alphabets No. 36, Are Also
Effective. 1976

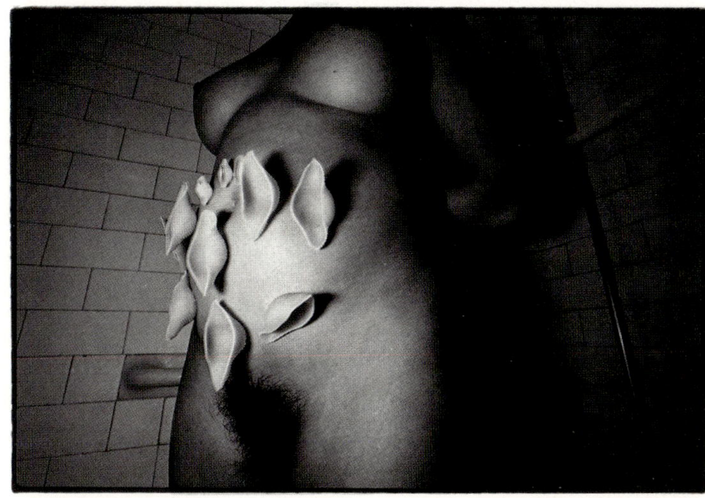

Giant Shells No. 54 Have Cured
Lymphomas, Sarcomas, and
Adenocarcinomas of the Stomach after
Special Impregnation with Allium
Sativum. Medium Shells No. 31
Speed the Process. 1976

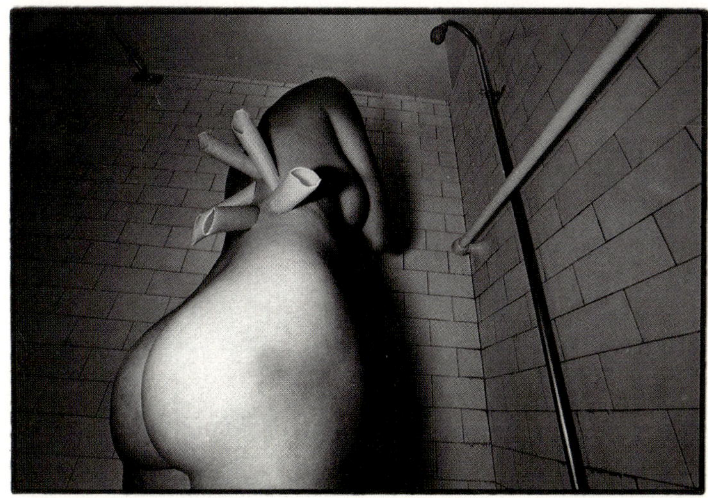

Hepatocellular Carcinomas of the
Liver Have Been Treated Successfully .
with Variegated Applications of
Manicotti. 1976

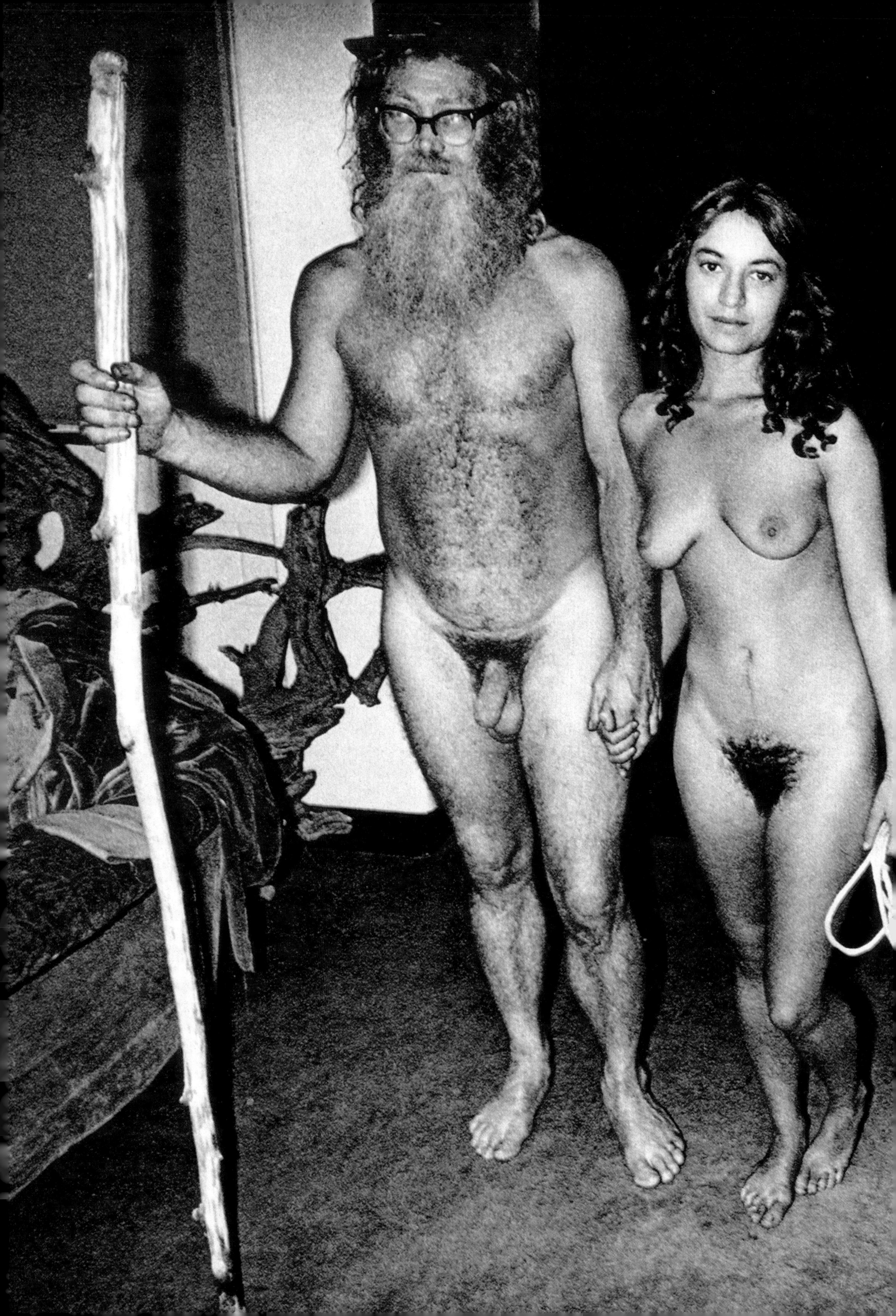

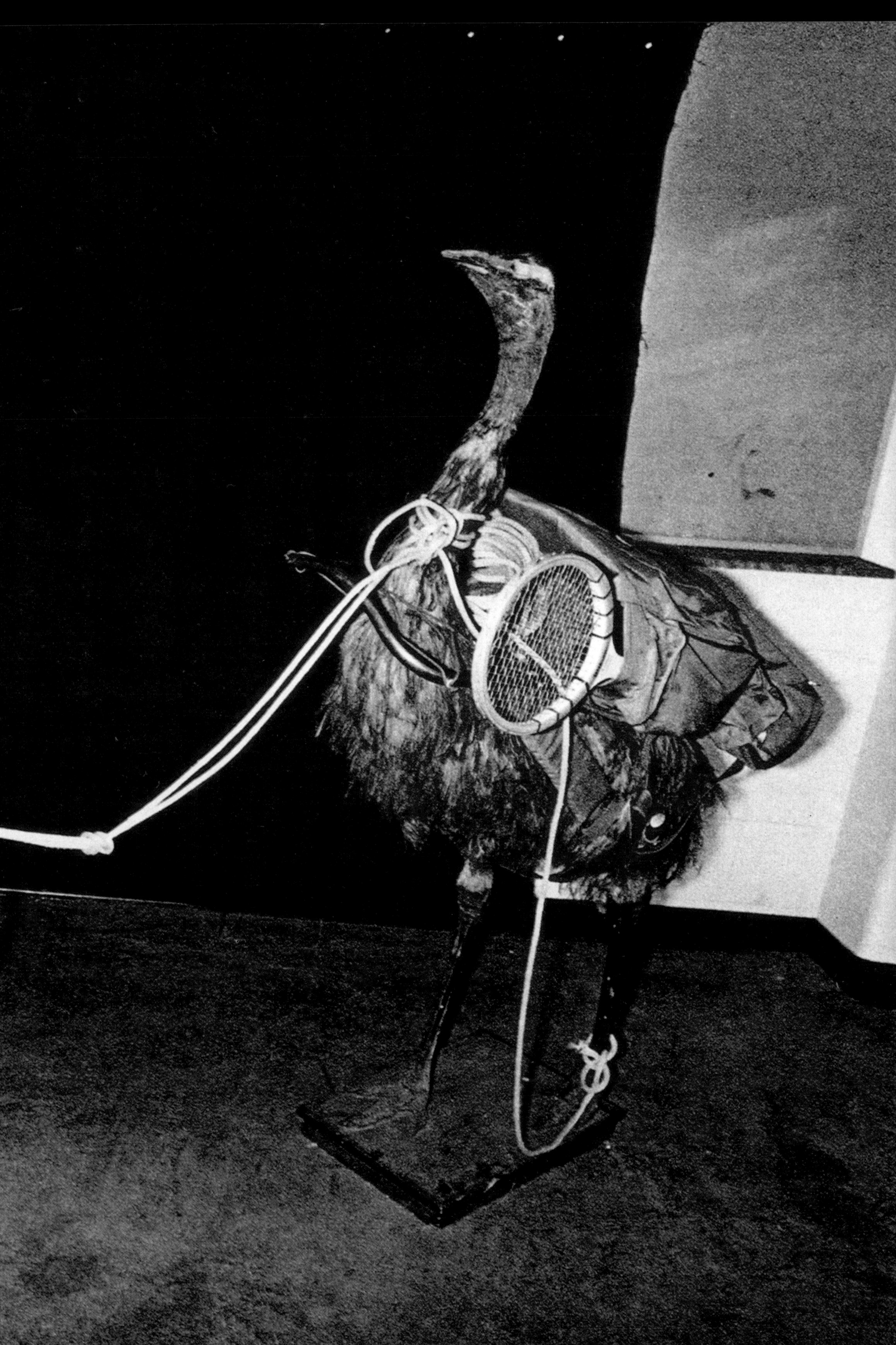

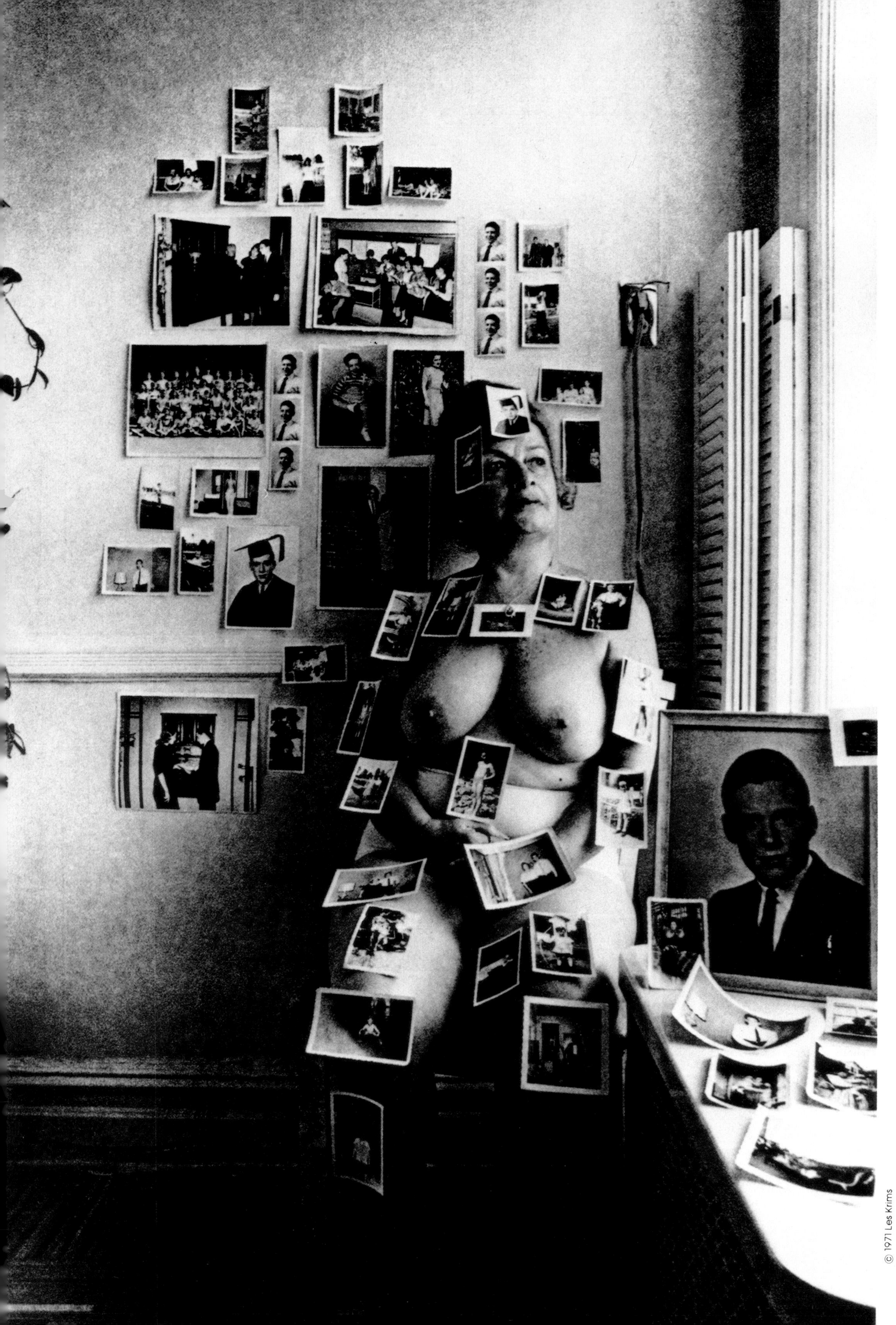

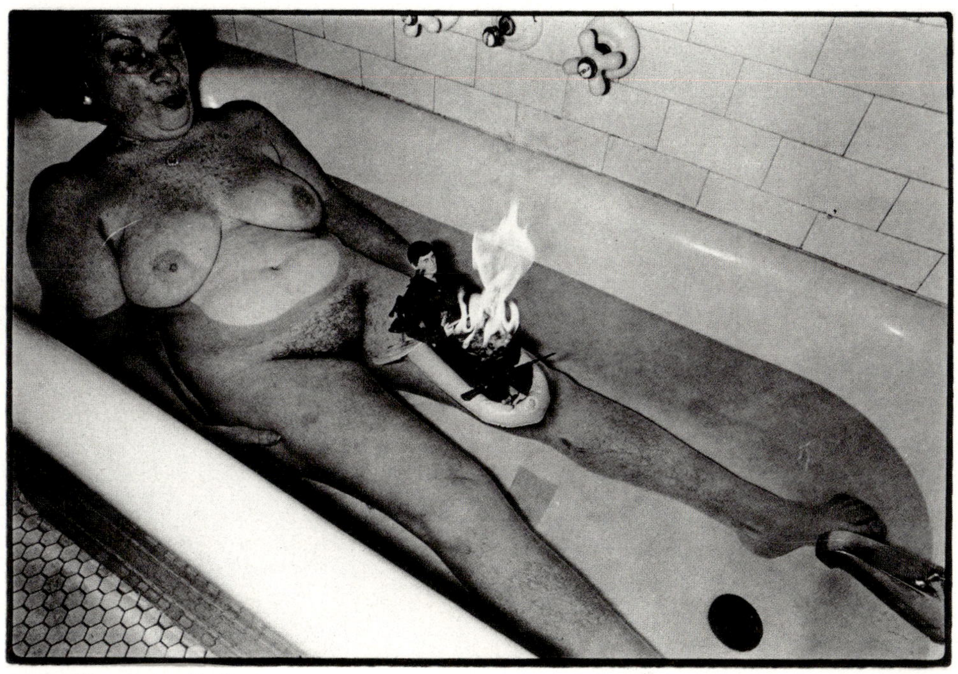

G.I. Joe Wounded and in Flames
Fleeing the Giant Nude
Monster (Kodalith Version), 1975

© 1975 Les Krims

Mom's Snaps Pasted, 1971

Self Operation Fiction, 1970-71

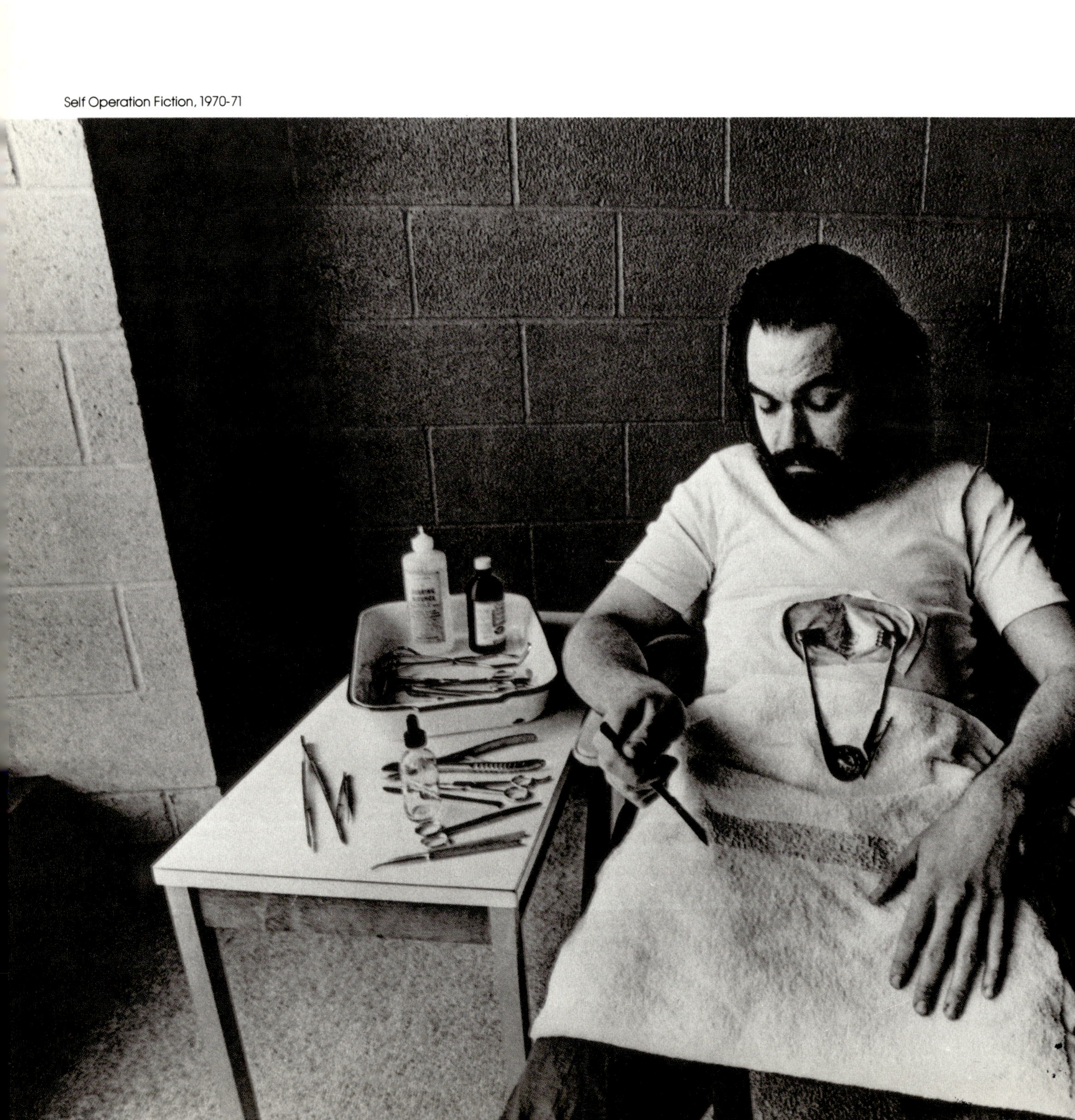

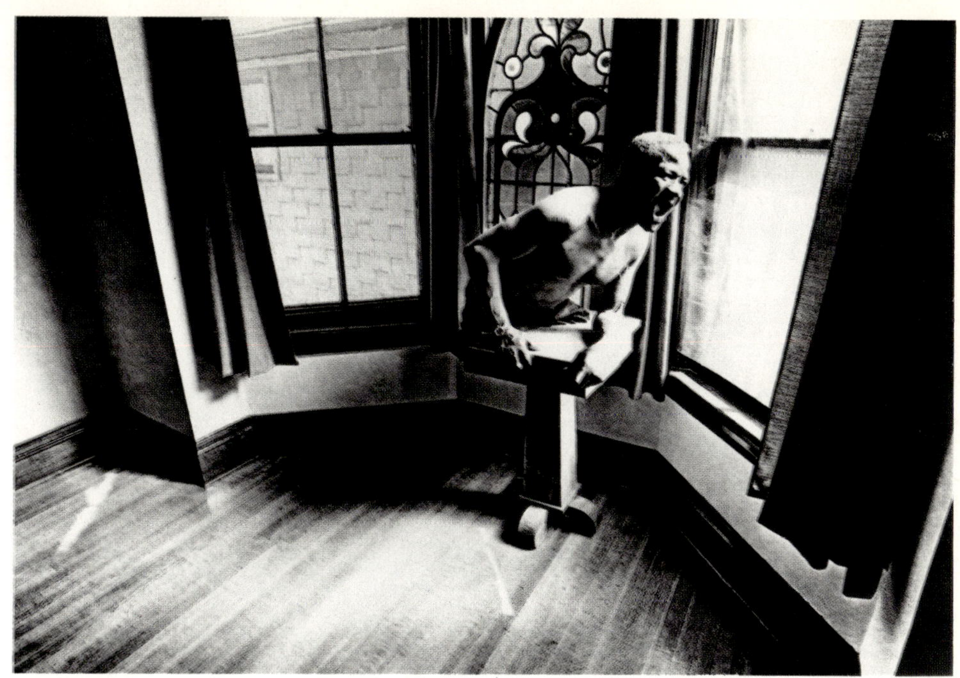

Human Being as a Piece of Sculpture, 1969

© 1969 Les Krims

© 1971 Les Krims

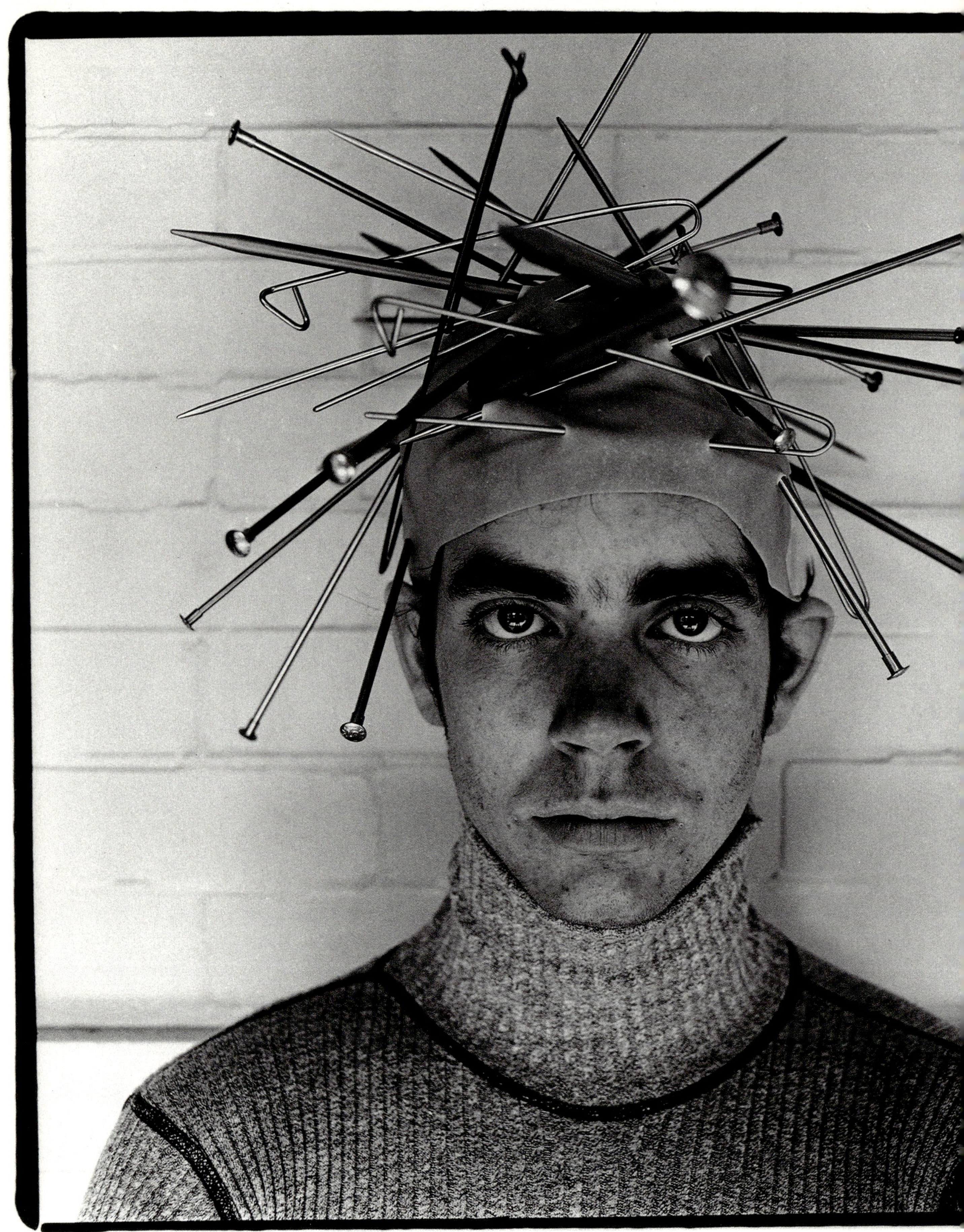

Untitled, 1976

Untitled, 1975

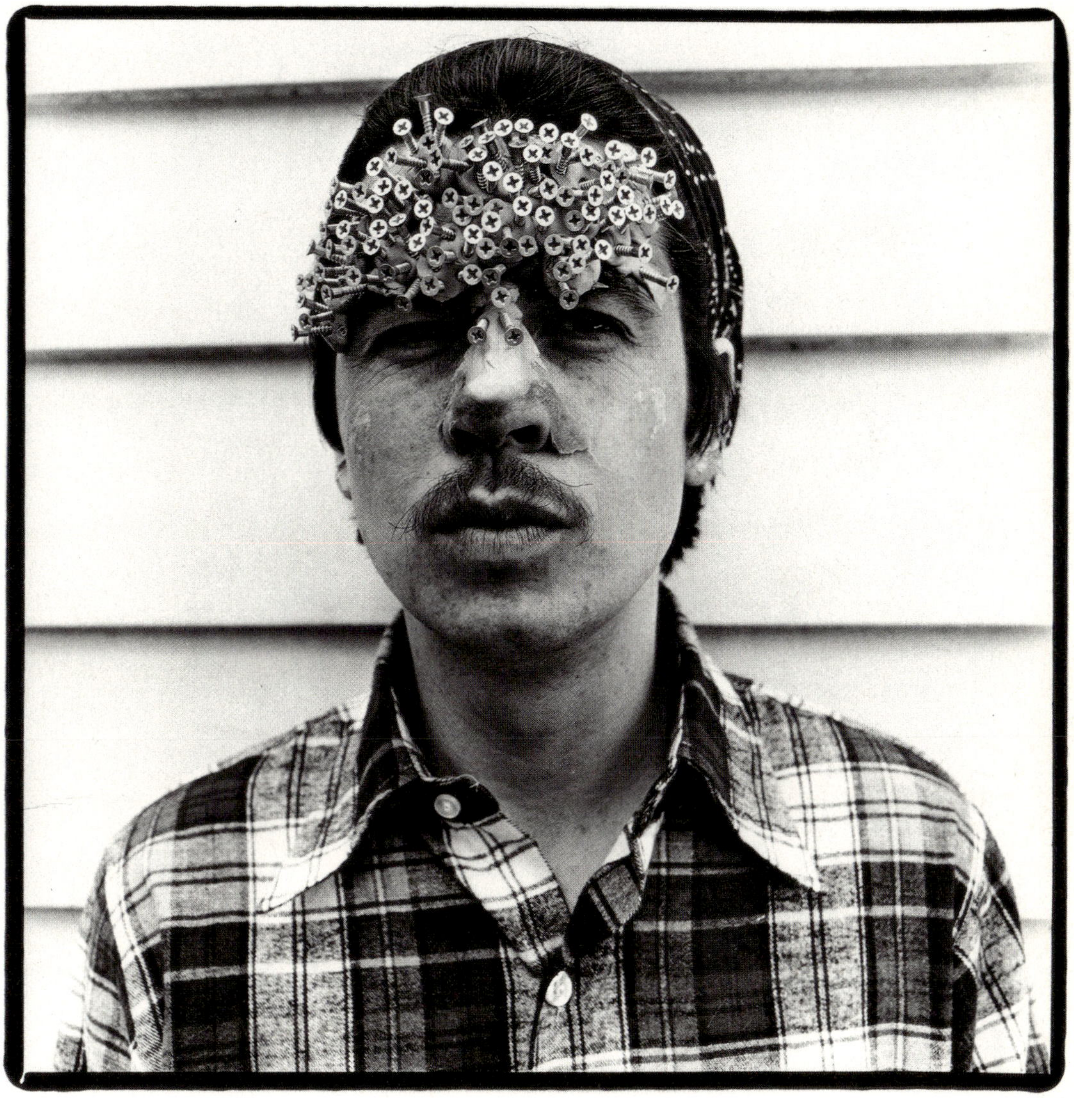

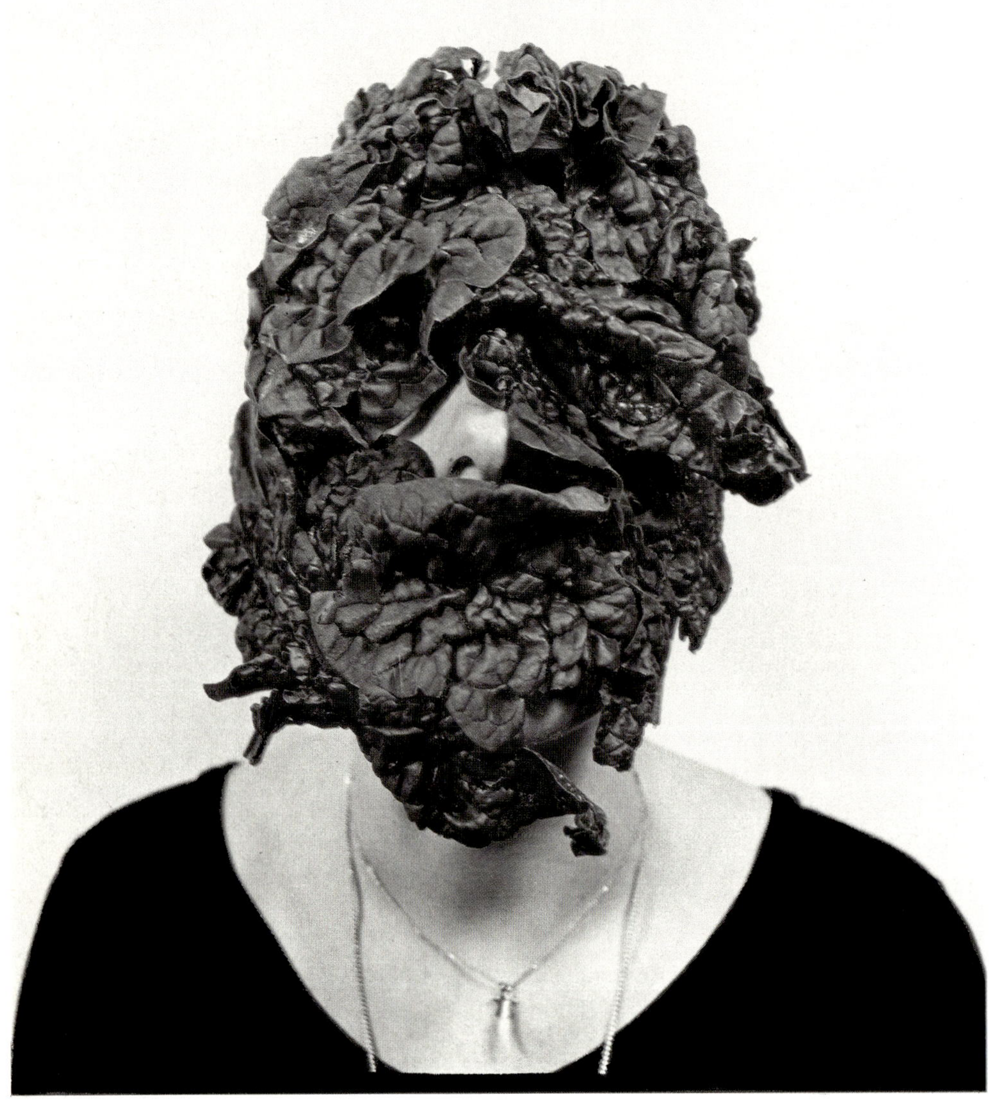

Untitled, 1975

© 1975 Ellen Carey

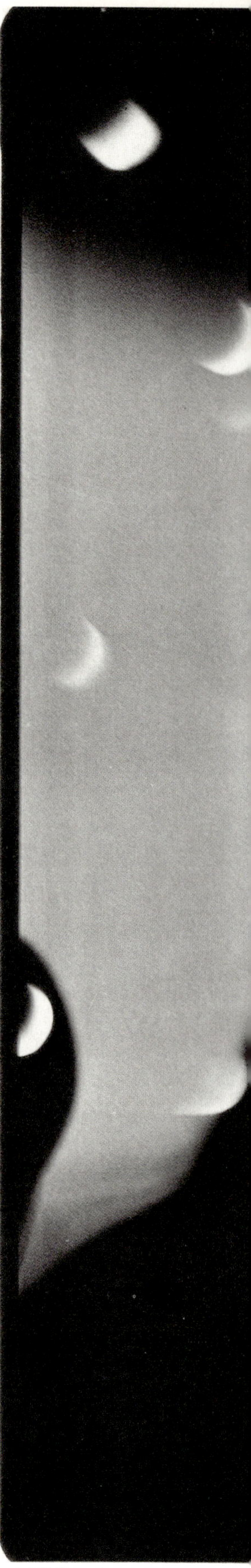

© 1976 Ellen Carey

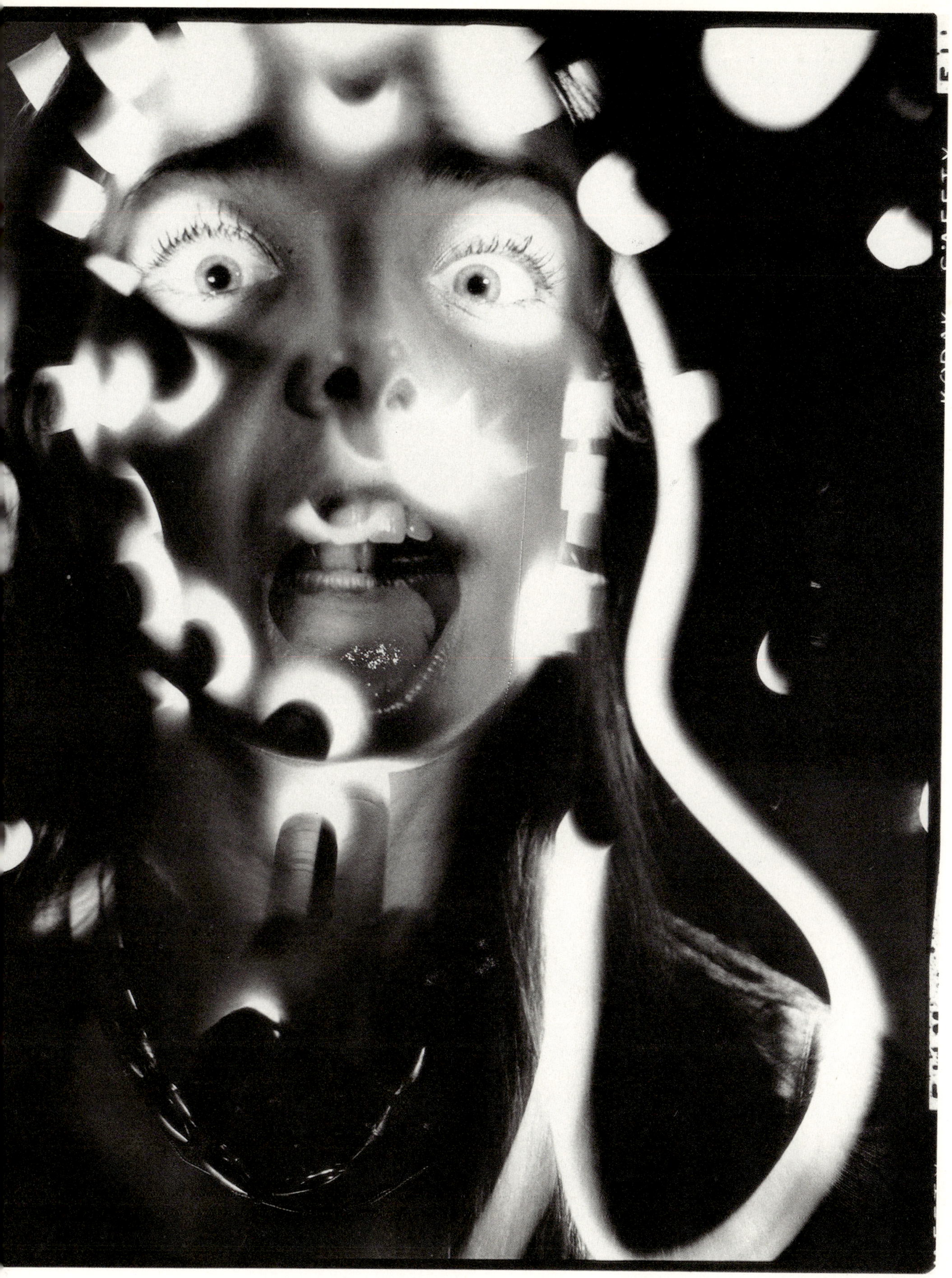

Light Portrait from the ''Black Hole in Space'' Series, 1976

Wet Veil, 1937

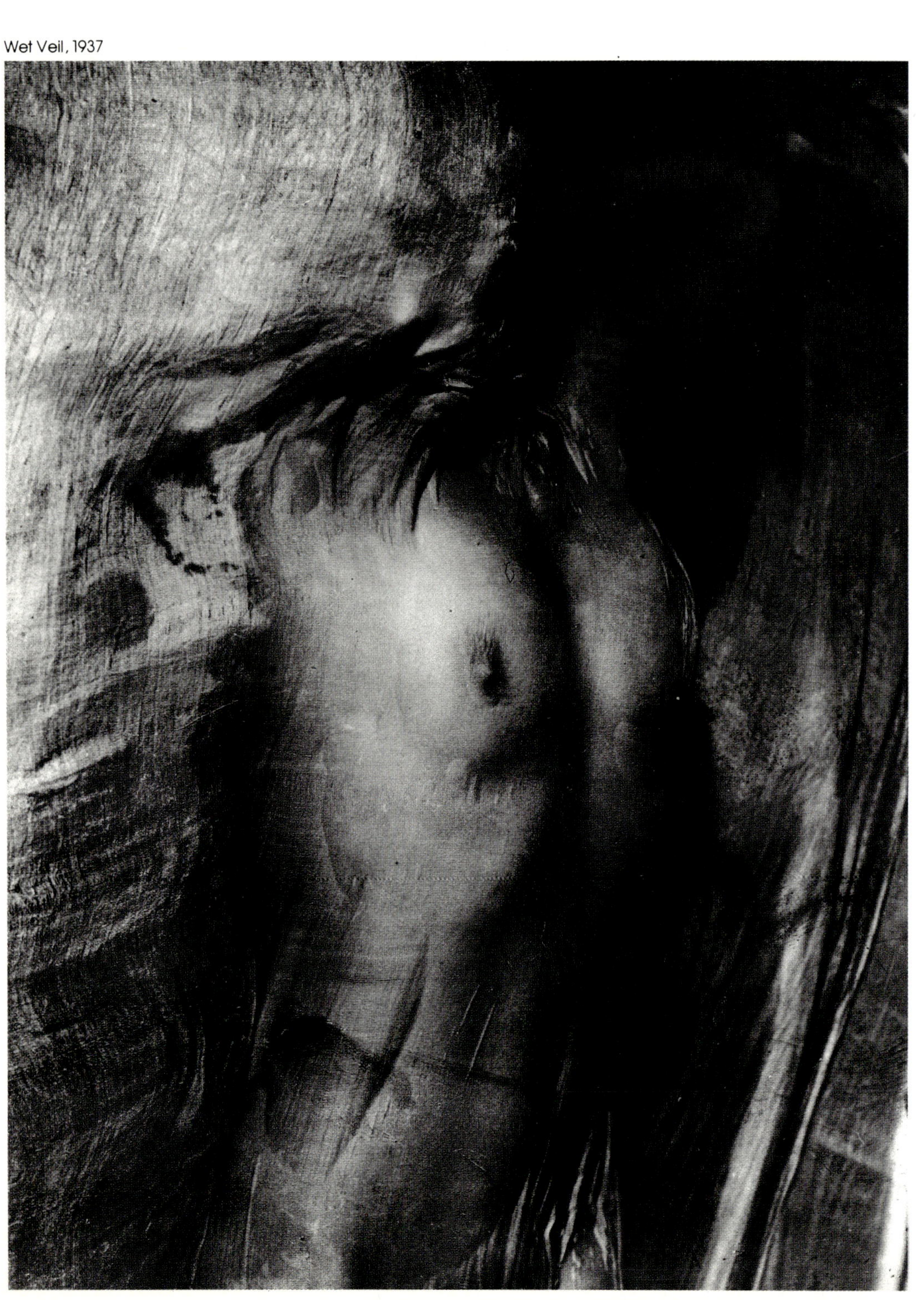

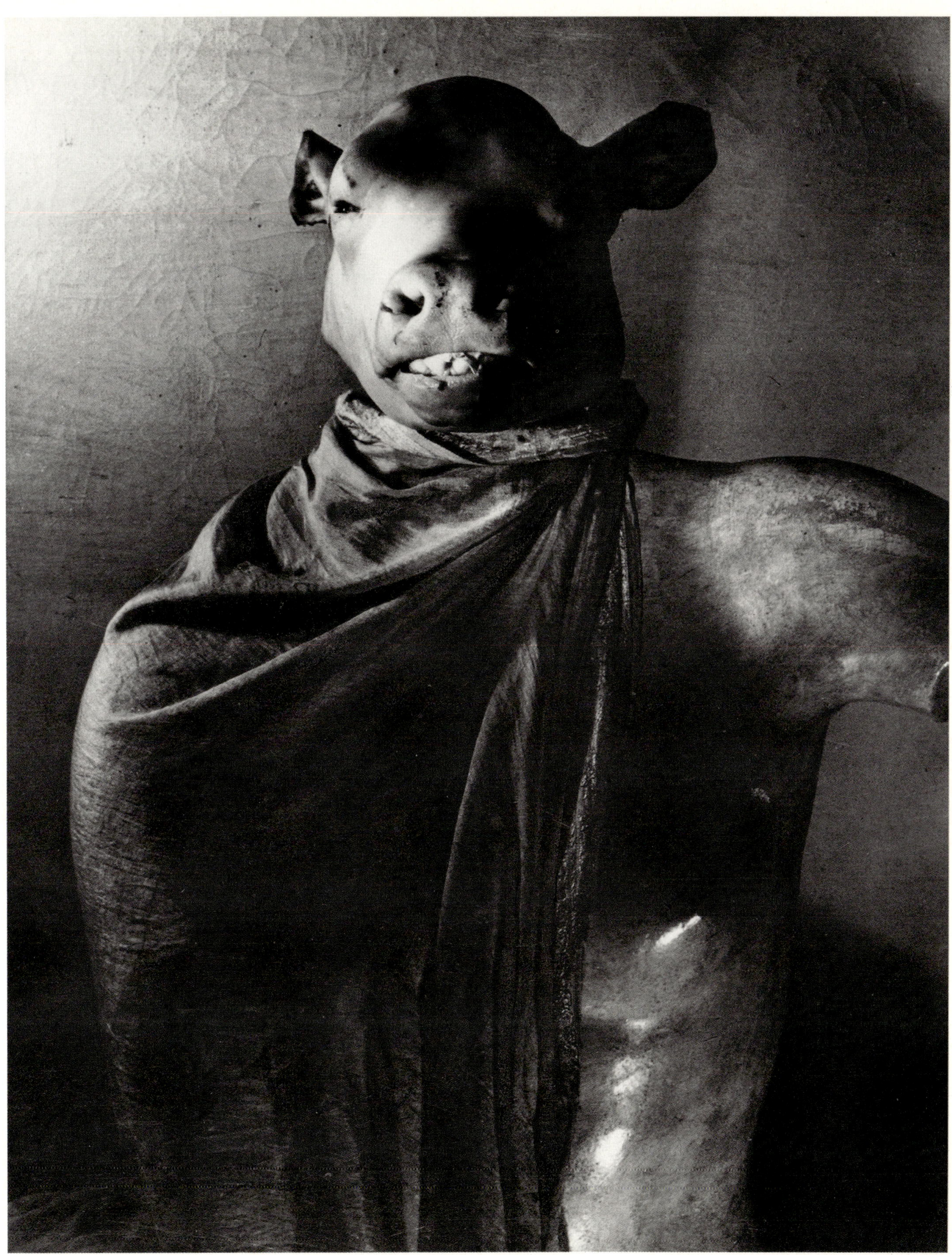

Minotaure (or The Dictator), Paris, 1937

Stefan Mihal's Suitcase

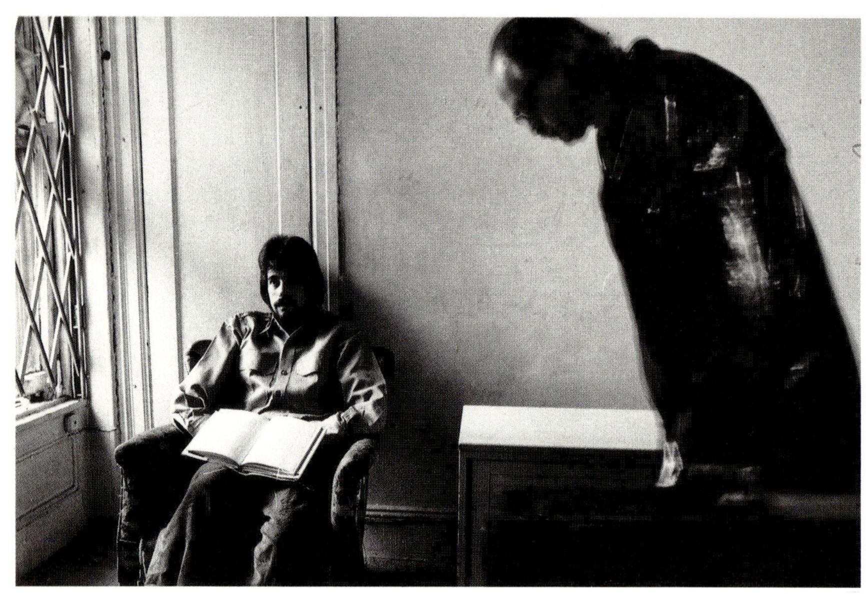

1

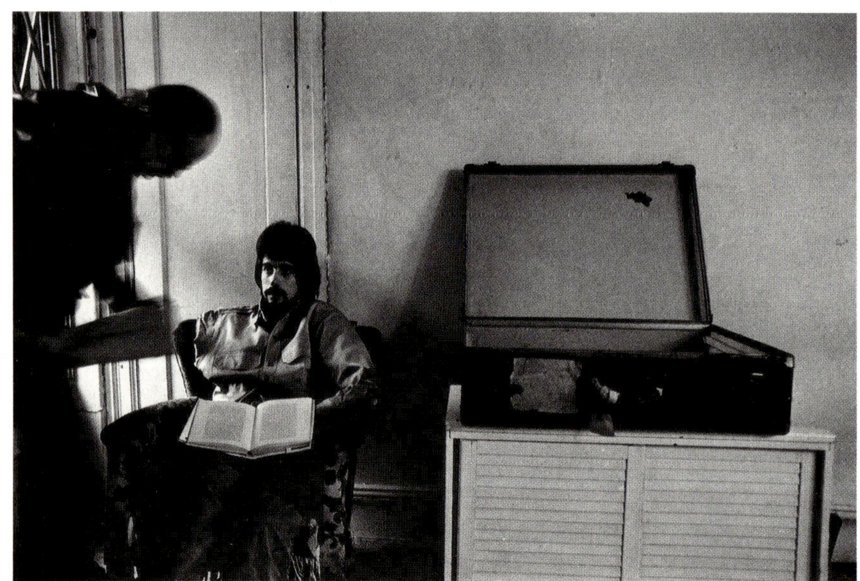

2

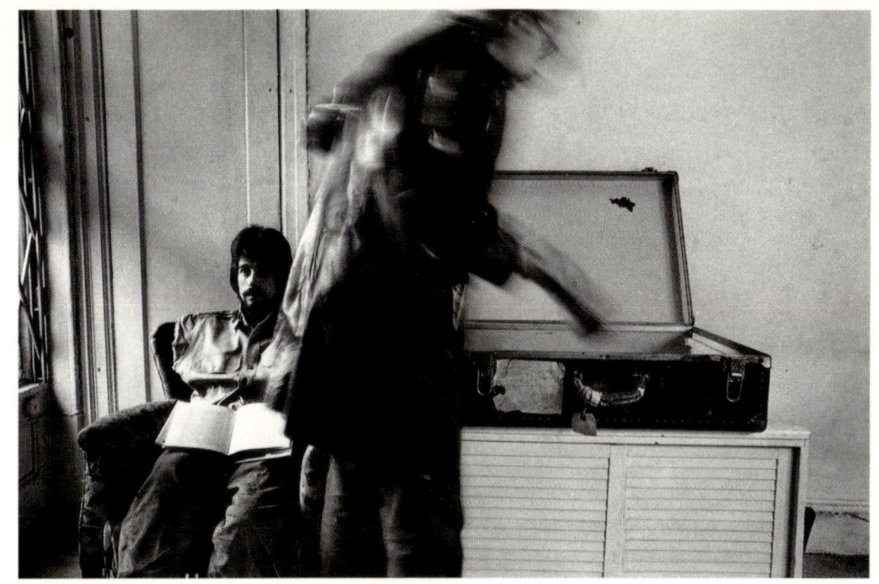

3

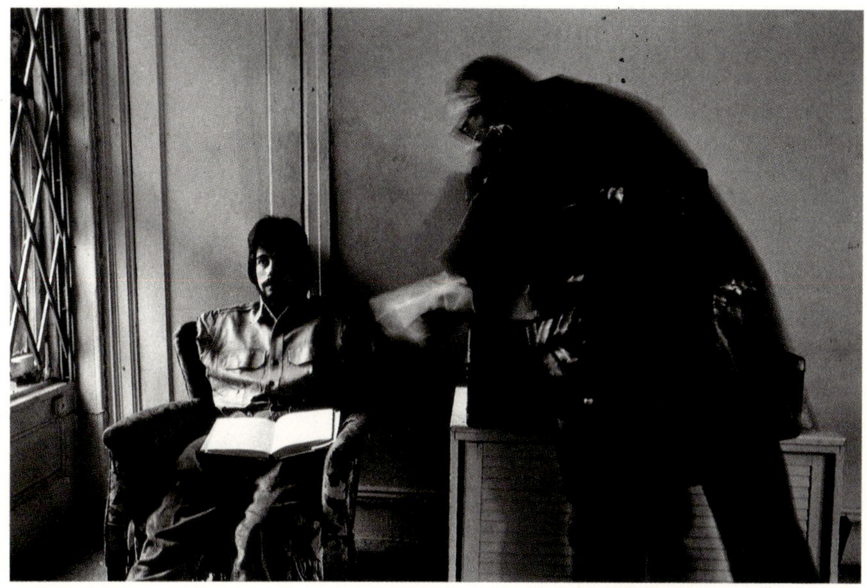

4

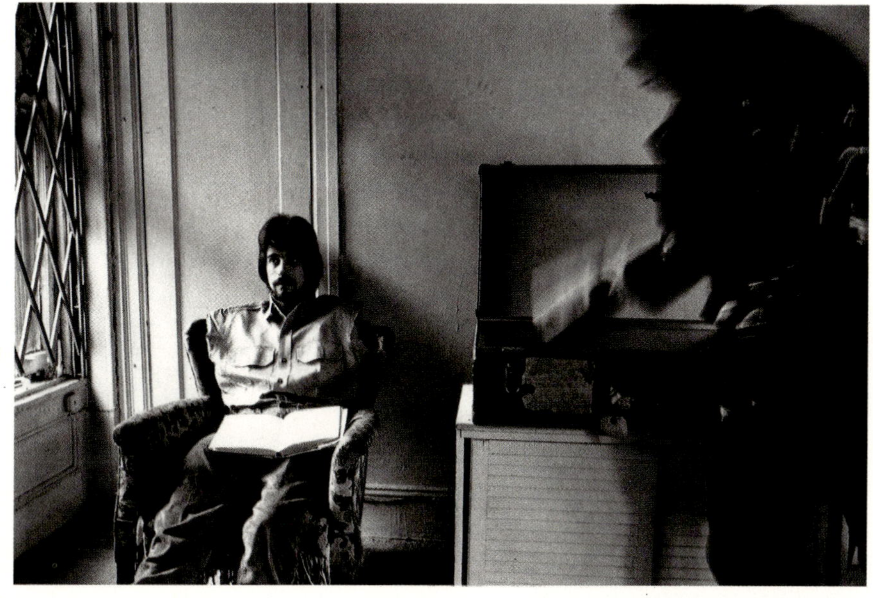

5

continued on following pages

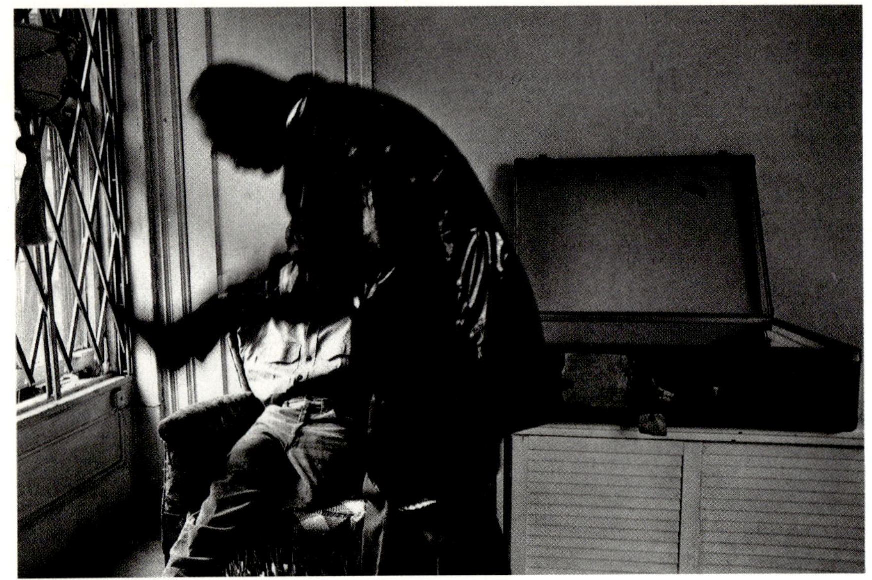

6

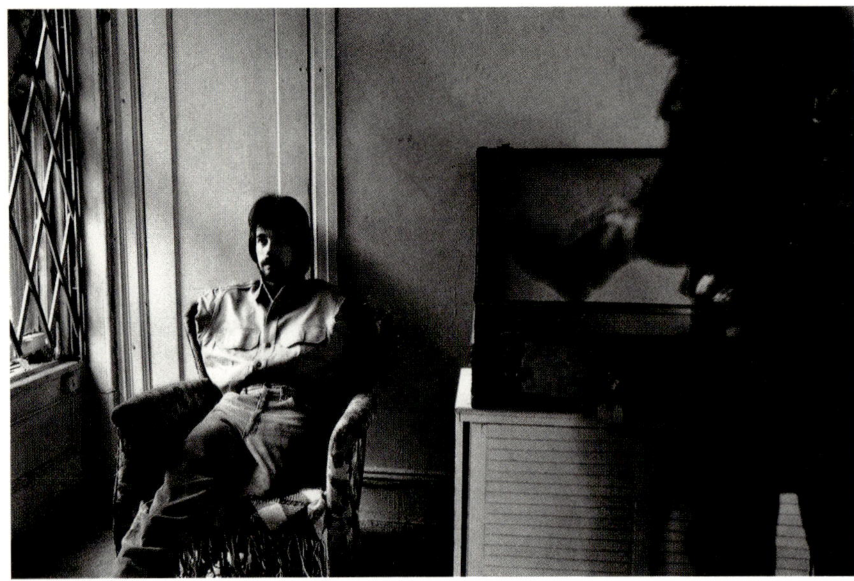

7

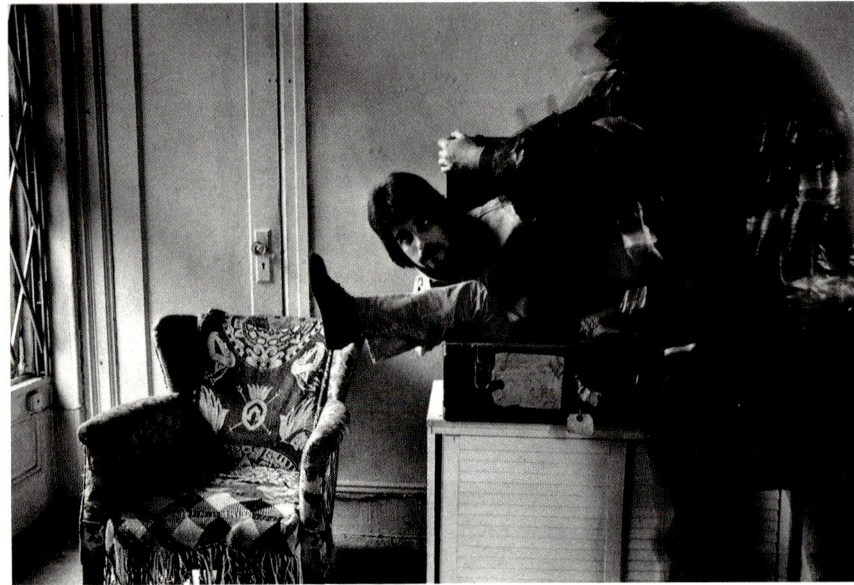

8

98

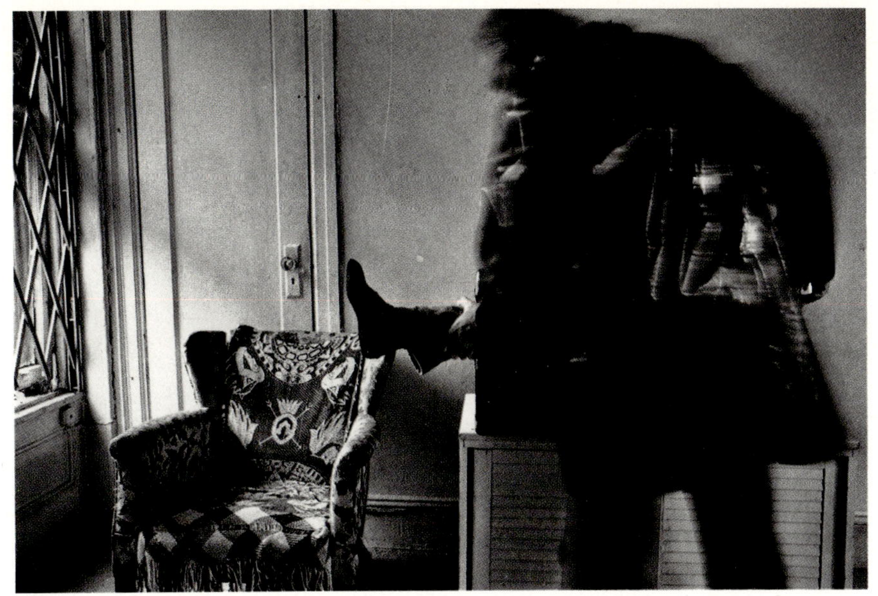

9

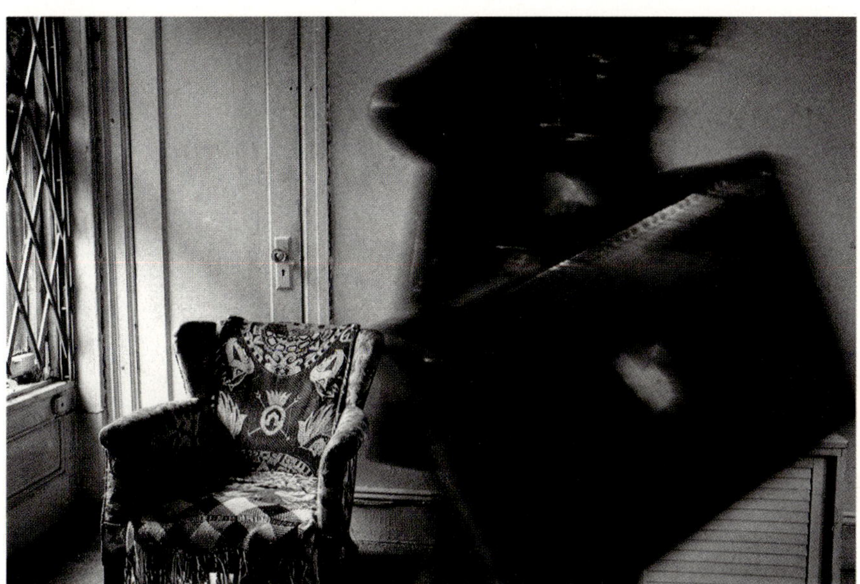

10

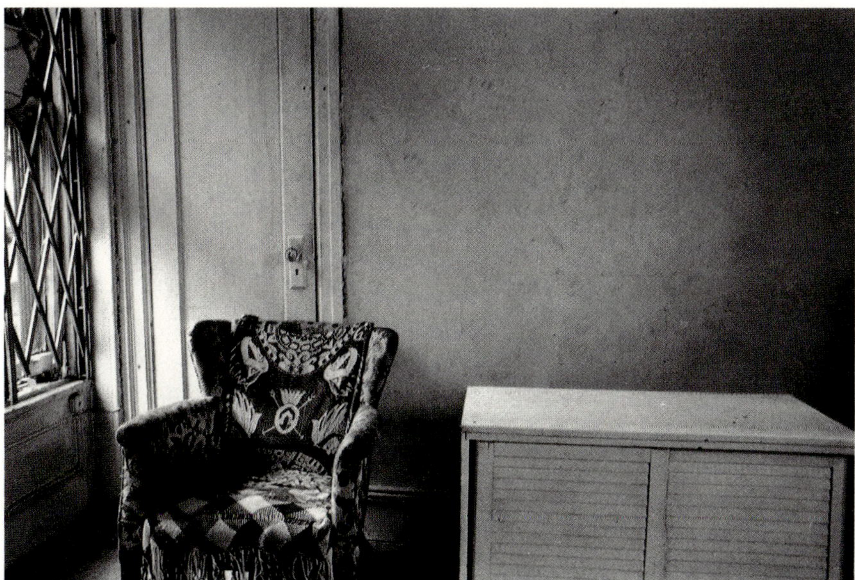

11

Distortion #40

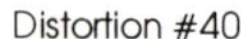

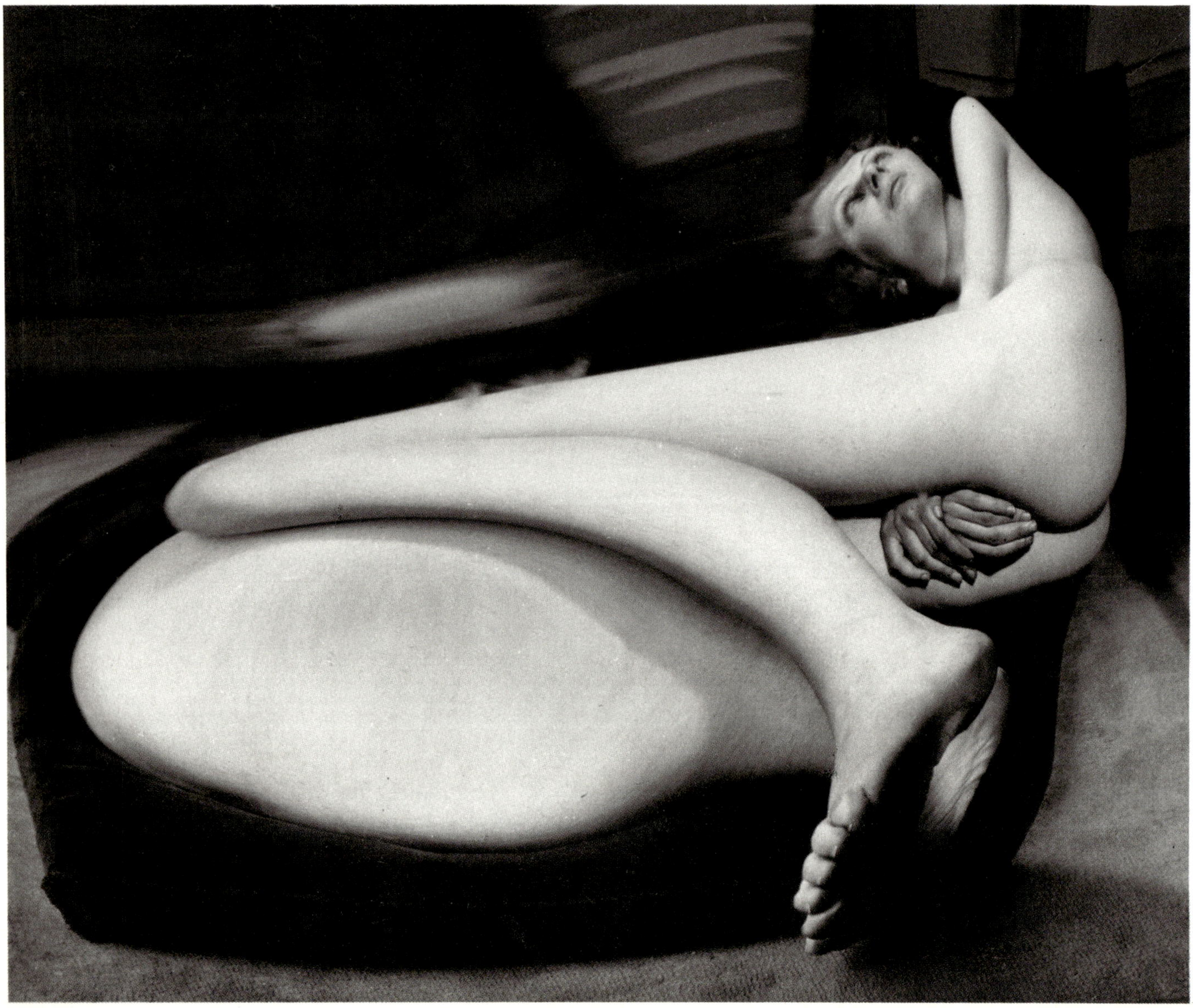

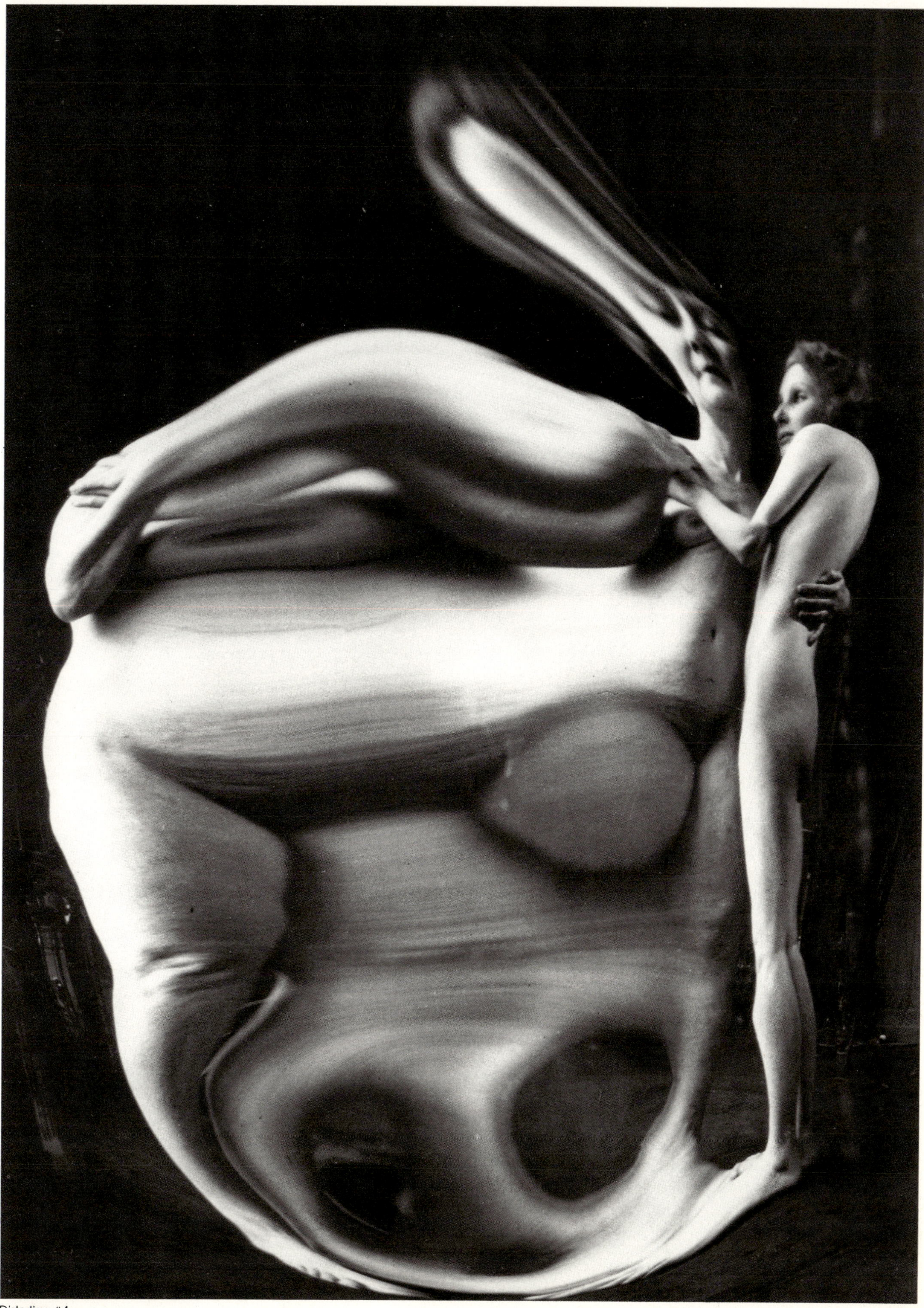

Distortion #4

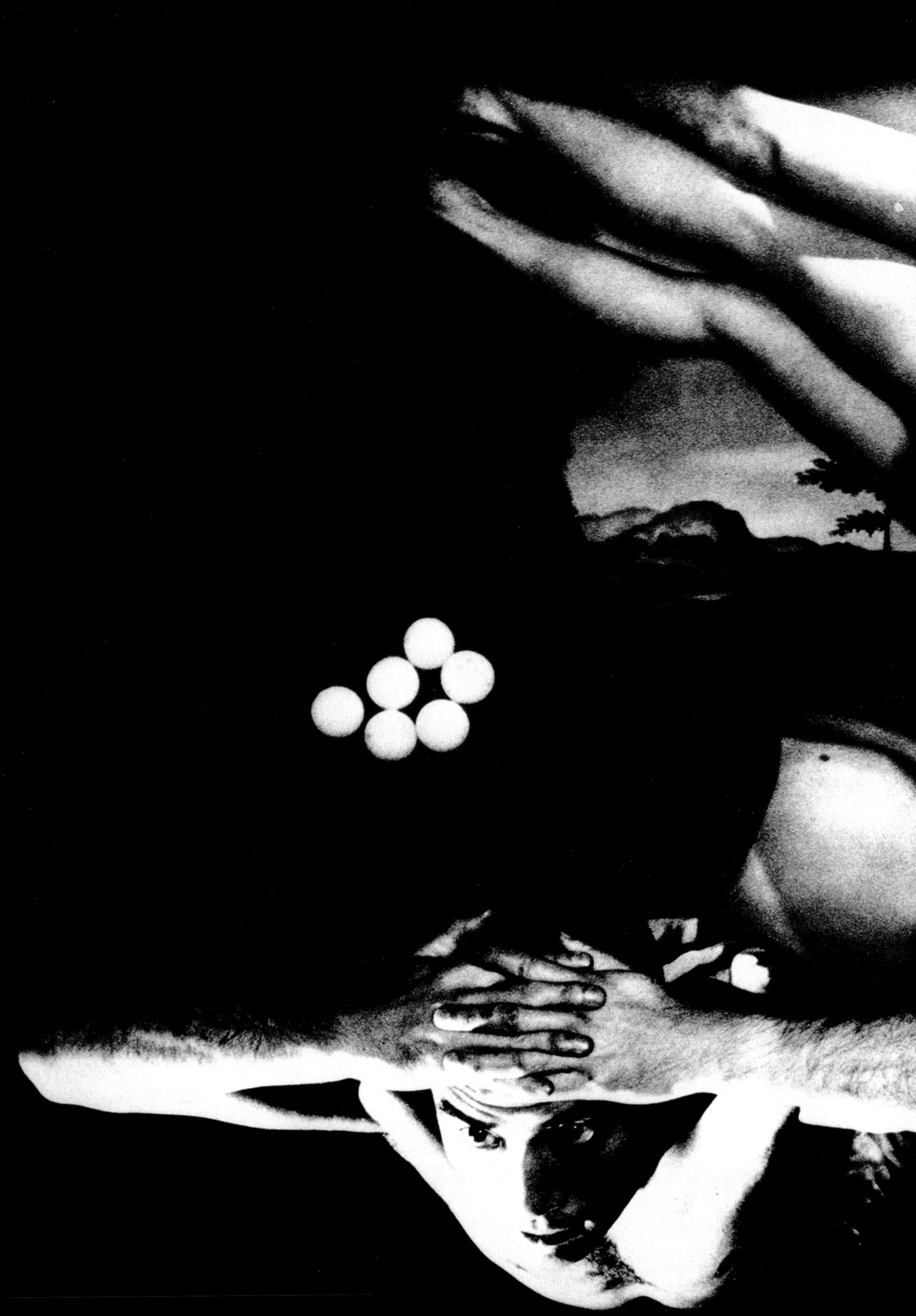

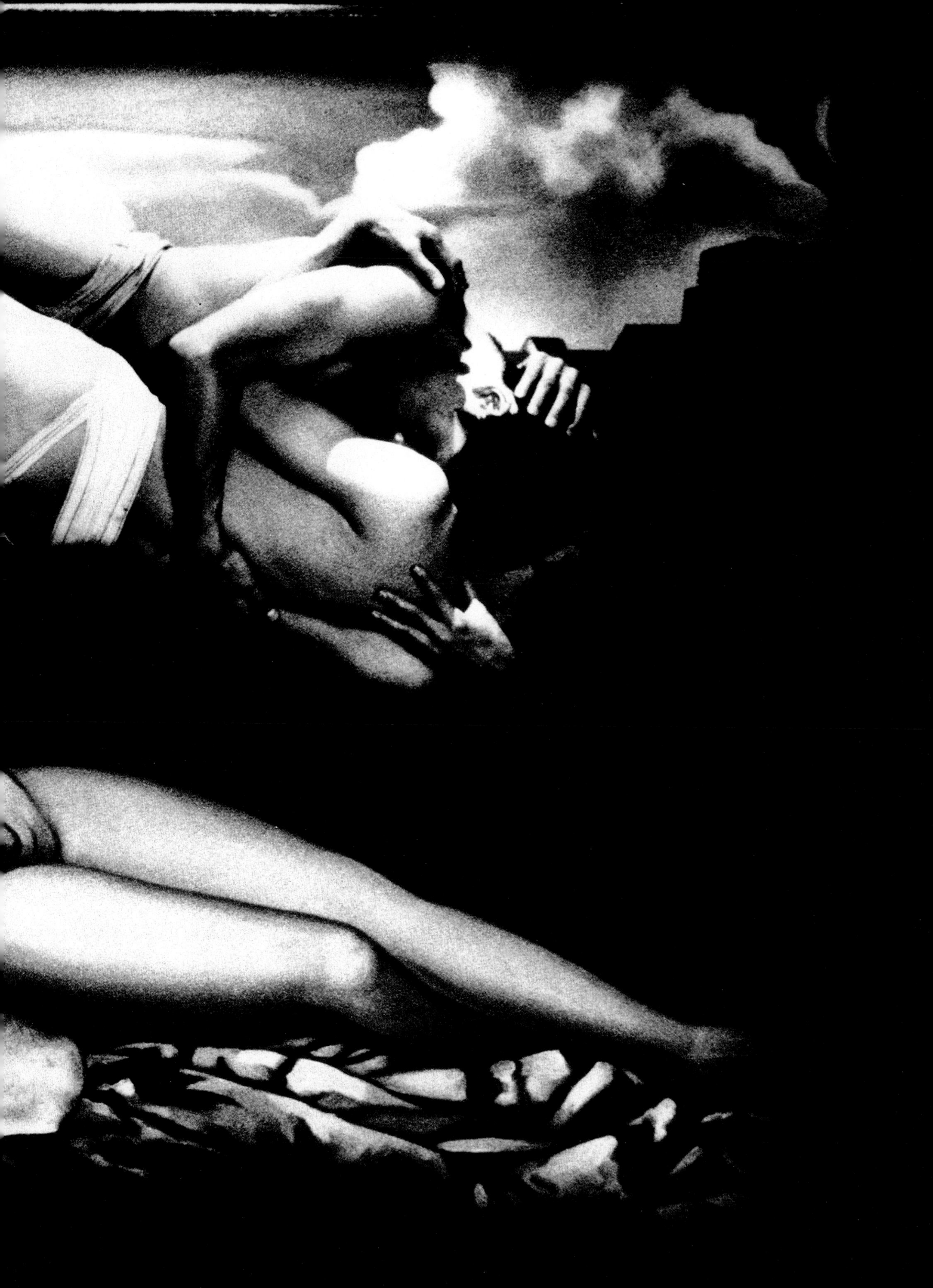

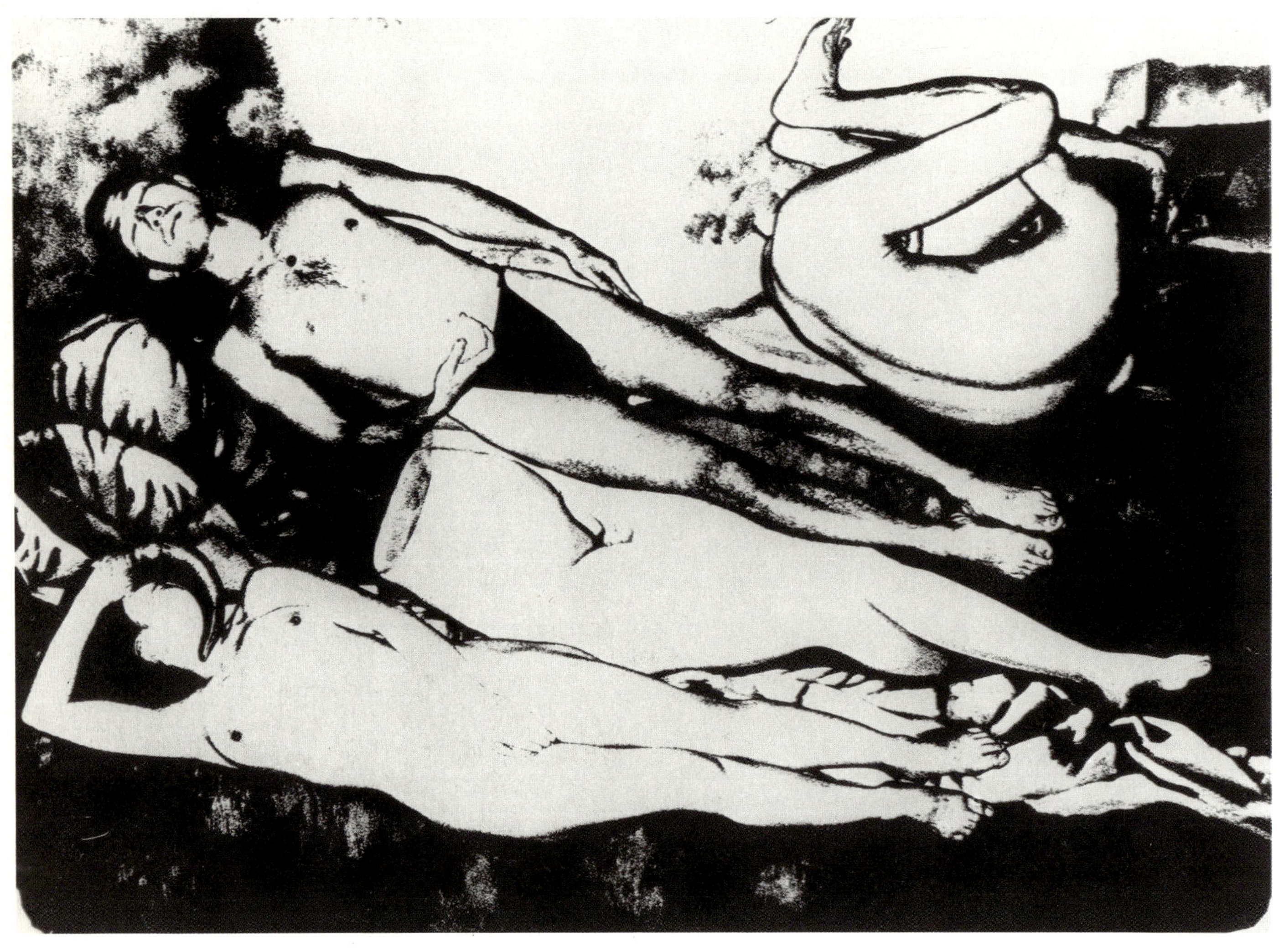

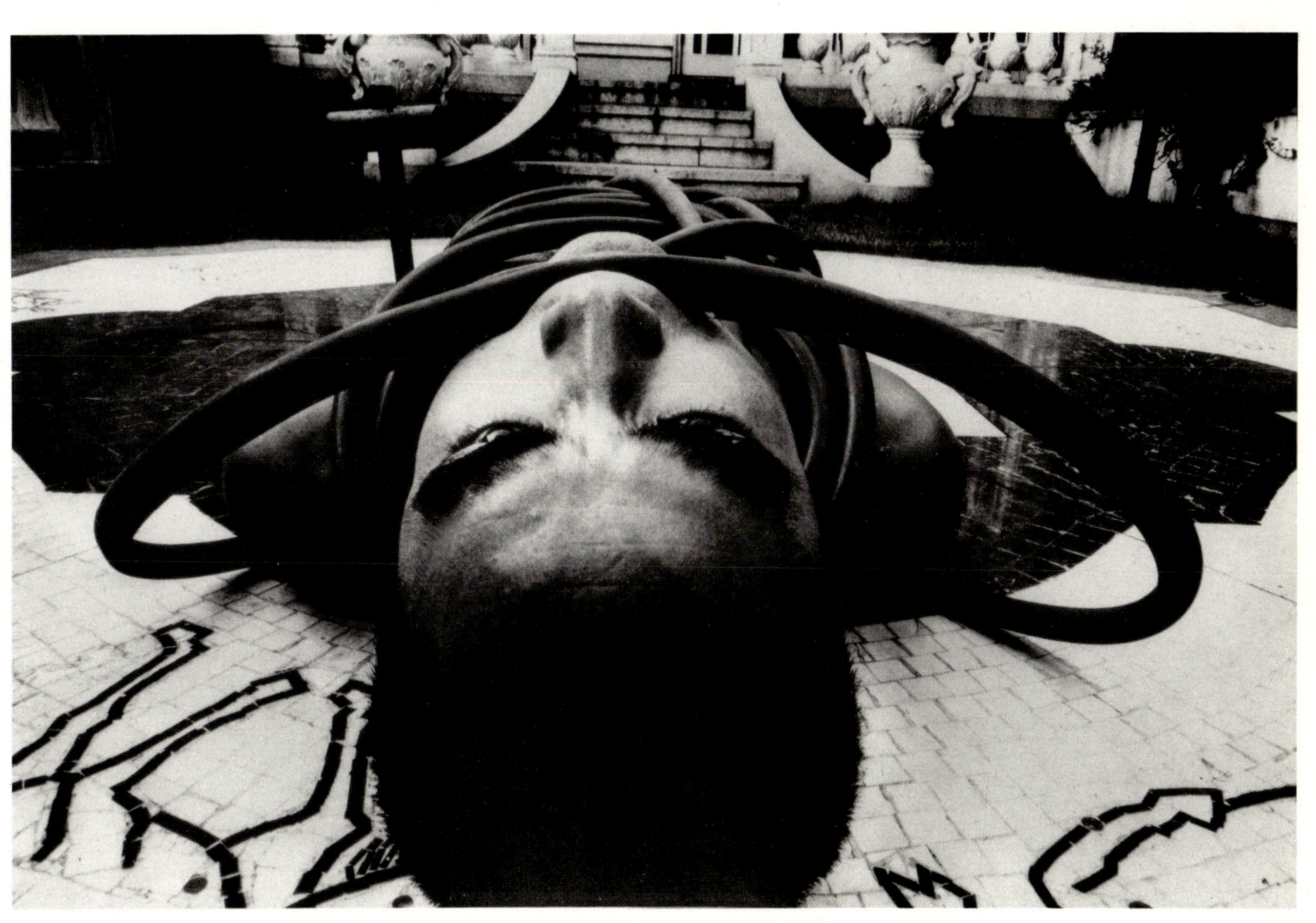

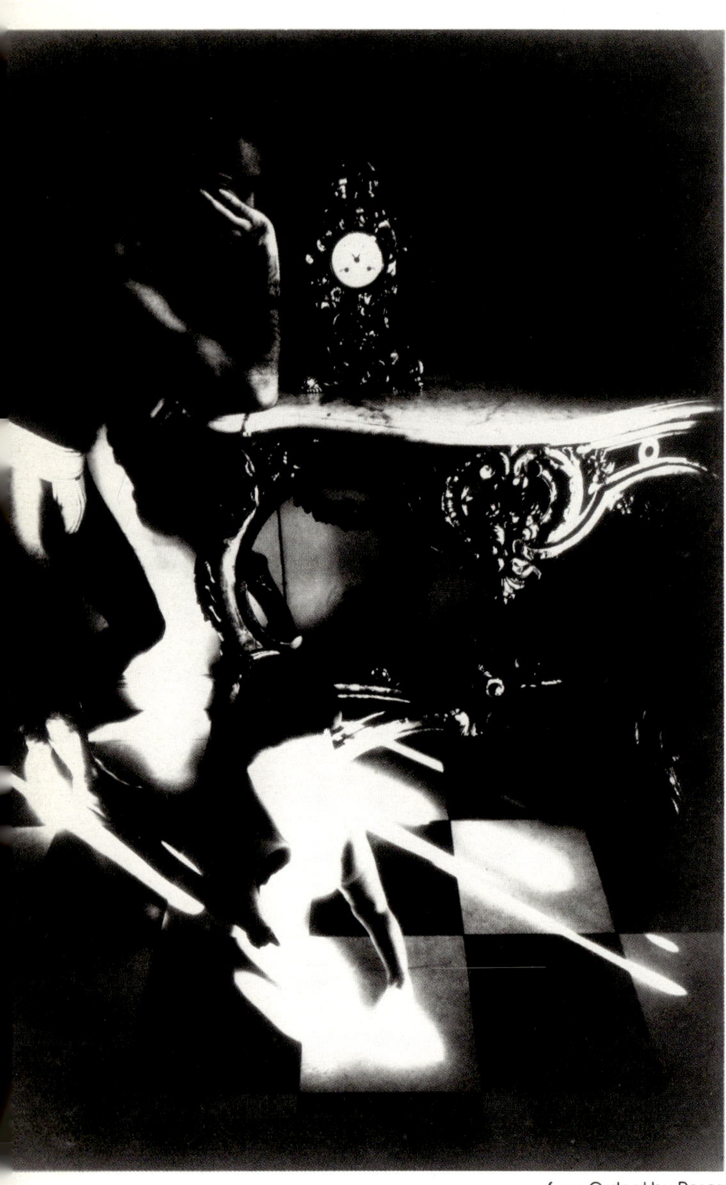

from Ordeal by Roses

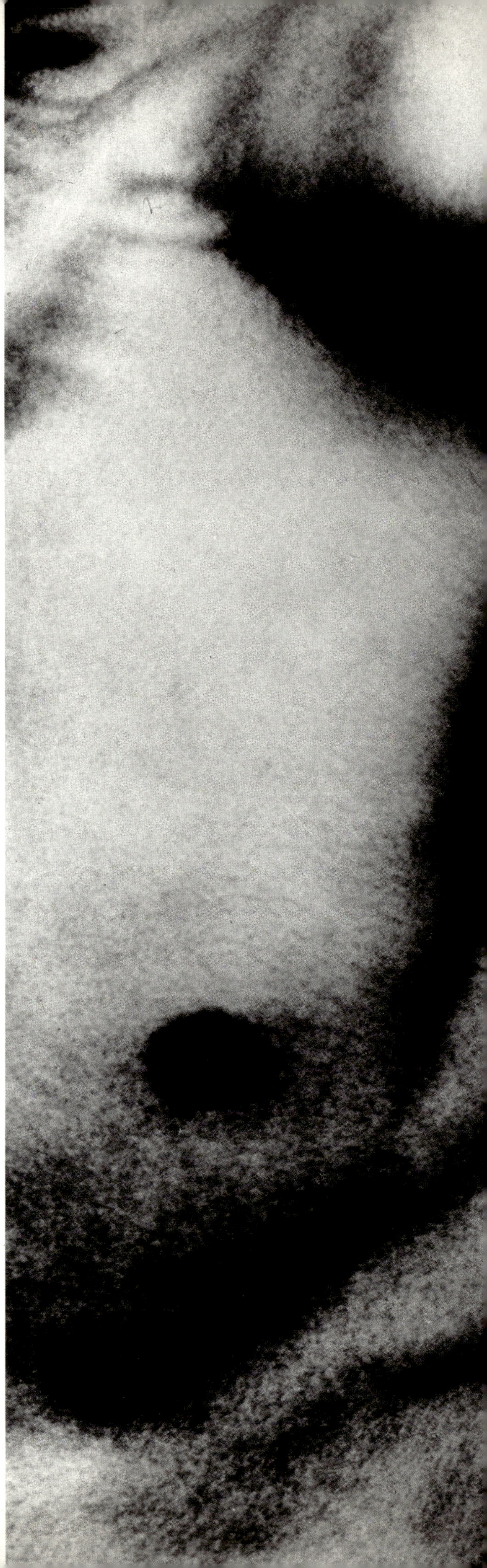

from Man and Woman

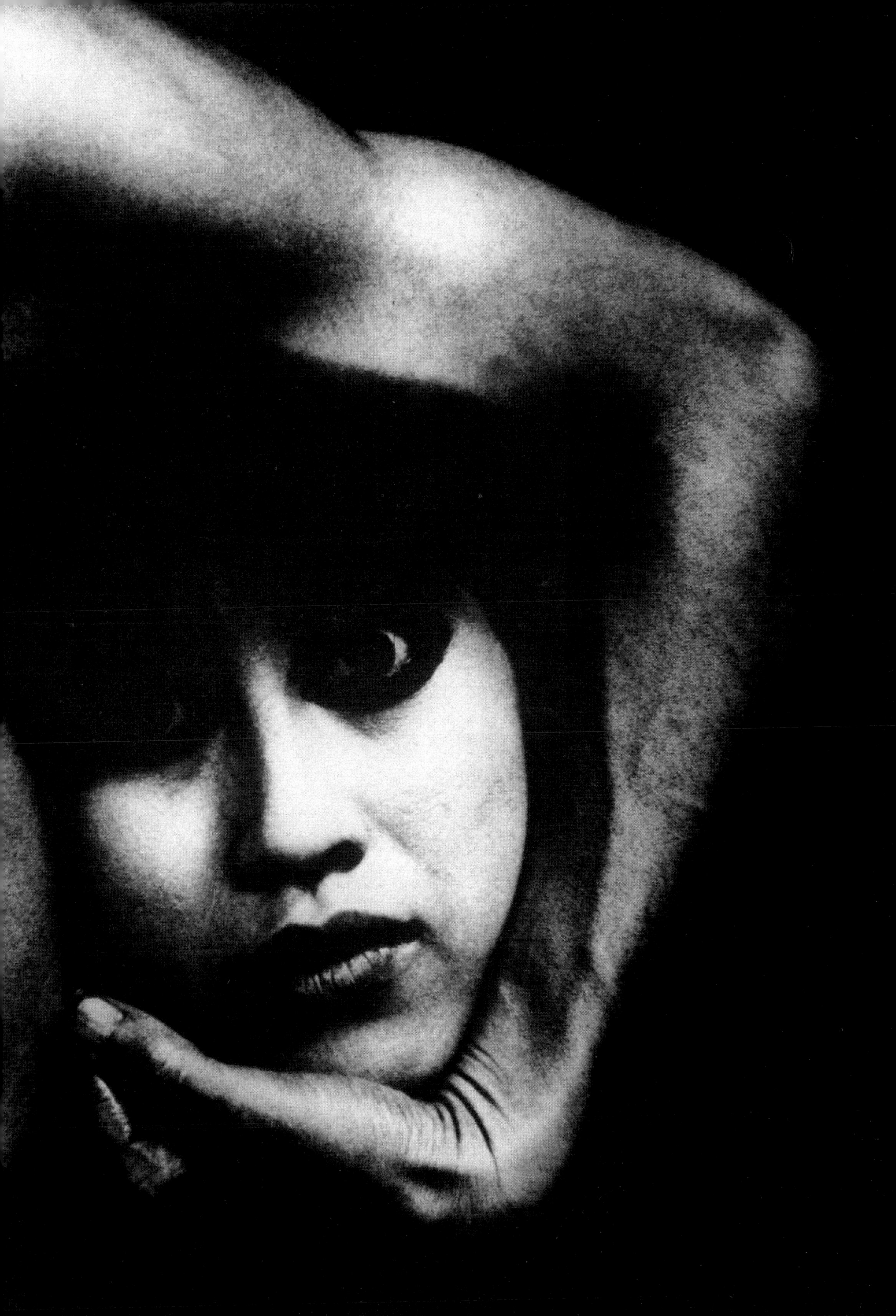

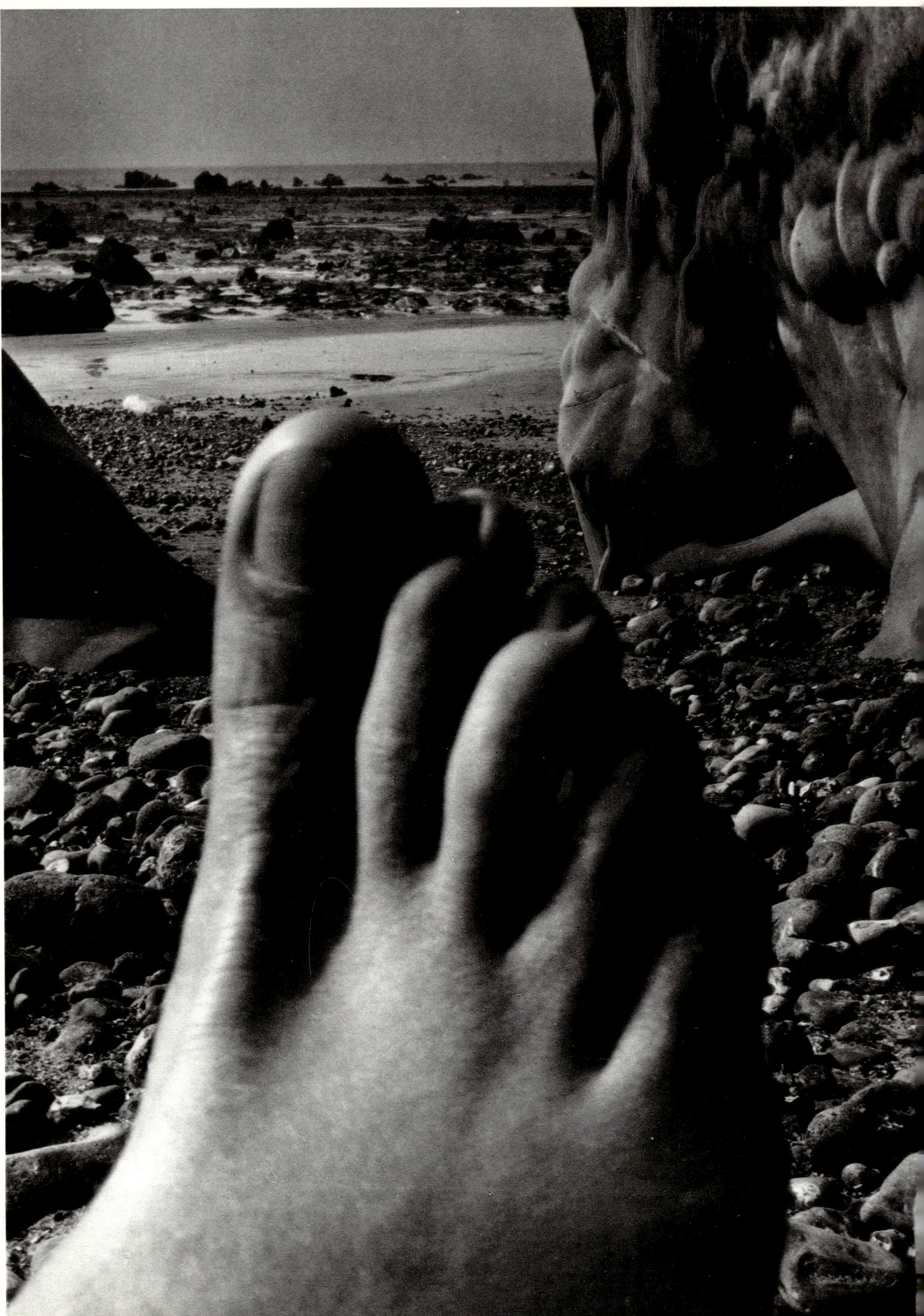

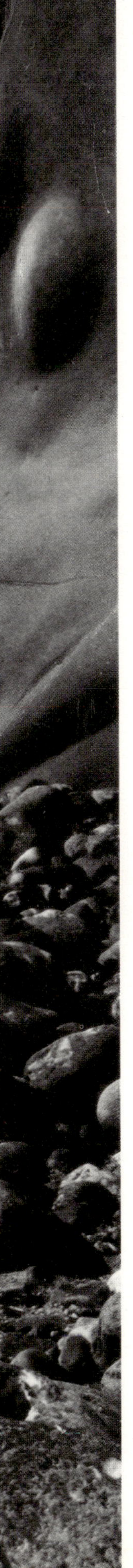

Greenwich Maritime Museum, London

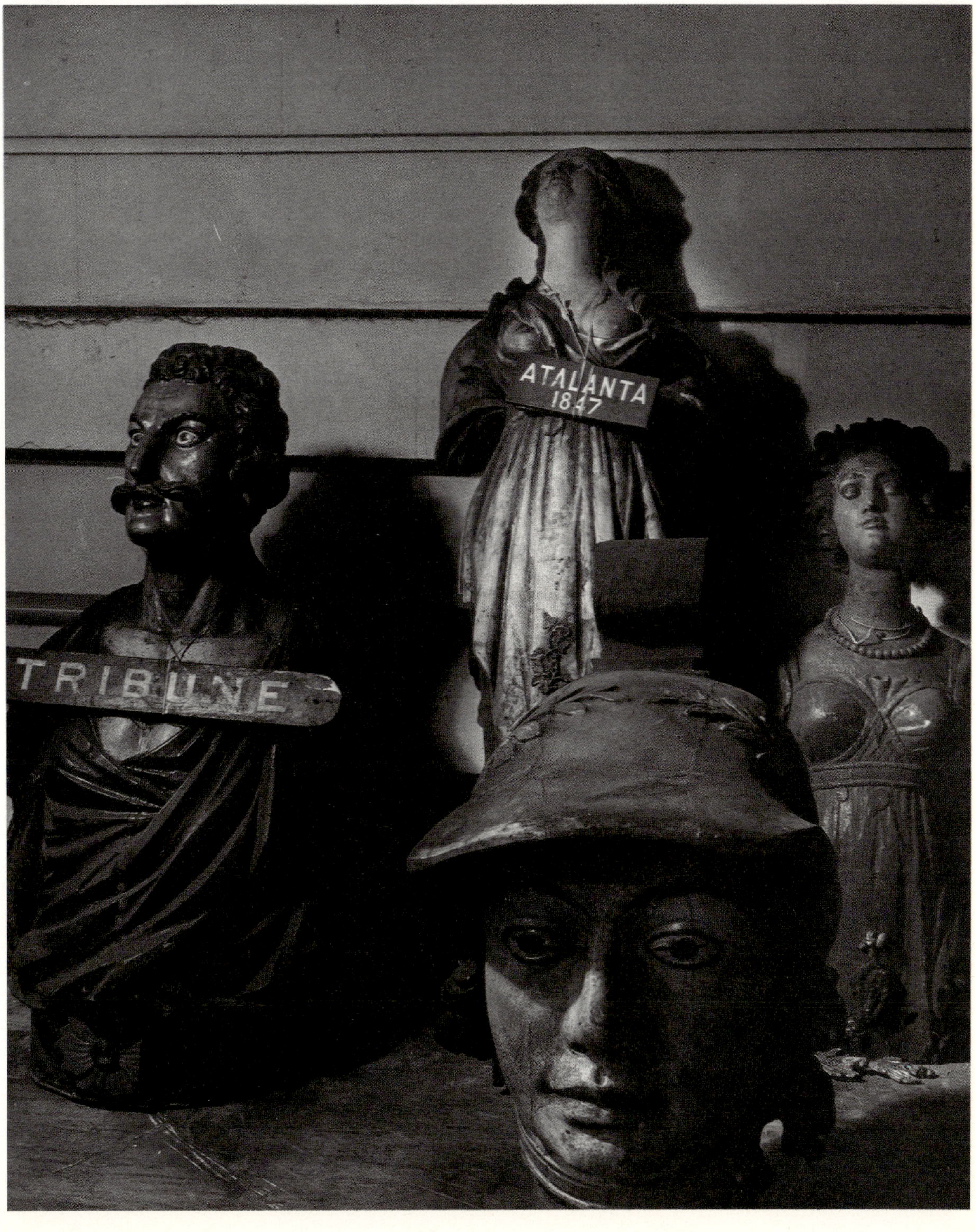

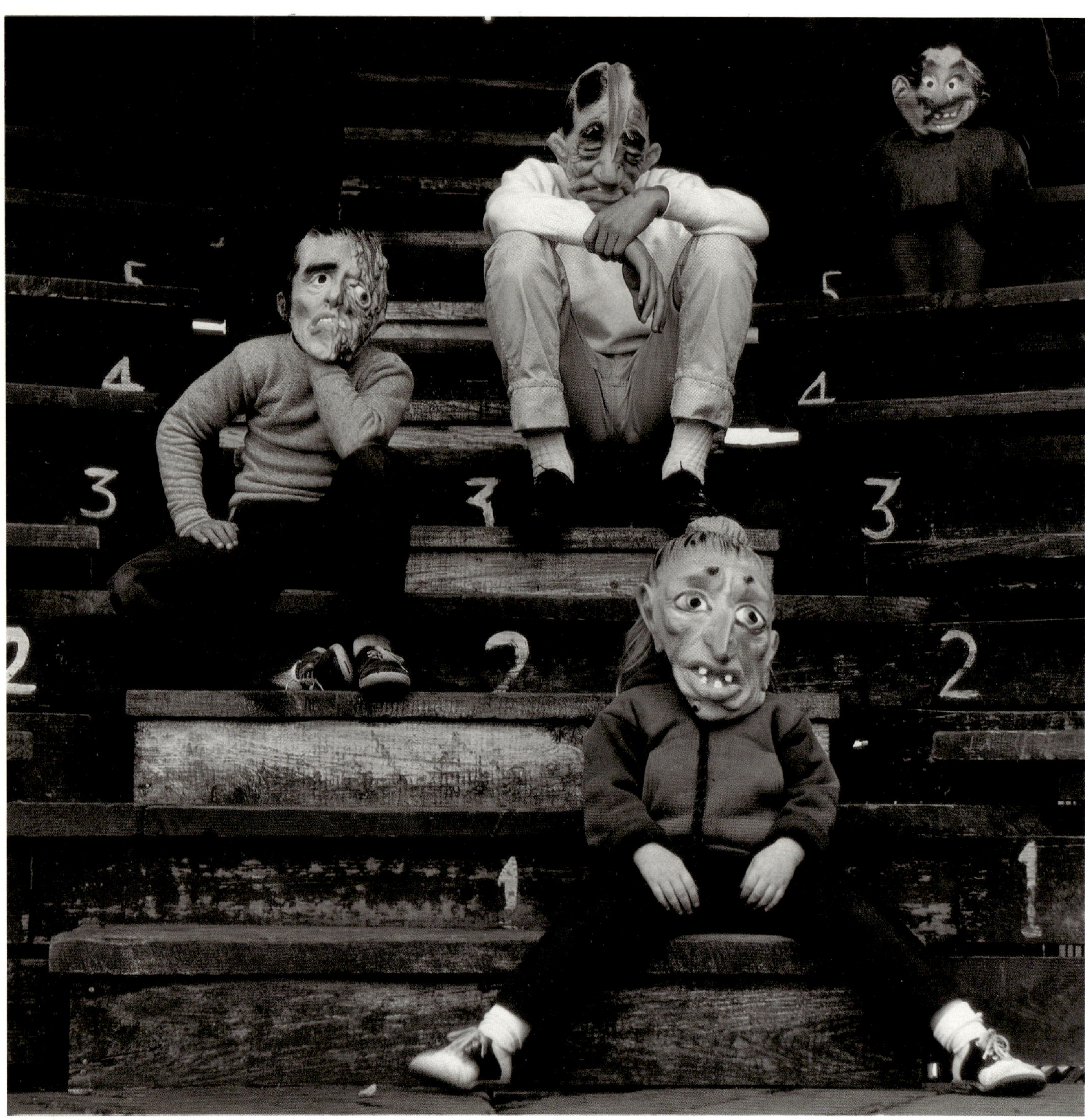

Ambrose Bierce # 3, ca. 1964

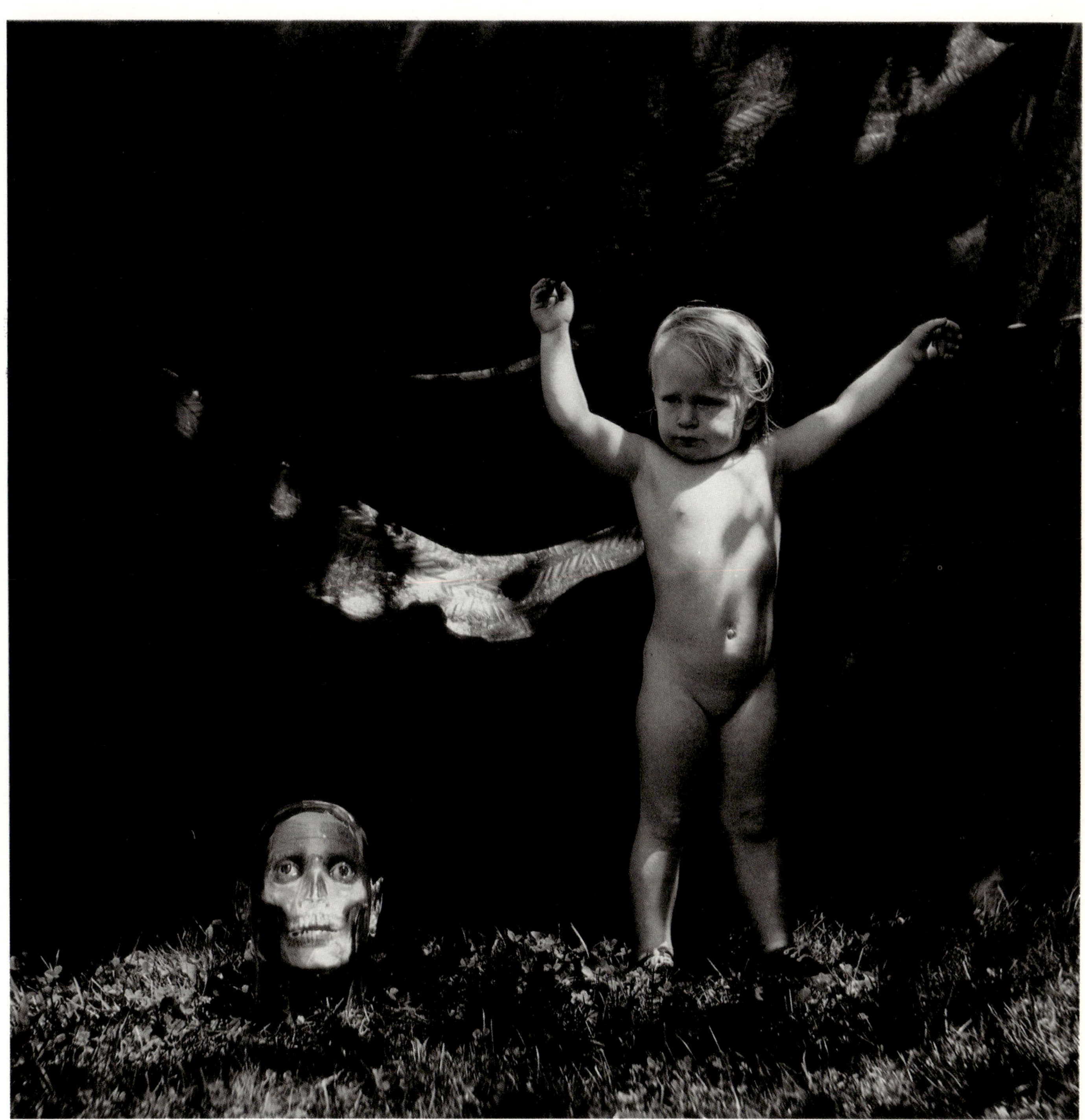

Untitled, ca. 1962

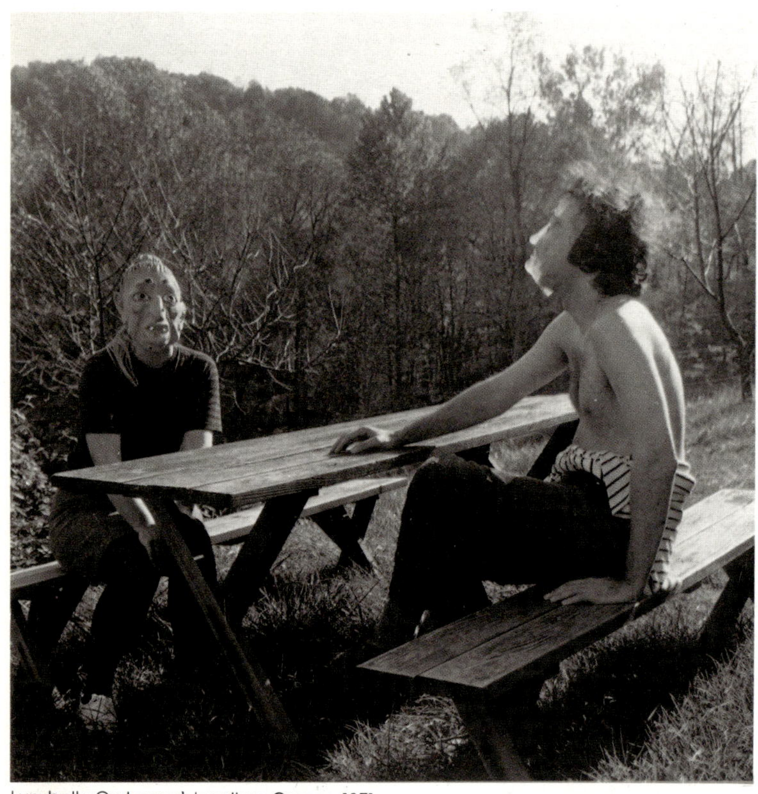

Lucybelle Crater and Jonathan Greene, 1971

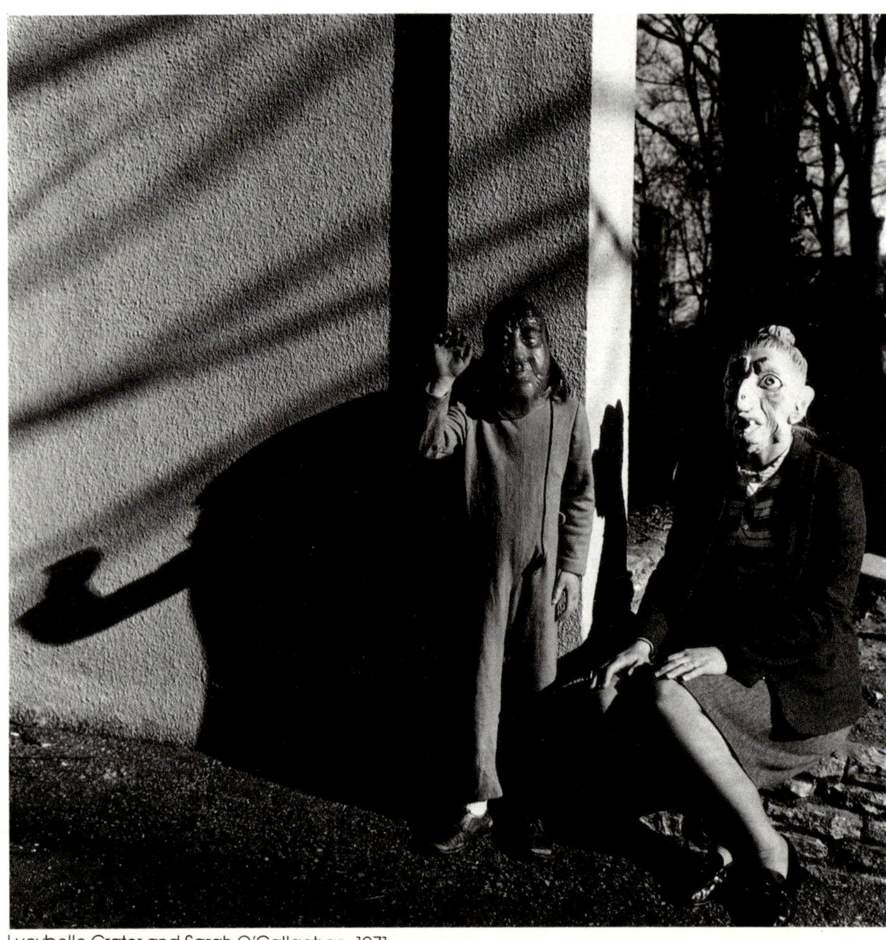

Lucybelle Crater and Sarah O'Callaghan, 1971

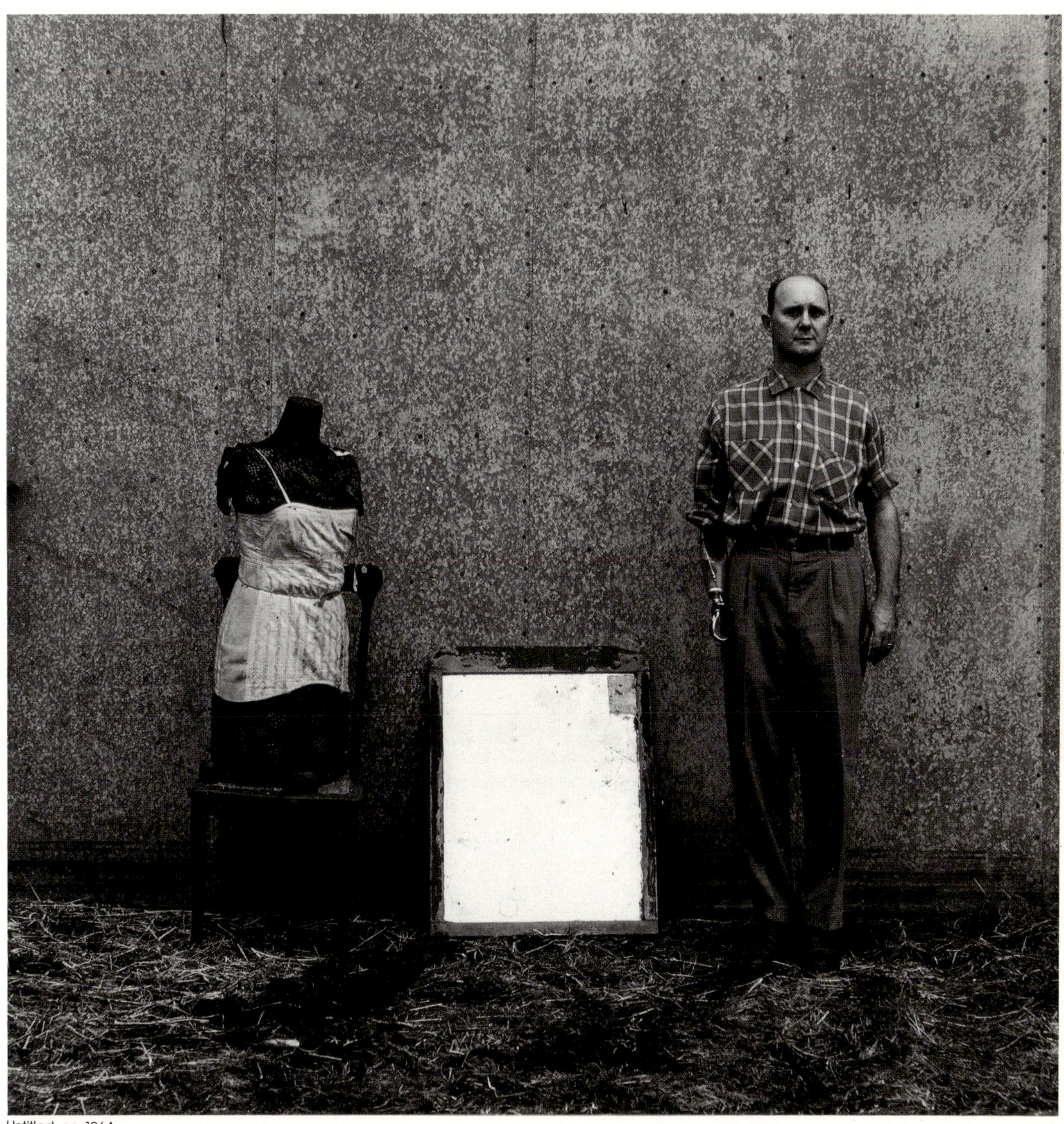

Untitled, ca. 1964

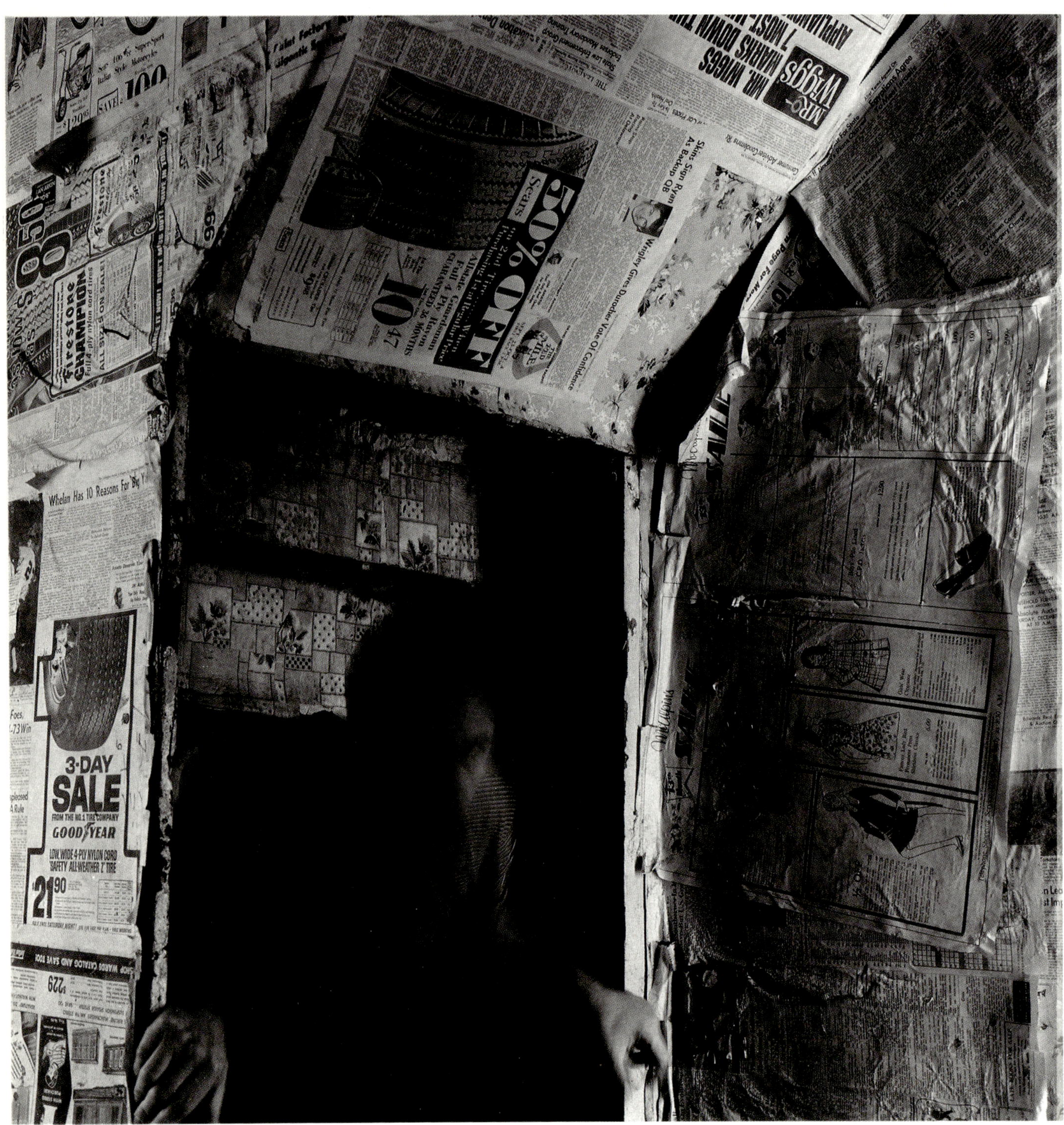

Untitled, 1970

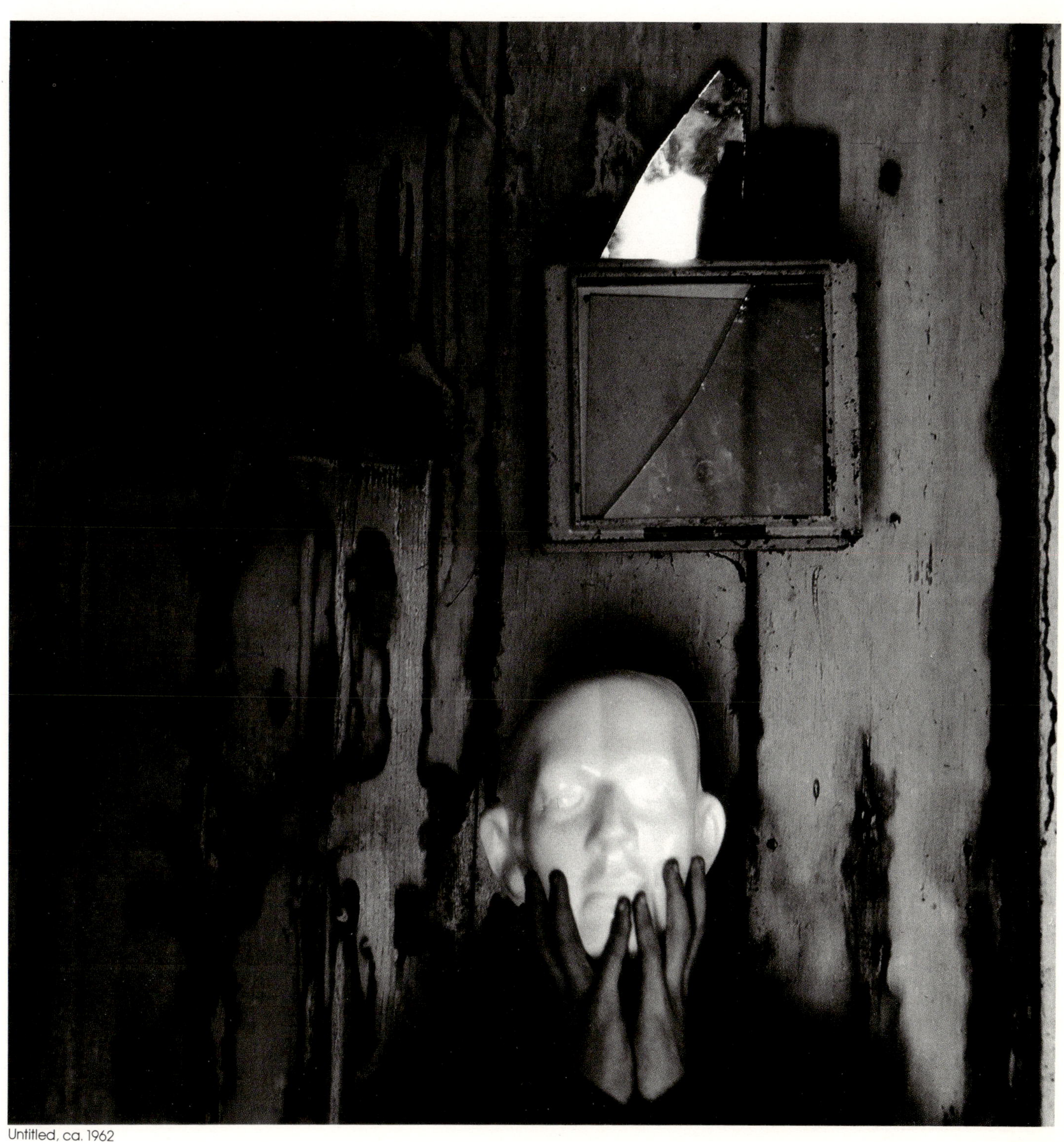

Untitled, ca. 1962

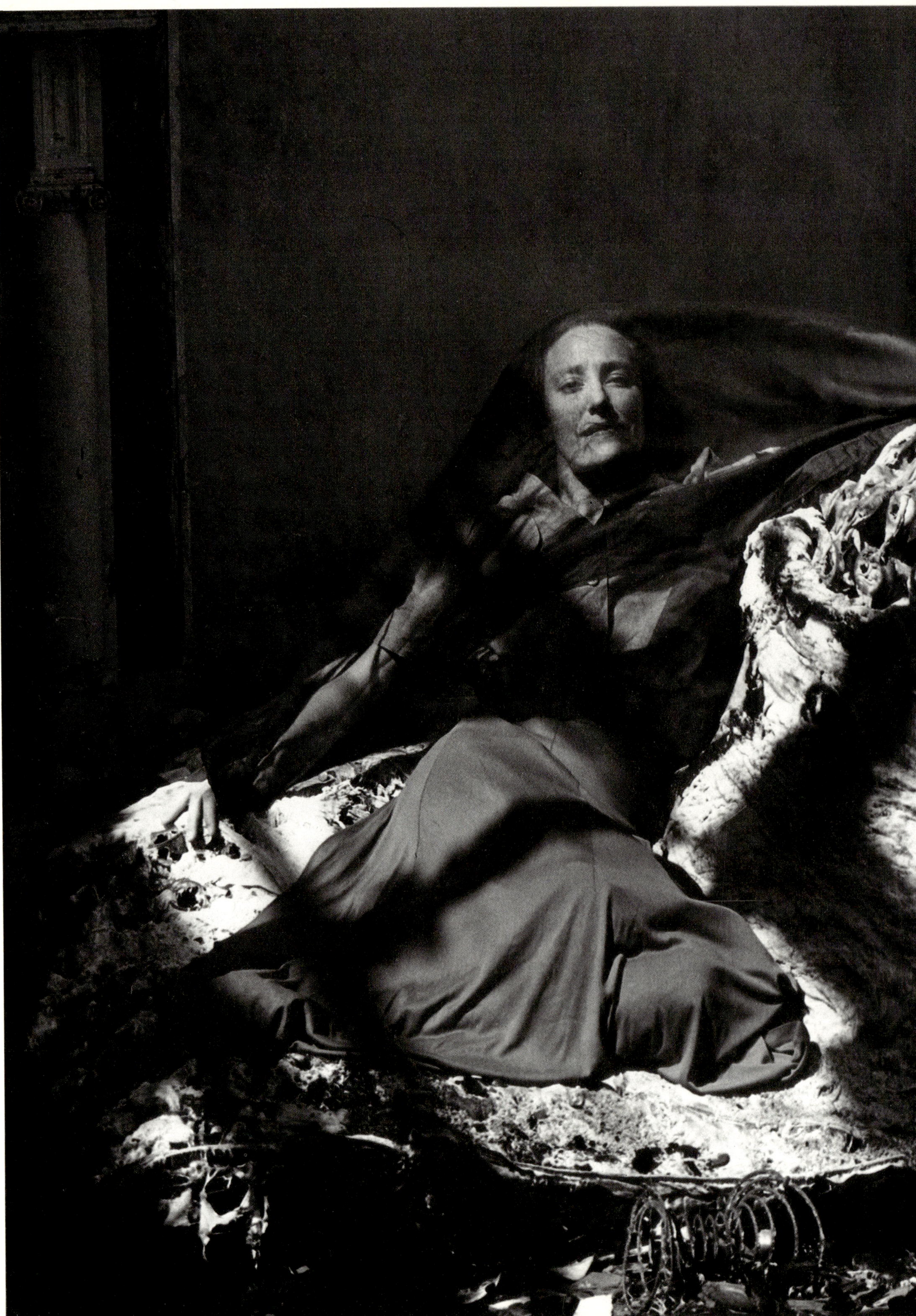

CLARENCE JOHN LAUGHLIN

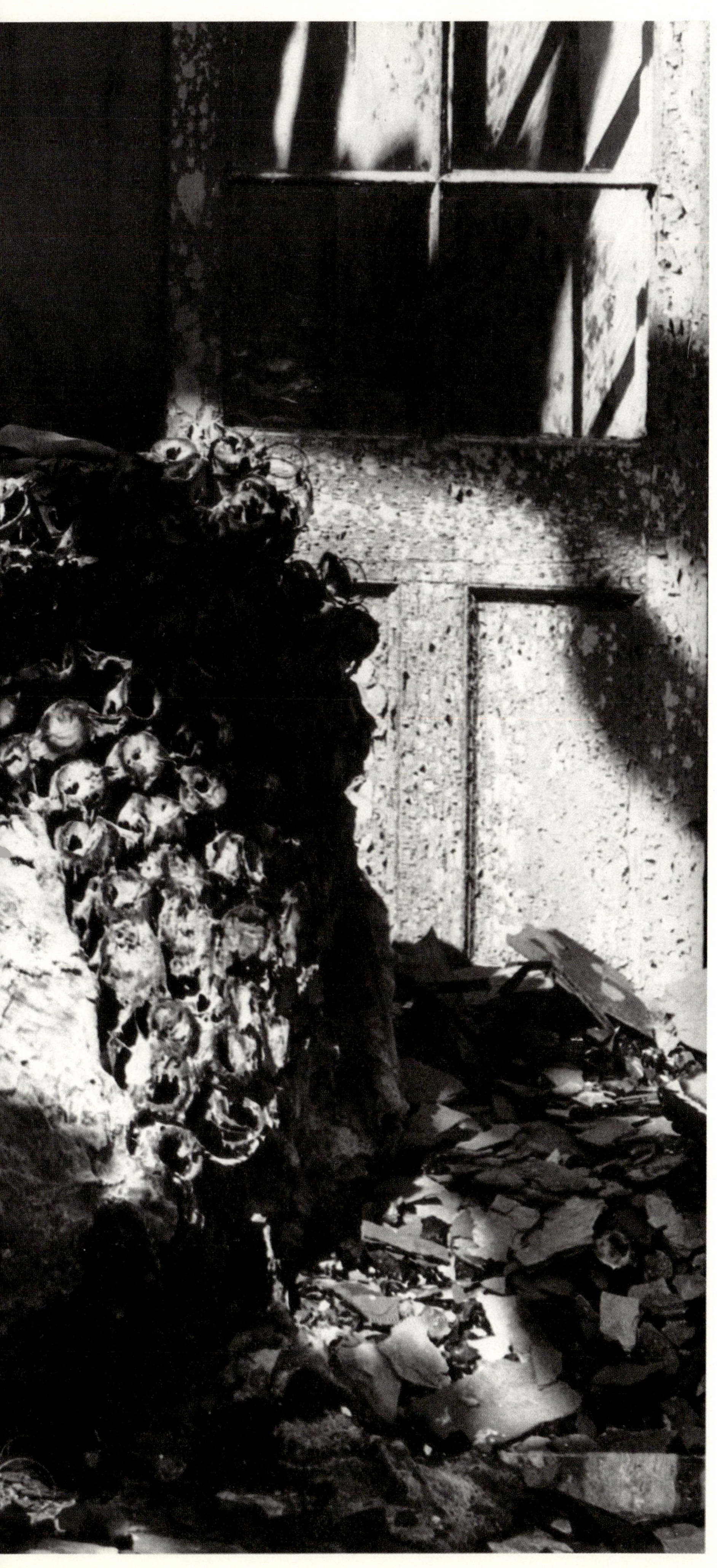

The Repulsive Bed, 1941
(From Group L: Poems of the Inner World)
This print becomes the symbol of marriage without
love, which is endured because of convention, or because of
economic compulsion. The house has corrupted, and
the marriage bed has disintegrated — becoming a monstrous head
of repulsion, whose snout rests on the hip of the
nameless figure in black, thus crystallizing the repugnance of
the bed to her. And the corroded mattress becomes
a supreme example of the grotesque. — C.J.L.
Copyright 1941 by Clarence John Laughlin.

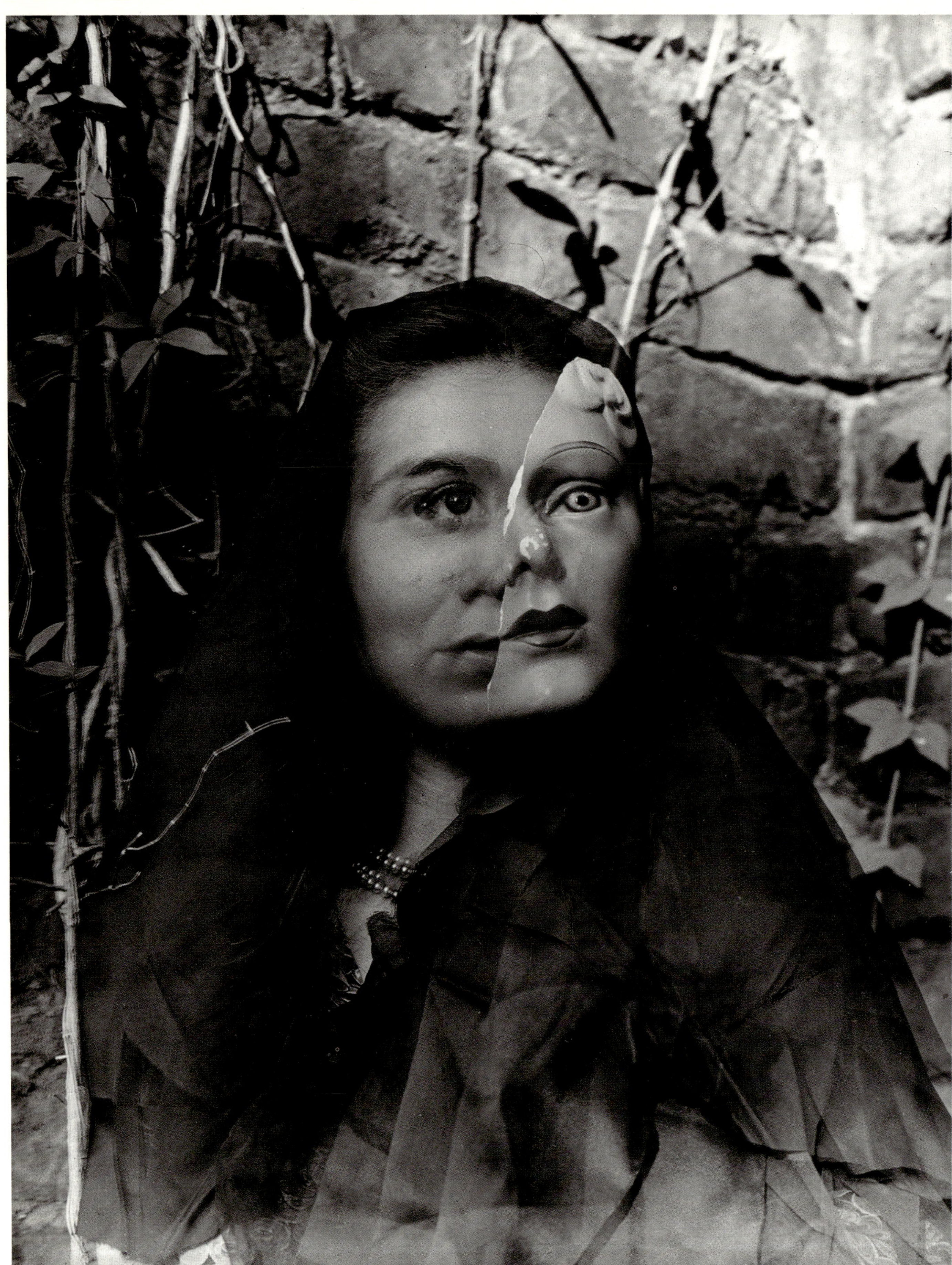

The Masks Grow to Us, 1947
(From Group L: Poems of the Inner World)
In our society, most of us wear protective masks (psychological ones) of various kinds,
and for various reasons. Very often, the end result is
that the masks grow to us, displacing our original characters with our assumed
characters. This process is indicated in visual and symbolic terms
here by several exposures on one negative — the disturbing factor being
that the mask is like the girl herself, grown harder and more superficial. — C.J.L.
Copyright 1947 by Clarence John Laughlin.

CLARENCE JOHN LAUGHLIN

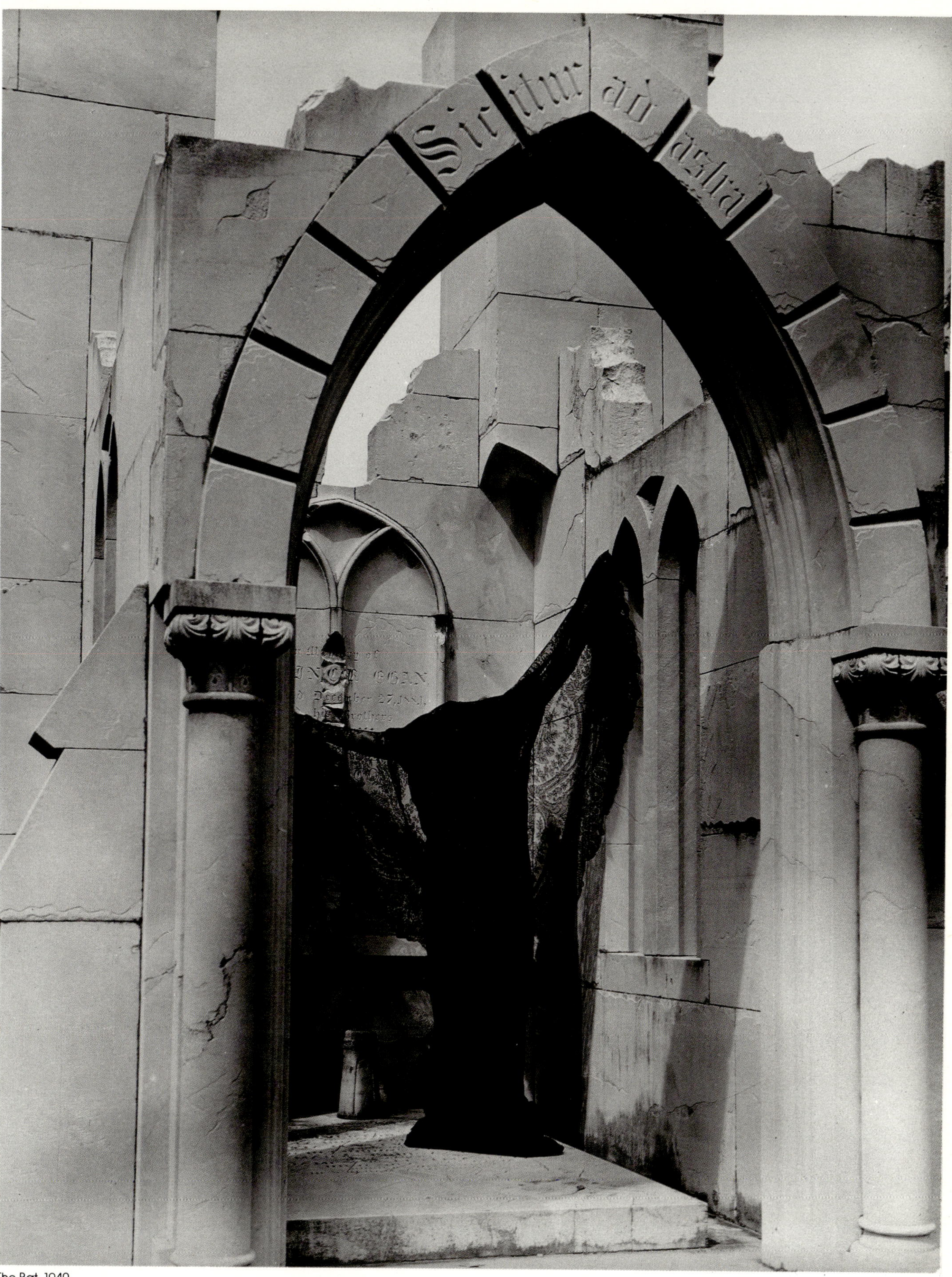

The Bat, 1940
(From Group L: Poems of the Inner World)
In an imitation ruined abbey in a New Orleans cemetery (even the cracks in the
walls are faked), this image of hypocrisy appropriately
appears. Batlike, hypocrisy flits everywhere, for it appears everywhere — in
church, state, big business — its head cunningly concealed (as with those who turn their
heads, hypocritically, from all that gives the lie to their own untruths).
And while they preach peace and humanity, the people of hypocrisy lead us, actually,
into confusion, war, and destruction. — C.J.L.
Copyright 1940 by Clarence John Laughlin.

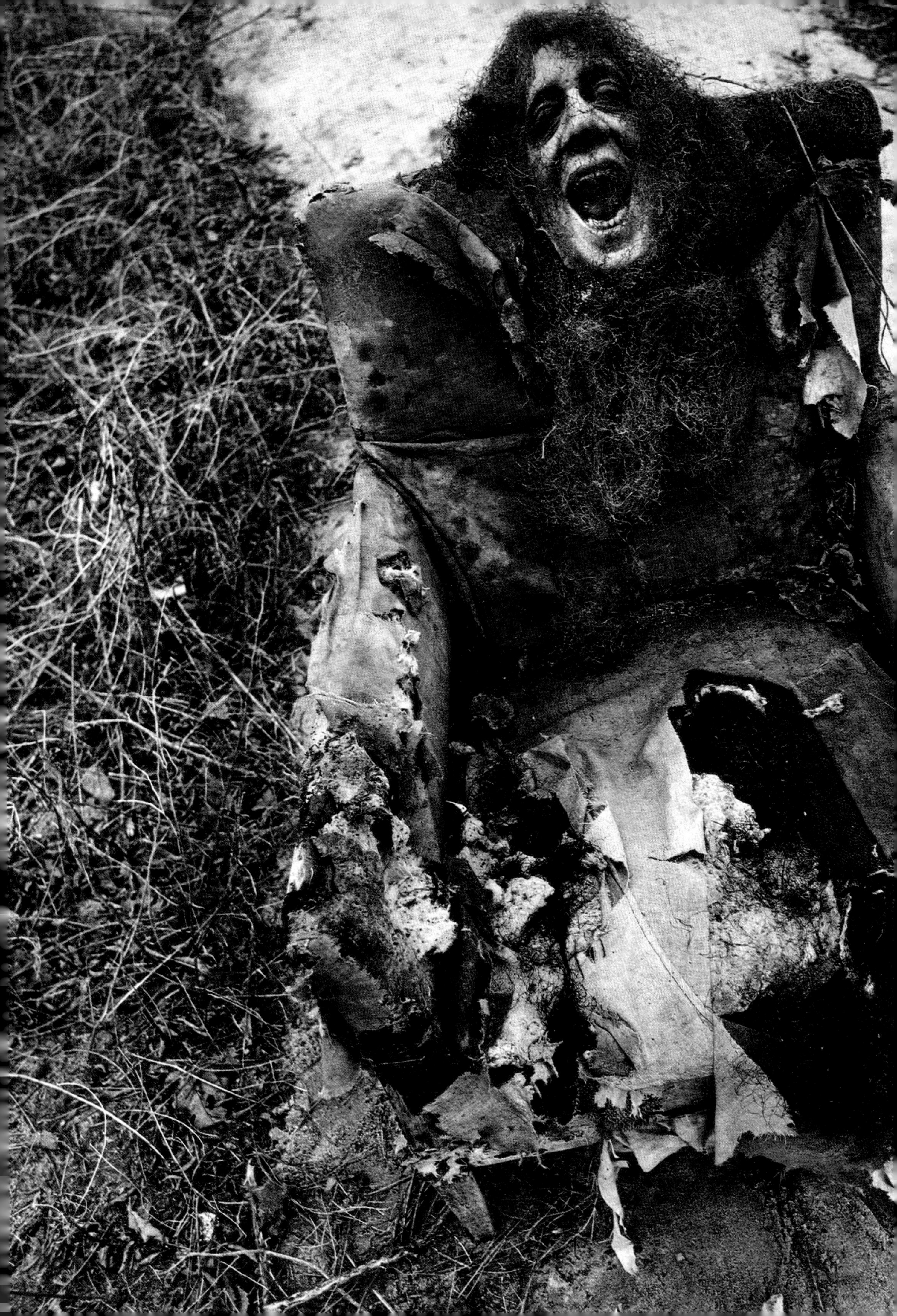

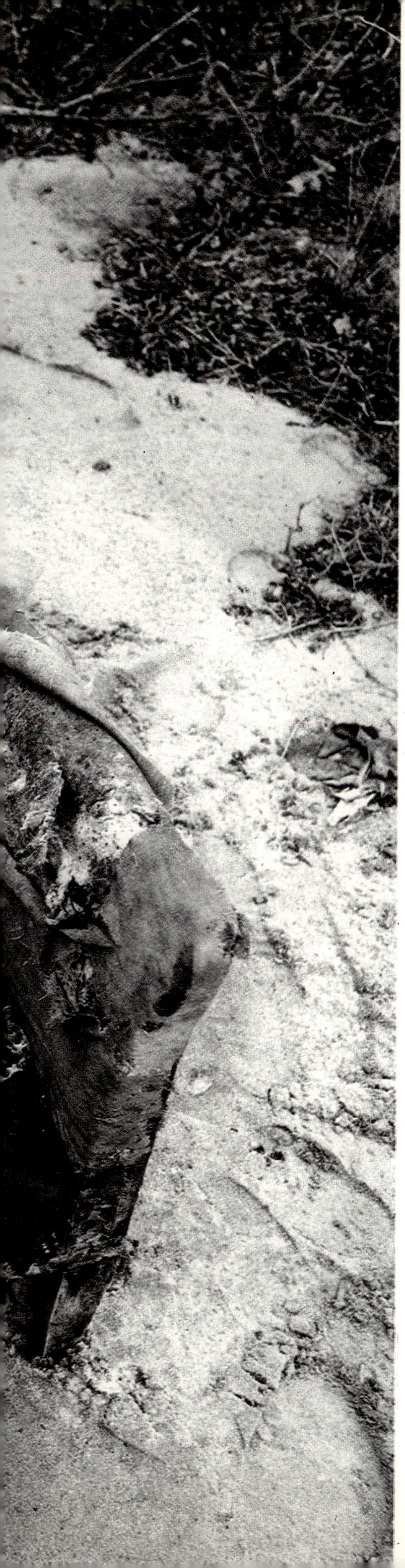

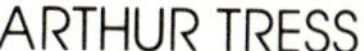

The Singing Chair

The Hypnotist

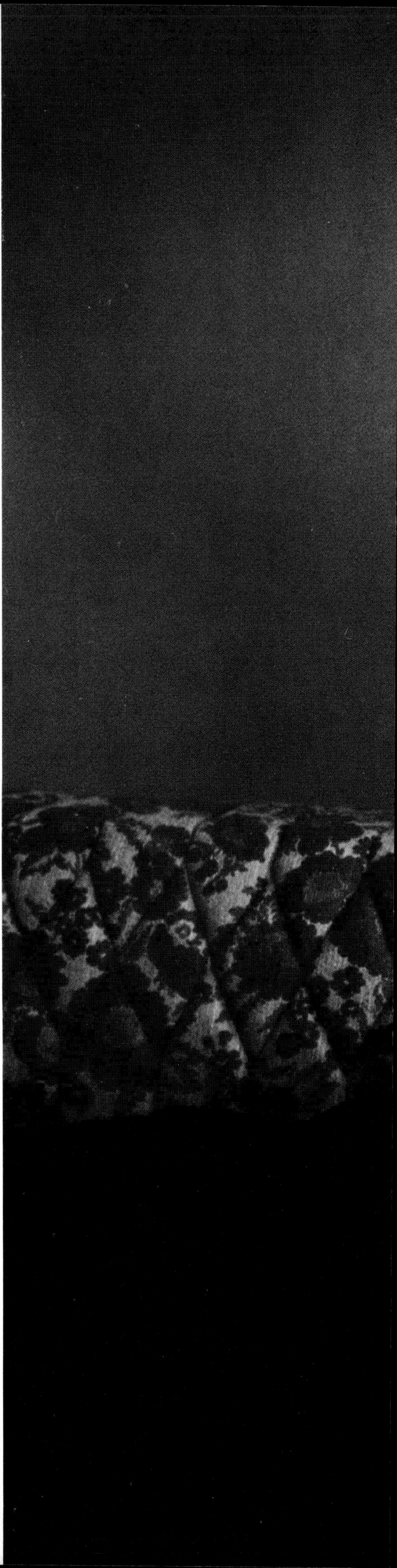

Portrait of a Woman

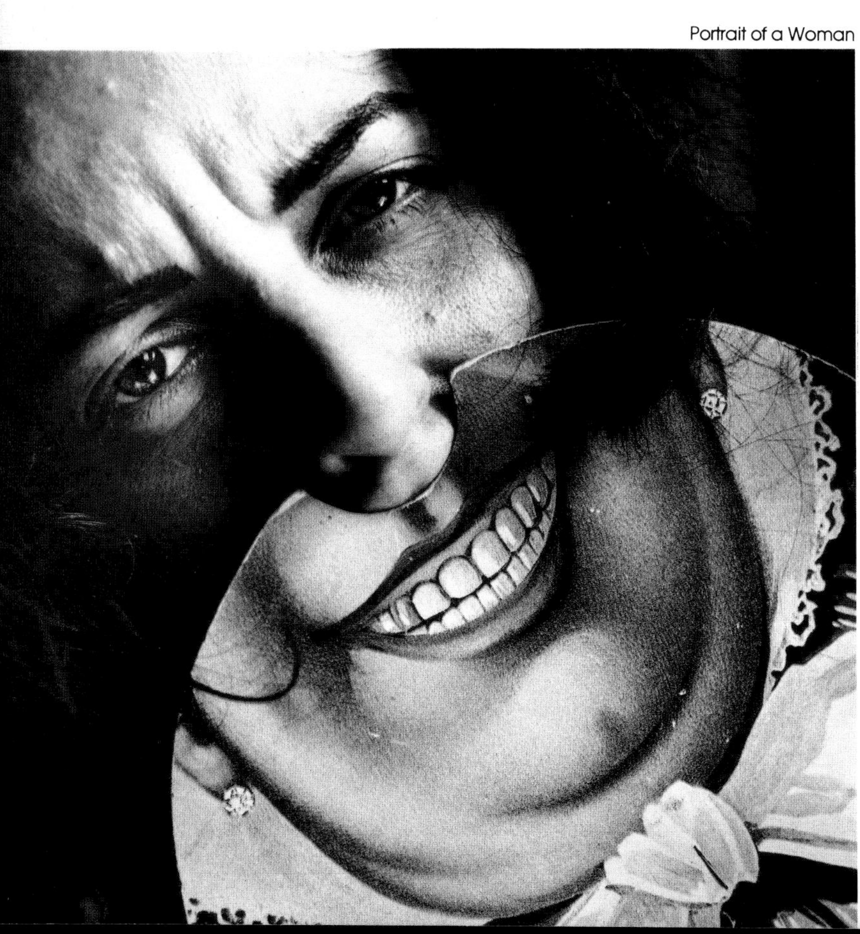

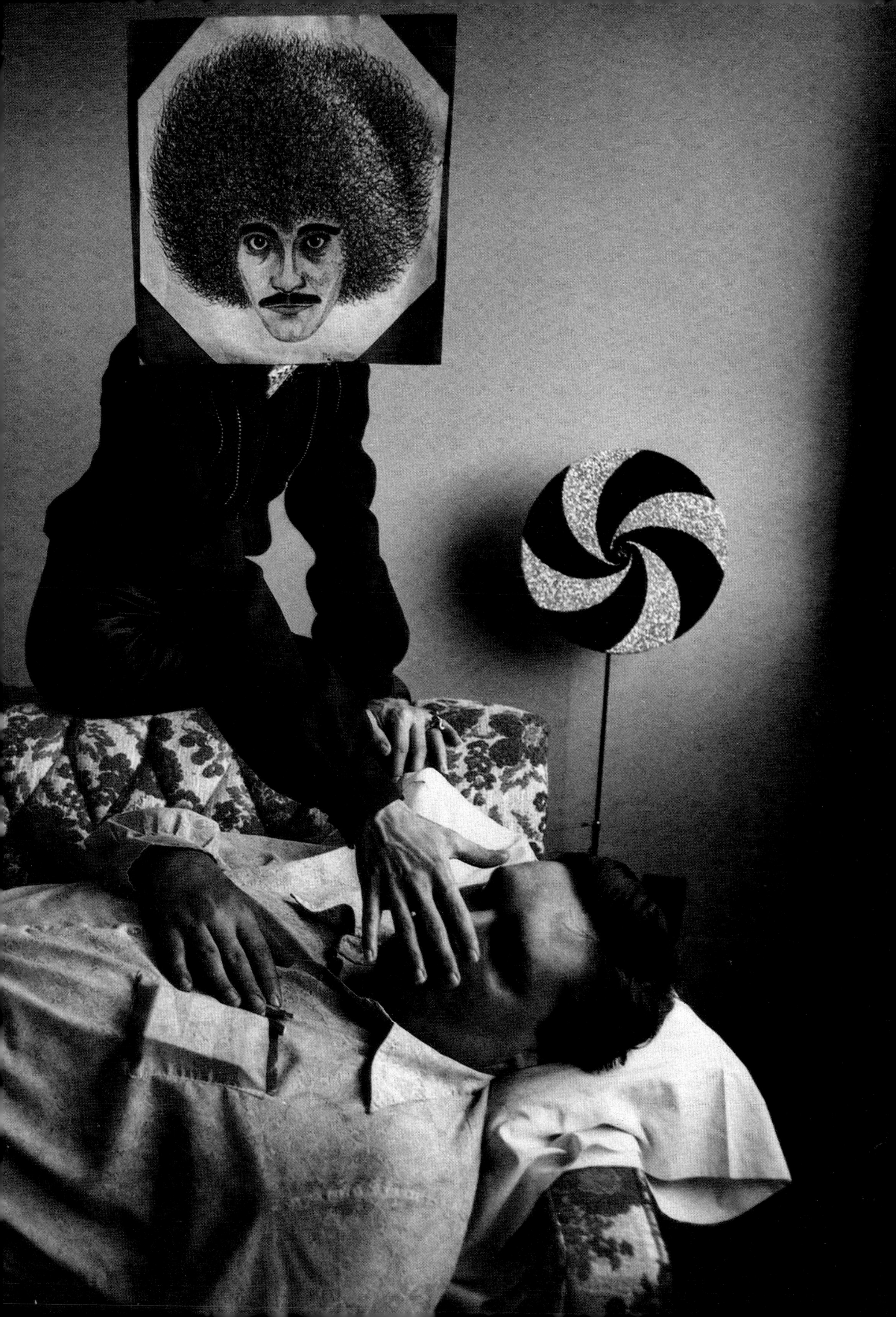

ARTHUR TRESS

Presidential Penis

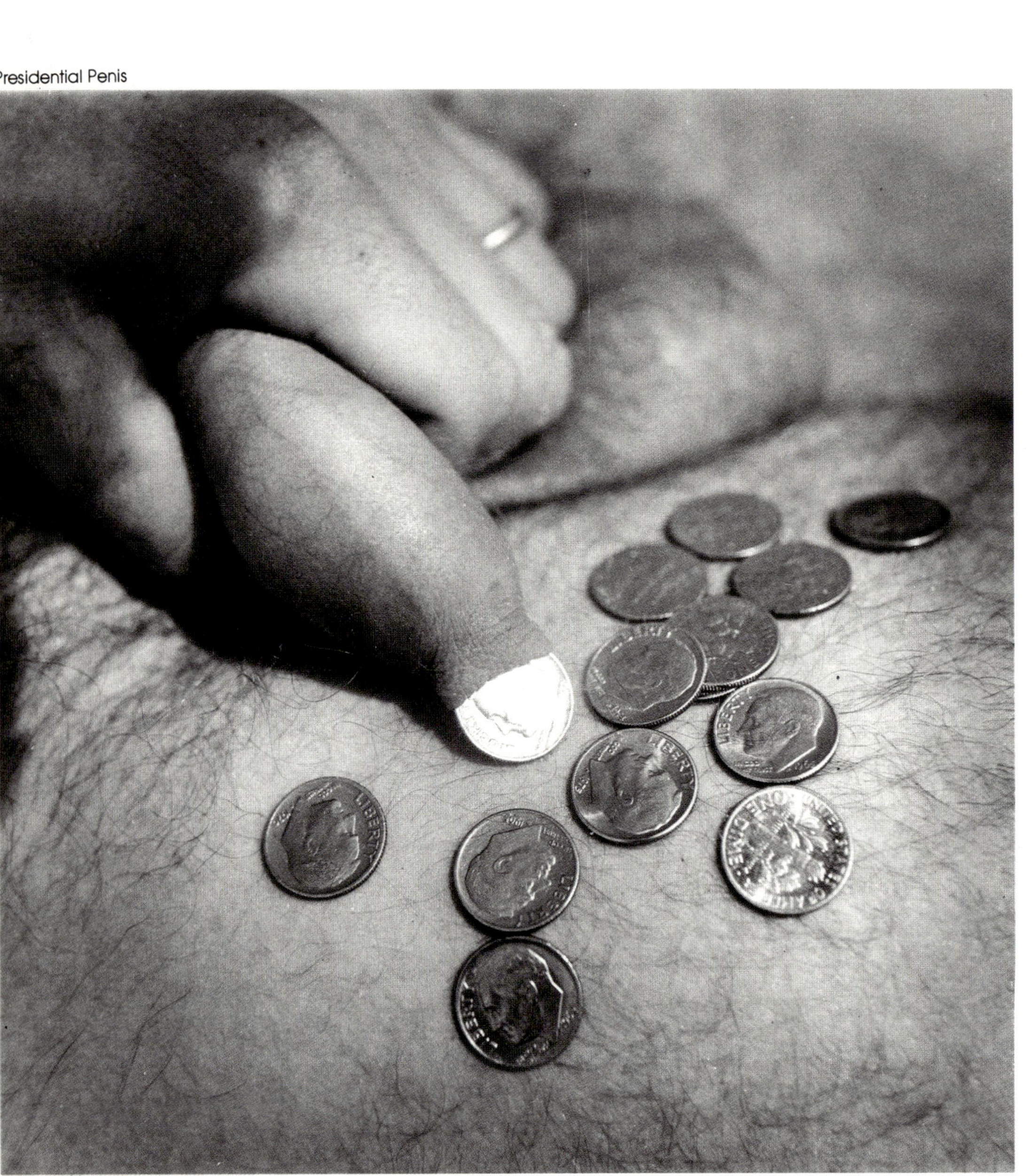

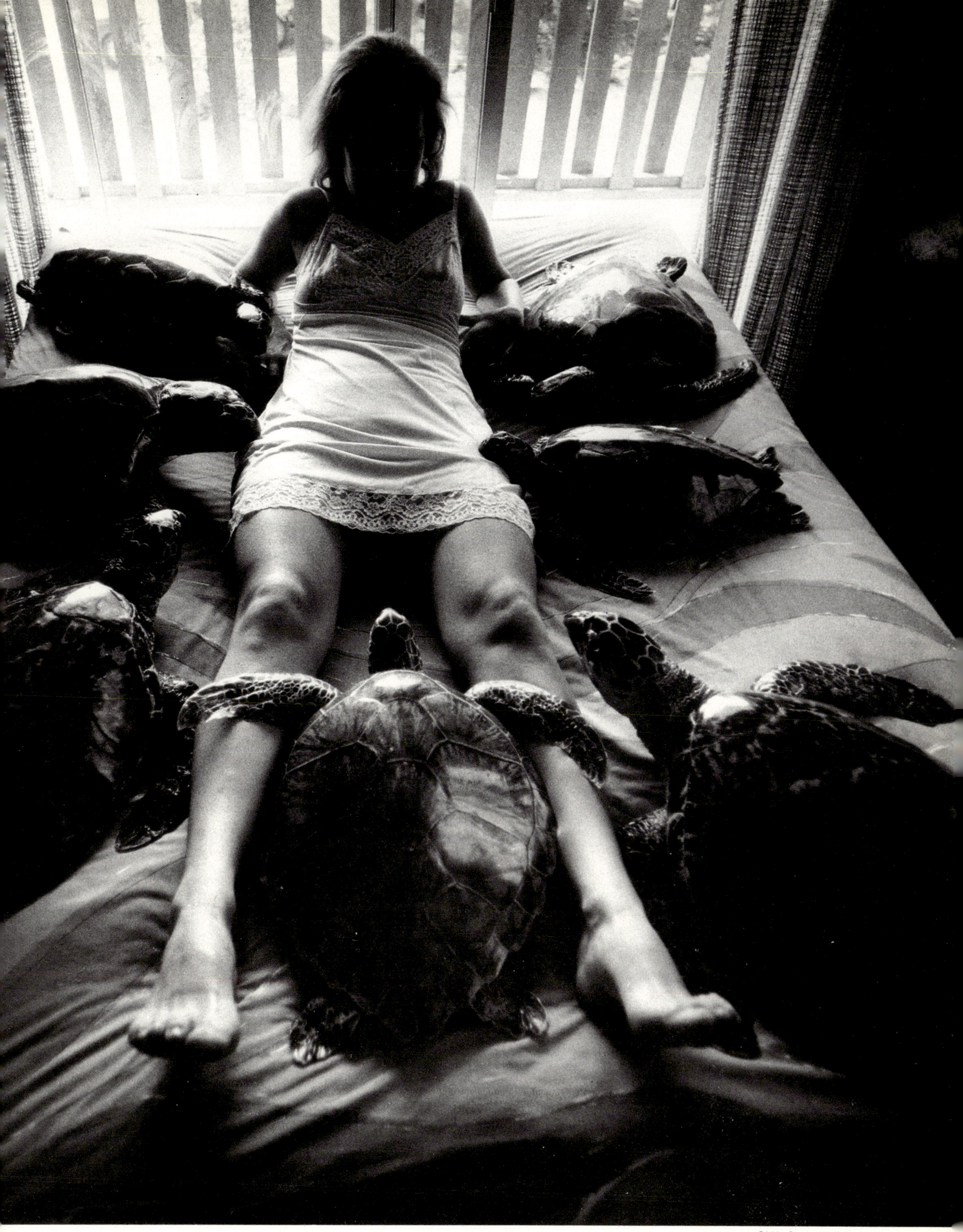

Girl in Bed with 7 Sea Turtles

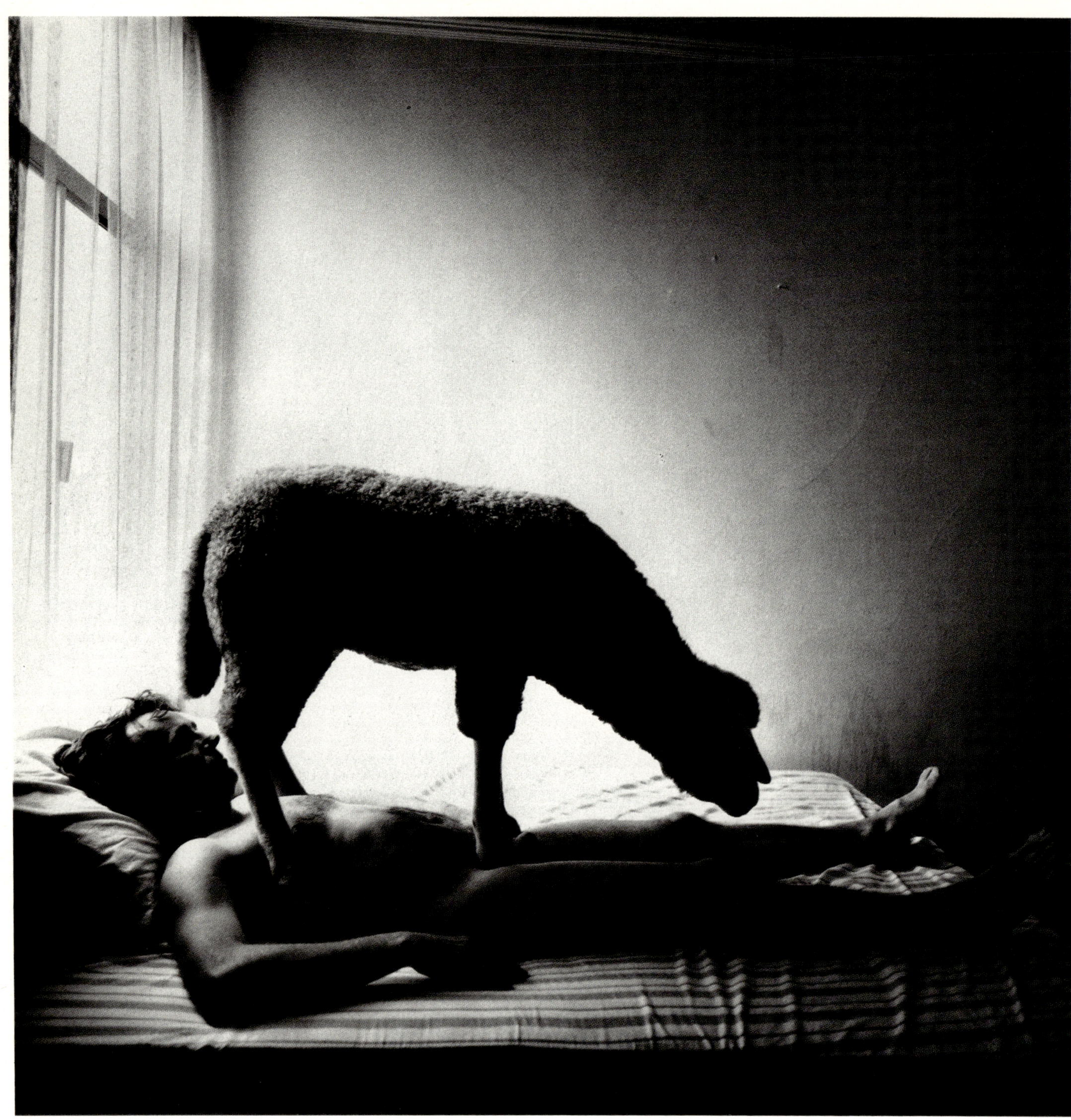

Man with Sheep

ARTHUR TRESS

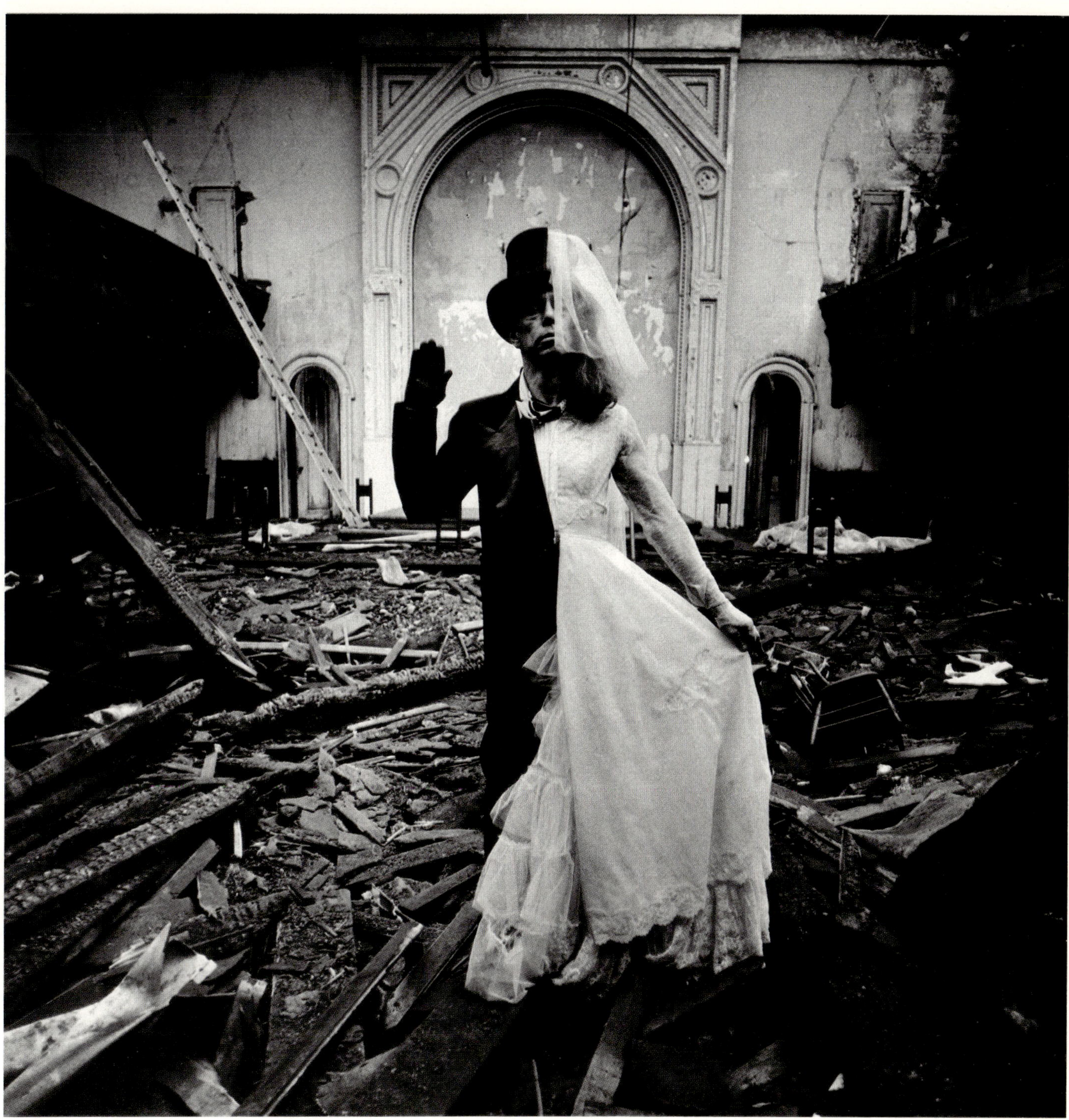

The Lovers

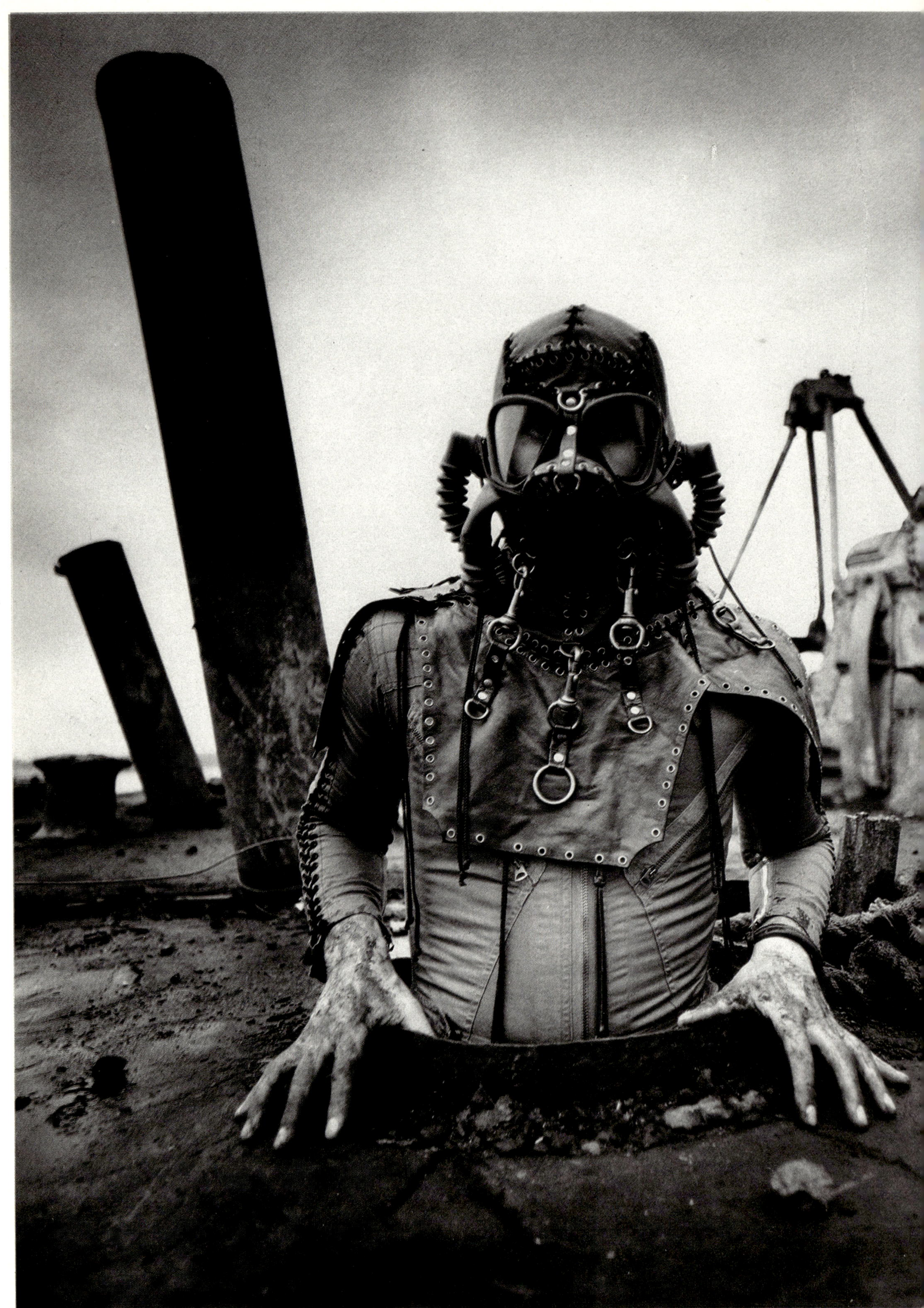

Portrait of a Leather Designer

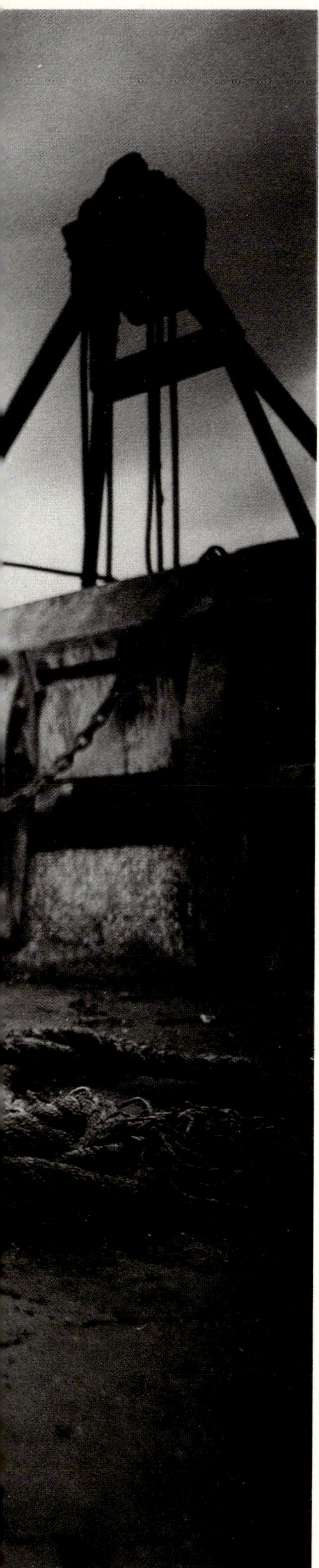

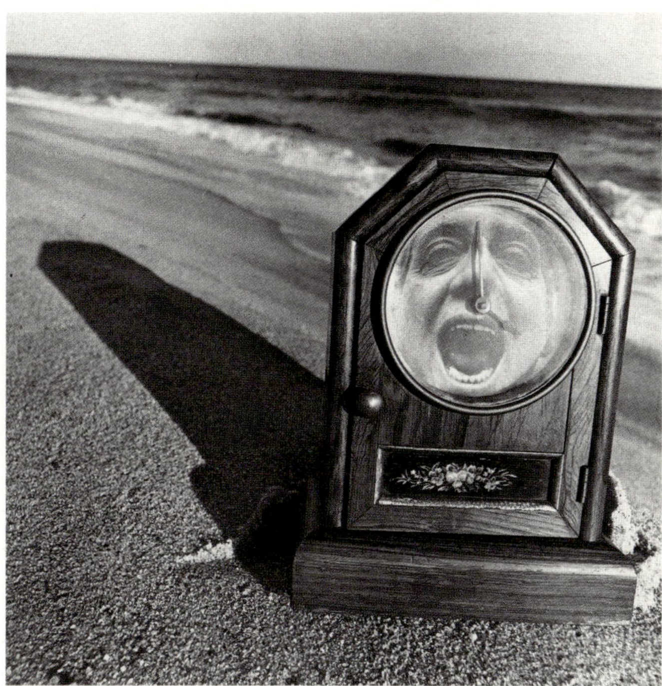

The Sands of Time

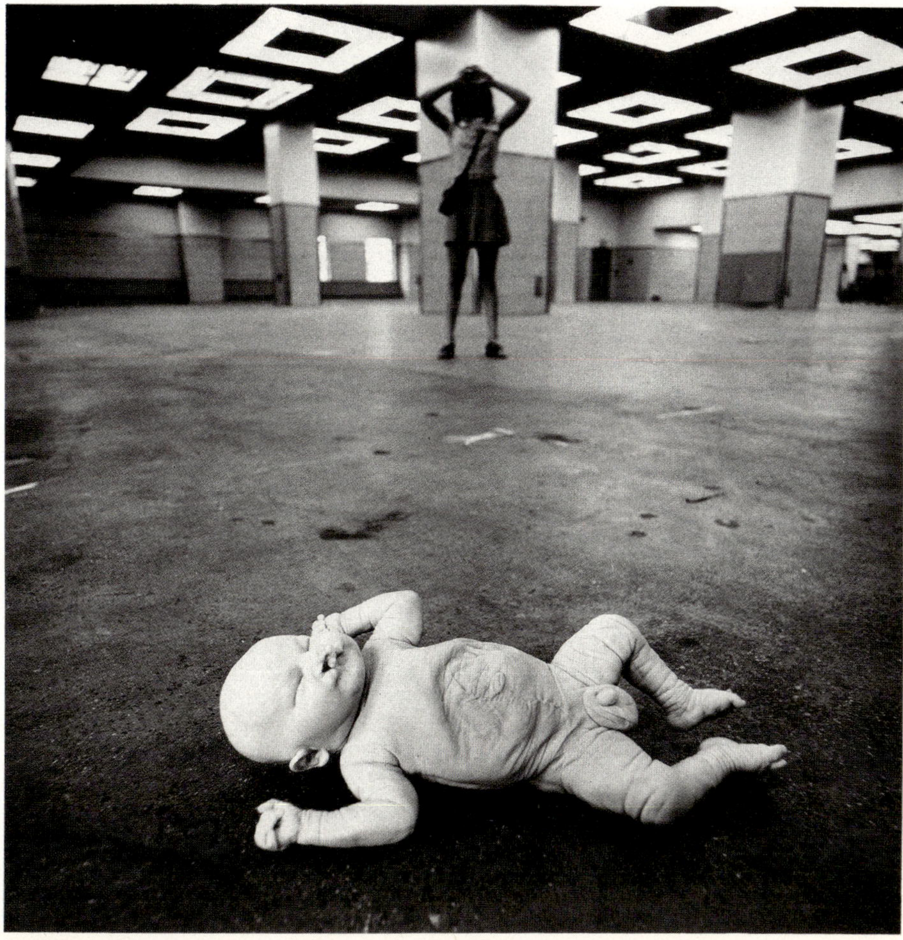

Student with Medical Doll

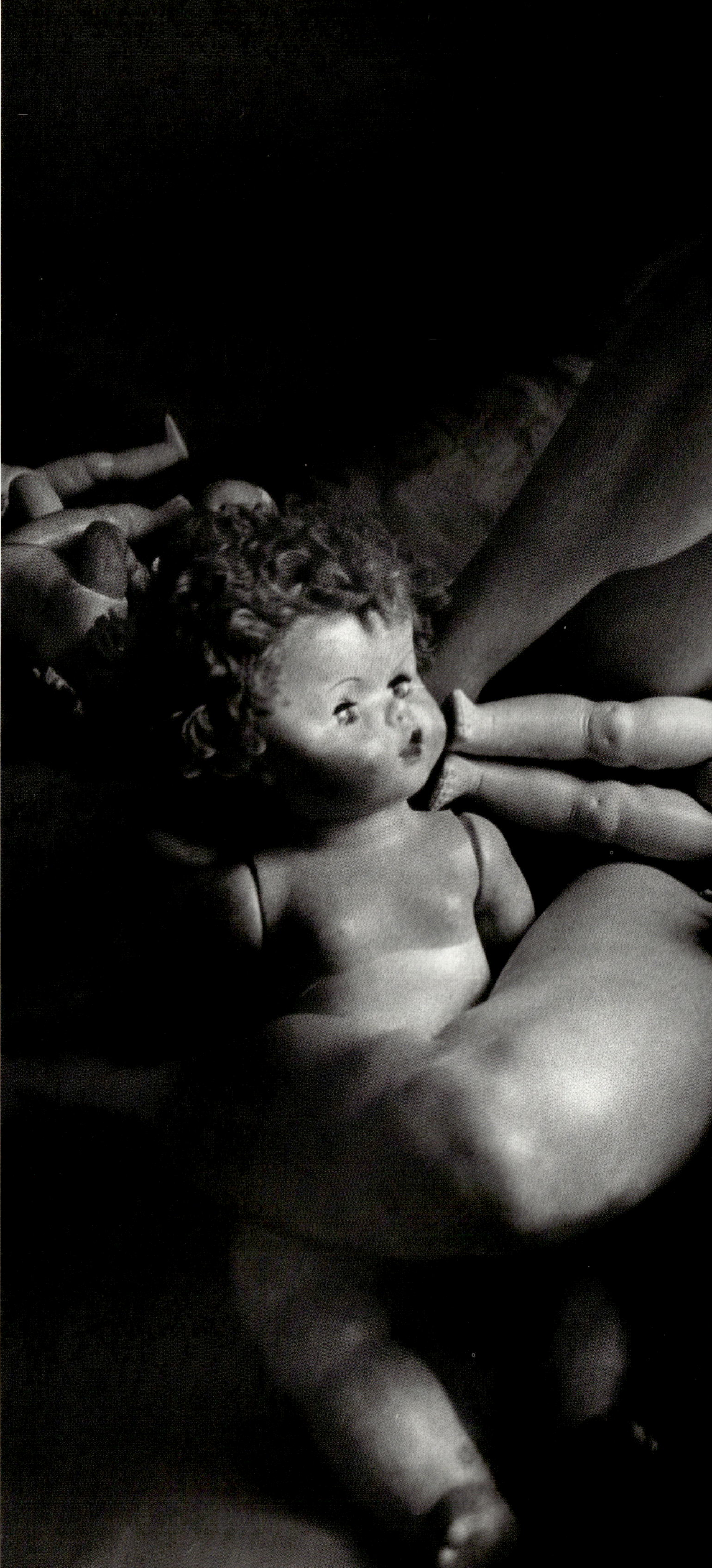

from Karen's Party

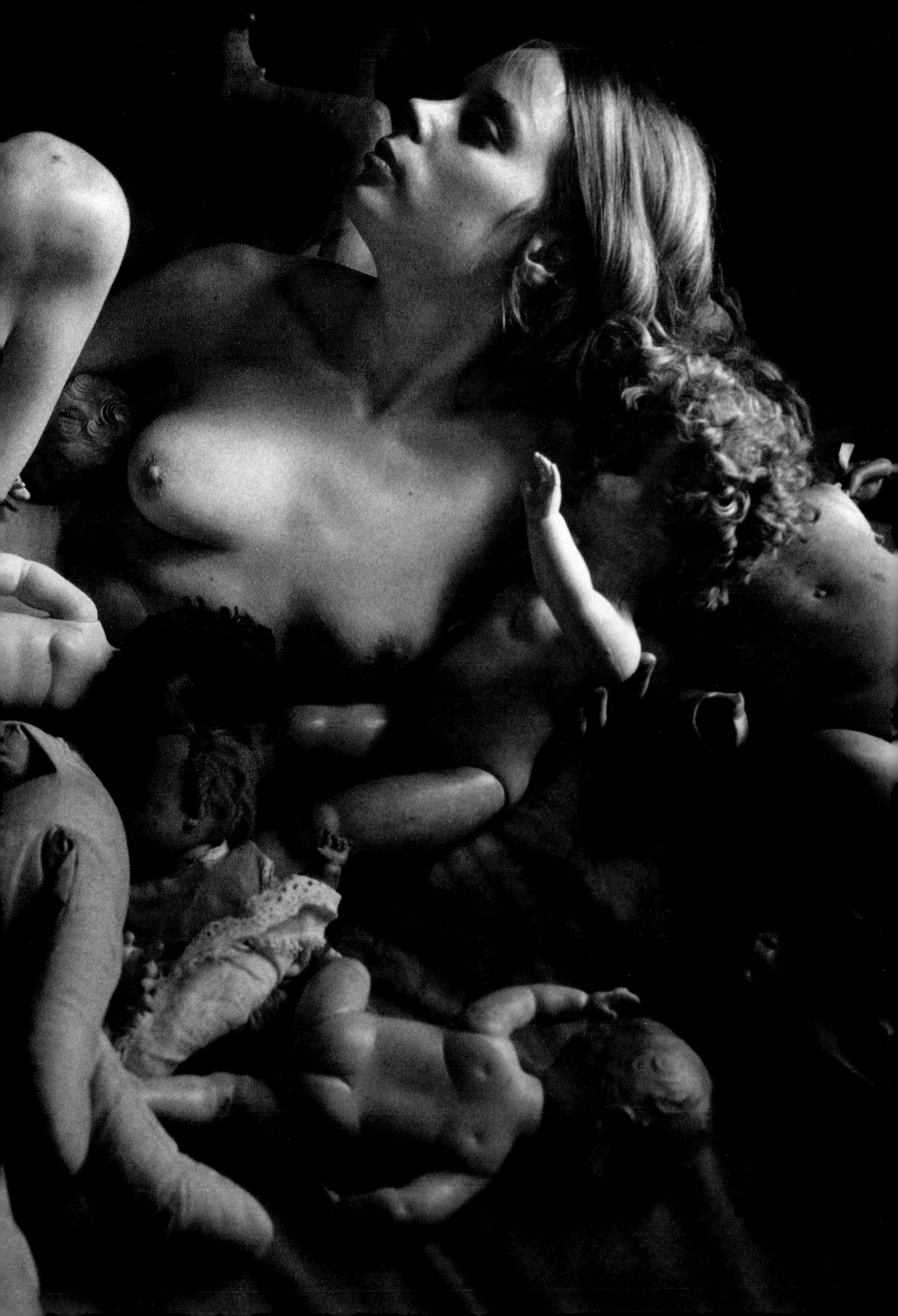

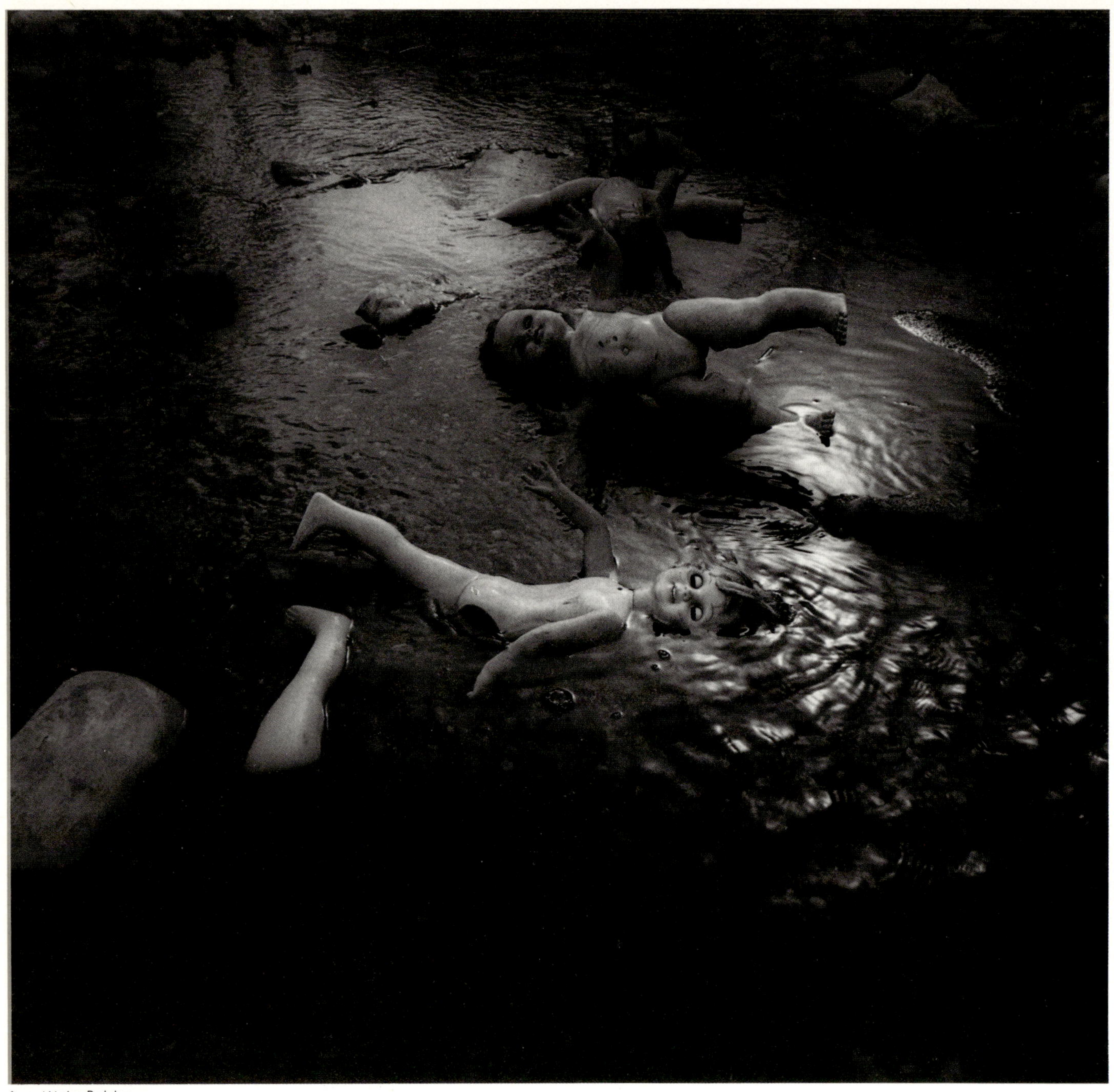

from Water Babies

M. RICHARD KIRSTEL

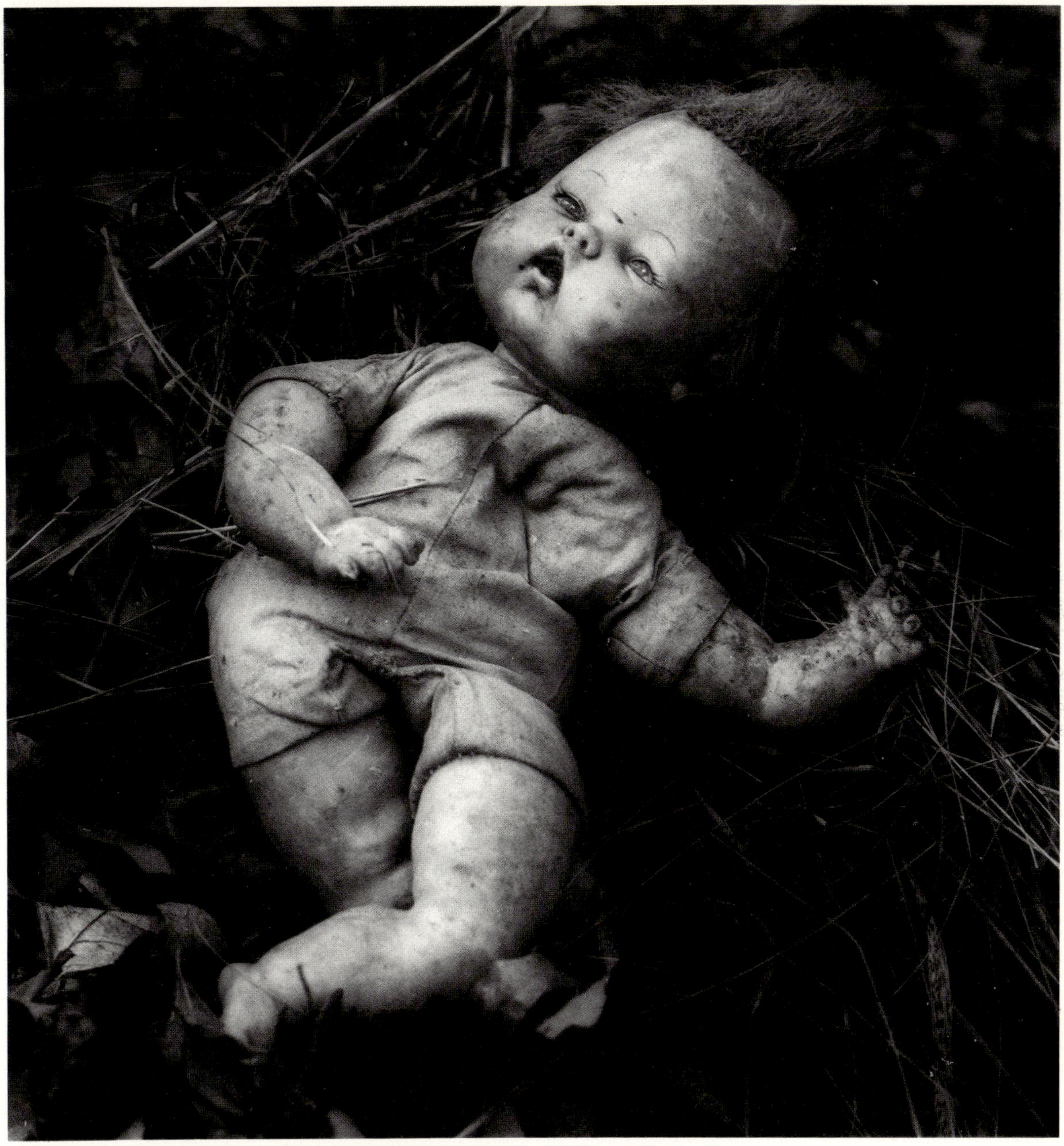

from Projections

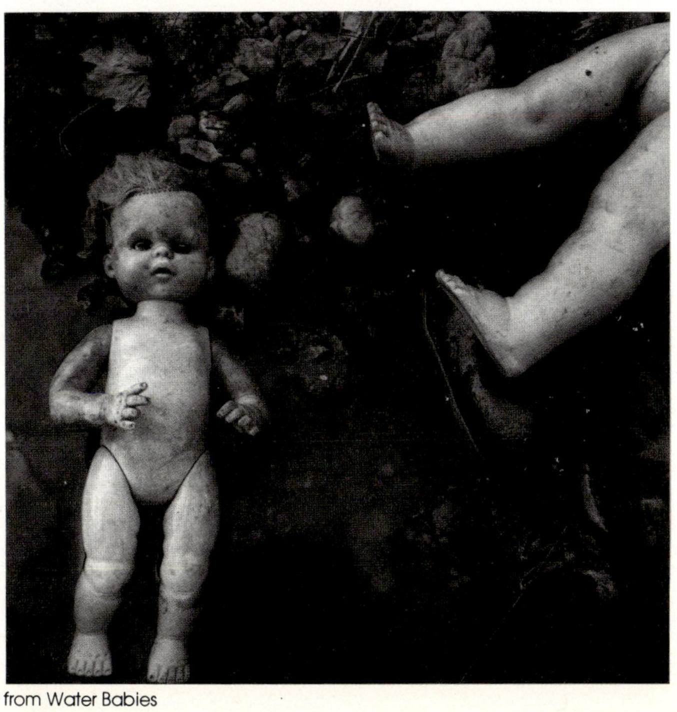

from Water Babies

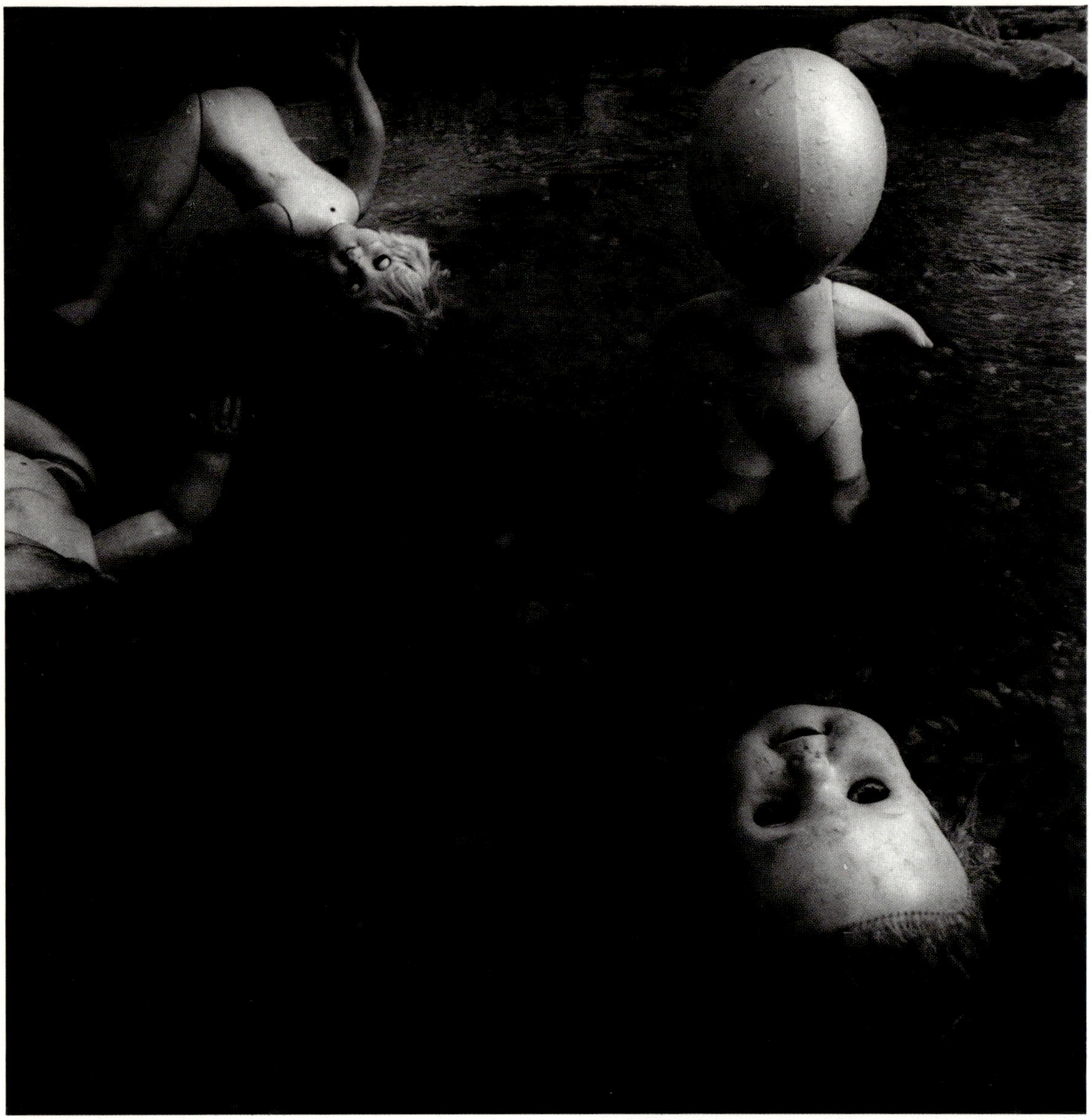

from Water Babies

from Water Babies

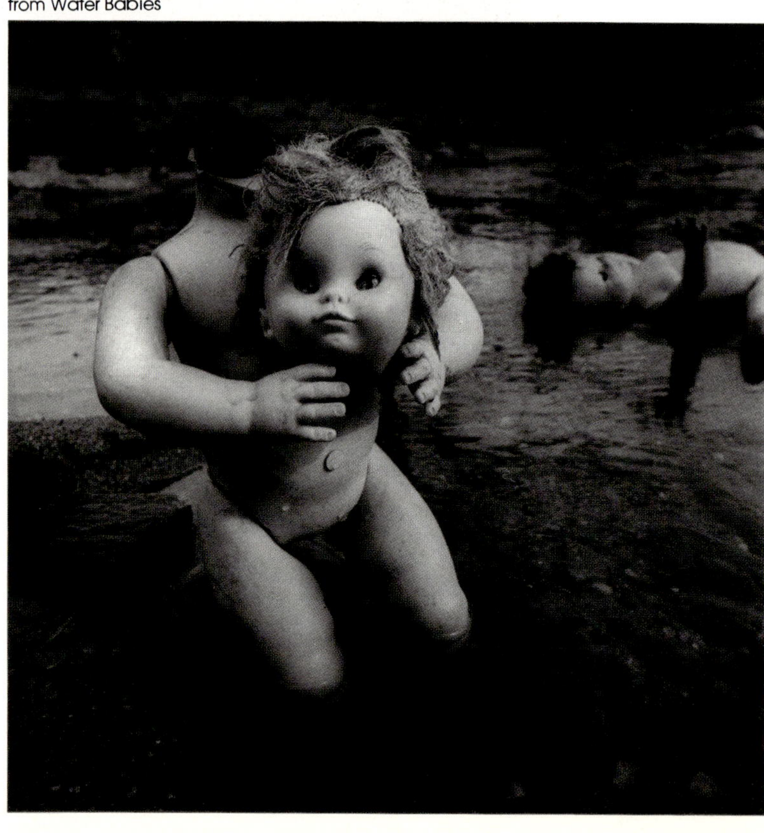

M. RICHARD KIRSTEL

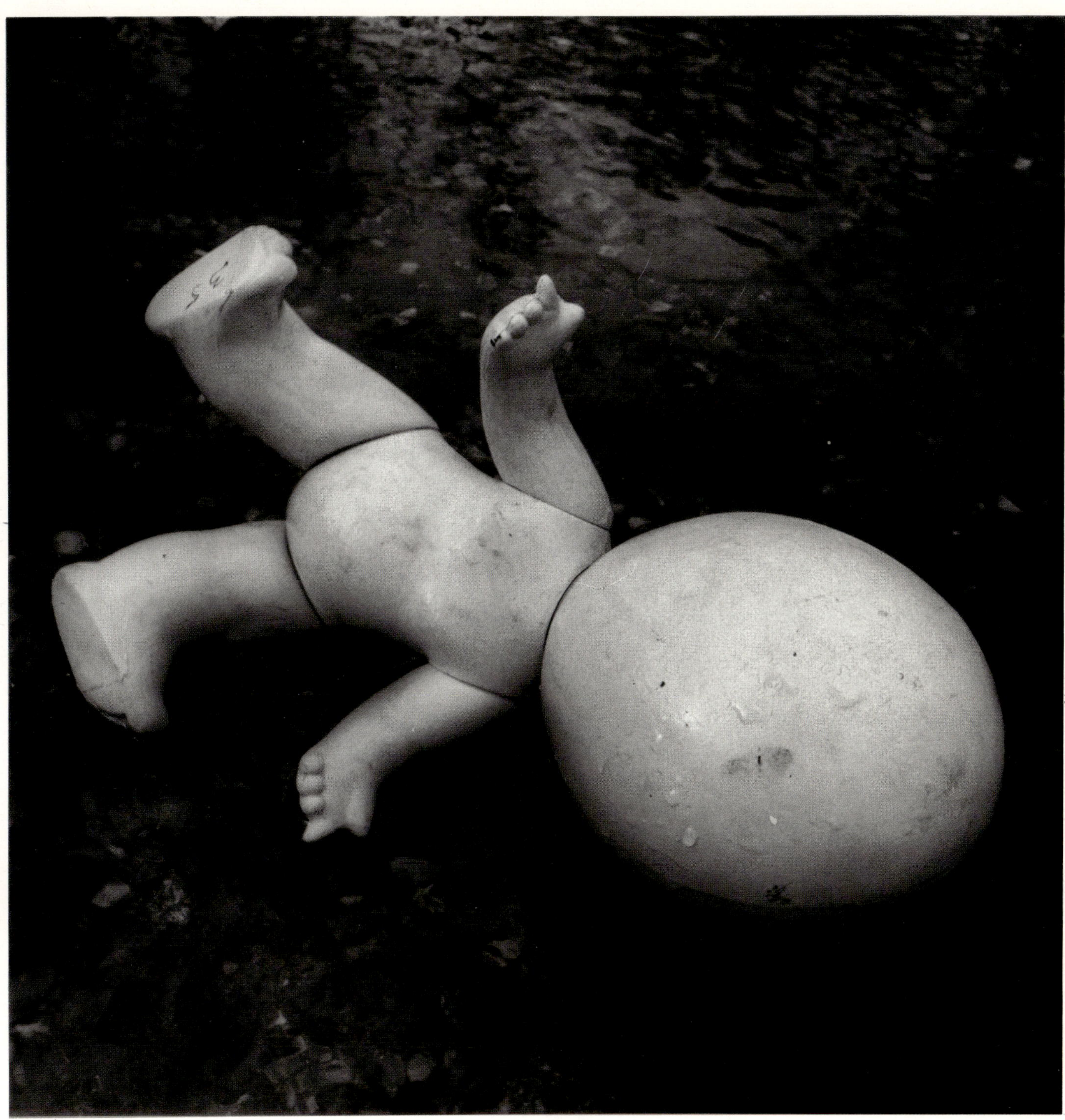

from Water Babies

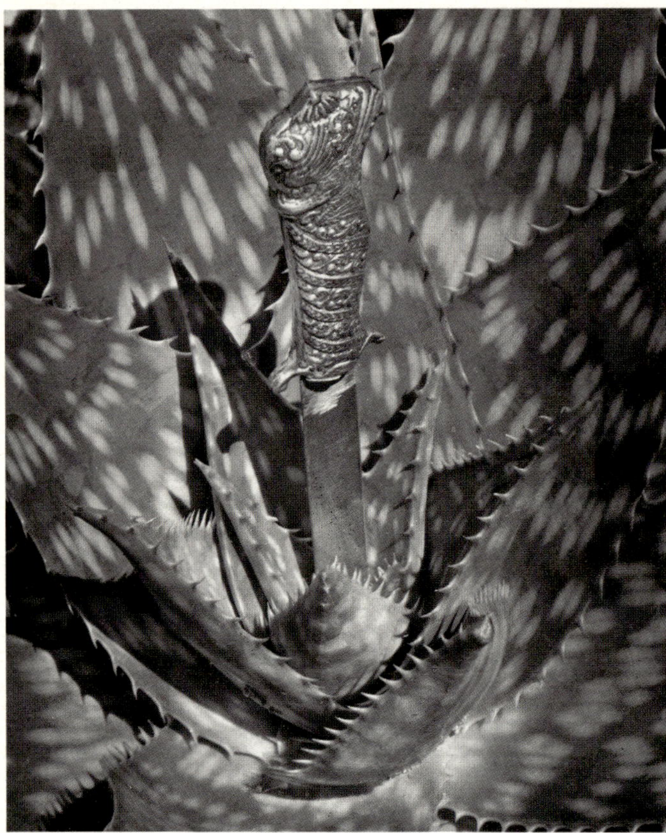

from Sirague City, Berkeley, 1964

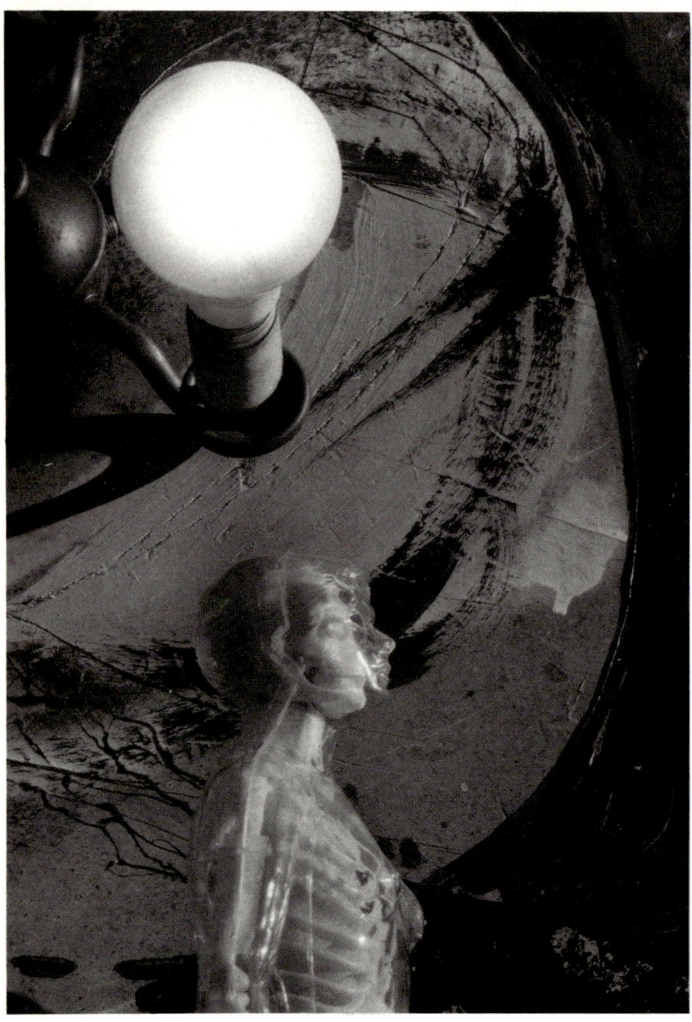

Séance, Berkeley, 1973

from Sirague City, Berkeley, 1964

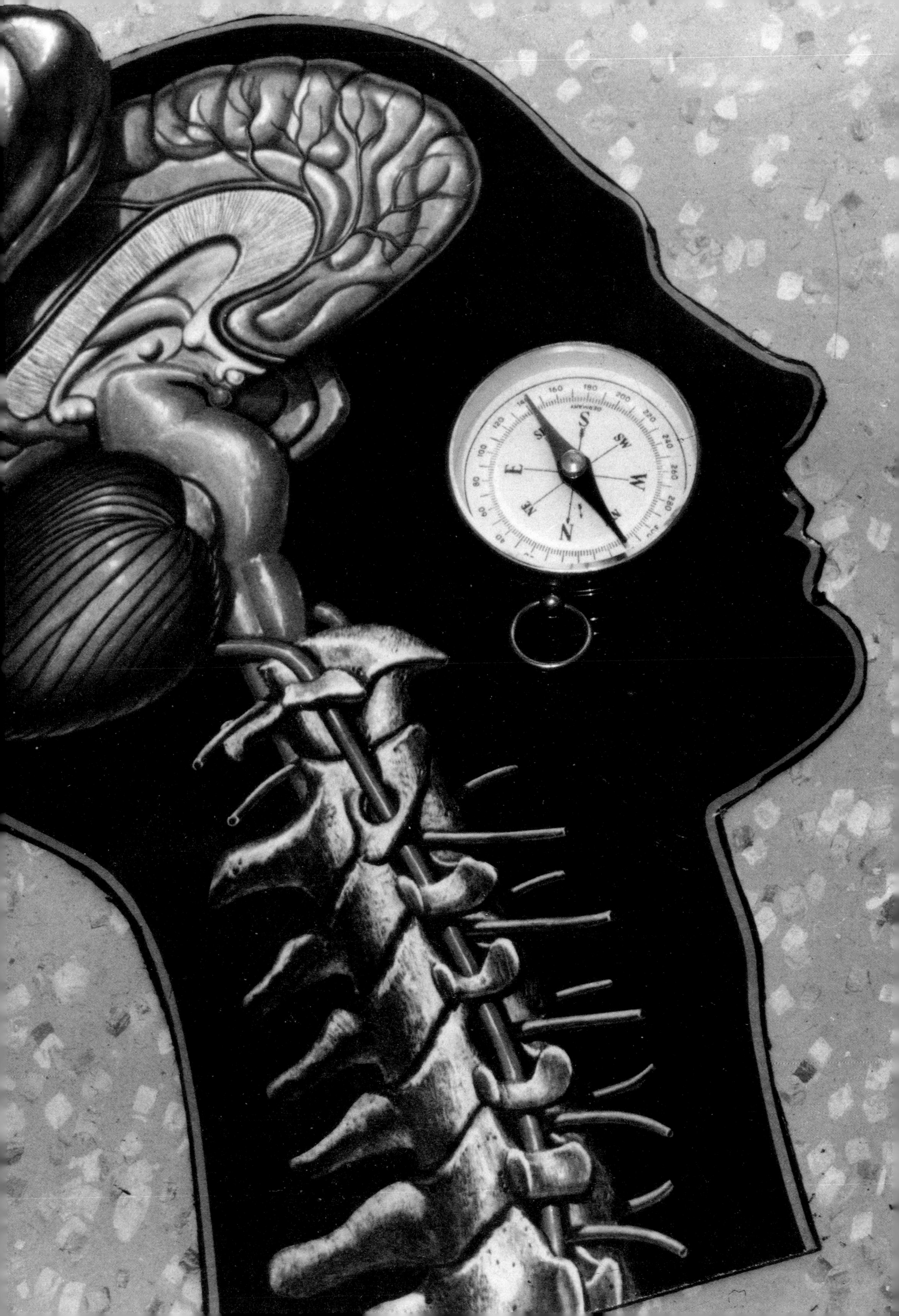

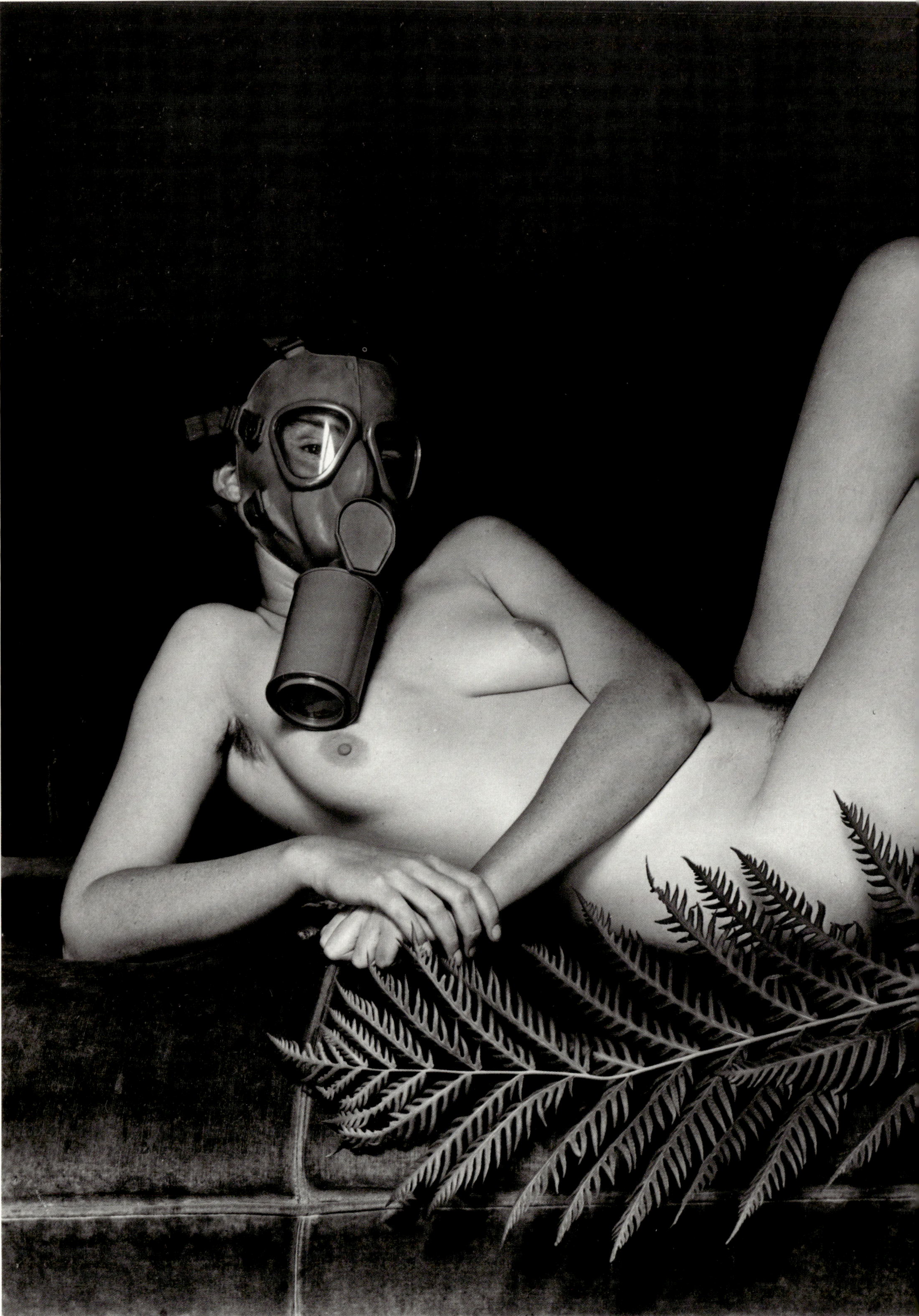

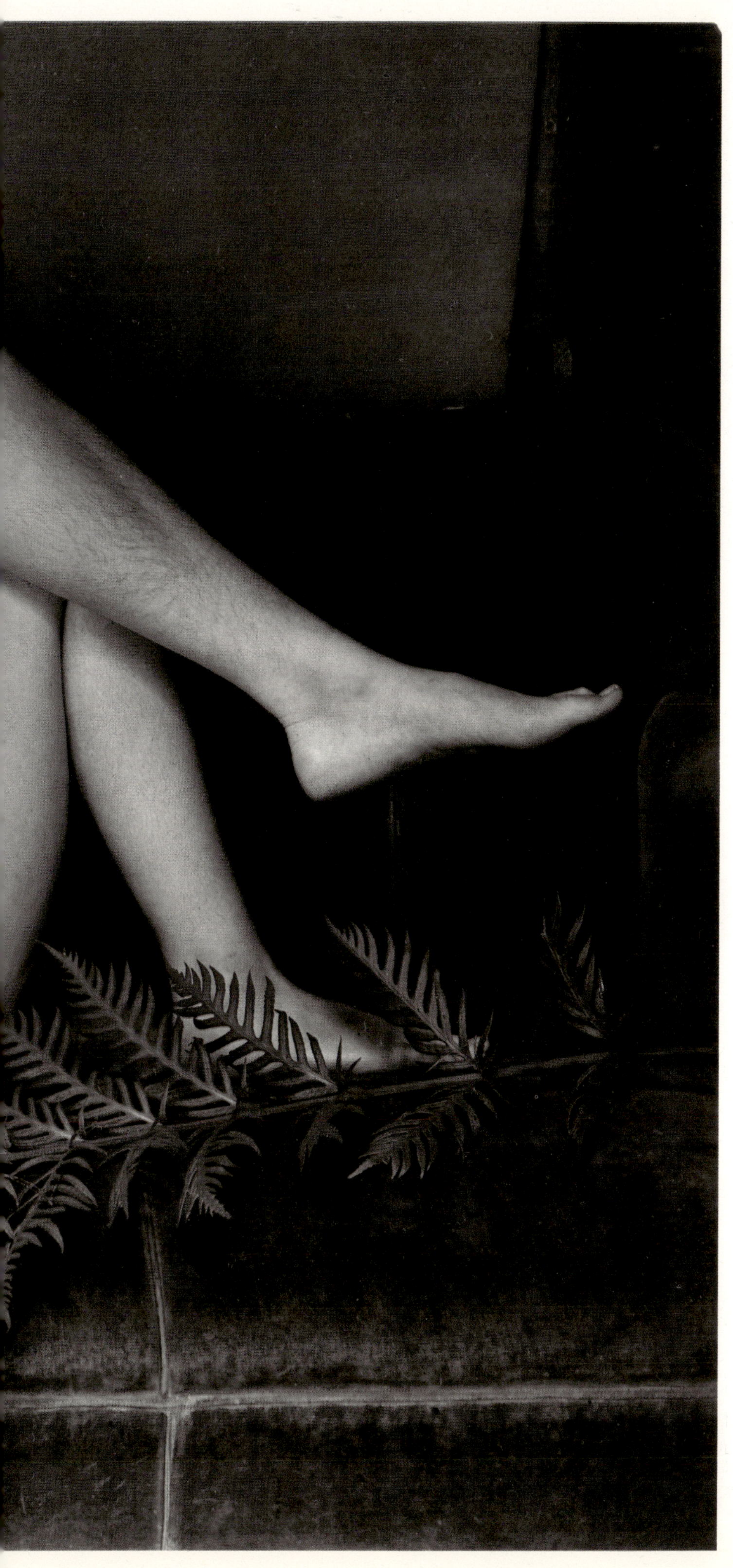

Civilian Defense, 1942

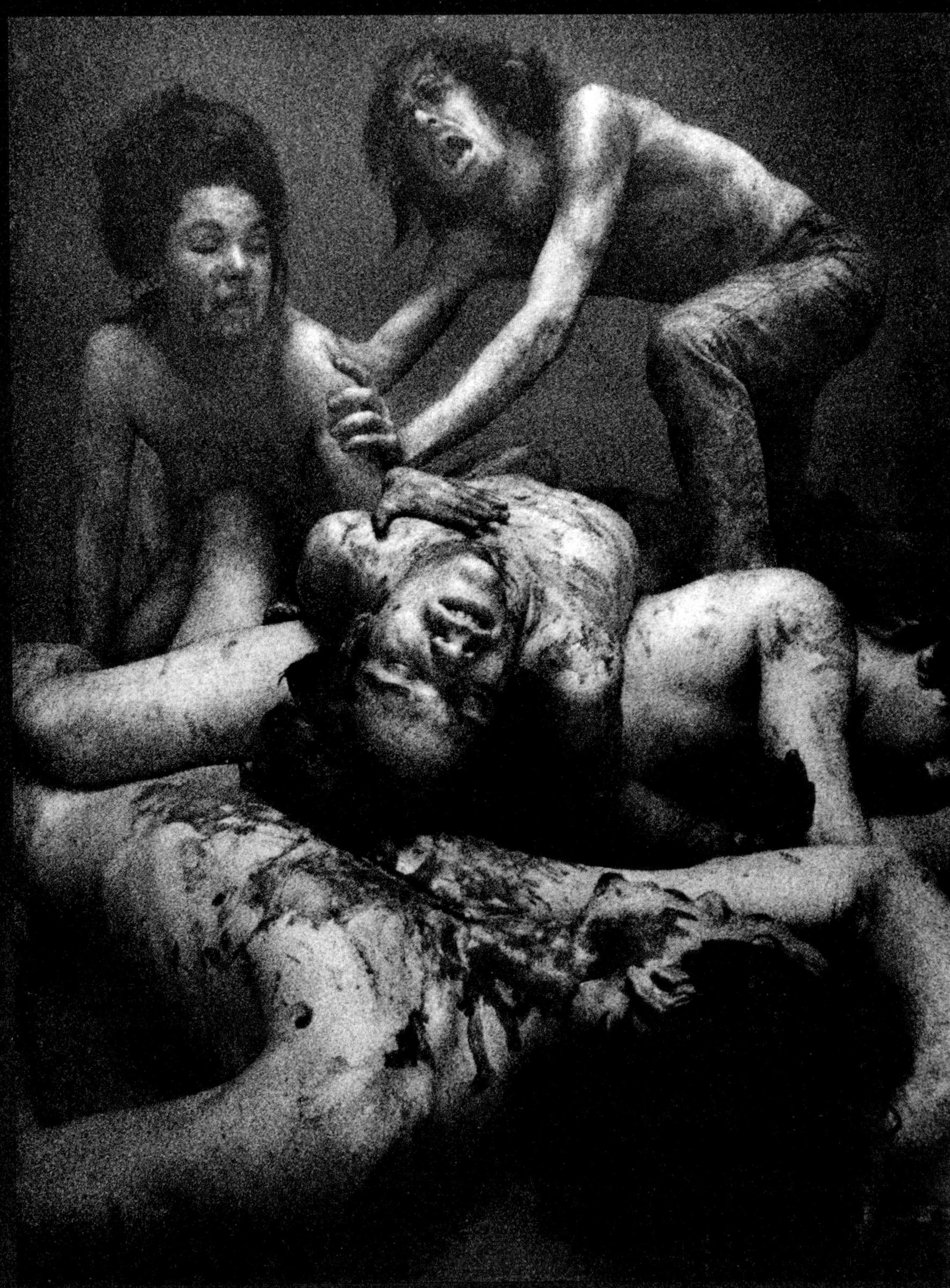

Dionysus in 69

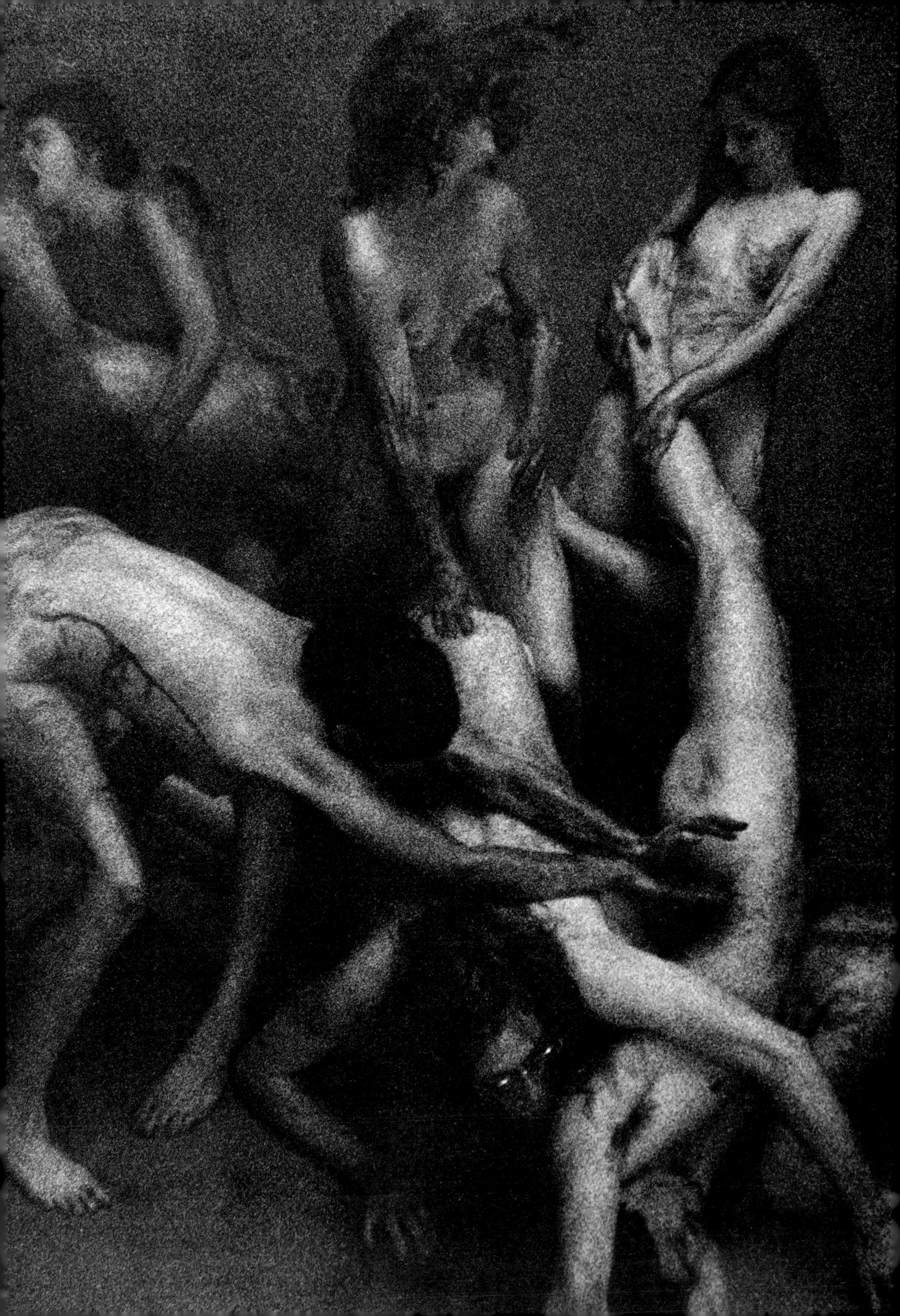

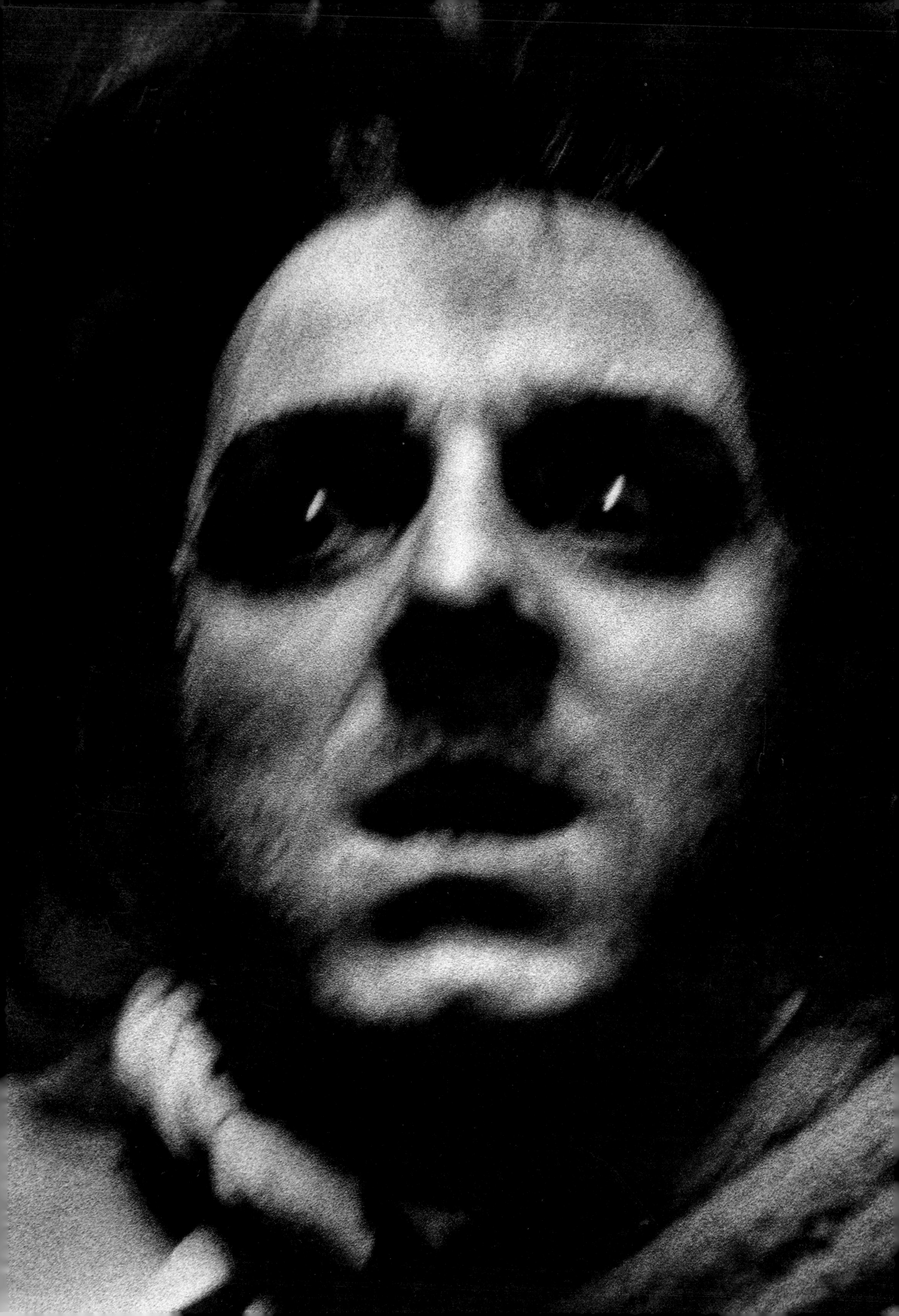

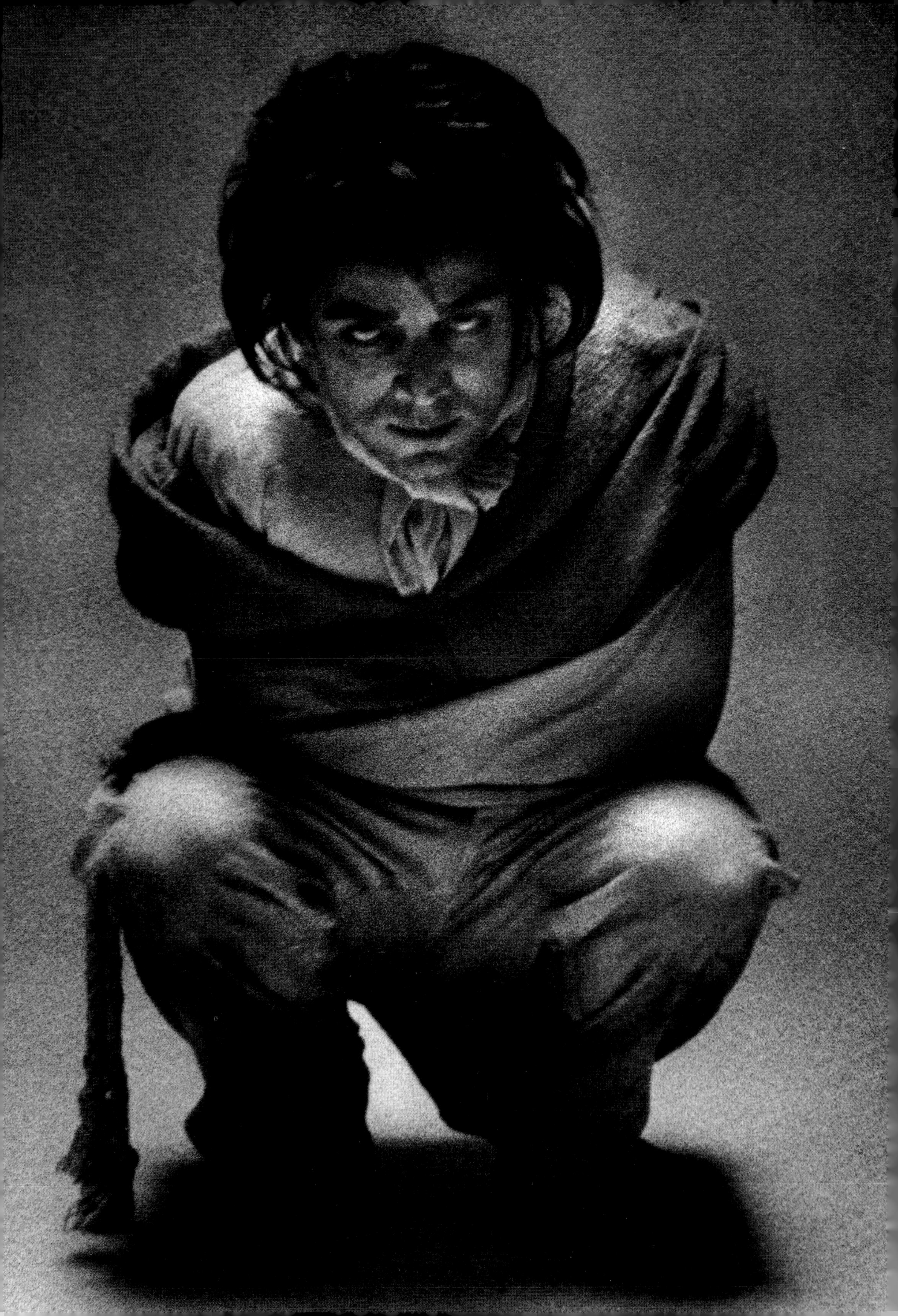

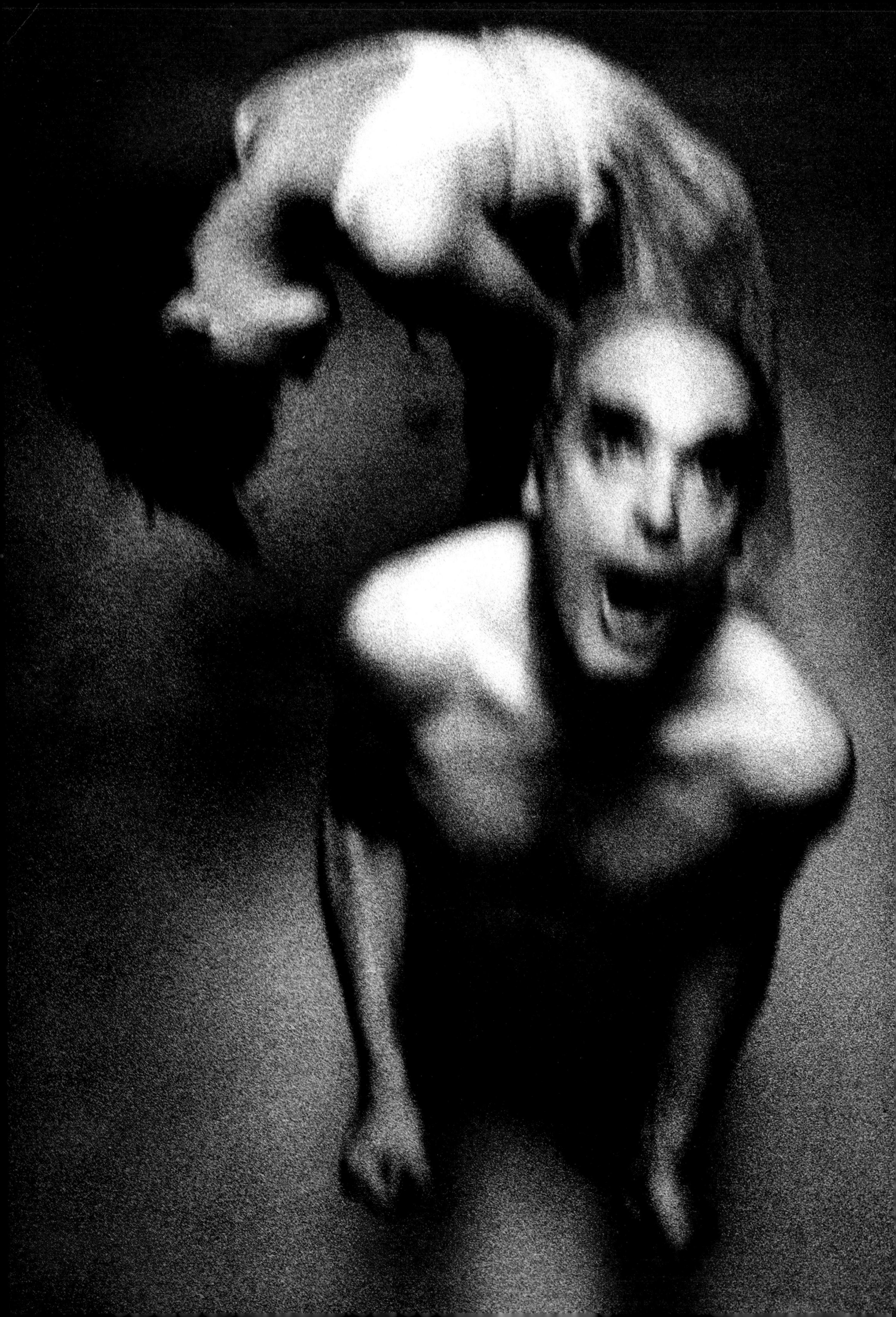

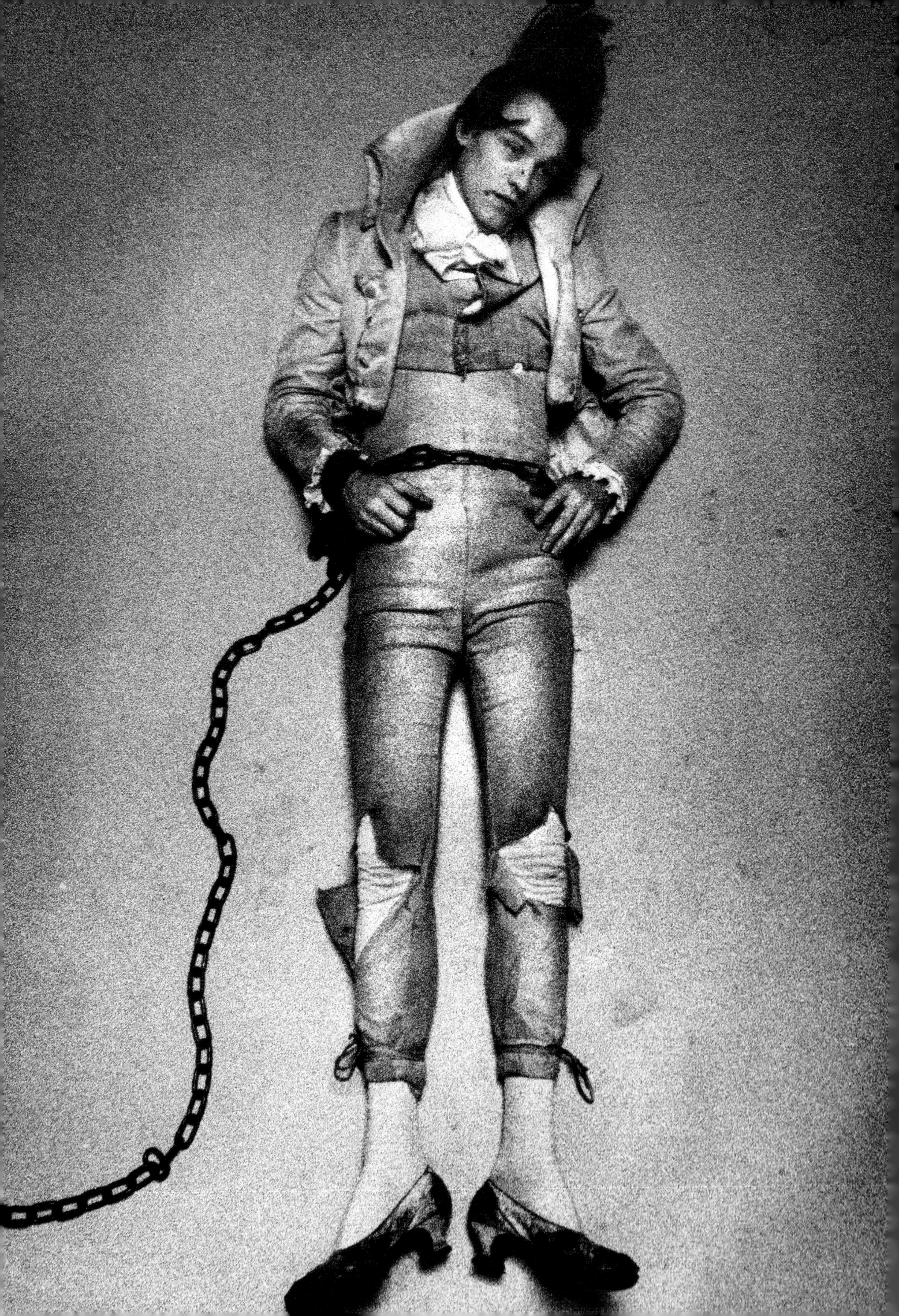

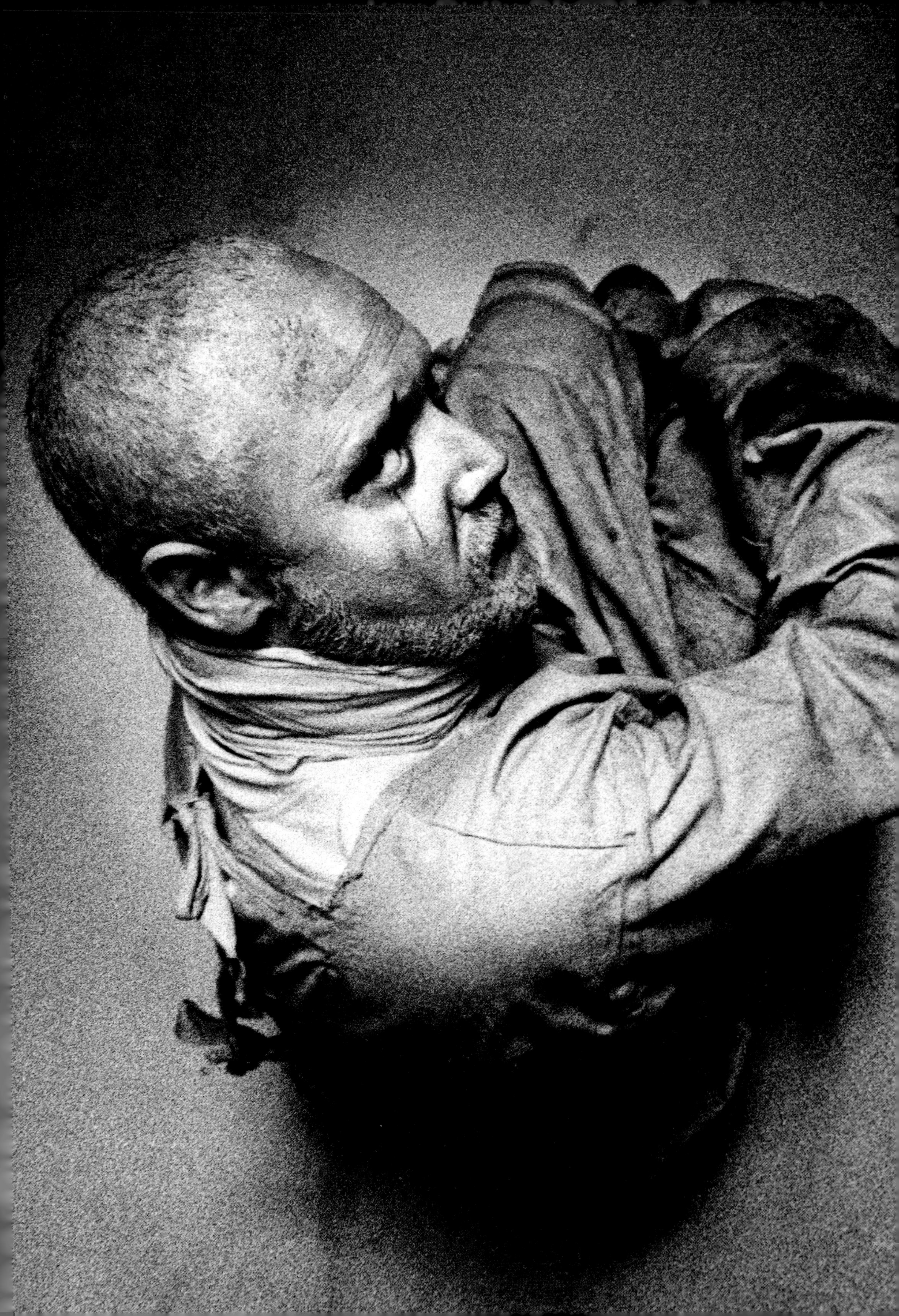

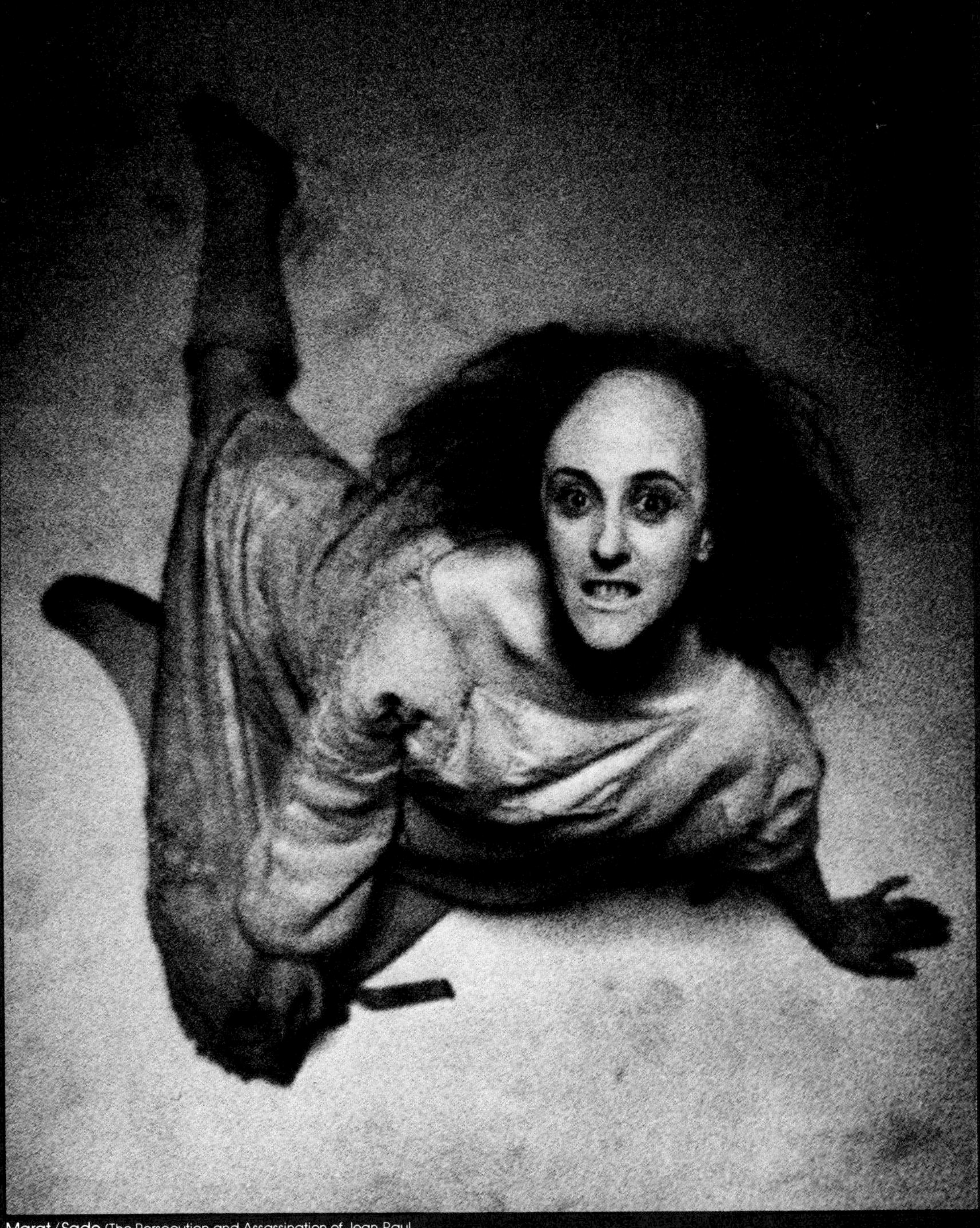

Marat/Sade (The Persecution and Assassination of Jean-Paul
Marat as Performed by the Inmates of the Asylum of Charenton
Under the Direction of the Marquis de Sade)
All photographs by Max Waldman, © 1966, 1969; from Waldman on Theater.

4 UNREALITIES

Paradoxically, although the camera must always address something in front of the lens, there are some photographic images that portray events that never happened.

Many photographic images in the grotesque mode are even more blatant in their outright illusionism than those defined as "constructed realities." In constructions, it is the event depicted that has been created or altered by the image-maker. The image itself is a more or less faithful rendering of the negative describing that event. But the images considered here are quite different in nature. In virtually all of them the unreality of what is depicted manifests itself rapidly, if not immediately. These images are not documents of any single moment of external "reality." Indeed, they deliberately undermine themselves in that regard. Sometimes this is achieved by presenting violations of the natural order of things so drastic as to be, simply, incredible. Sometimes they declare their multiple or hybrid origins more openly.

The creators of these images share an obvious lack of devotion to any realistic imperative connected to photography. A few of them take pains to manufacture deceptively seamless images that at first, and even second, glance may be perceived as literal documents. But their purpose is not to delude the viewer into the permanent conviction that that is how things really looked. Instead, they are setting the viewer up for a delayed perceptual double take. By thus contradicting the viewer's assumptions concerning the predictability and literalness of the photograph, they redirect attention to the specific image itself. This heightens awareness of its artificiality and evokes important questions in regard to its purpose.

For the others—those who leave the seams of their reconstructed worlds showing—the intent is less to create an effective illusion of reality than to refer to different aspects of reality by combining portions of different photographic images, which encode the surface appearance of those aspects. It is in the nature of photographs to particularize. But when fragmented, mixed, and reorganized, they can be made to generalize as well, to symbolize classes of things in addition to representing the single instance that is their subject.

Regardless of approach, images in this form declare themselves to be unrealistic. They are descriptions of inner states rather than external phenomena. Of all the images in this book these come closest to the traditional meaning of *the grotesque* in art-historical terms: non- or antiliteral evocations of dreams, fantasies, visions, and hallucinations.

It is possible to group these image-makers in several different ways. For example, they can be differentiated according to the sources of the raw material they use as components in their images. Some use only "found" photographic imagery from newspapers, magazines, and other such sources, and thus are not themselves photographers. Some work exclusively with their own images. Some combine the two.

They may also be distinguished by the choice of technique. Some are photocollagists. Some are photomonteurs or combination printers. Some employ other methods altogether, including direct manual manipulation of the print or negative surface. There have even been grotesque photograms—cameraless images made on light-sensitive paper—by Man Ray, George Obremski, and others.

None of these distinctions is hard and fast, and more important than any such divisions is what these image-makers have in common. They all use photographic imagery either exclusively or primarily in their work. They alter or combine it in ways which require a healthy irreverence for the documentary integrity of the original negative or the inviolability of the print. (As Man Ray once wrote: "A certain amount of contempt for the material employed to express an idea is indispensable to the purest realization of this idea.") Yet though they may fragment or otherwise manipulate that imagery to a great extent, its photographic origin is obviously important to them. Thus, although their methods and intentions vary widely, it is apparent that they are all aware of and actively utilizing the peculiar psychological effect of the photographic image, whose factuality and temporality always refer the viewer to its source in a specific time and place.

The works by Weegee, Paul Diamond, Jerry Uelsmann, Adál, and Todd Walker involve the most specifically photographic techniques.

Weegee's brash, humorous inventions (pages 172–173) were created by way of a wide range of methods and devices. Some of these—kaleidoscopes, patterned glass, and distorting lenses—were utilized during exposure of the negative. Others—mirror reflection, easel tilting, photomontage—he used in the darkroom. These are generally whimsical images, obviously a form of play for Weegee and perhaps a release from some of the grimmer aspects of his professional work.

The superimposition of one image on another is called *montage*. Sometimes this term is used interchangeably with *collage*, but they are not identical. Sometimes photomontage can be achieved simply with collage techniques—i.e., by gluing one image on top of another. Often, however, it requires more elaborate photographic methods. One of these is double exposure, done while the negative is still in the camera. That is how Paul Diamond created "Victor's Faces" and "Half Lost" (pages 160–161). There are also other darkroom montage processes, such as multiple printing or the "sandwiching" of negatives (printing two superimposed negatives simultaneously, as in Emmet Gowin's image on page 37). In such cases both the image components and the techniques involved are purely photographic in nature.

The latter techniques are among those employed by Jerry Uelsmann (pages 184–193). Combination printing, one of the methods he employs most consistently, was originated in the nineteenth century and brought to a peak by such masters as Henry Peach Robinson and O. J. Rejlander. Even in its early days it was controversial. With the rise of the purist camp in photography early in this century it fell out of favor. A few creative photographers continued to use it—Edmund Teske, Val Telberg, and Clarence John Laughlin among them—and were consequently relegated to limbo by hidebound historians and critics.

Uelsmann devoted a great deal of study, experimentation, and energy to reviving the process in the early 1960's. Surviving severe criticism and outright rejection of his initial efforts by his peers, he has forged a major body of work in this form over the past decade.

There are consistently grotesque motifs throughout Uelsmann's imagery. These include apparitions of disembodied human parts and the merger of human beings with various natural objects—rocks, trees, and the like. These are traditional grotesque themes, used here to convey the feeling of subconscious states of awareness.

A similar effect is achieved by Adál, whose disorienting images also present photographically credible visions although their information cannot be reconciled with common sense. This young Puerto Rican artist dissects some of his photographs precisely and replaces parts of them with bits of other images (pages 196–199). His symbology is highly personal, often autobiographical, and his attitude ironic. Self-contained and authoritative, his images seek to provide, in his own words, "the evidence of things not seen."

The ghostly female figures in Todd Walker's images (pages 194–195) appear always to be on the verge of fully materializing—or dematerializing, as the case may be. These figures seem to exist in the half-light of some limbo that can only be glimpsed. Walker achieves this by employing the Sabattier effect (often called solarization), which involves exposing prints or negatives to light during development. This causes a reversal of tones in areas of the print and can be controlled with considerable precision. Walker often translates the resulting images into offset lithographic color prints, a conversion that further heightens their eerie effect.

Though all five of these photographers utilize one form or another of post-exposure manipulation of prints and/or negatives, their work is devoid of overt signs indicating the physical alterations of optical reality. The same is true of other photographers who have explored the grotesque: Fredrich Cantor, Kunié, Henry Holmes Smith, Cecil Beaton, and Mario Giacomelli among them. Others, however, have allowed their hands to show, both figuratively and literally.

Brassaï's "Transmutations," for example, self-evidently combine photographic elements with hand-drawn imagery. These works were created by another nineteenth-century technique called *cliché-verre*, whereby a drawing was actually scratched into the emulsion of an unexposed glass-plate negative, which in turn was used to make photographic prints of the hand-drawn image.

In this instance, the negatives were some of Brassaï's already-exposed nude studies, portions of which he left intact and portions of which were reworked. In writing of these images (pages 166–169), which he made in 1934–35, Brassaï says, "That which attracted me in this adventure was not the process itself . . . but the possibility of introducing something indefinable which belongs only to photography. . . . Unlike my predecessors, I discarded the virgin plates, which suggested nothing to me, to tackle negatives which were already impressed with a subject which tempted me." Best known for his photography, Brassaï is also a sculptor, writer, filmmaker, and graphic artist. His kinship with his close friend Pablo Picasso can be felt in these works.

William Mortensen also reworked his negatives

manually, adding hand-drawn graphic elements and sometimes even words and titles to the image itself. He
functioned directorially in relation to his models, then altered the resulting images (pages 162–165) by the above
means and also through a diversity of printing procedures.
Madness, satanism, and the occult are frequent themes in
his work. His was an almost medieval sensibility, which
met with little sympathy from a modernist- and purist-
oriented photographic establishment during the 1920's and
1930's, when his finest work was done. He has been seriously neglected by historians and critics. Although he was
an influential teacher and writer his name appears in none
of the standard reference works on the medium.

If Mortensen's sensibility can be described as
medieval, that of Lucas Samaras is surely Renaissance.
Samaras works in many media—tapestry, writing,
sculpture, and photography among them. His photographic work is exclusively self-portraiture, employing
only Polaroid materials. By now Samaras has created hun-
dreds of what he calls "autopolaroids," using both the older
Polaroid system and the new SX-70.

The SX-70 print is composed of a chemical
"batter" sandwiched between two sheets of plastic. In
exploring this material, Samaras (along with many other
photographers, including Les Krims) discovered that it
remains malleable for several hours before hardening permanently. Consequently, the image can be altered by pres-
sing firmly on the surface of the print in order to move parts
of the image around. That is how the peculiar, horrific
distortions of his face and body in the images reproduced
here (pages 174–179) were generated.

Although they embrace relatively unorthodox
methods for doing so, the image-makers discussed here so
far—and, indeed, in this book—are employing techniques
that are, by and large, essentially photographic. The Sabattier effect, the *cliché-verre* process, combination printing,
indeed, even the manipulation of SX-70 pigments, are all
based on phenomena that are intrinsic to the medium of
photography. And the images they produce thereby, in
their nature as objects, are undeniably photographs.

But this survey could not even pretend to com-
prehensiveness within its medium or its mode if it failed to
consider a remarkable group of image-makers who share a
high degree of photographic content and awareness although they often use methods that are not essentially
photographic, and equally often produce works that,
strictly speaking, are not photographs.

Some of these image-makers are nominally
categorized as photographers. Some are not. The technique
on which they rely most heavily is photocollage. They
approach it in a variety of ways.

Like photomontage, photocollage can be traced
back to the nineteenth century. The terms themselves were
originated early in this century by the Dadaists in Europe.
Often used interchangeably, the terms are difficult to separate. Even practitioners of the same method frequently
define their process differently.

For our purposes, let us simply say that photocollage involves the cutting up and reassembling of parts of
photographic prints or reproductions of photographs. In
itself, this does not necessarily require any specific photographic activity. All that is consistently photographic in
such images is the origin of the component parts.

Some of those who work in this form conceive
of the original collage as a matrix from which to derive
photographic copy prints with a unified surface. Some
conceive of it as the finished work. Some incorporate parts
of images they did not generate themselves, or even non-
photographic elements—paint, colored paper, objects, and
so forth—into their works. Suffice it to say that, again like
photomontage, photocollage is not a medium for purists.

Because some forms of such imagery can be
generated without the use of a camera or a darkroom, it has
attracted many visual artists from outside the perimeters of
photography, ranging from Max Ernst to Richard Hamil-
ton and Robert Rauschenberg. Indeed, it is perhaps not
altogether coincidental that the form of the grotesque mode
in photography that is most akin to the tradition of the
grotesque in art is also the form that has been most accessible to photographers and nonphotographers alike.

Hannah Höch is often credited—along with
Raoul Hausmann—with being the inventor of photocollage. Though argument still rages among historians over
the precise lineage of the form, there is no question that
Höch was among the first and most influential of photocollagists. Grotesque elements have appeared in her works
from the very beginning, as can be seen in those reproduced
here (pages 206–207). Color plays an increasingly important role in her more recent collages, no doubt an echo of her
concerns as a painter; and her imagery has grown more
abstract. In contrast, these early works seem stark and
spare. Höch is still living in Germany, and continues to
make and exhibit a diversity of work.

Erwin Blumenfeld, whose work also appears in

the previous chapter, died in 1969. A photographer and writer, Blumenfeld was a German Jew who fled the holocaust and came to New York City. Here he carved out a triumphant career as a fashion photographer. A technical virtuoso, Blumenfeld—not unlike Man Ray—explored all photographic processes without inhibition: collage, solarization, and (as in "Face in Mirror," on page 171) multiple printing as well. Much of his personally motivated work is highly political in orientation—witness "Minotaure (or The Dictator)" on page 95, and "Hitler Skull." The latter image (page 170) is a rephotographed collage, made on the occasion of Hitler's election. Distributed in large quantities as an anti-Nazi poster, it earned Blumenfeld a place on the Gestapo's "most wanted" list.

Allen Dutton and Robert Heinecken are collagists who, by their own choice, are usually grouped with photographers. The grotesque is also a central theme for both of them. Heinecken, from California, is an influential teacher and theorist. He indicates that "everything I've done is grotesque." His images (pages 200–205) incorporate collage, drawing, and painting. Additionally, some of the pieces illustrated are three-dimensional, sculptural works, jigsaw puzzles made up of segments of human figures that can be rearranged at will.

Often his two- and three-dimensional works combine his own imagery with vernacular photographs from magazines and newspapers. The themes of sex and violence are recurrent in his work, much of which is directed toward exploring the connections between pornography, brutality, and a consumer society.

In terms of technique, Allen Dutton (pages 152–159) can be considered a transition figure in this form. Some of his imagery is directorially oriented but technically "straight." The work represented here is collage in origin, primarily composed of images Dutton generates himself but also including fragments of "found" photographs. From these he reconstructs a visionary's universe, reflected in outlandish dreamscapes populated with remarkable creatures. These collages are then rephotographed, so that what Dutton presents to the viewer is, literally, a photograph. Its unified surface suggests that it has not been tampered with, but this is belied by the impossible incongruities encapsulated therein. This conflict between object and image is consciously exploited by Dutton for its emotional impact.

Robert Delford Brown is a representative example of the many twentieth-century artists who, though not actually photographers themselves, have worked with photographic imagery in a variety of ways. Delford Brown's interest has persistently been directed toward the more bizarre manifestations of the vernacular photograph—particularly forensic and fetish photographs, which he enlarges to life size and laboriously hand-tints in lurid colors, and such collages as those reproduced here (pages 180–183). Like Samaras, Delford Brown is a Renaissance sensibility, working in many different media of which photography is only one.

The coexistence of irreconcilably different image segments within one final composite image creates an unsettling, dislocating effect within the viewer. Indeed, it could be said to be a central tactic of artists pursuing the grotesque in all media. Since it is also intrinsic to the technique of collage, it would not be unreasonable to suggest that there is a fundamental link between photocollage and the grotesque. That relationship has been deliberately amplified by such diverse artists as Romare Bearden, the brilliant black American painter; John Heartfield, the acidulous German political satirist, and Miecyzslaw Berman, his Polish disciple; and such others as Stefan and Franciszka Themerson, Frantisek Vobecky, Bohumil Stepân, Henryk Hermanowicz, Carolee Schneeman, and Verlon. It is also possible to point out grotesque elements in works by many other collagists for whom the grotesque was not a major theme per se: Herbert Bayer, Man Ray, and Laszlo Moholy-Nagy are only a few of these.

But to give these works the full consideration they merit would require, in addition to their placement within the grotesque mode of photography, an examination of the impact of photography on twentieth-century art. That is beyond the scope of this book. Perhaps it will become the subject of another. But the existence of so many works that bridge the boundaries of photography and the other graphic arts is in itself sufficient proof of the connection between the grotesque mode in photography and its counterpart in the other media. The diversity of work encompassed in this survey demonstrates, I believe, that the grotesque in photography is not merely a stylistic or subject-related attribute, but is in fact a mode in its own right, with its own intrinsic cognitive and performative functions. And because photography has since its inception profoundly affected the ways in which we apprehend the world, I hope this survey has indicated the extent to which our definitions of *the grotesque* have been shaped by the medium. If it succeeds in raising that question and its numerous ramifications, it will have achieved its purpose.

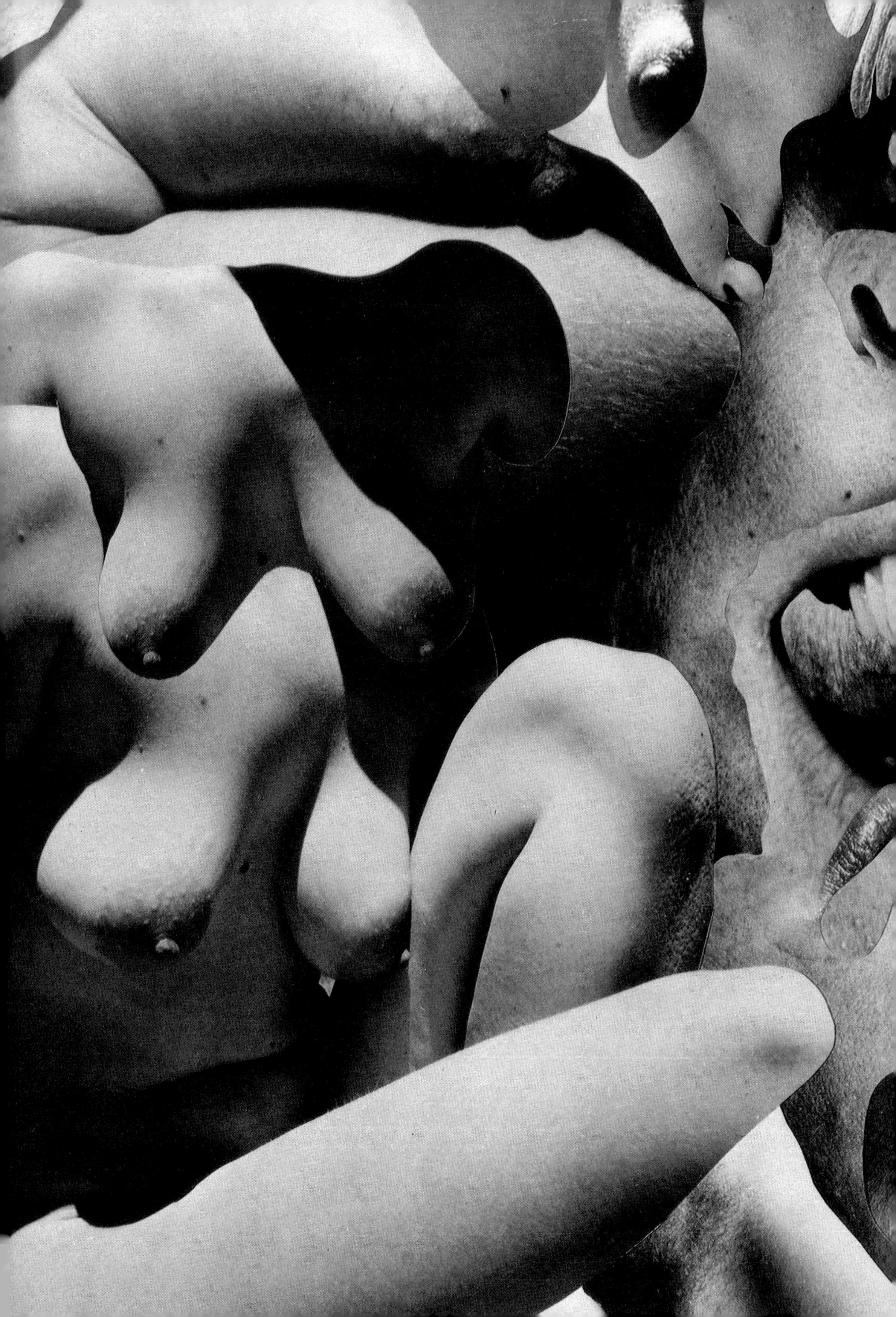

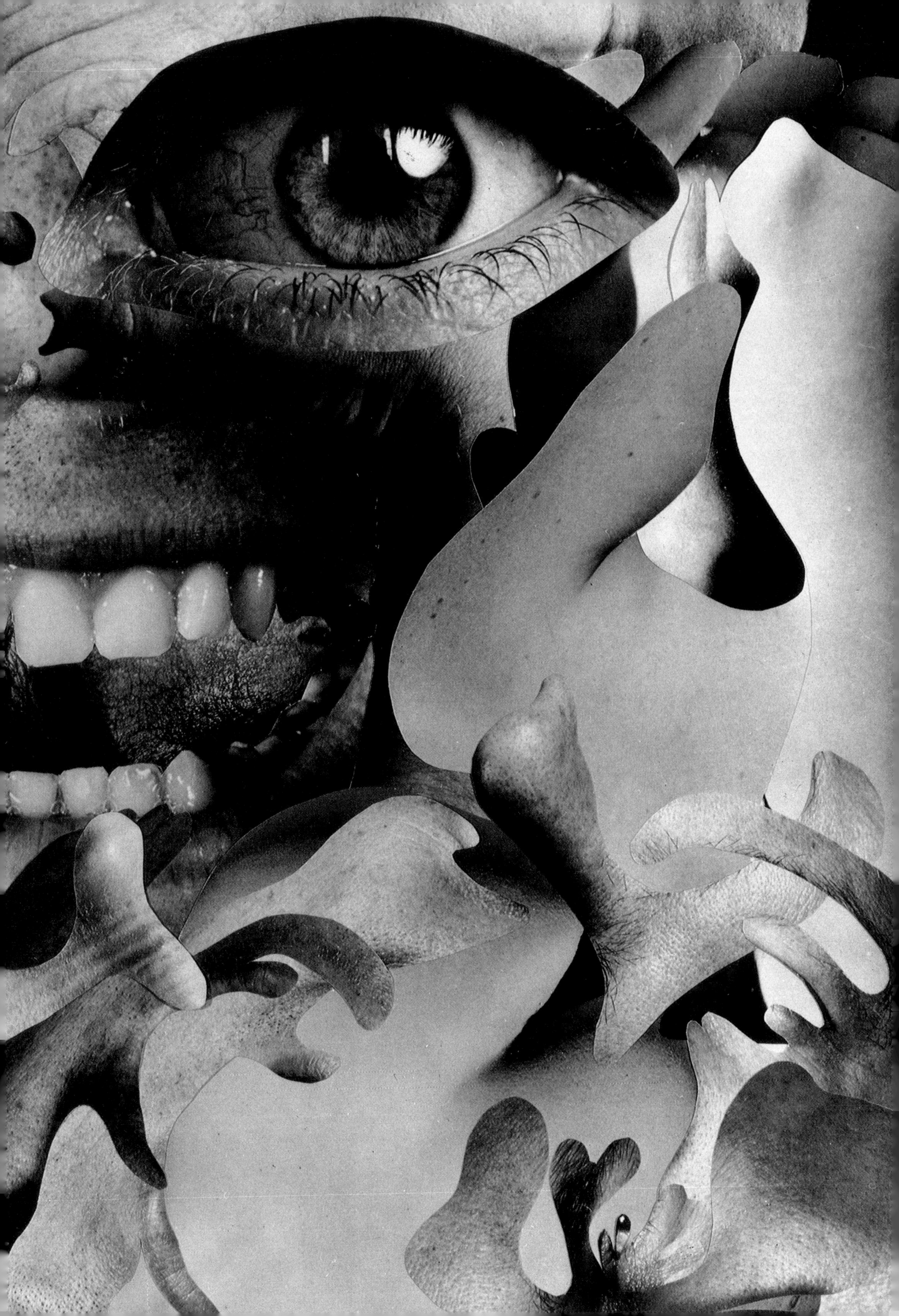

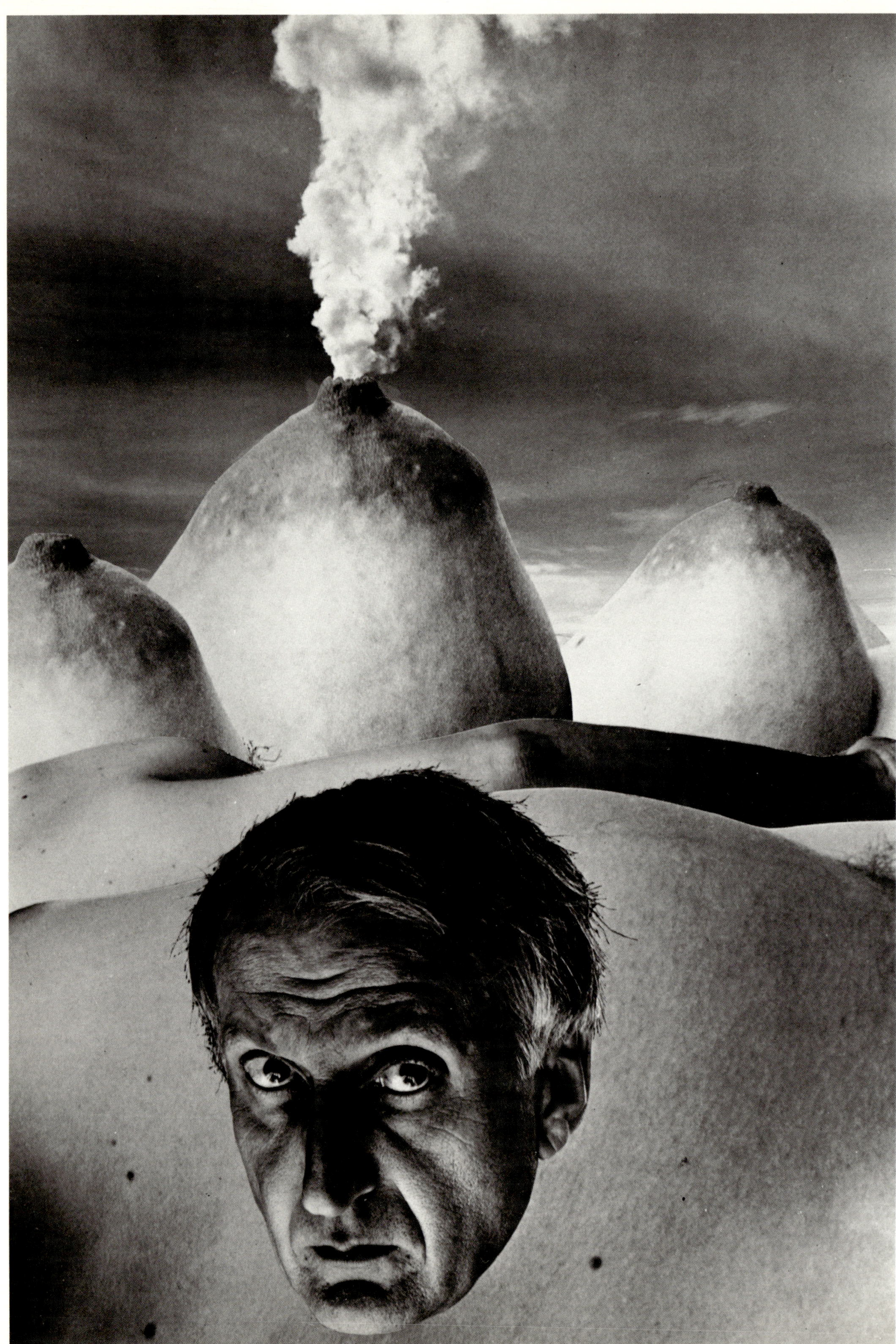

The Specter of Tumid Titans

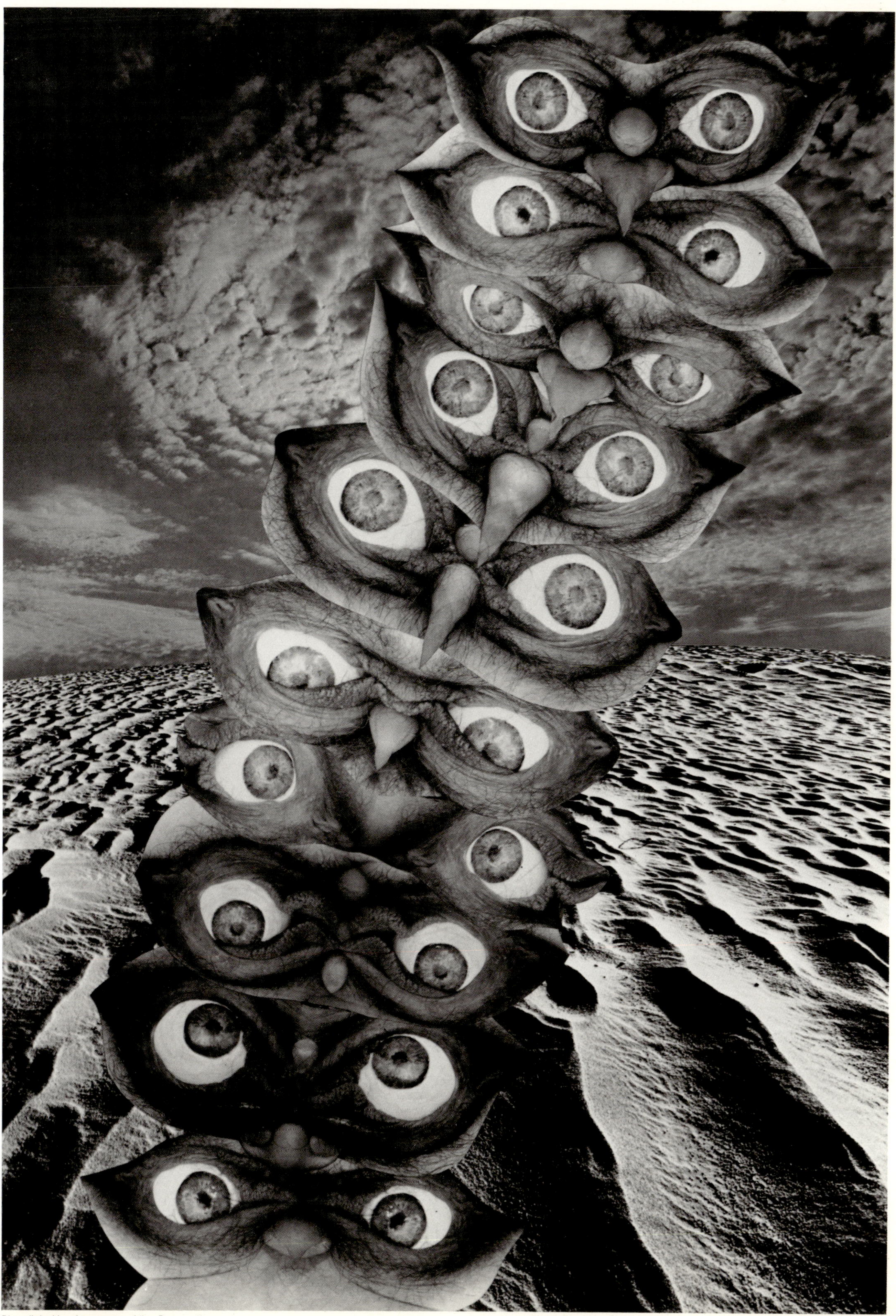

Plausible Humbuggery of the Perceptive

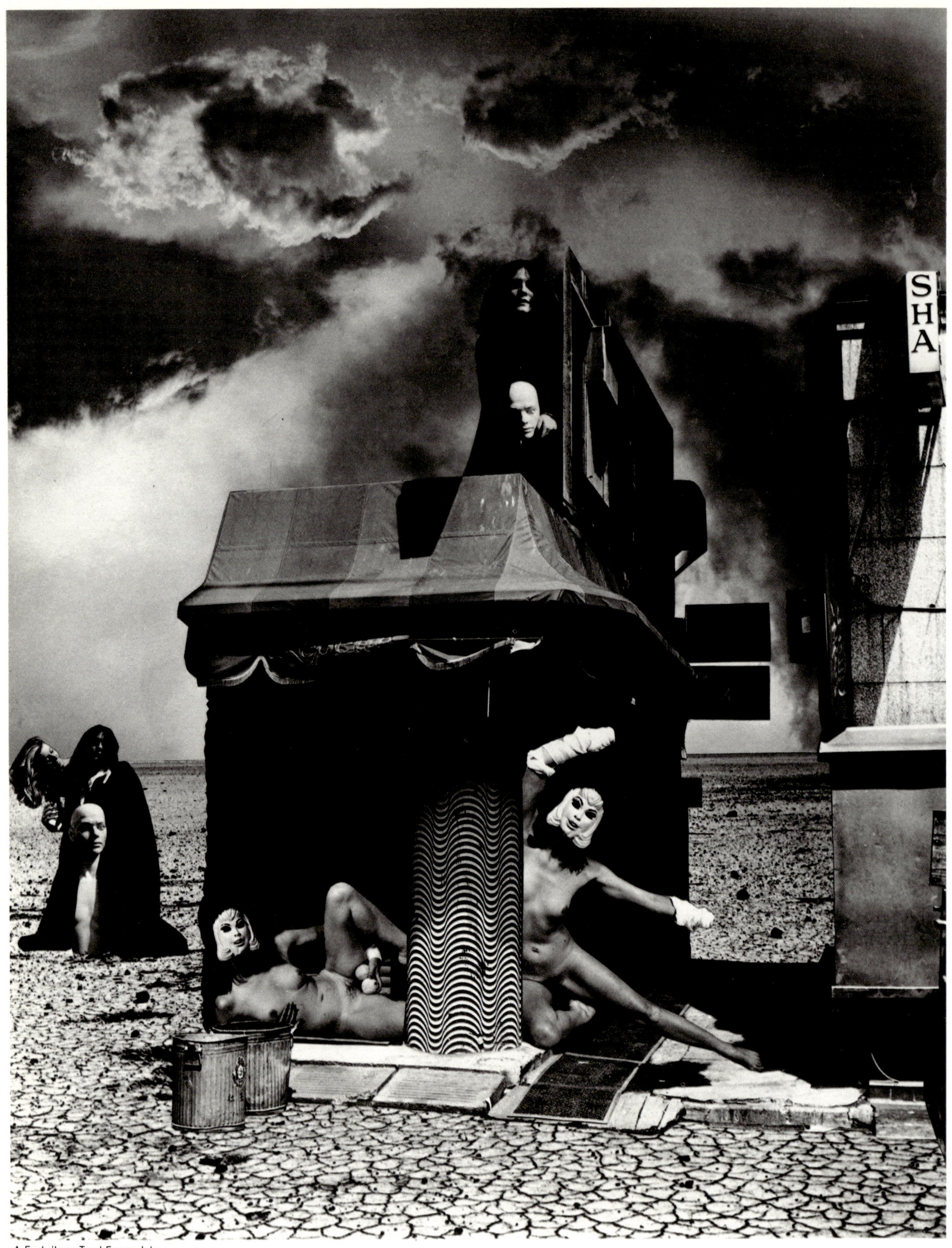

A Fortuitous Tout Ensemble

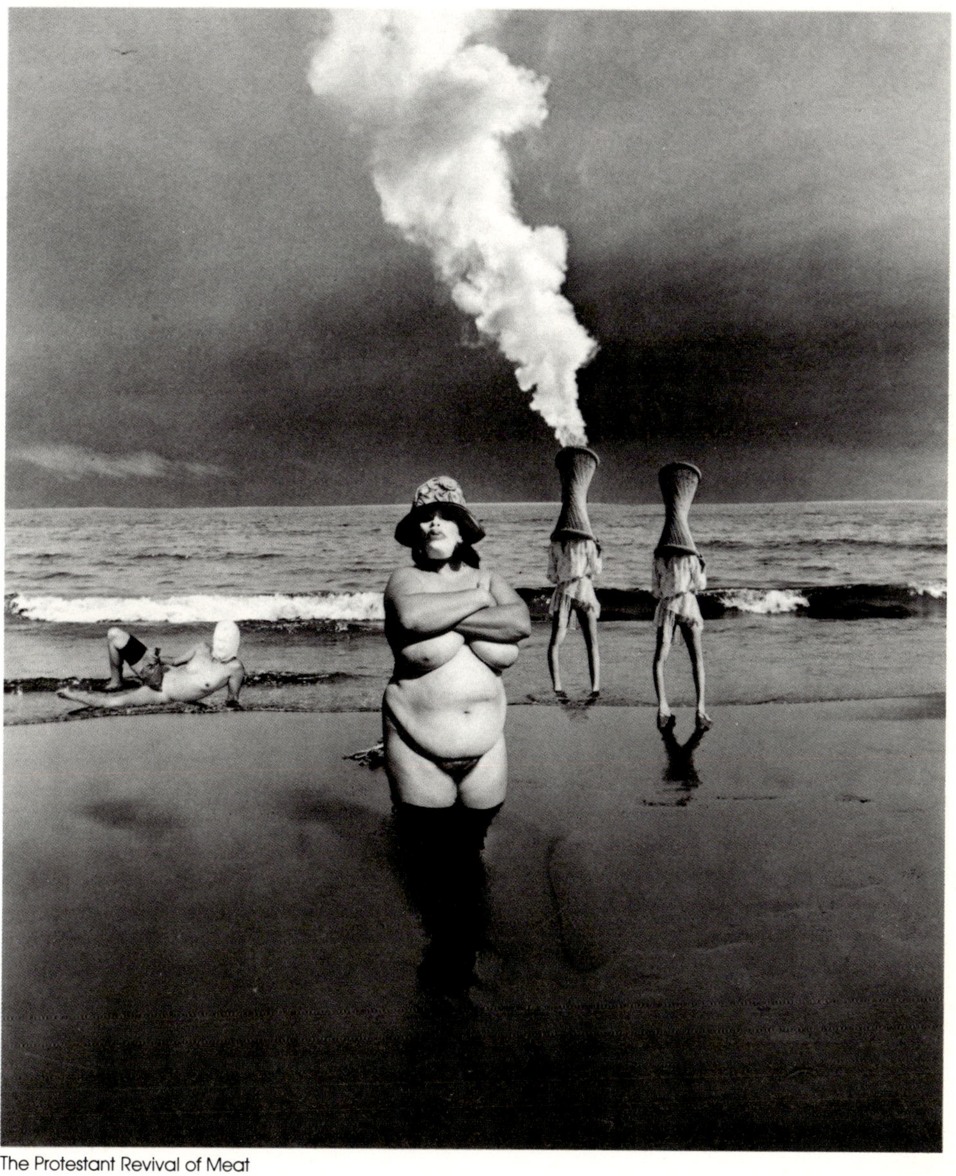

The Protestant Revival of Meat

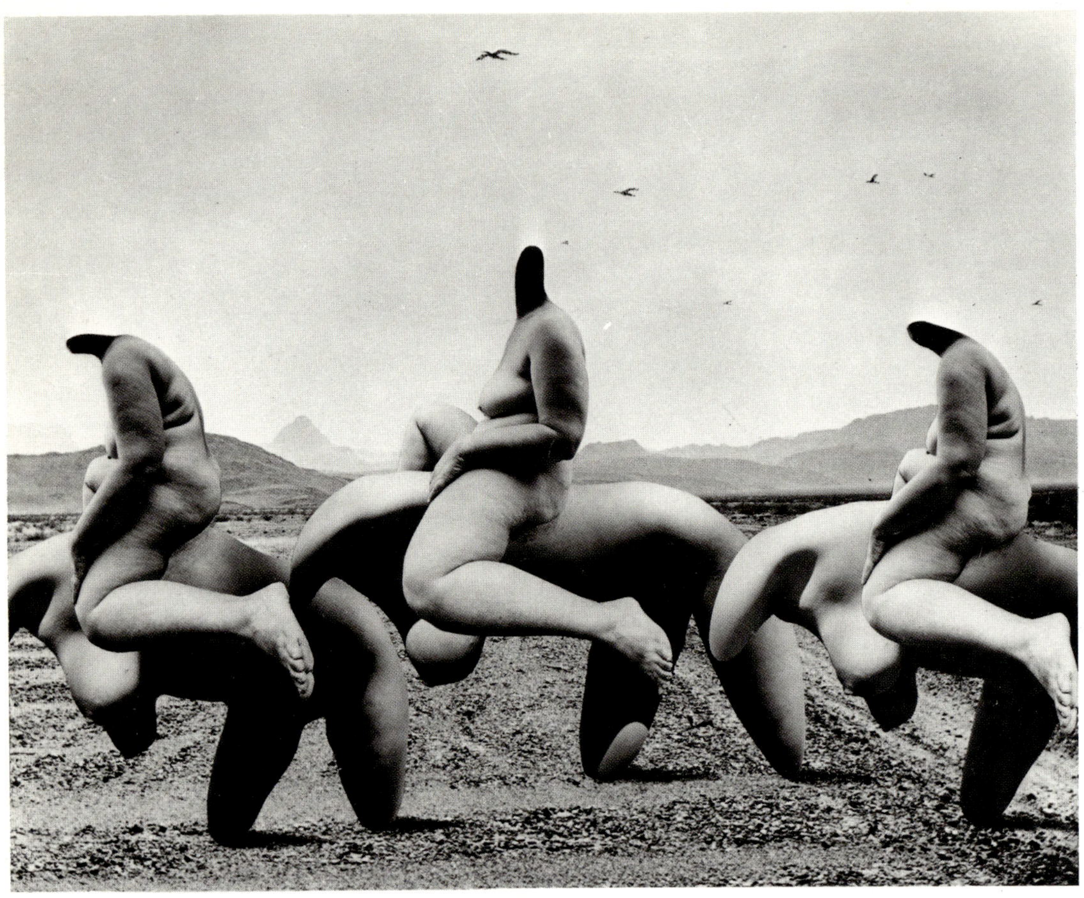

Perspicacity Requires a Head

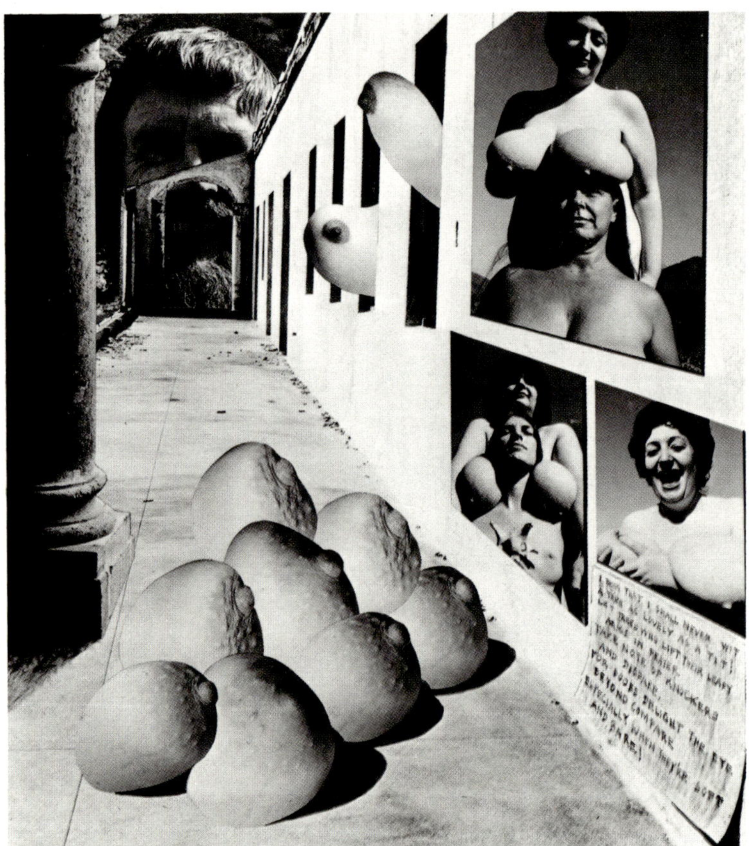

I Think That I Shall Never Wit

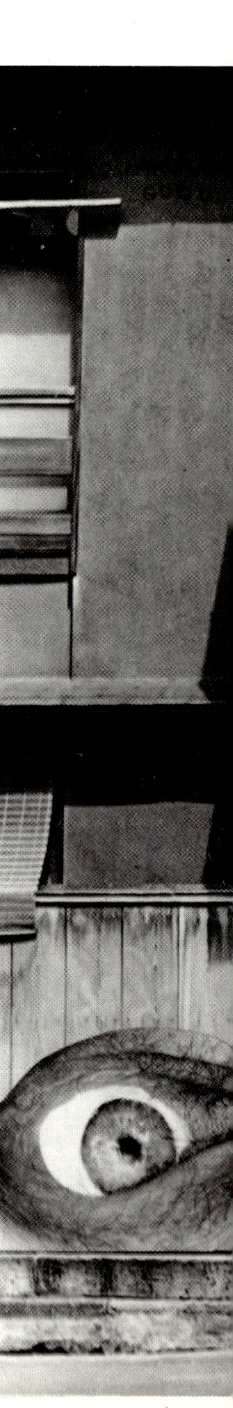

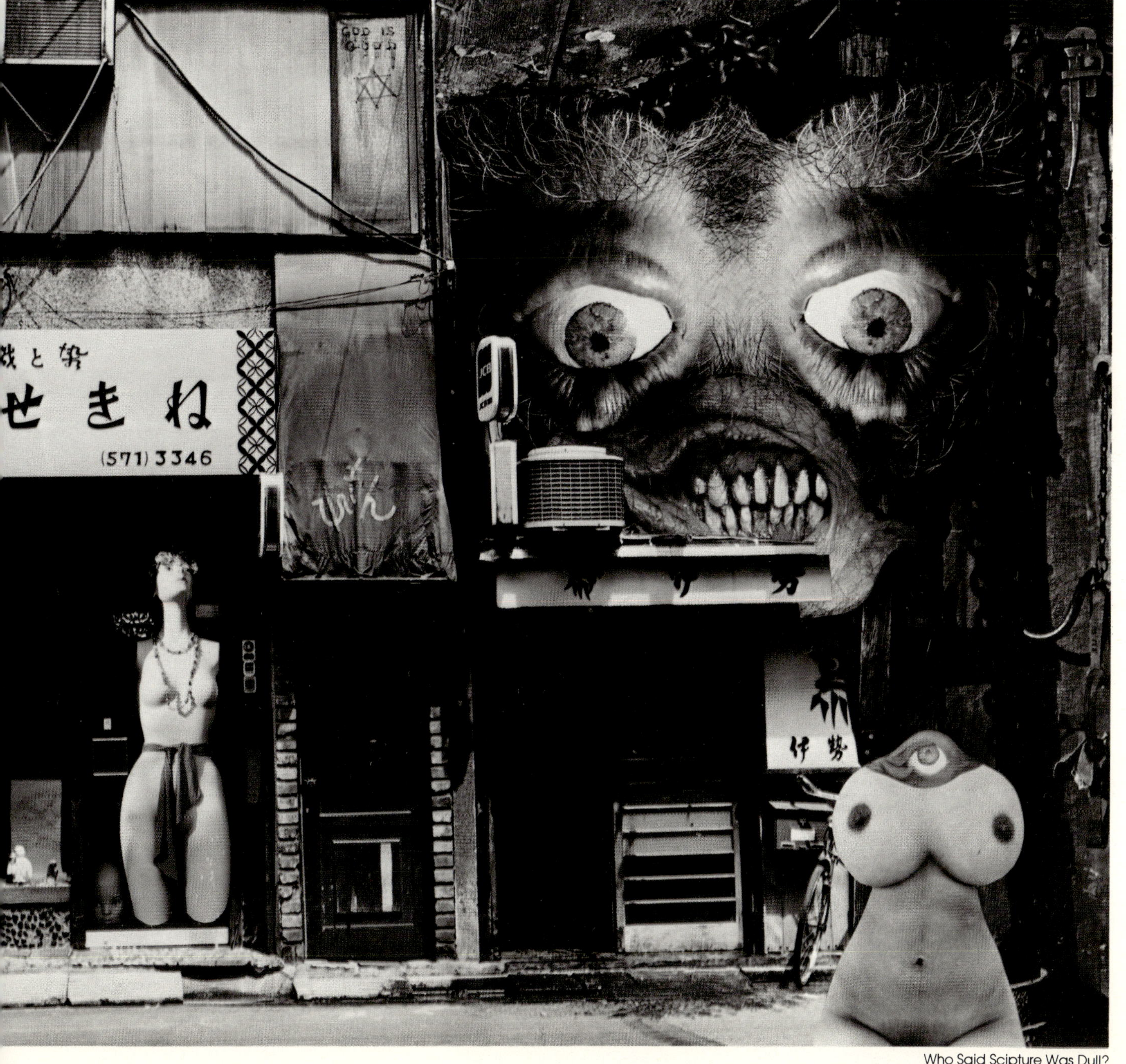

Who Said Scipture Was Dull?

Victor's Faces, Nashville, 1971

Half Lost, SF, 1974

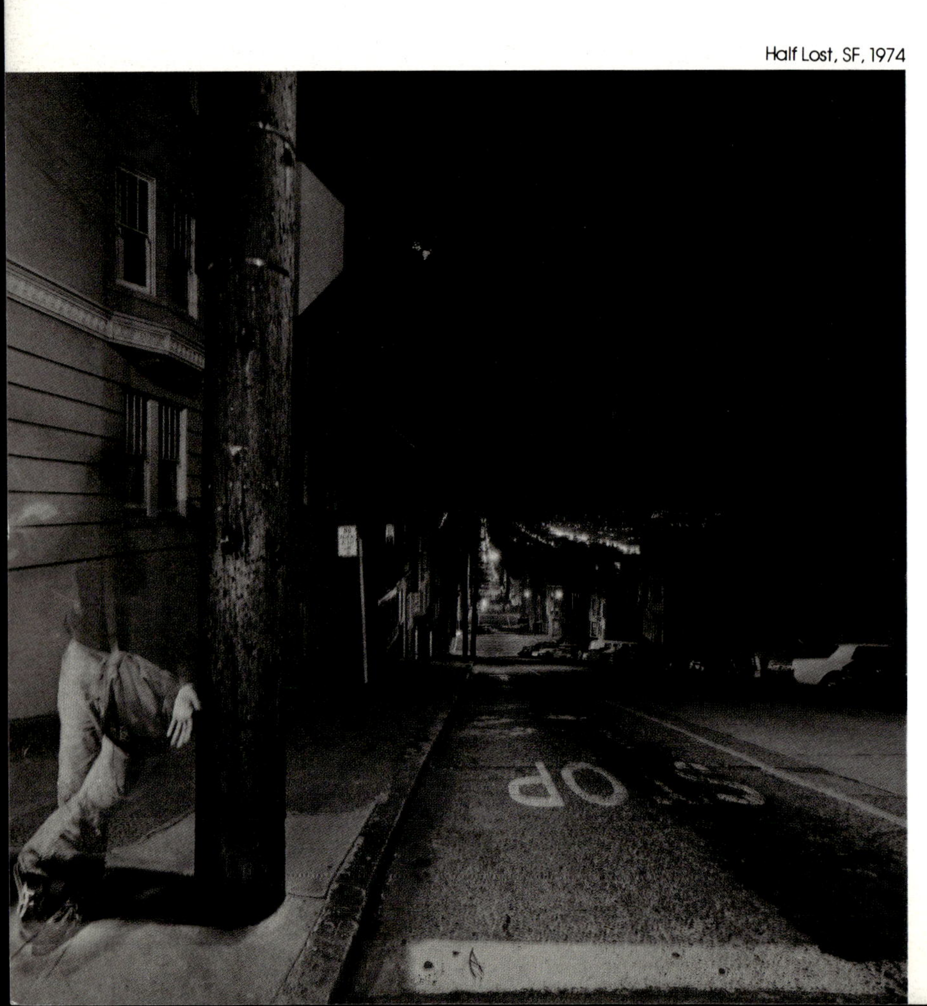

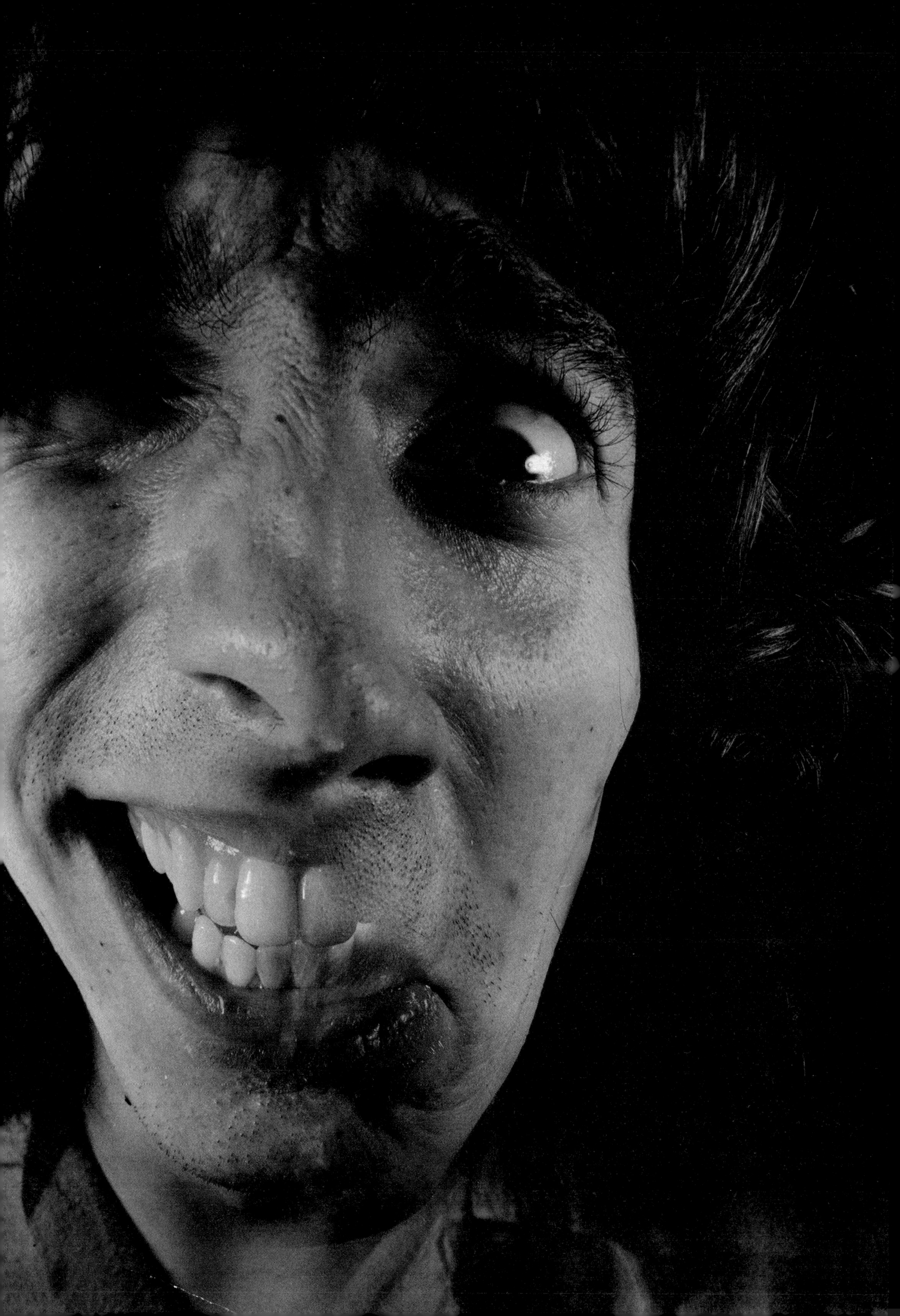

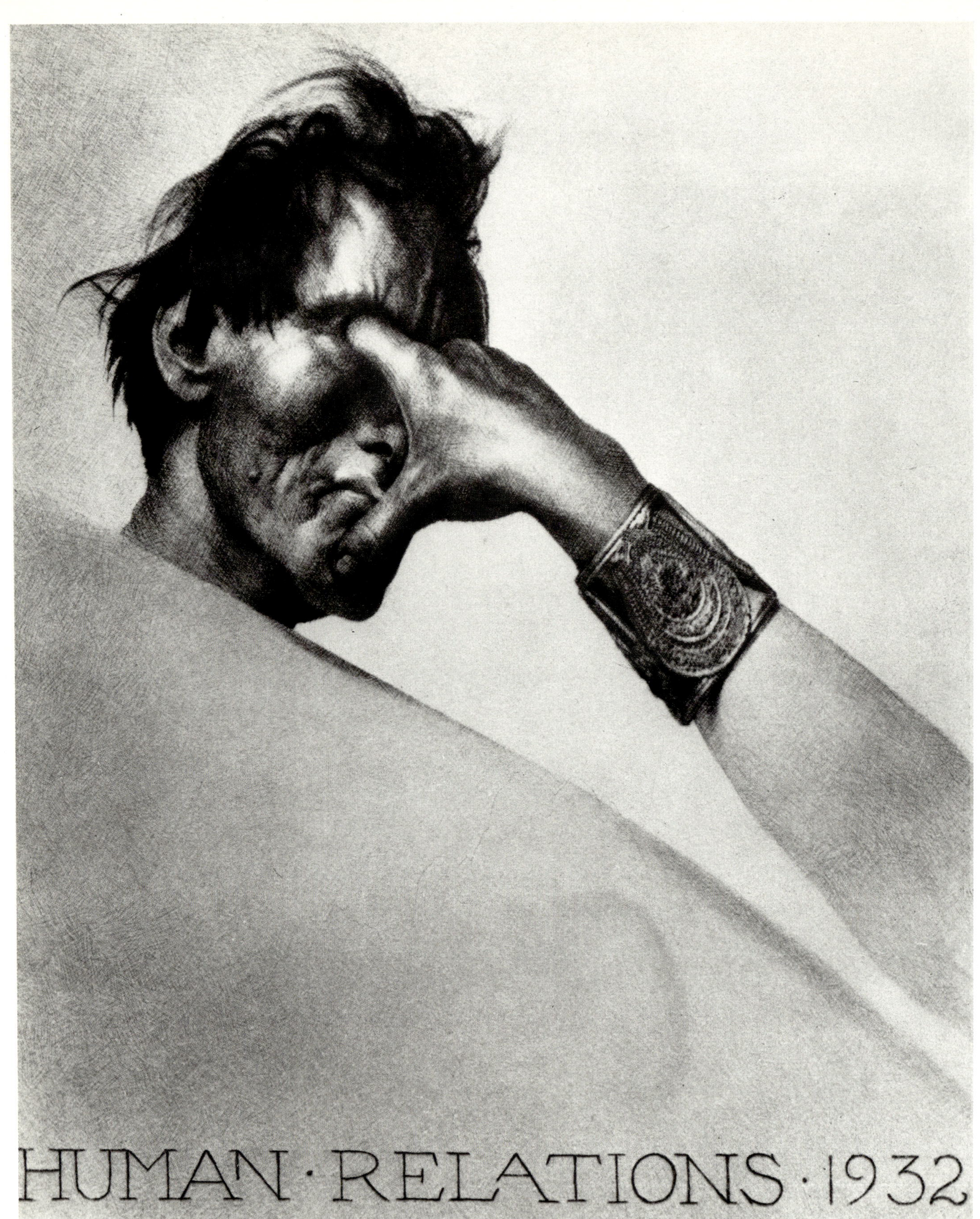

HUMAN · RELATIONS · 1932

The Spider Torture

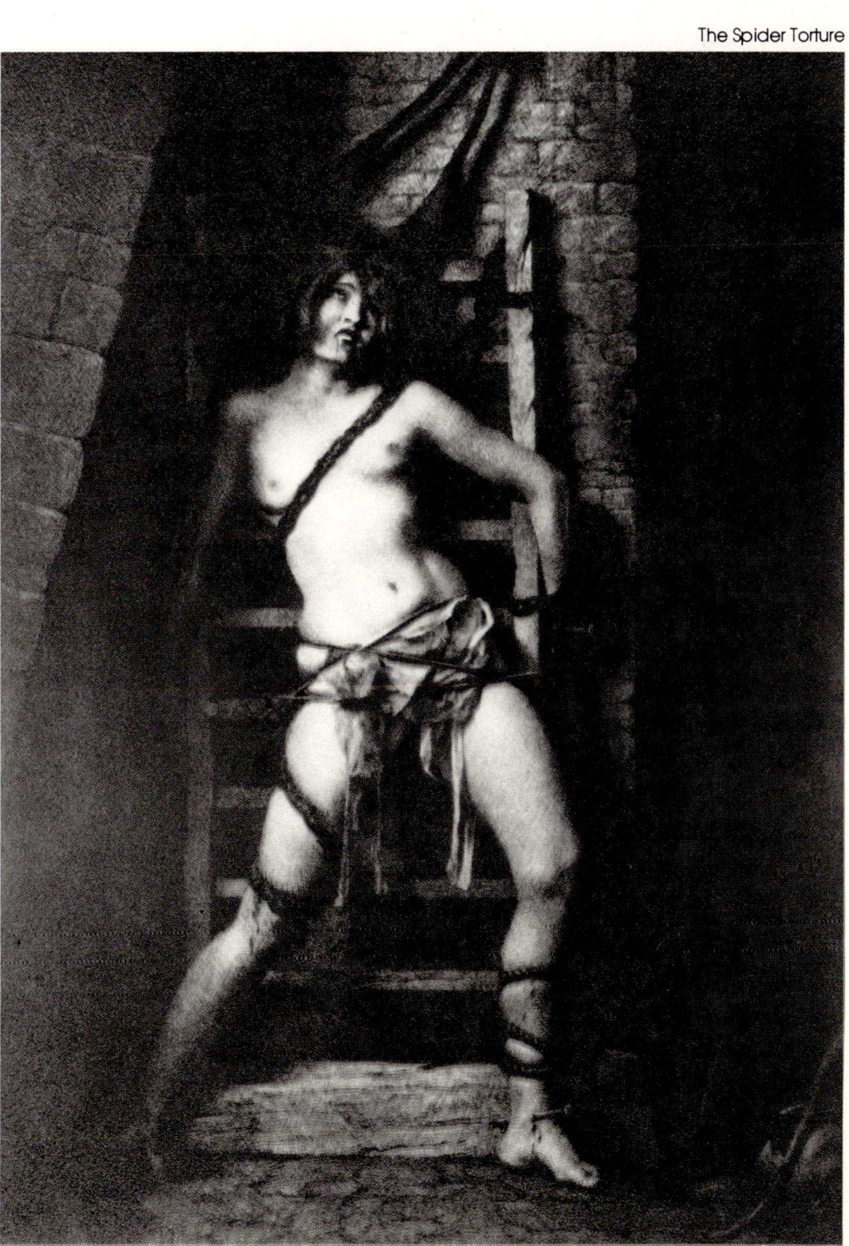

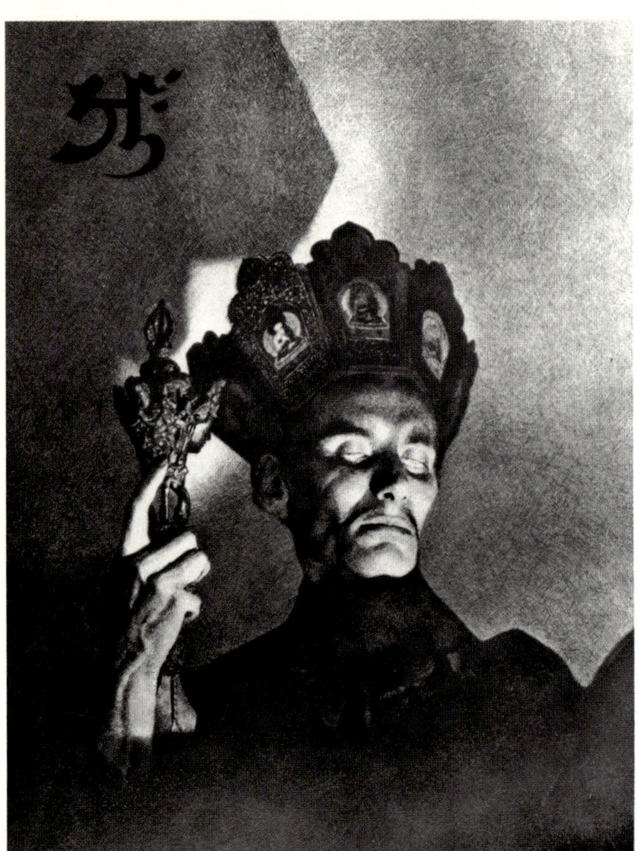

Tantric Sorcerer

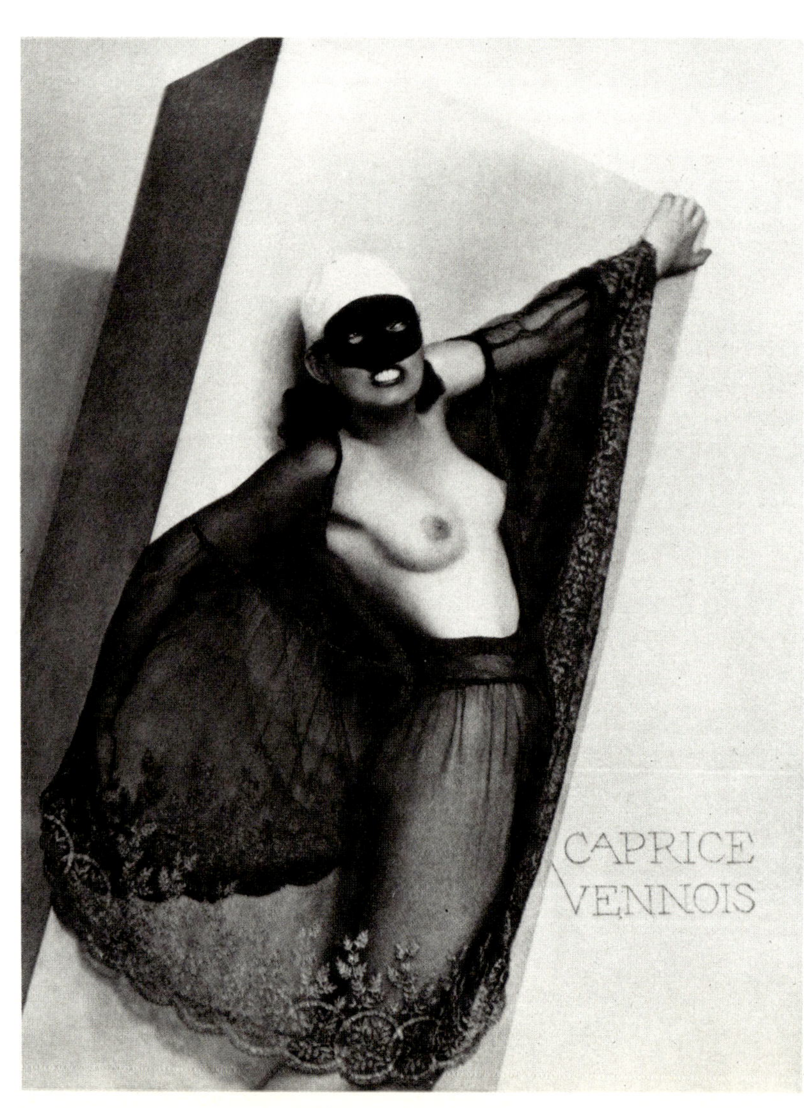

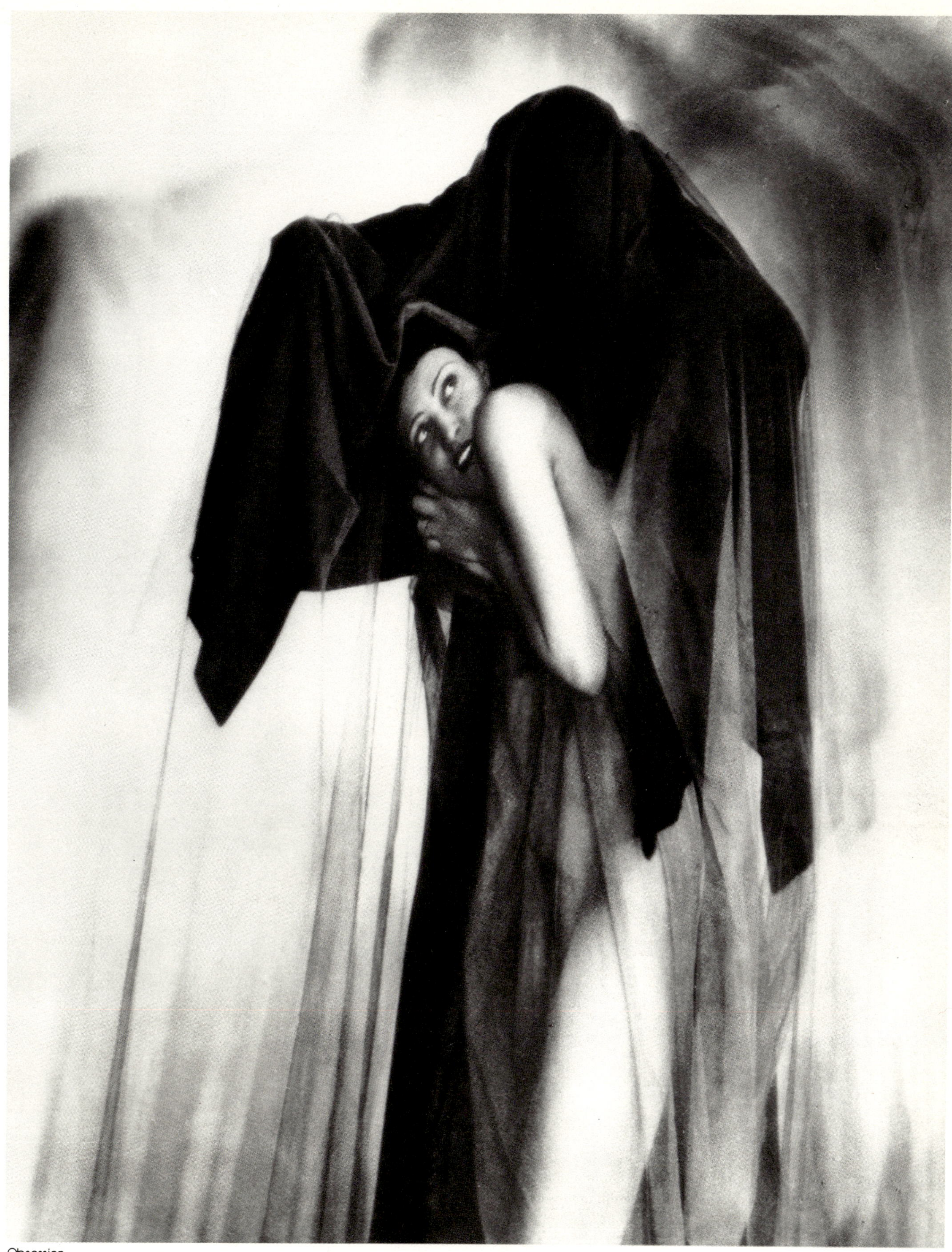

Obsession

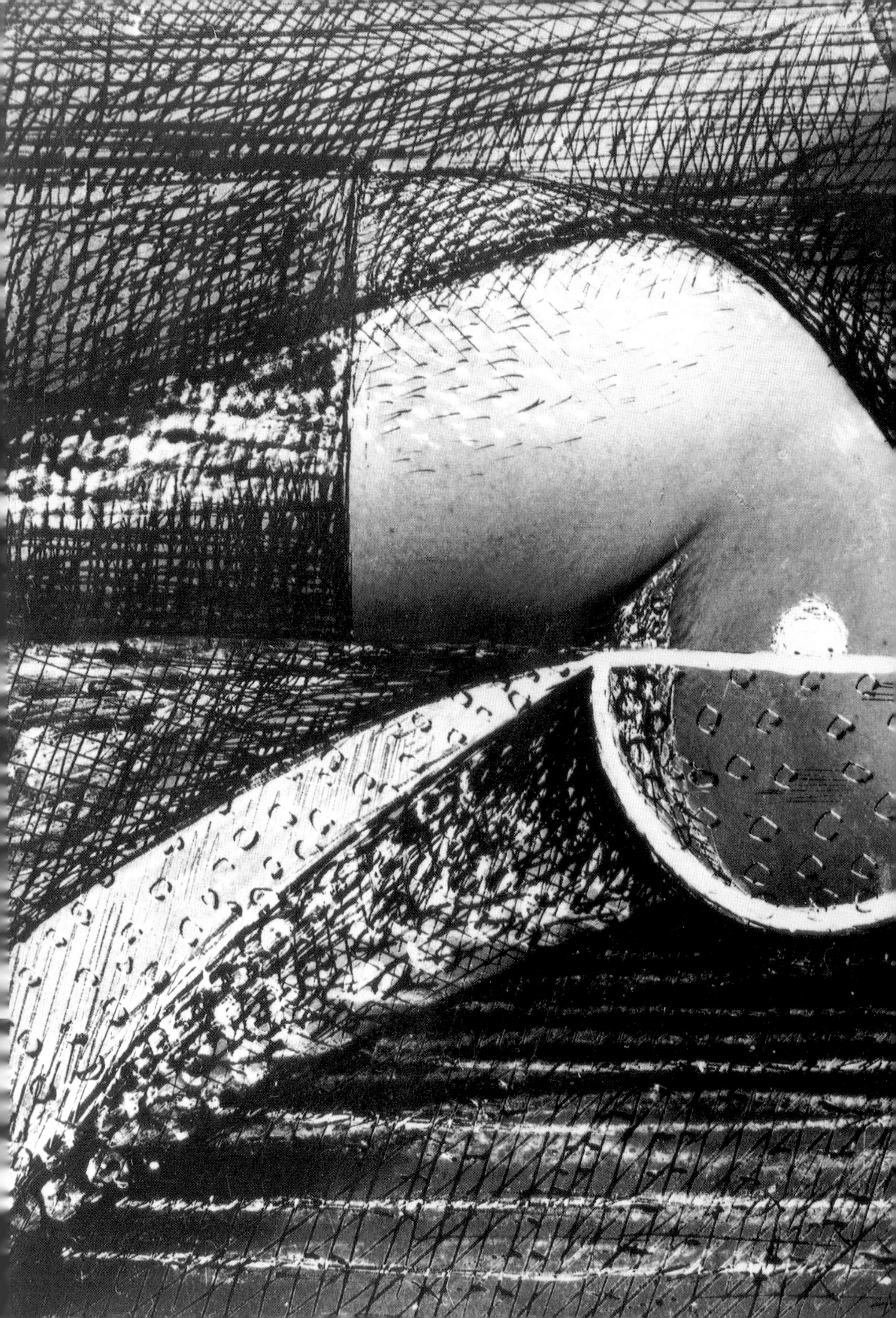

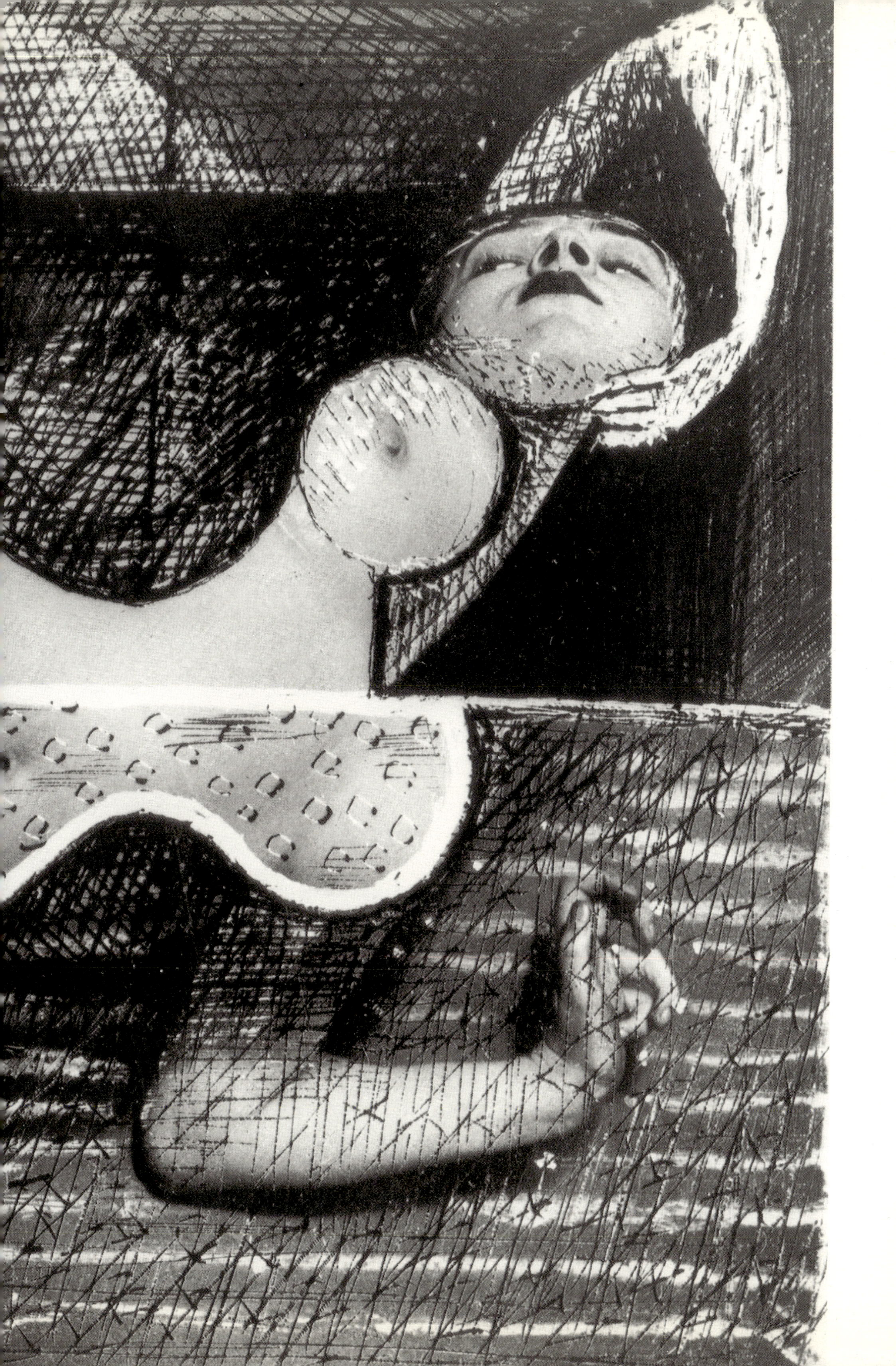

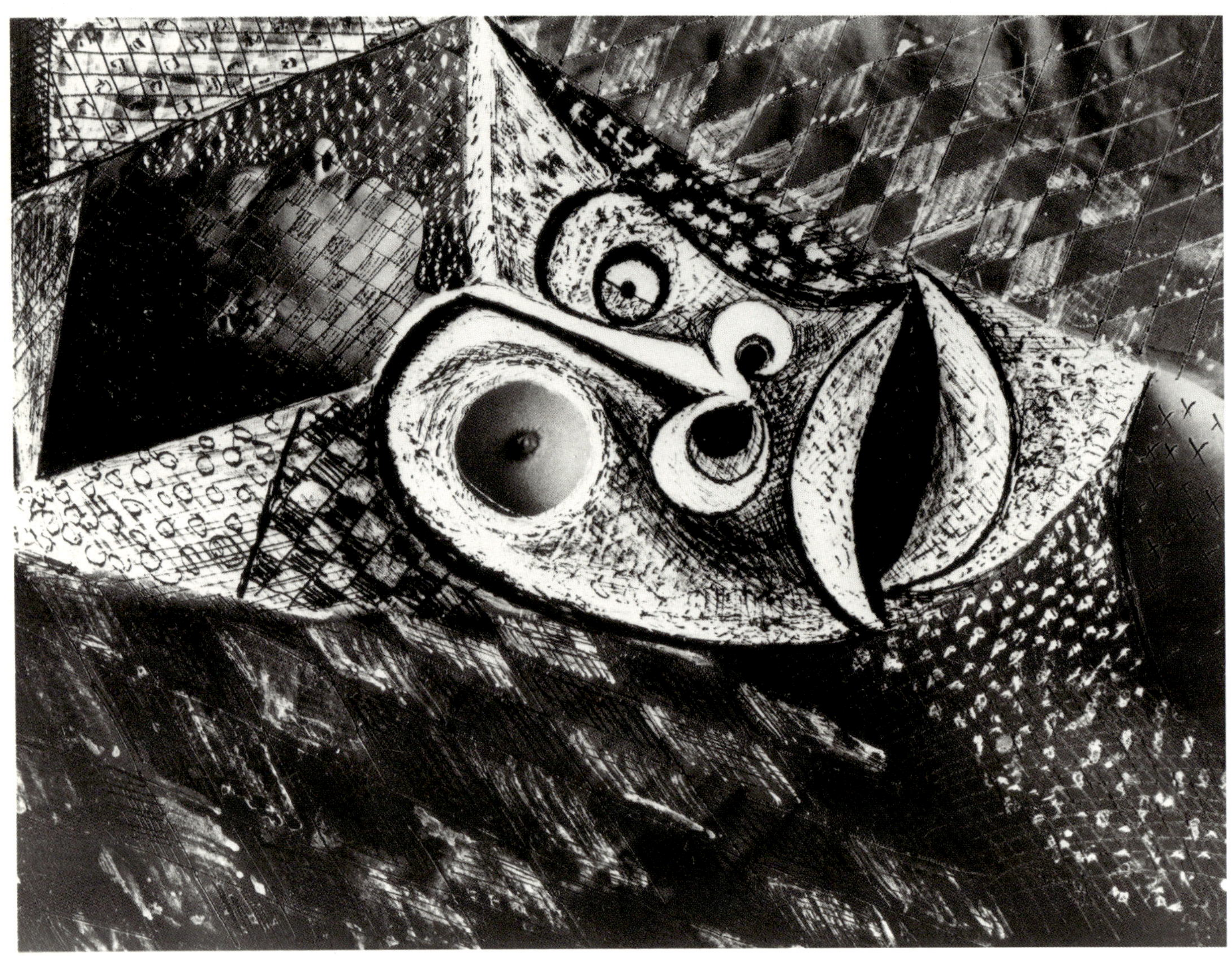

Tentation de Saint Antoine, 1934–35

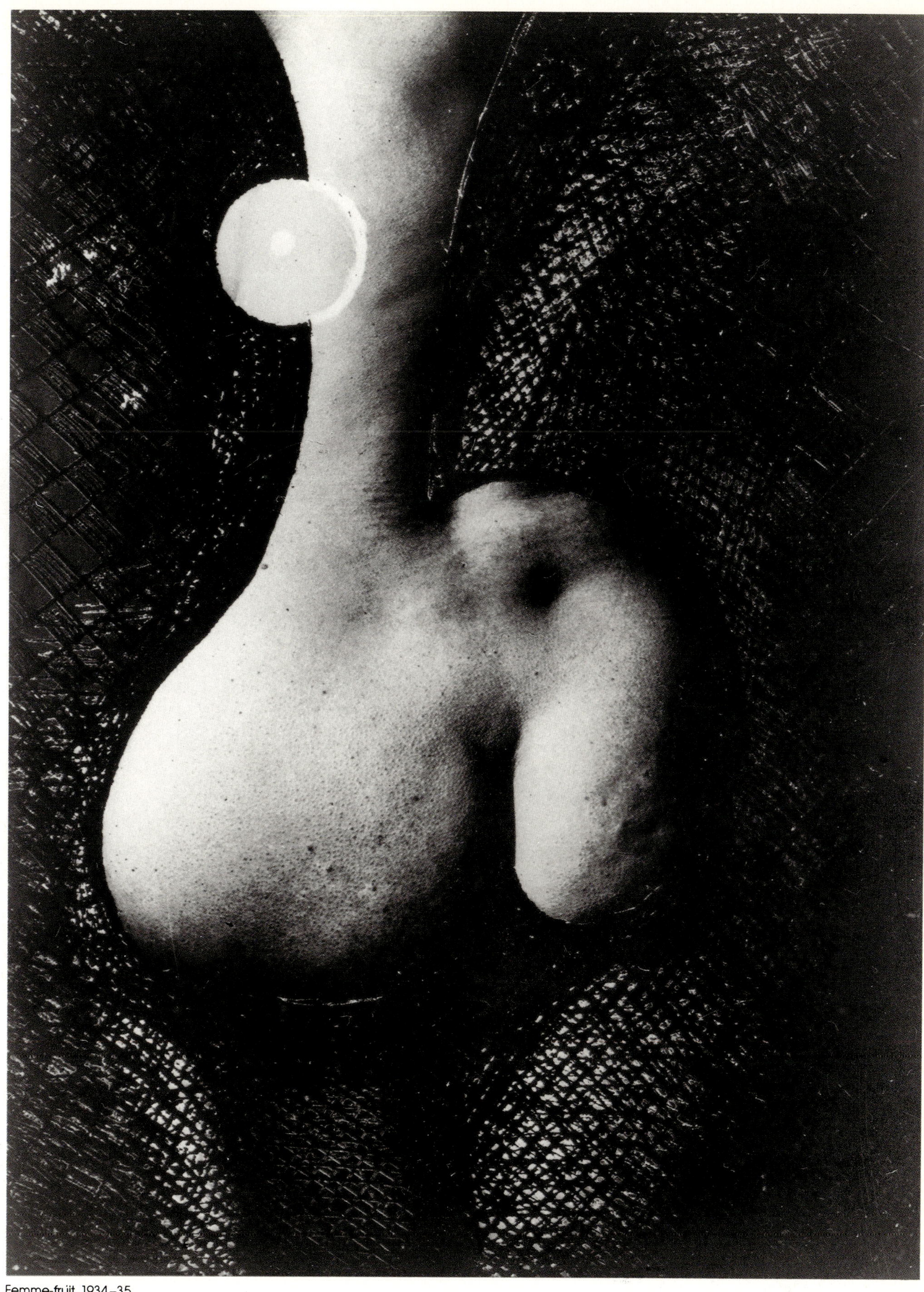

Femme-fruit, 1934–35

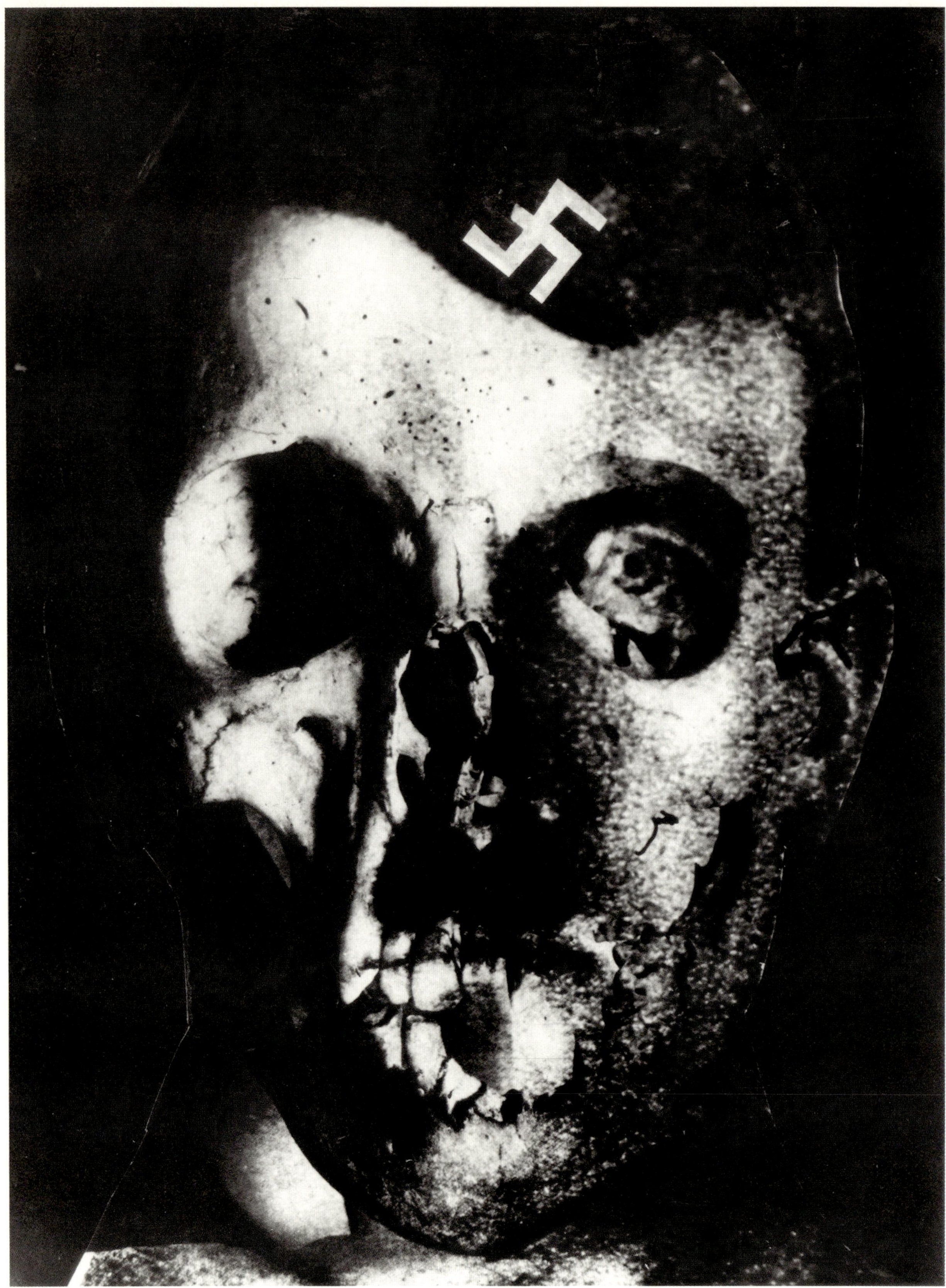

Hitler Skull, 1933

ERWIN BLUMENFELD

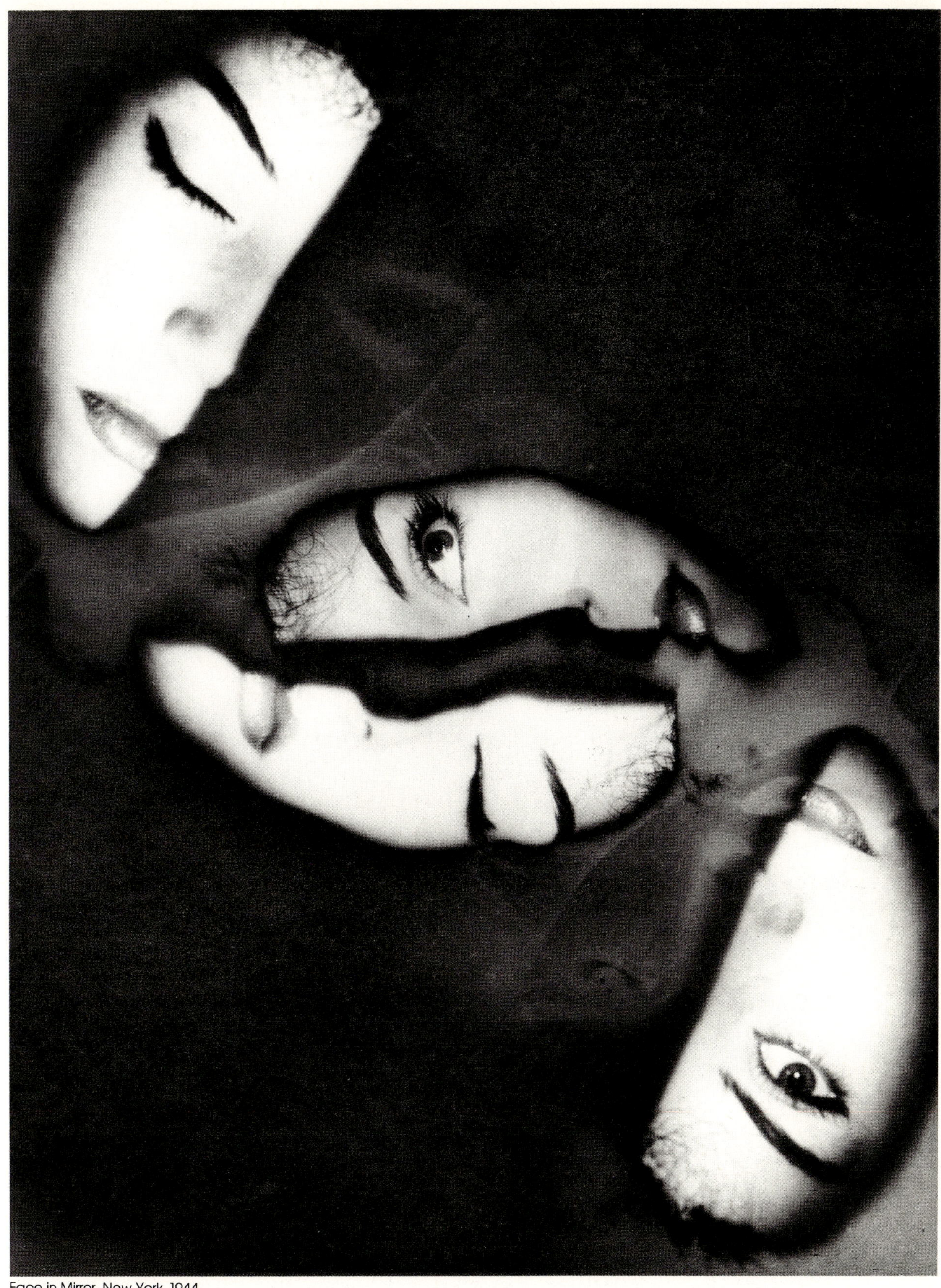

Face in Mirror, New York, 1944

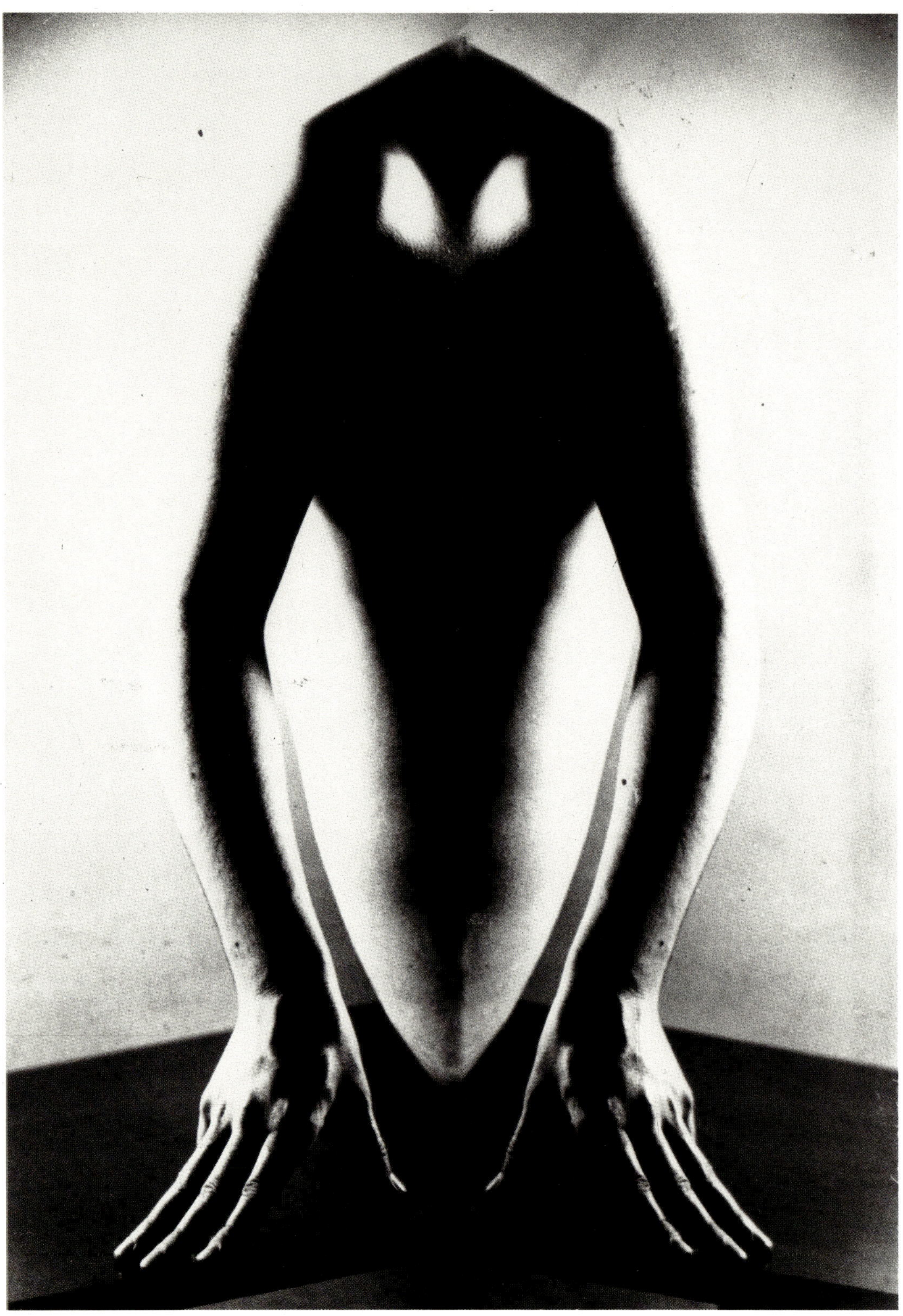

Mother-in-Law

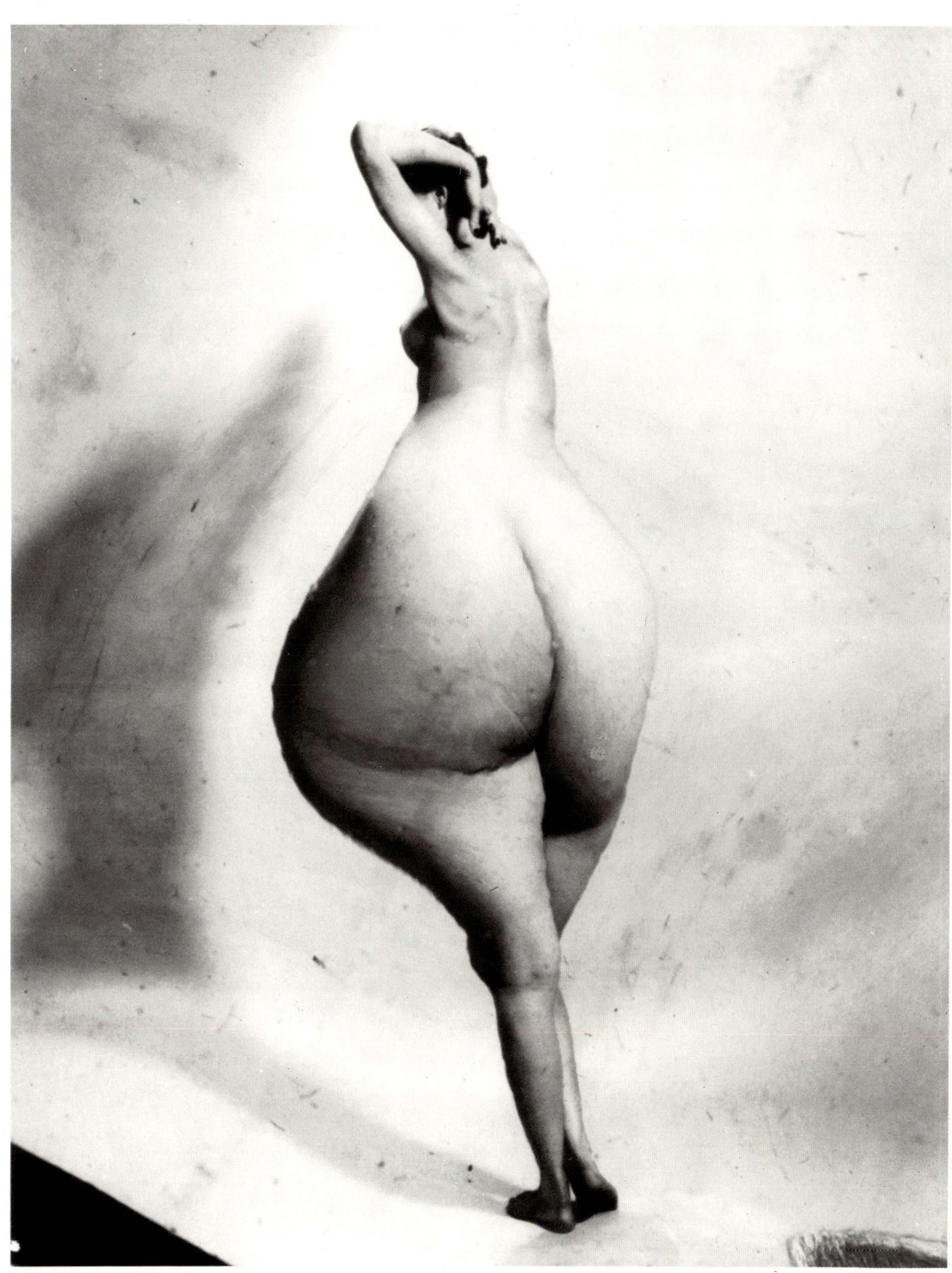

From "Human Sculpture" Series

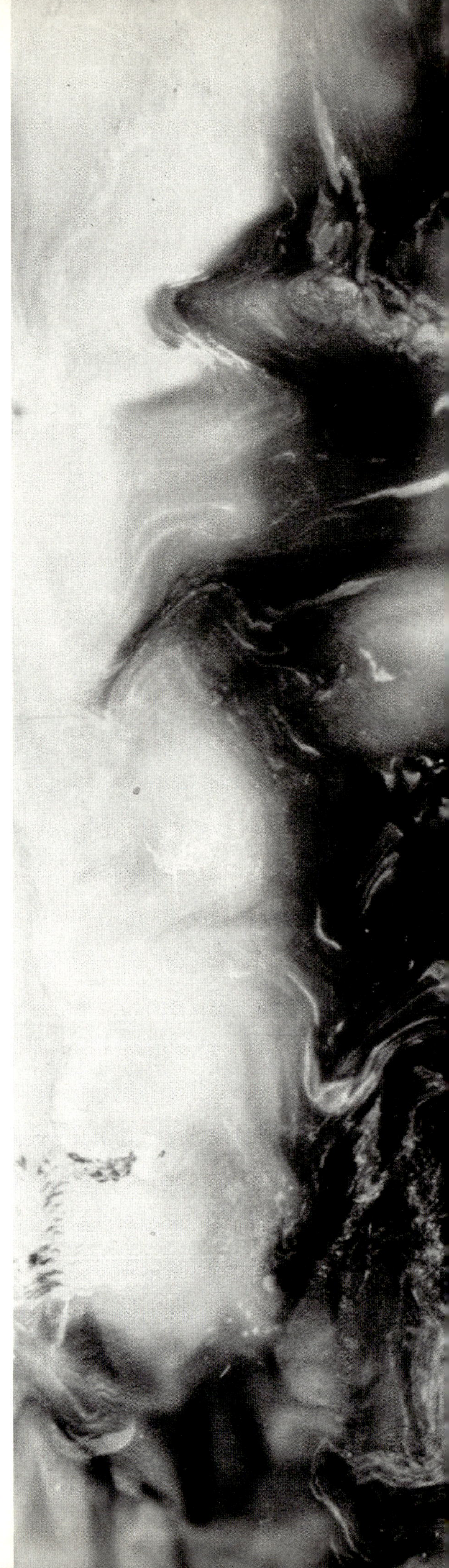

Phototransformation, 11 / 7 / 73

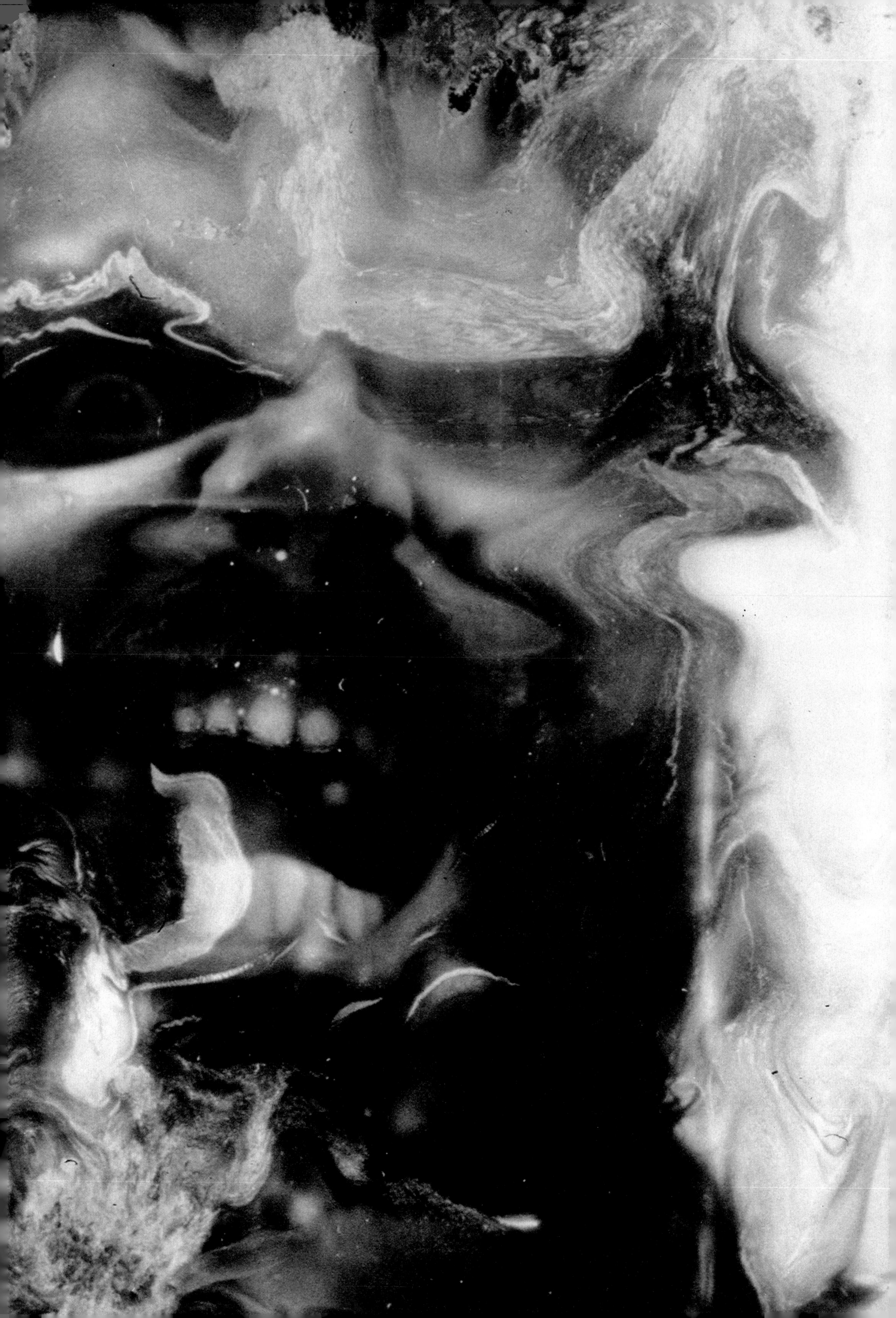

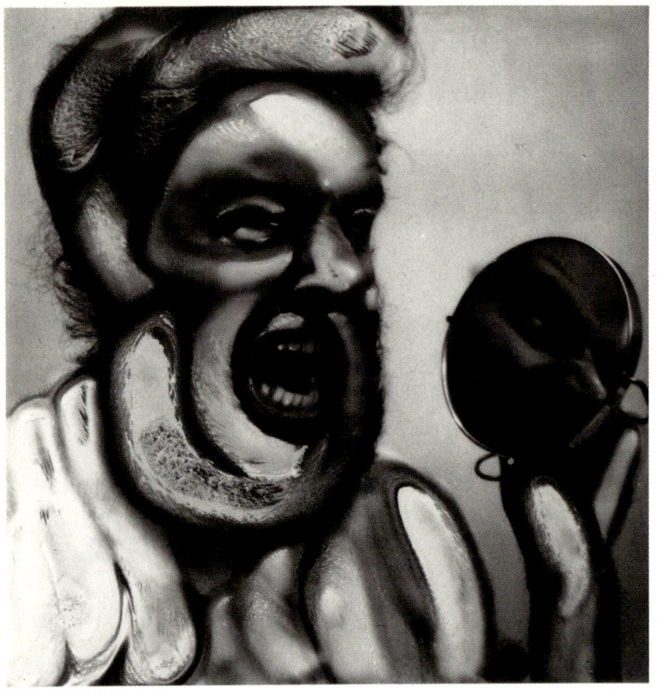

Phototransformation, 11/12/73

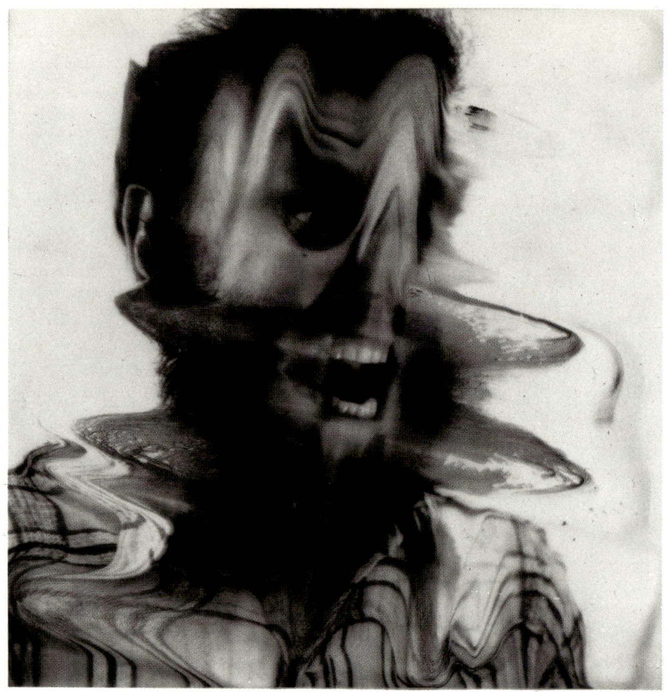

Phototransformation, 1973

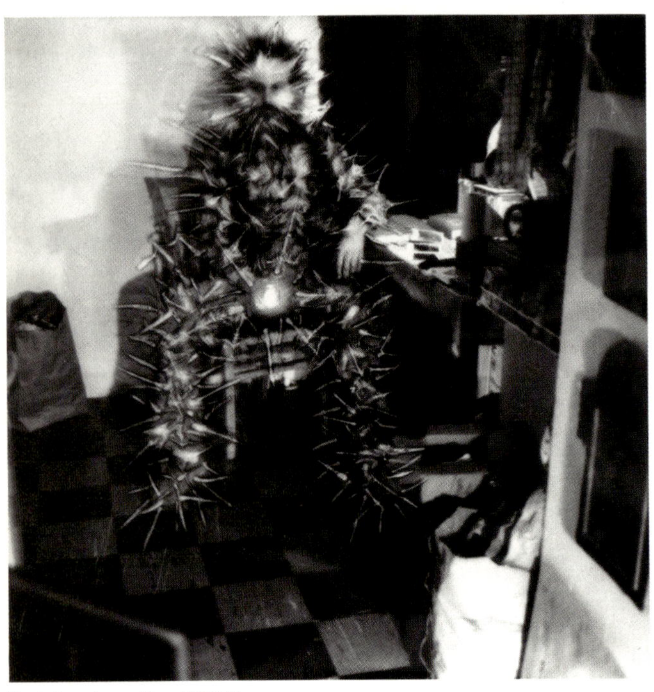

Phototransformation, 1973/4

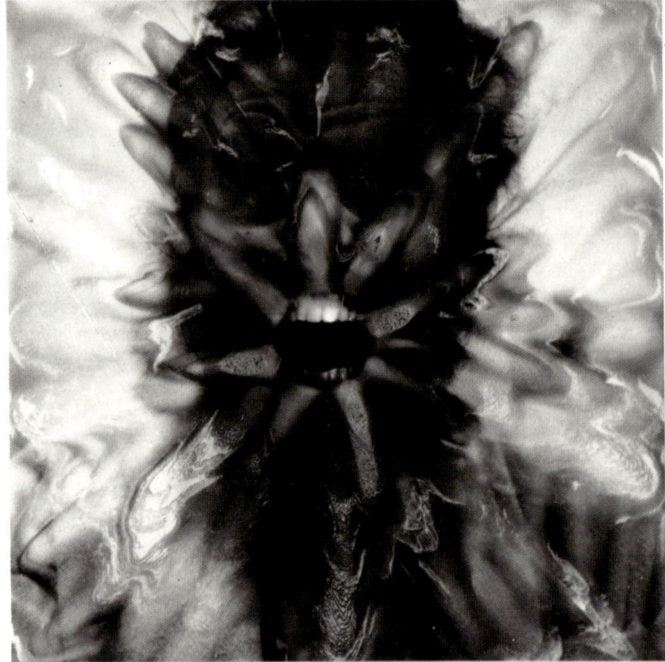

Phototransformation, 10/28/73

LUCAS SAMARAS

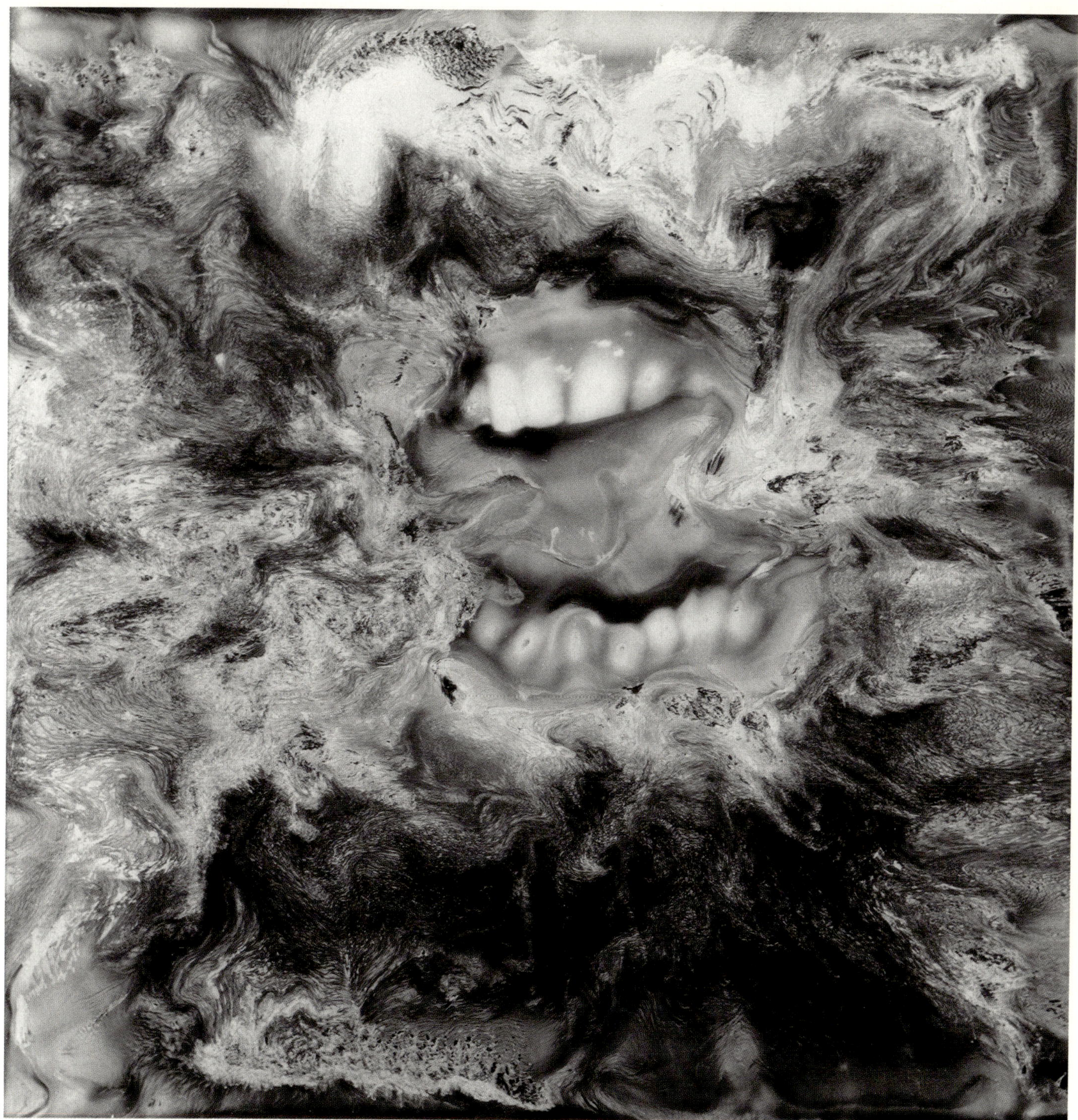

Phototransformation, 11/3/73

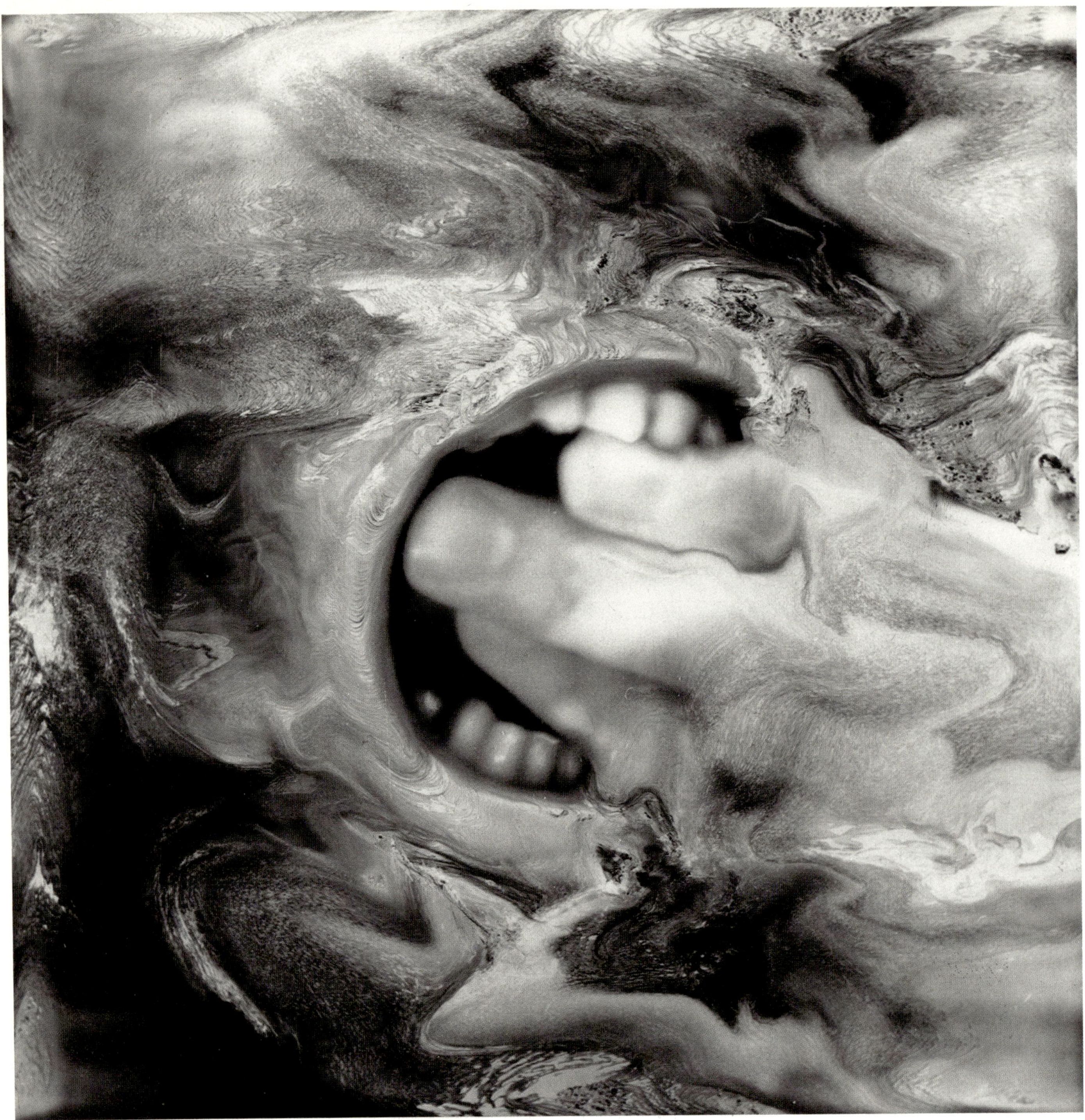

Phototransformation, 11/3/73

LUCAS SAMARAS

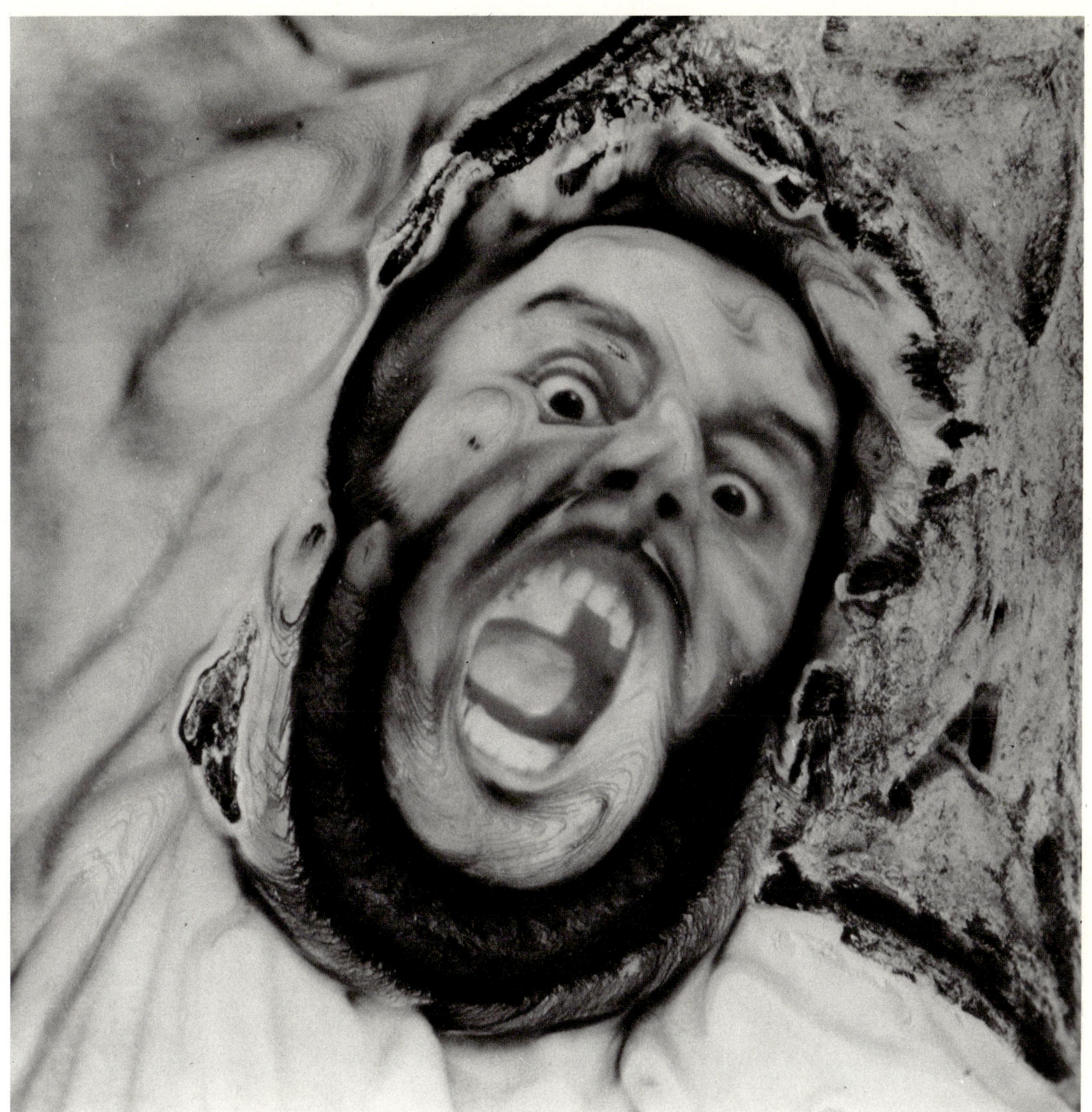

Phototransformation, 11/13/73

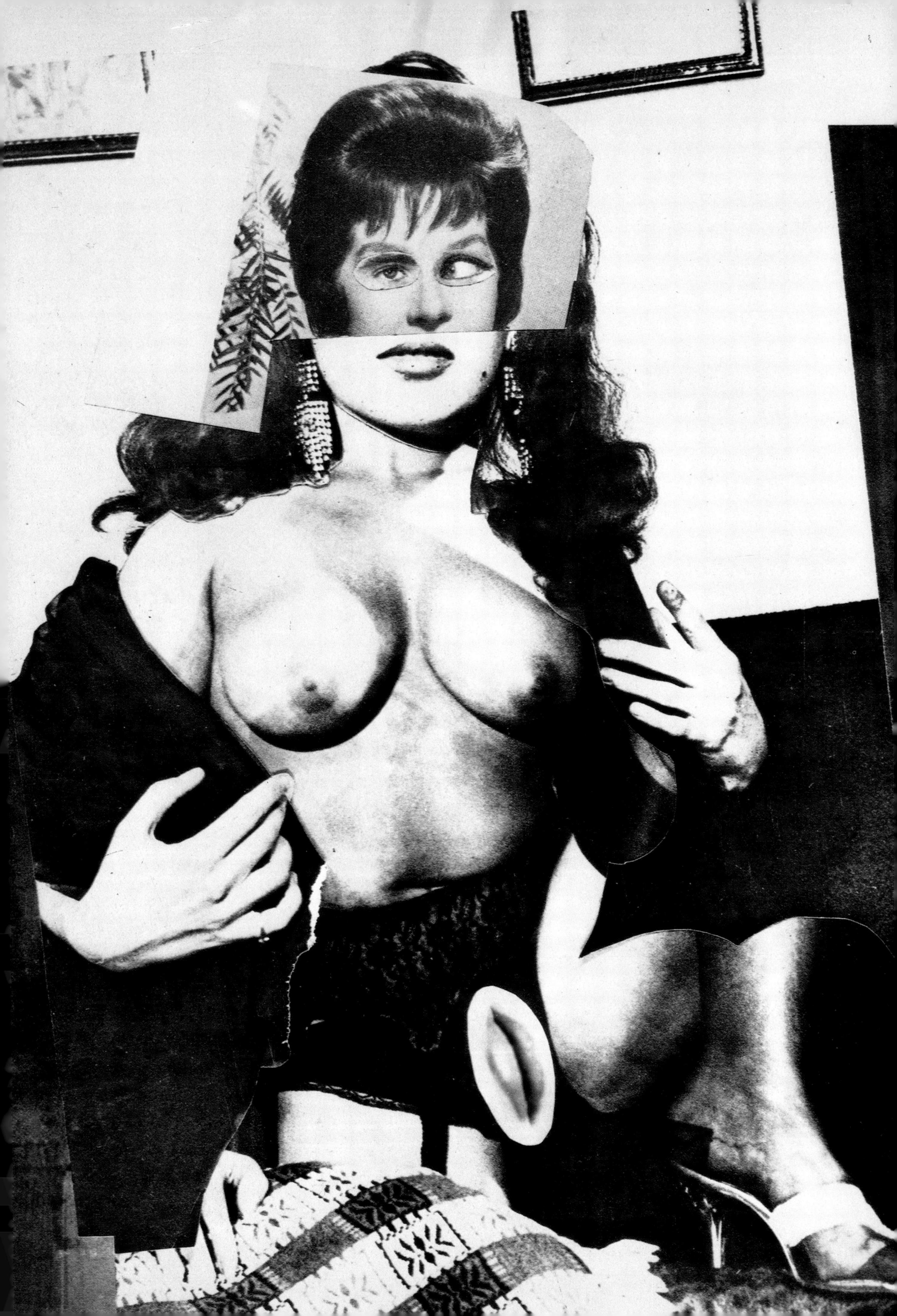

Altered Odalisque, 1963

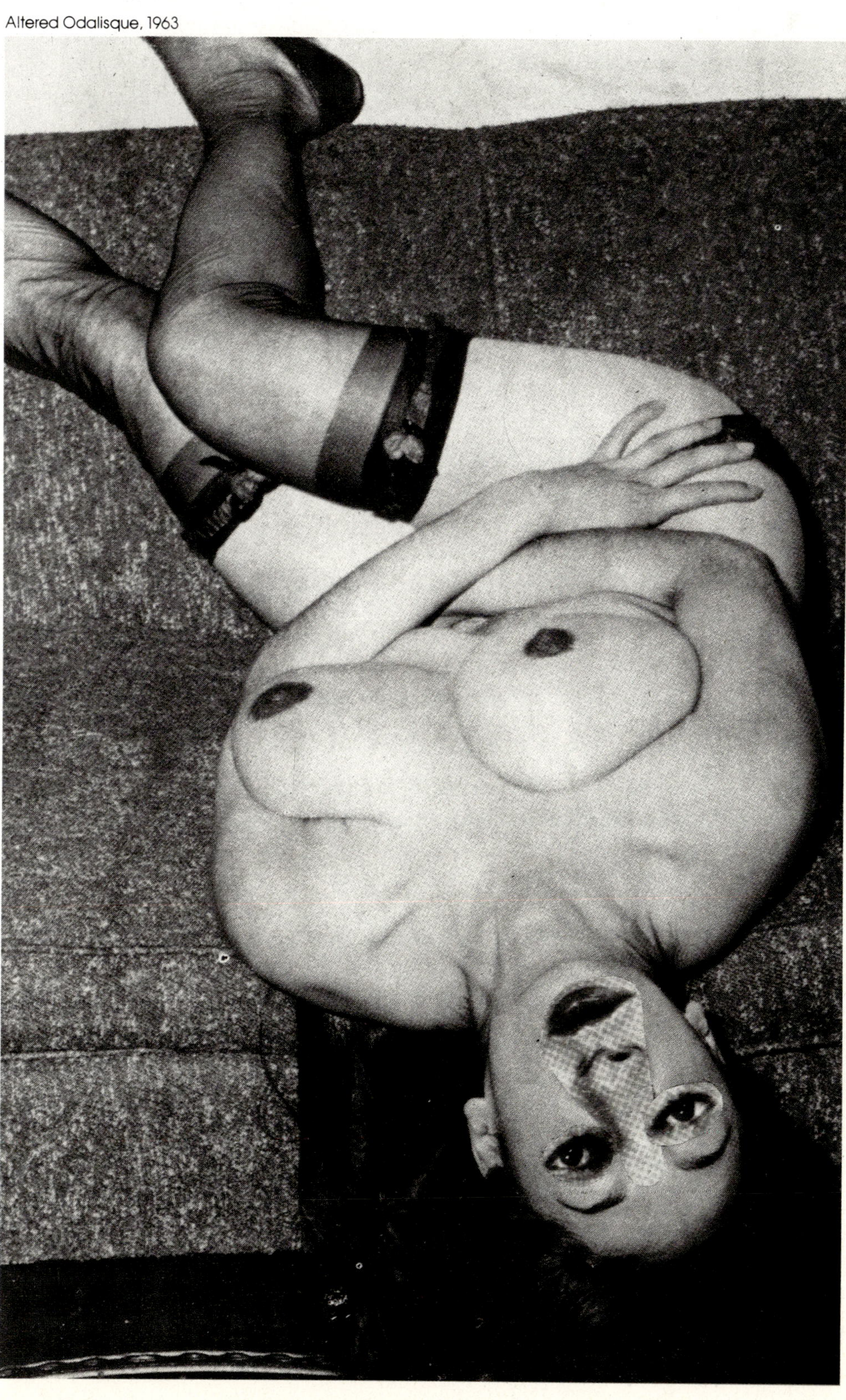

Portrait of My Wife, 1964

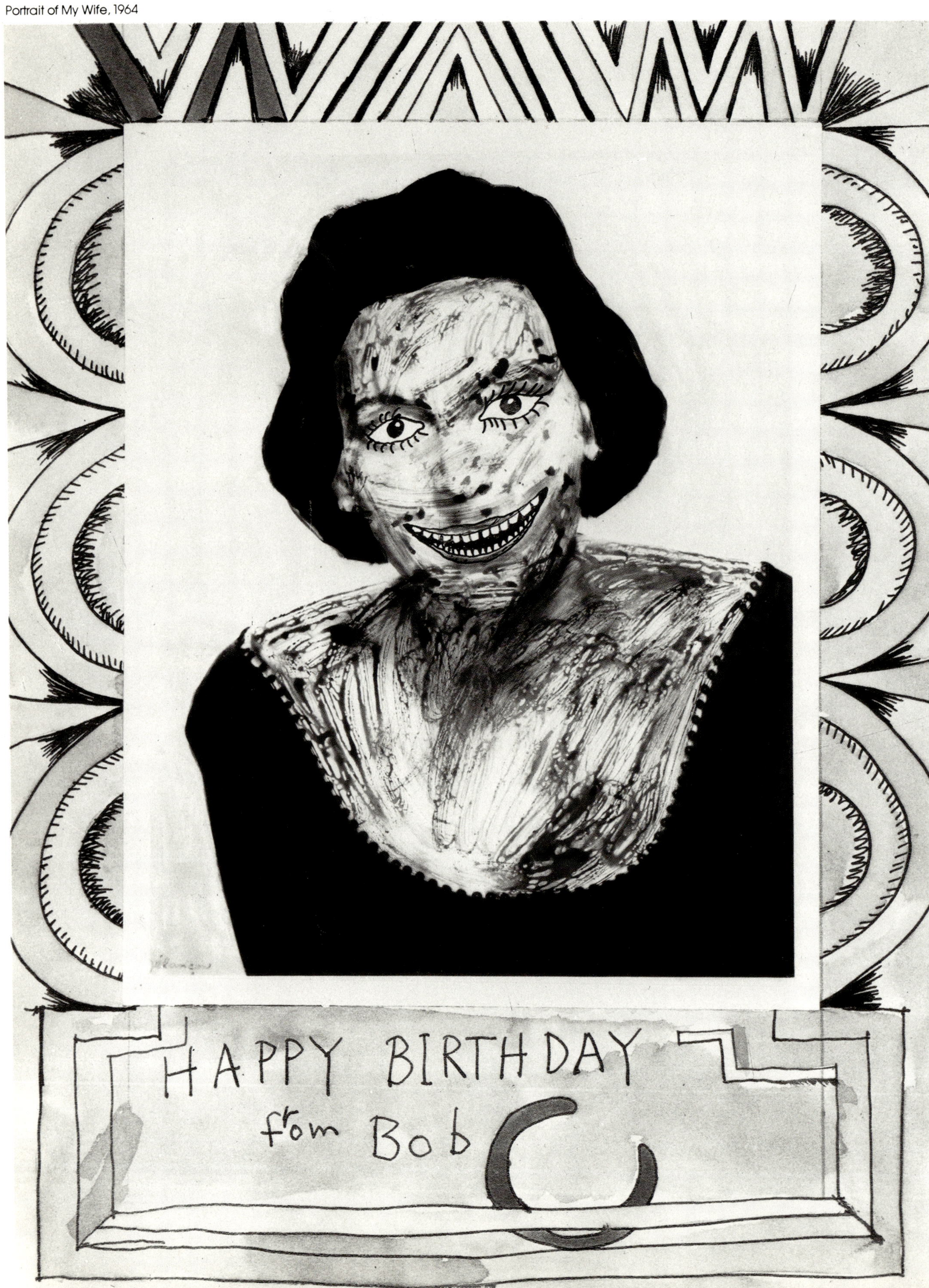

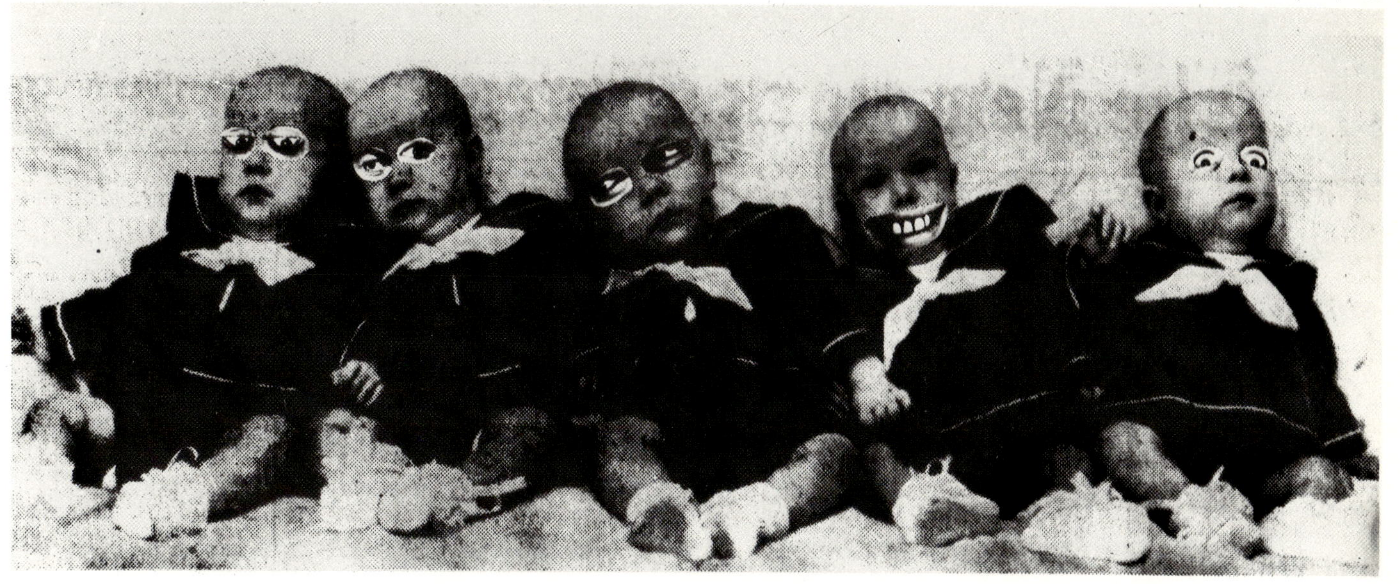

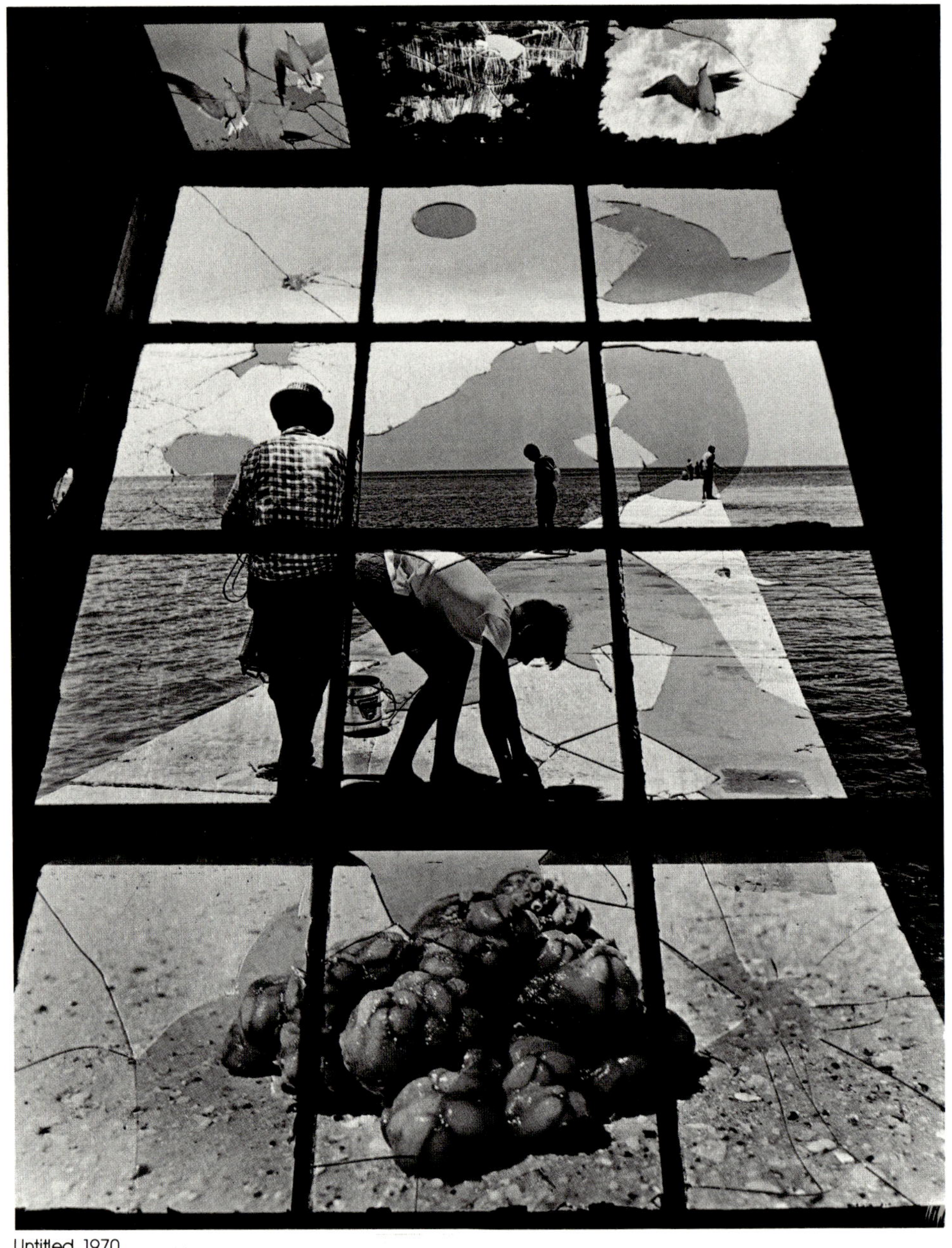

Untitled, 1970.

Self-portrait, 19

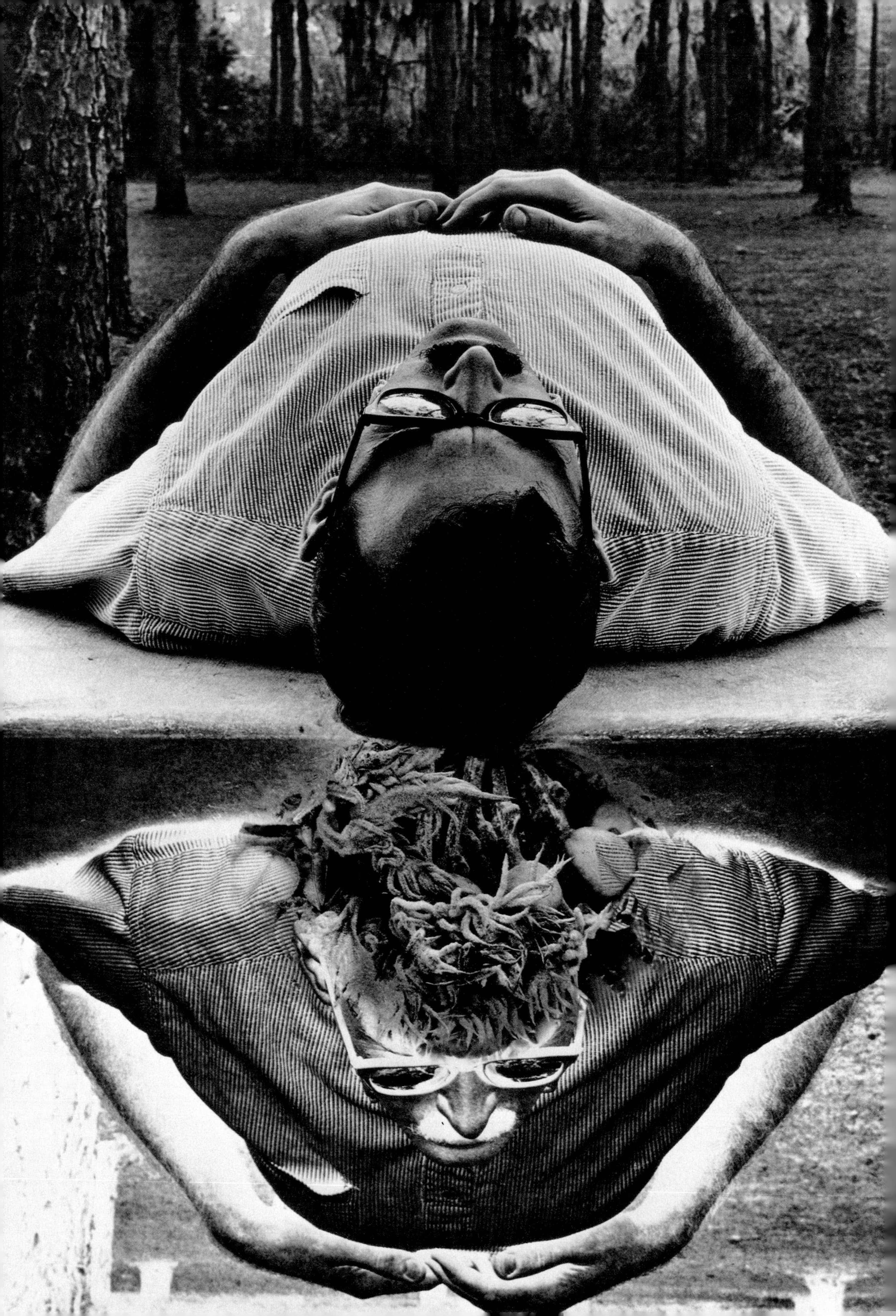

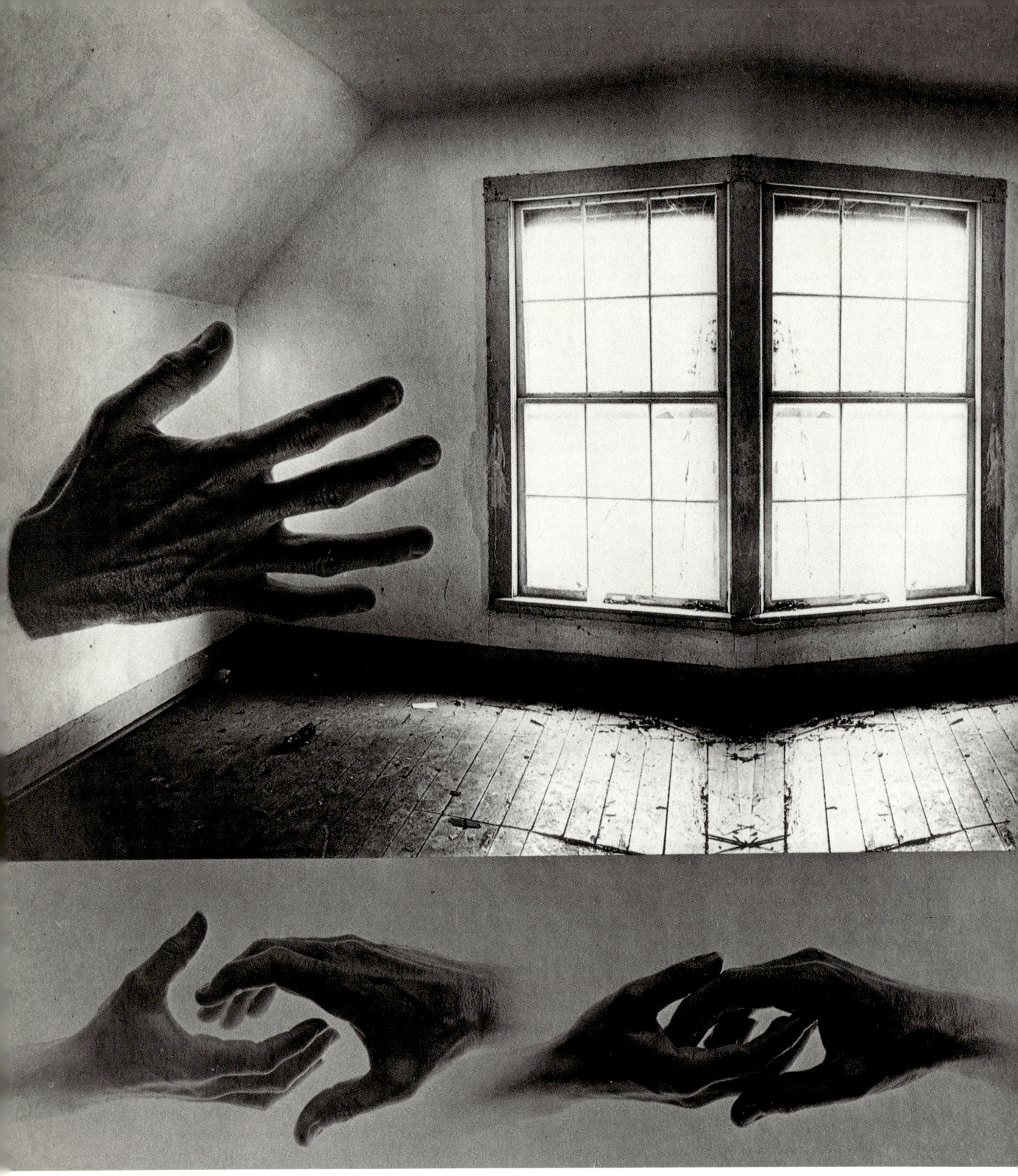

Questioning Moment, 1971

186

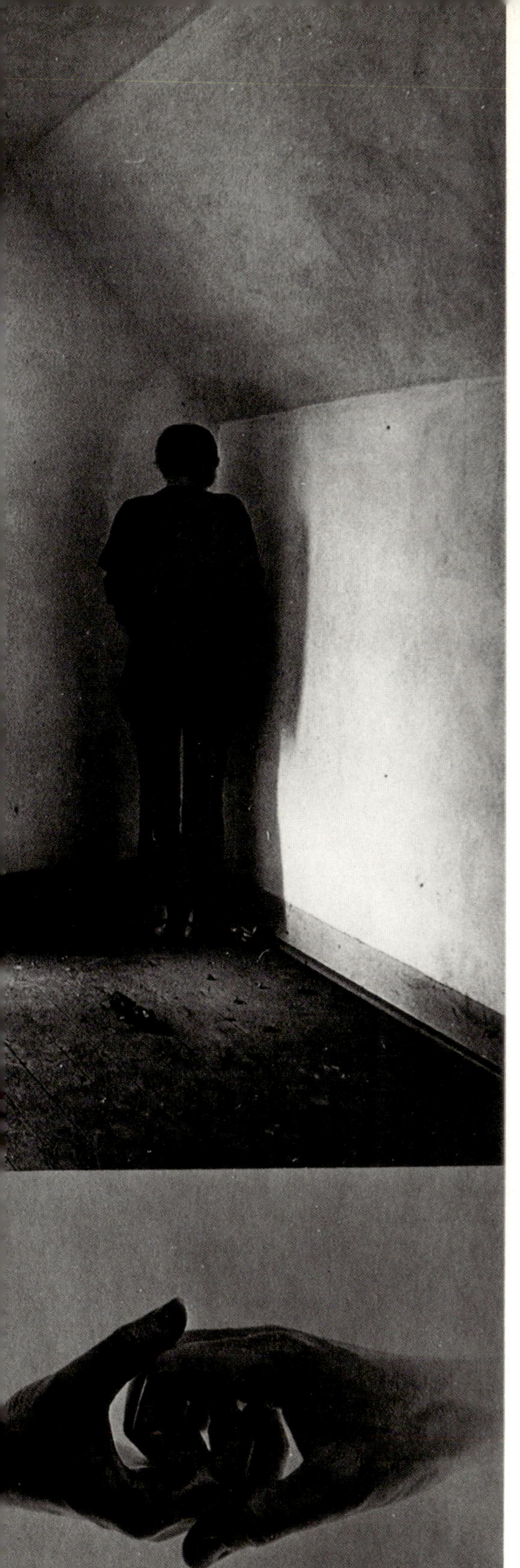

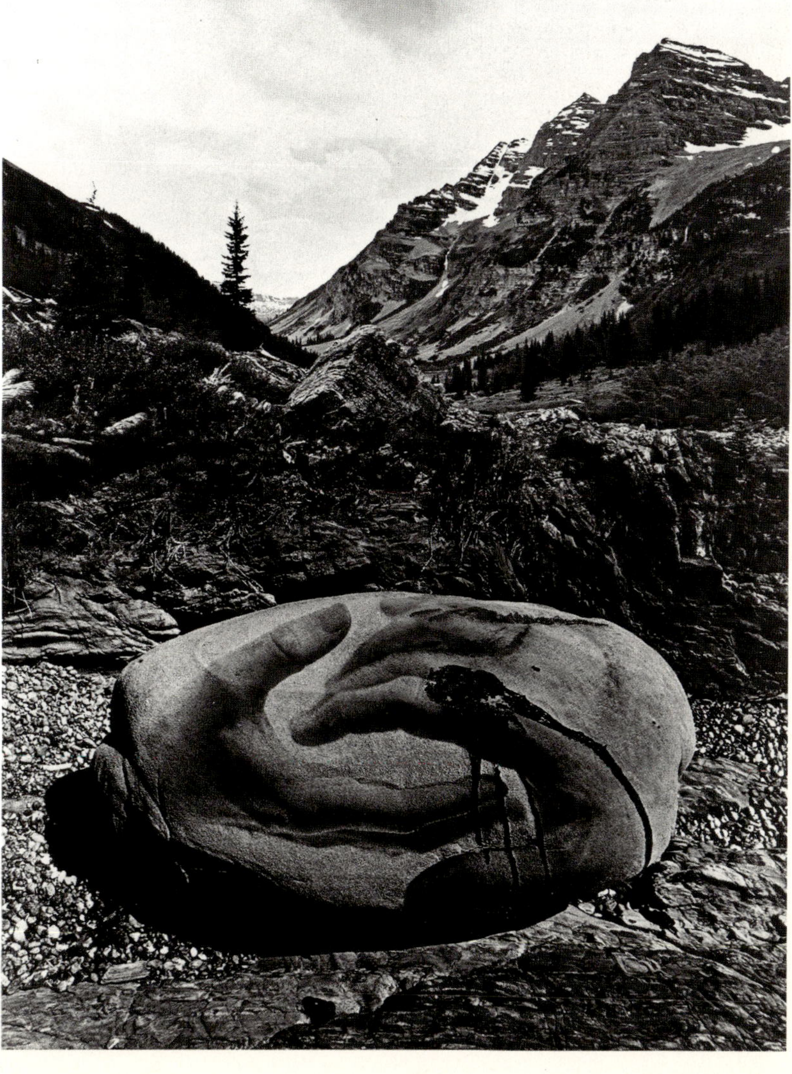

Untitled, 1970

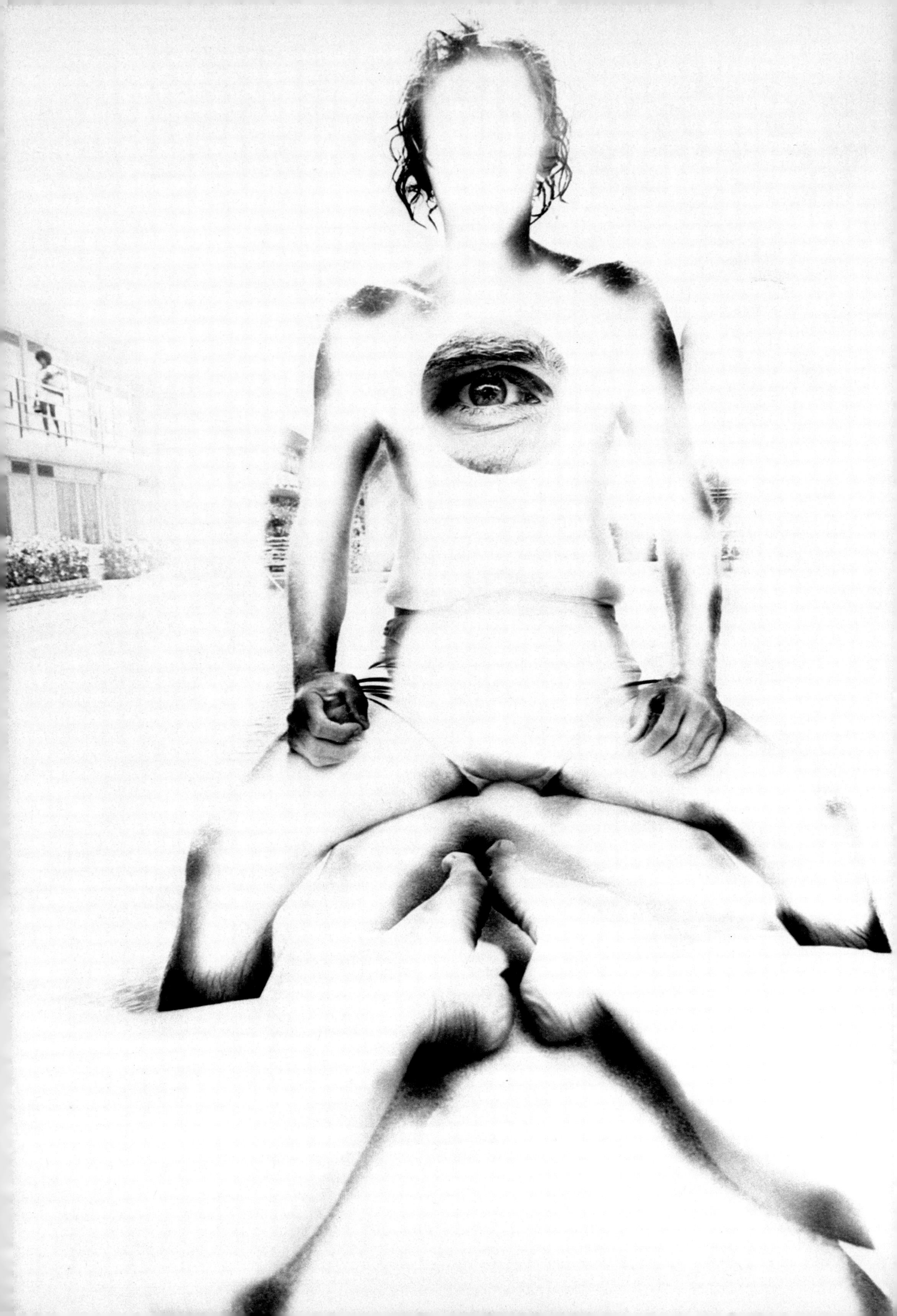

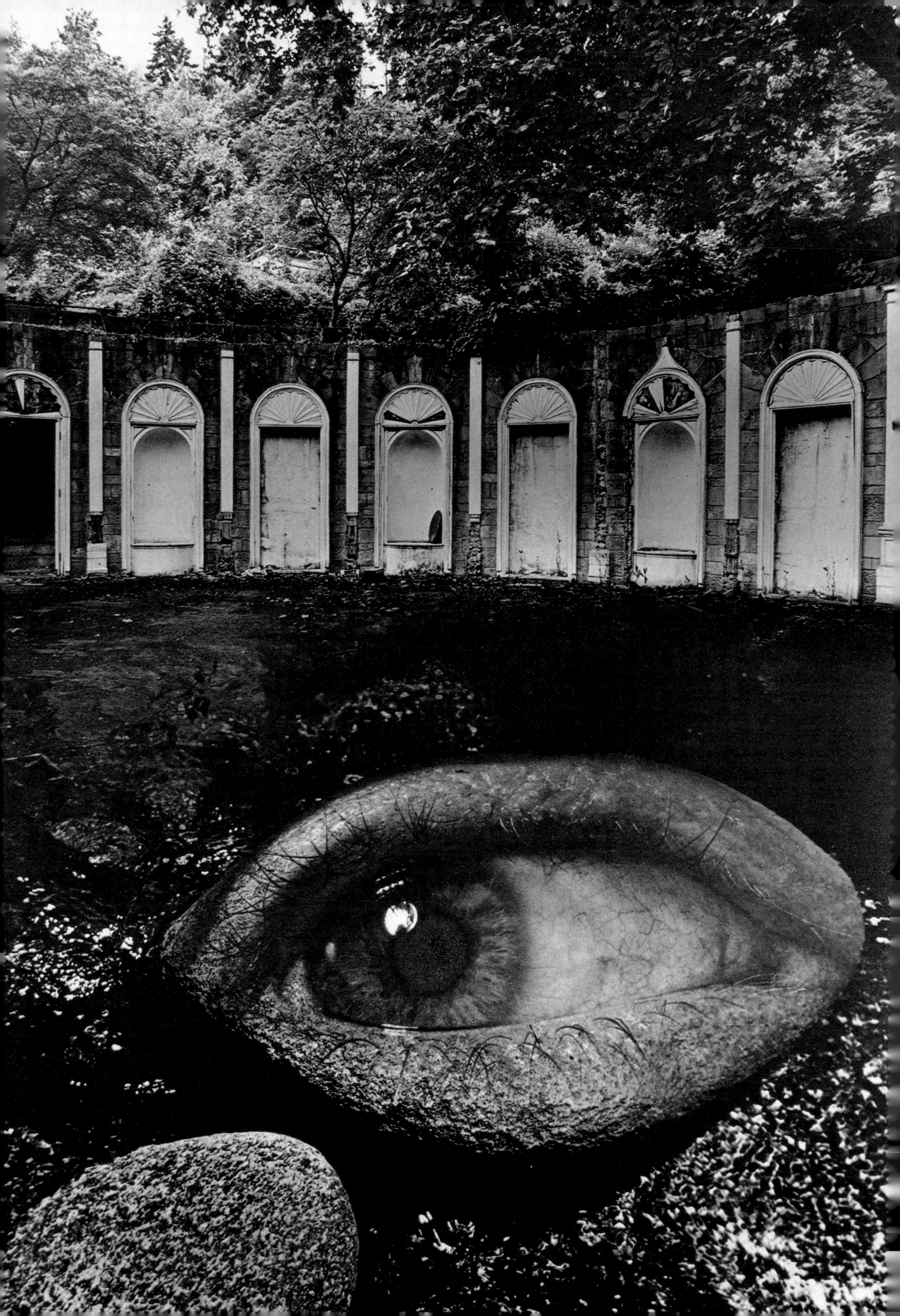

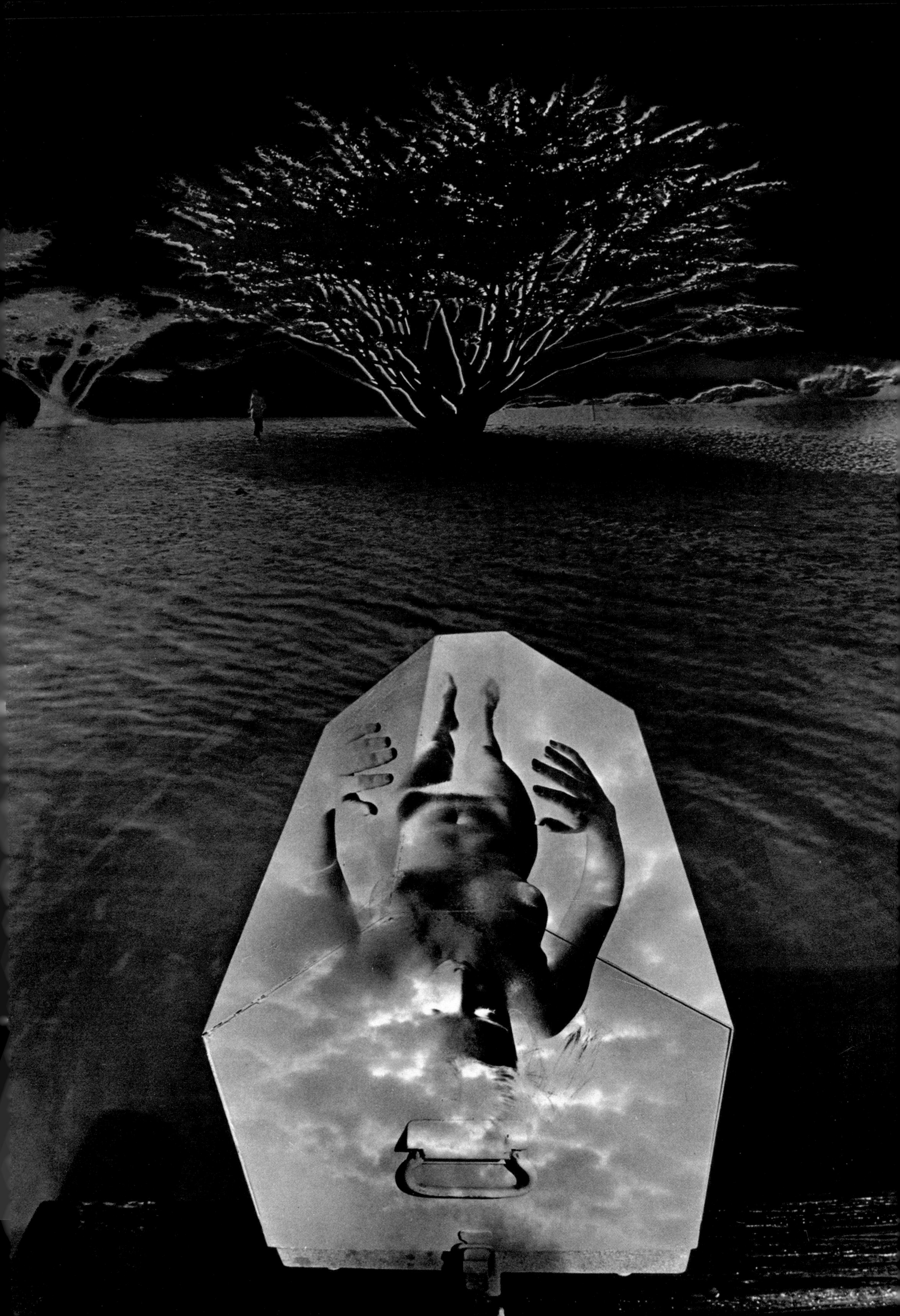

JERRY N. UELSMANN

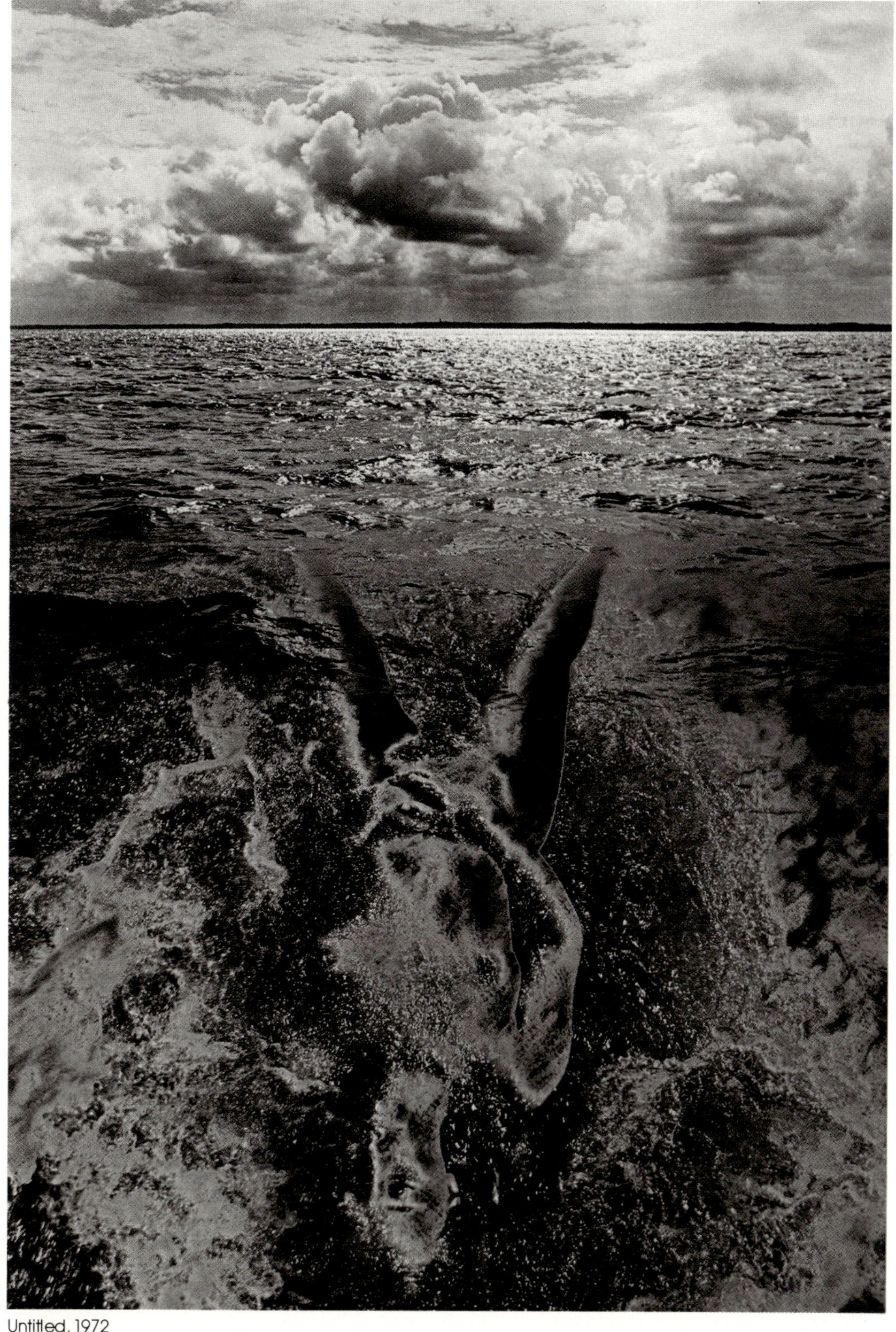

Untitled, 1972

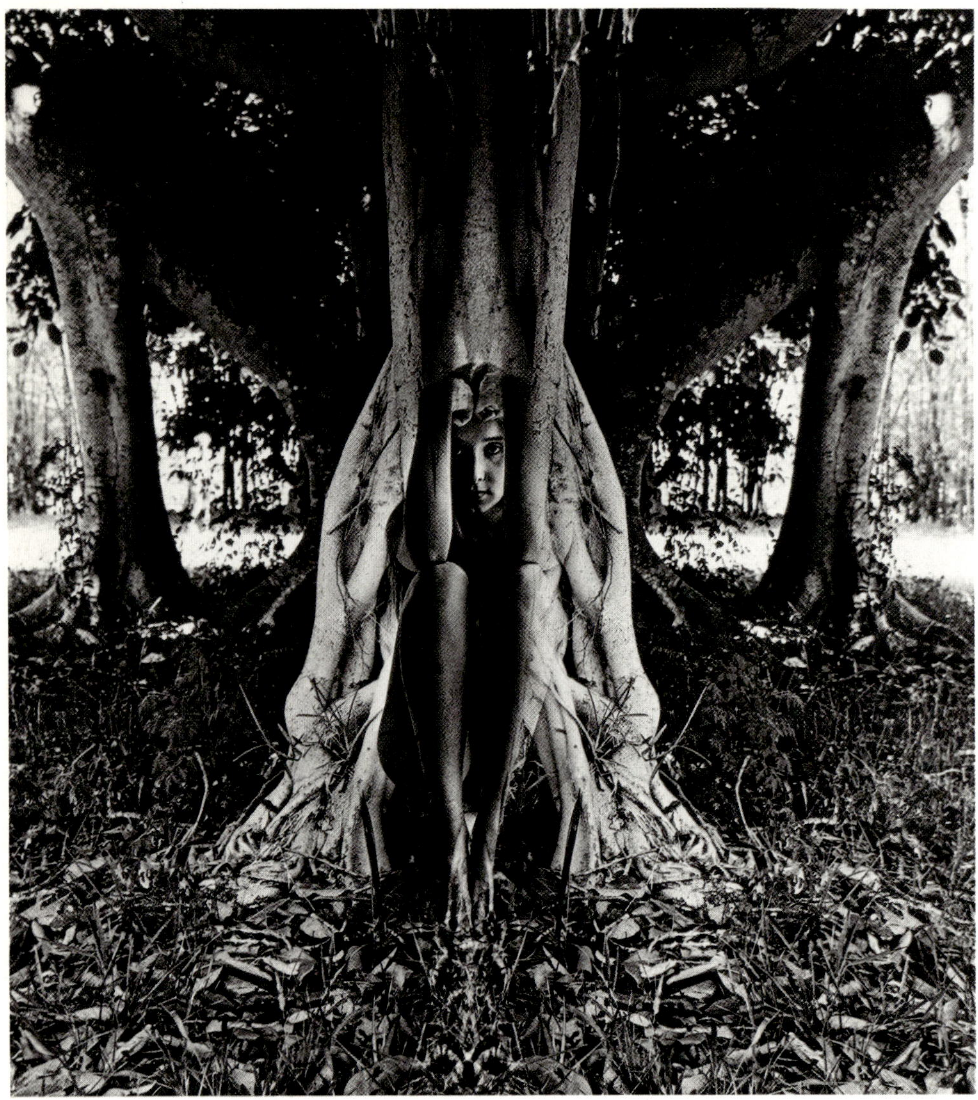

Untitled, 1972

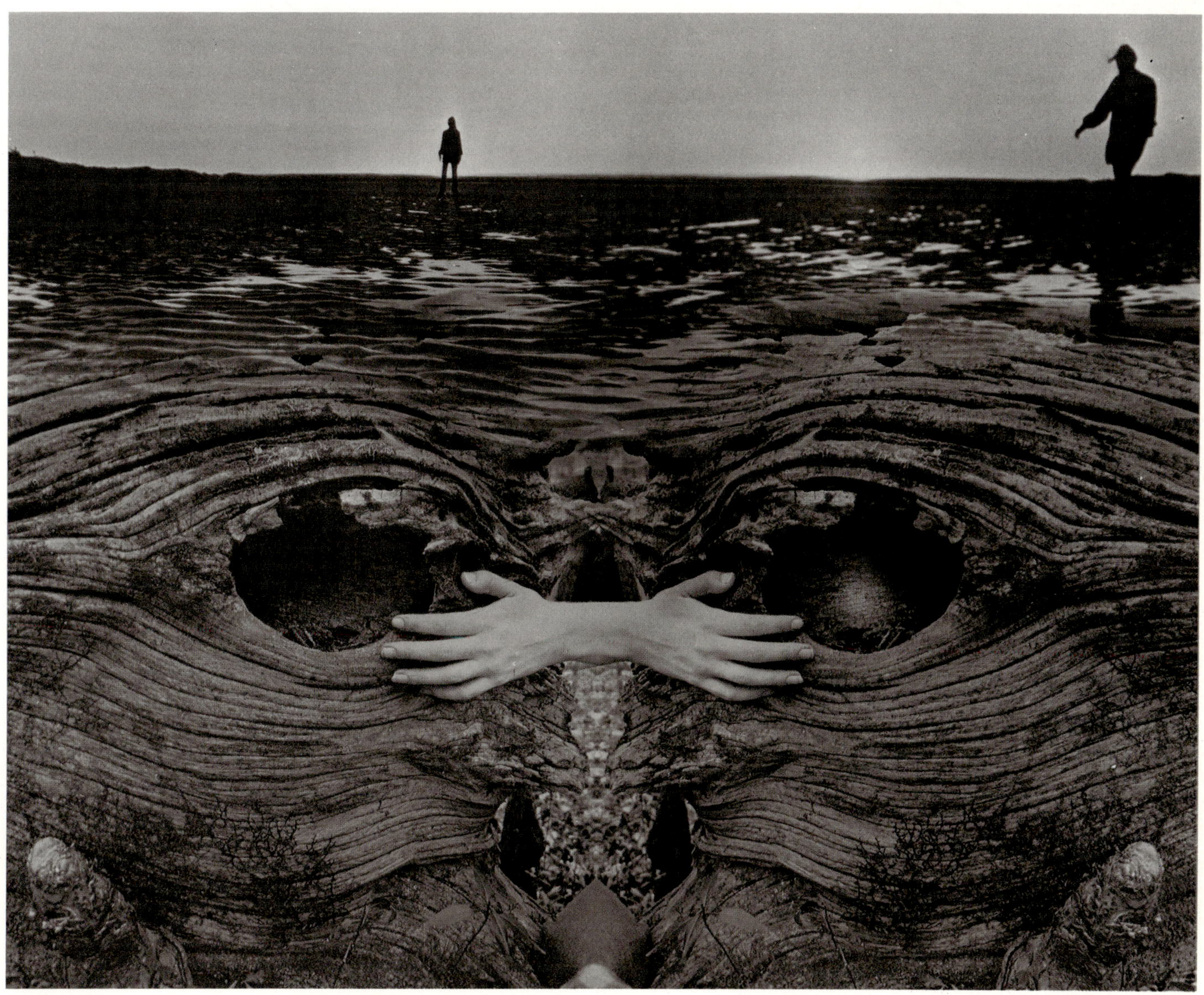

Untitled, 1974

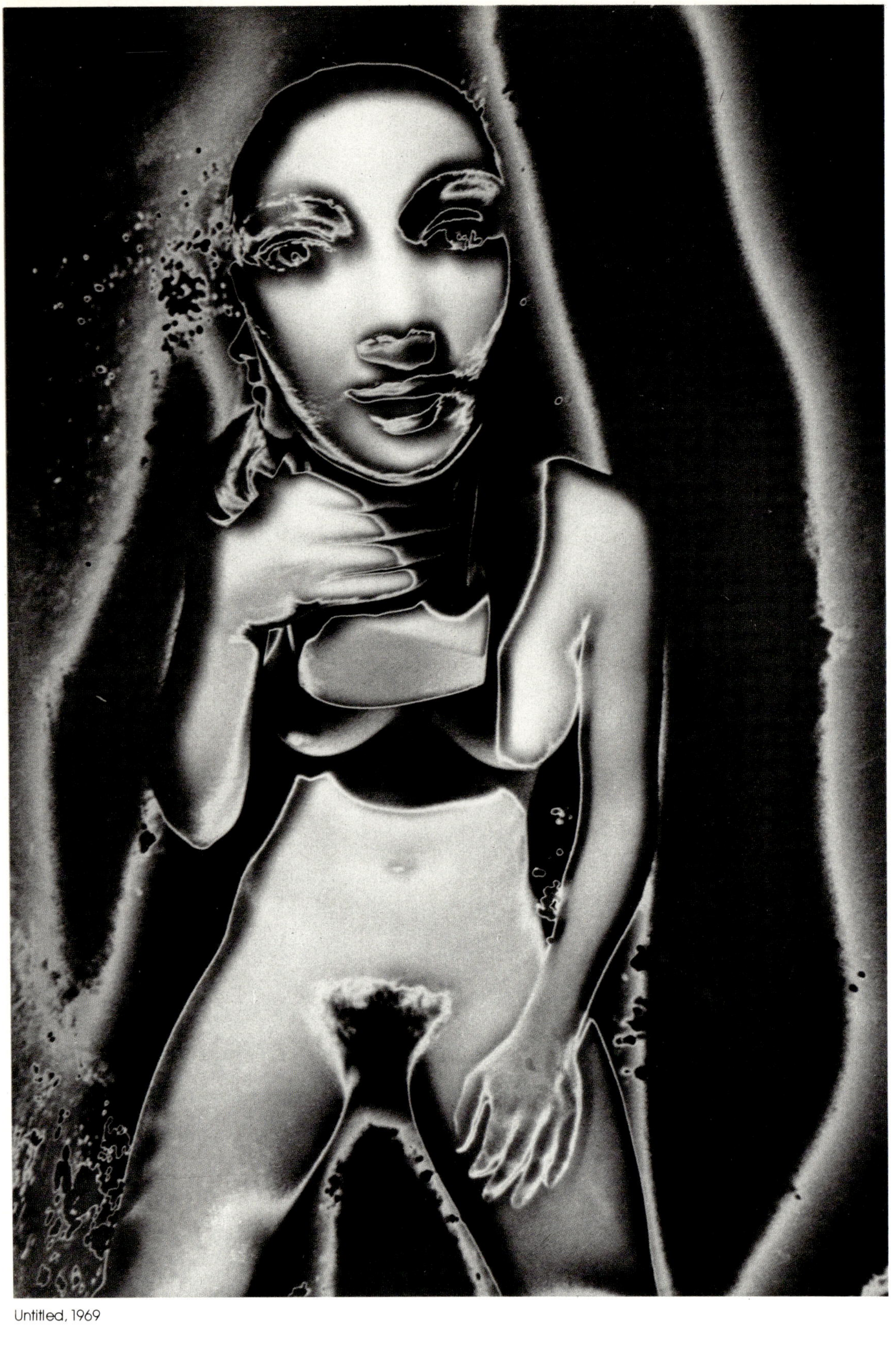

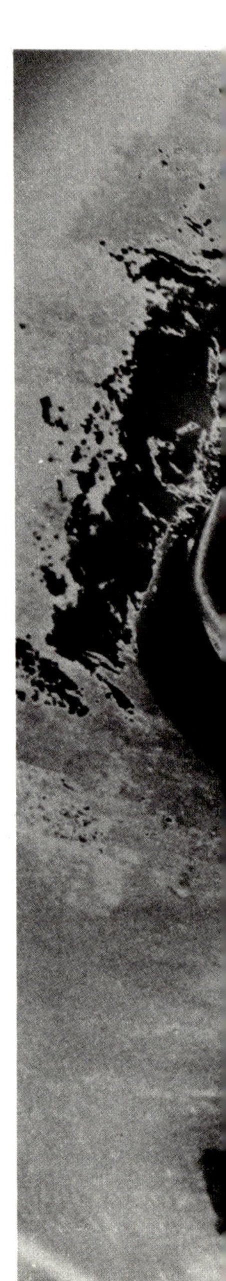

Untitled, 1969

Untitled, 1969

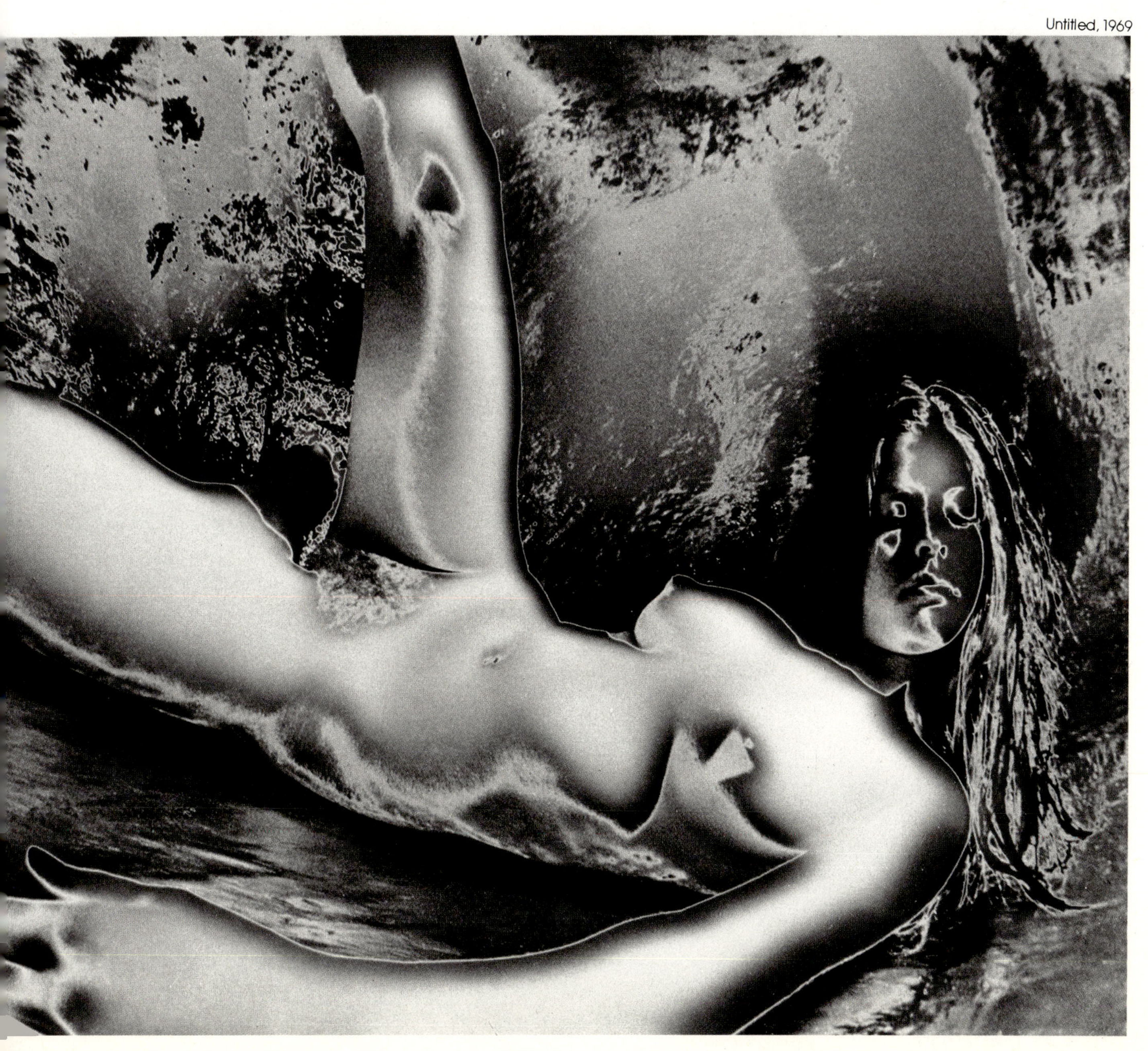

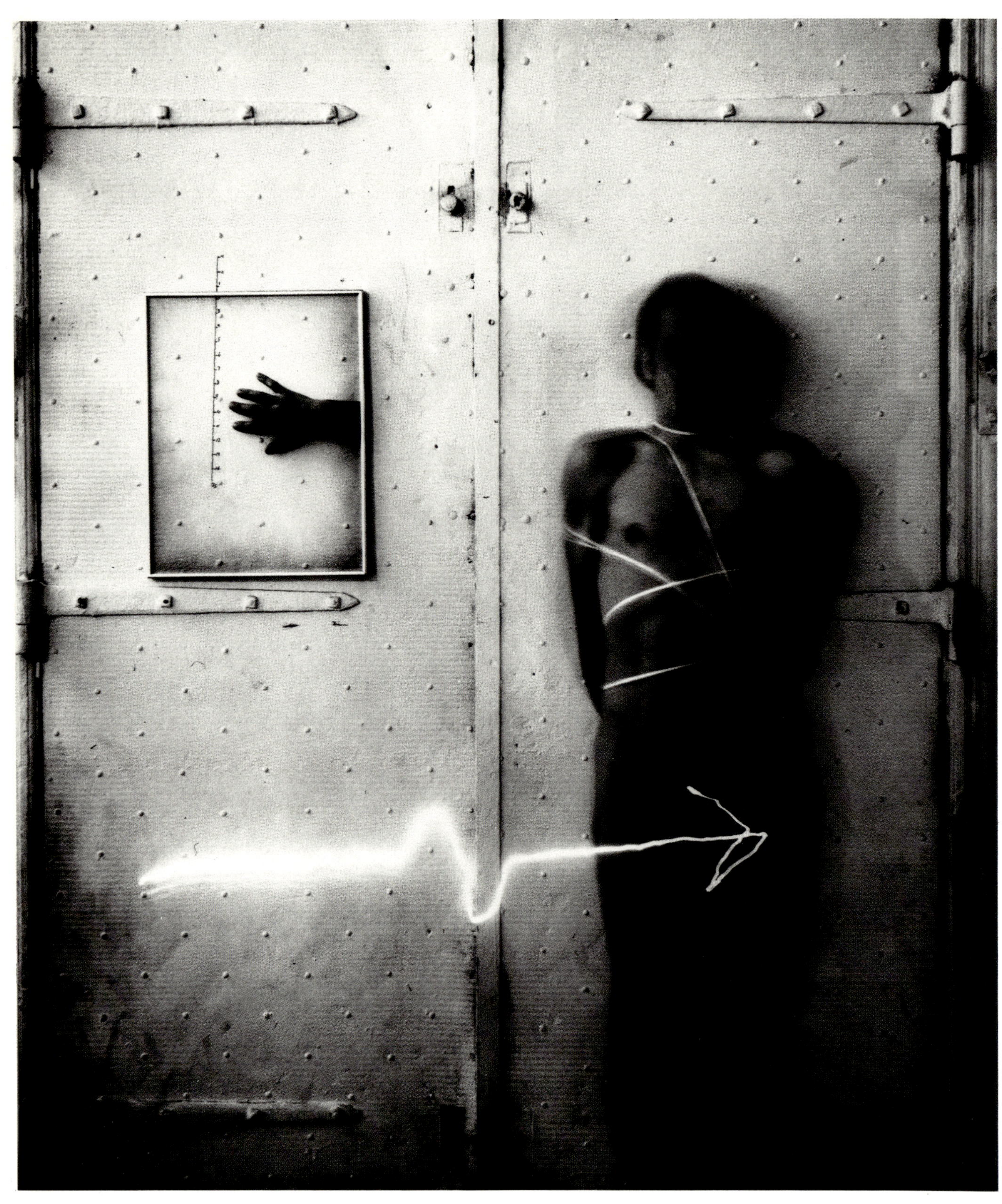
A Self-Defeating Gesture

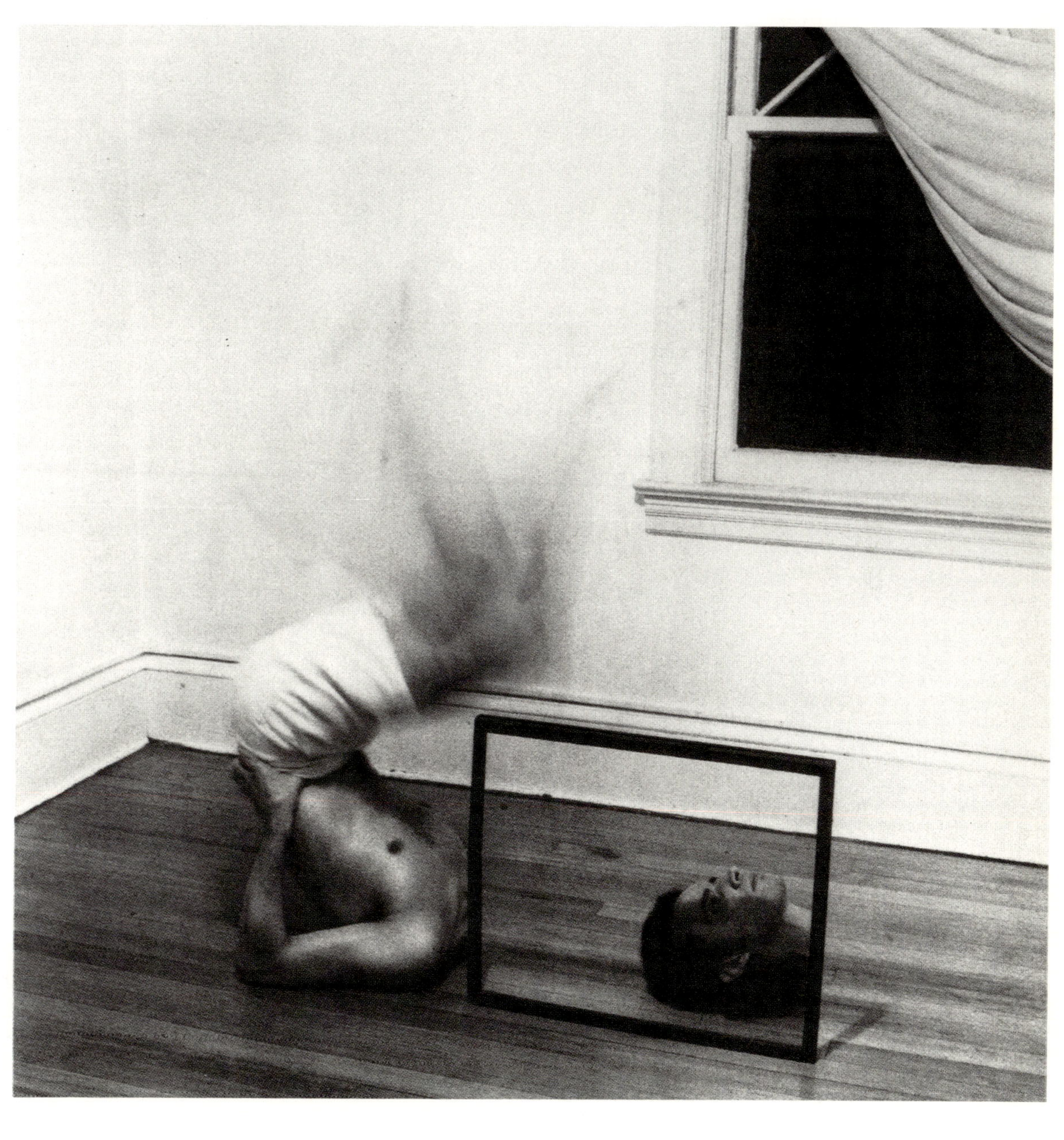

cuarto que guarda recuerdos

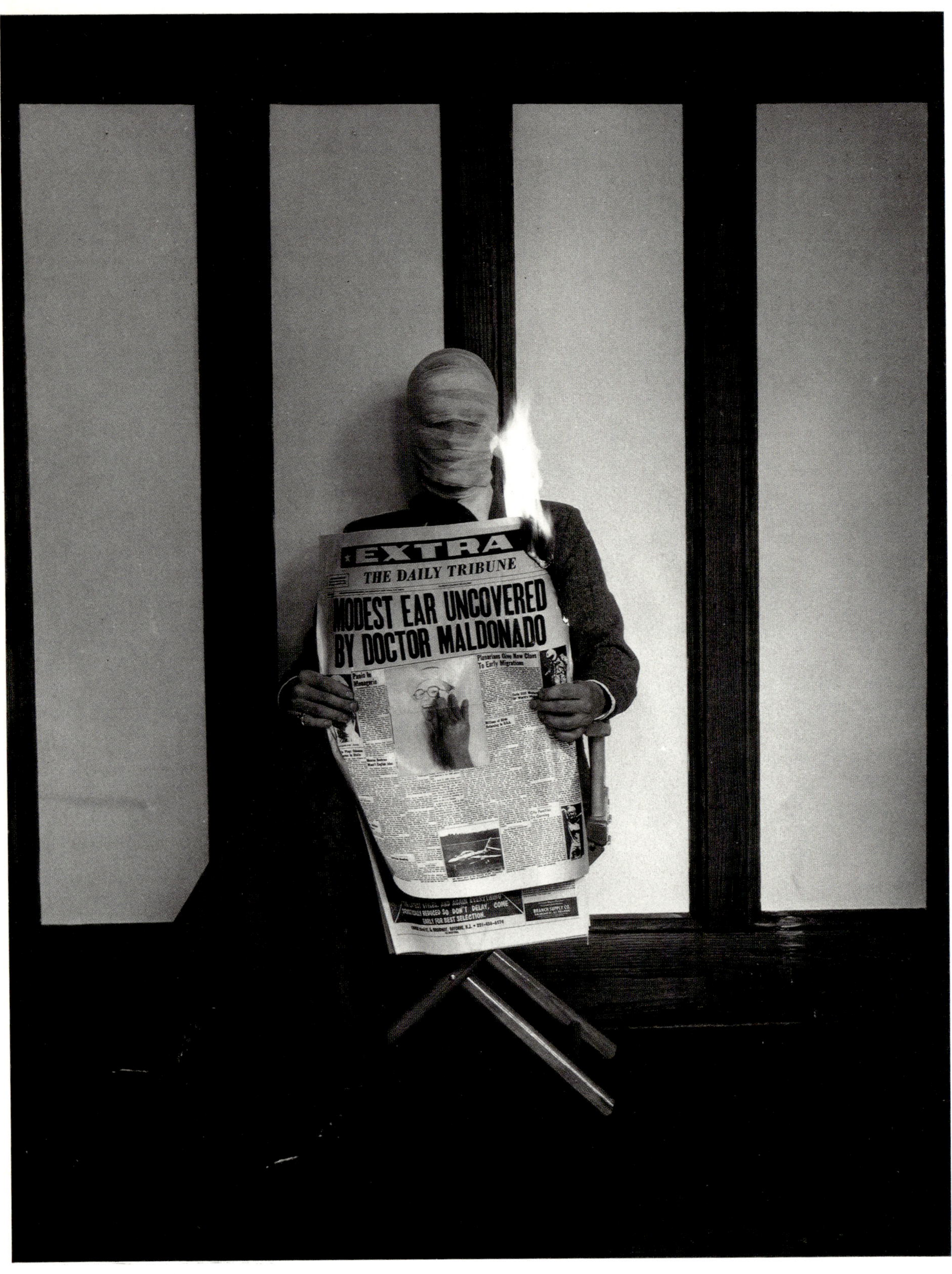

ADÁL

Paquete numero 825

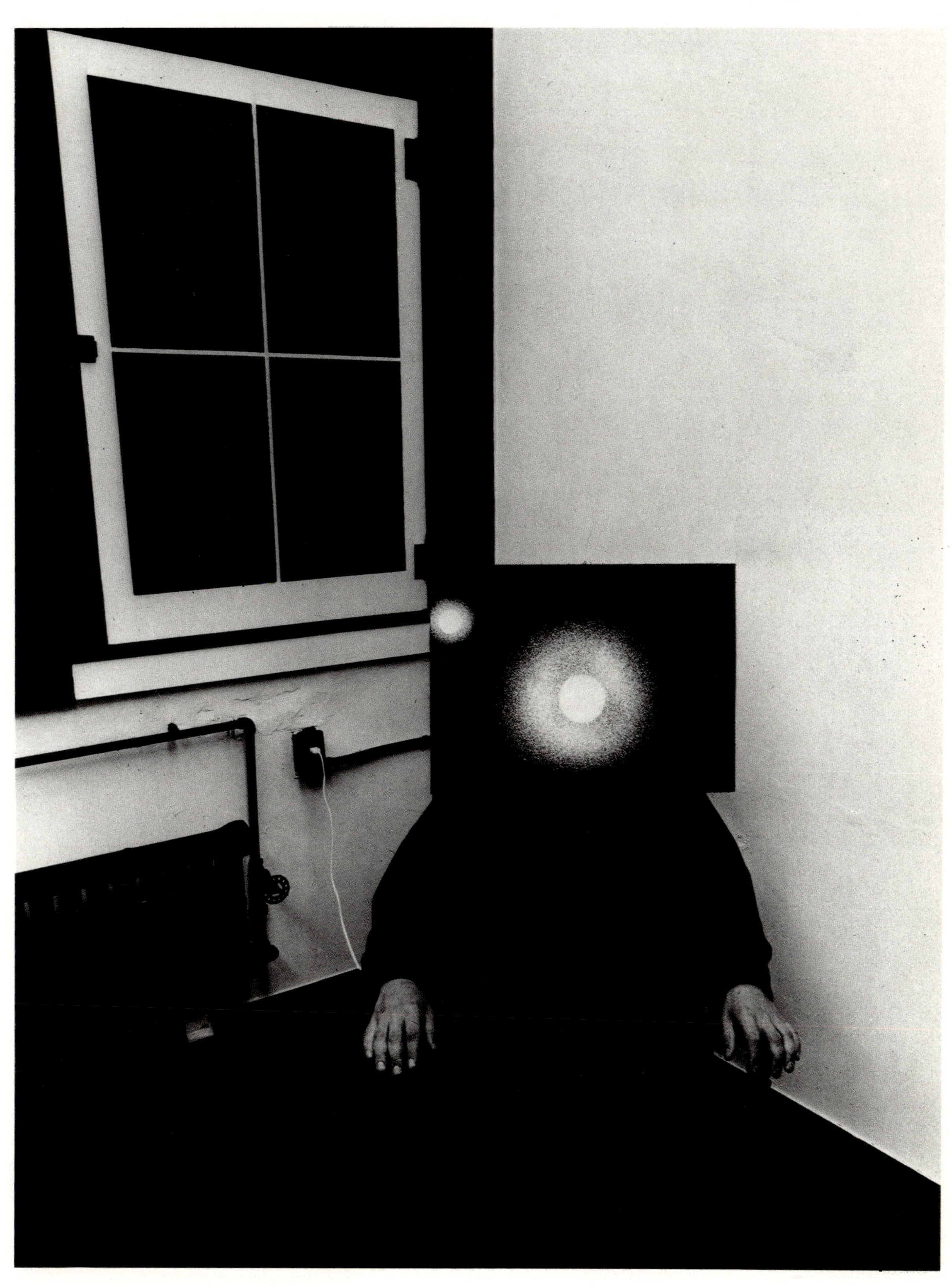

A Threat and a Promise

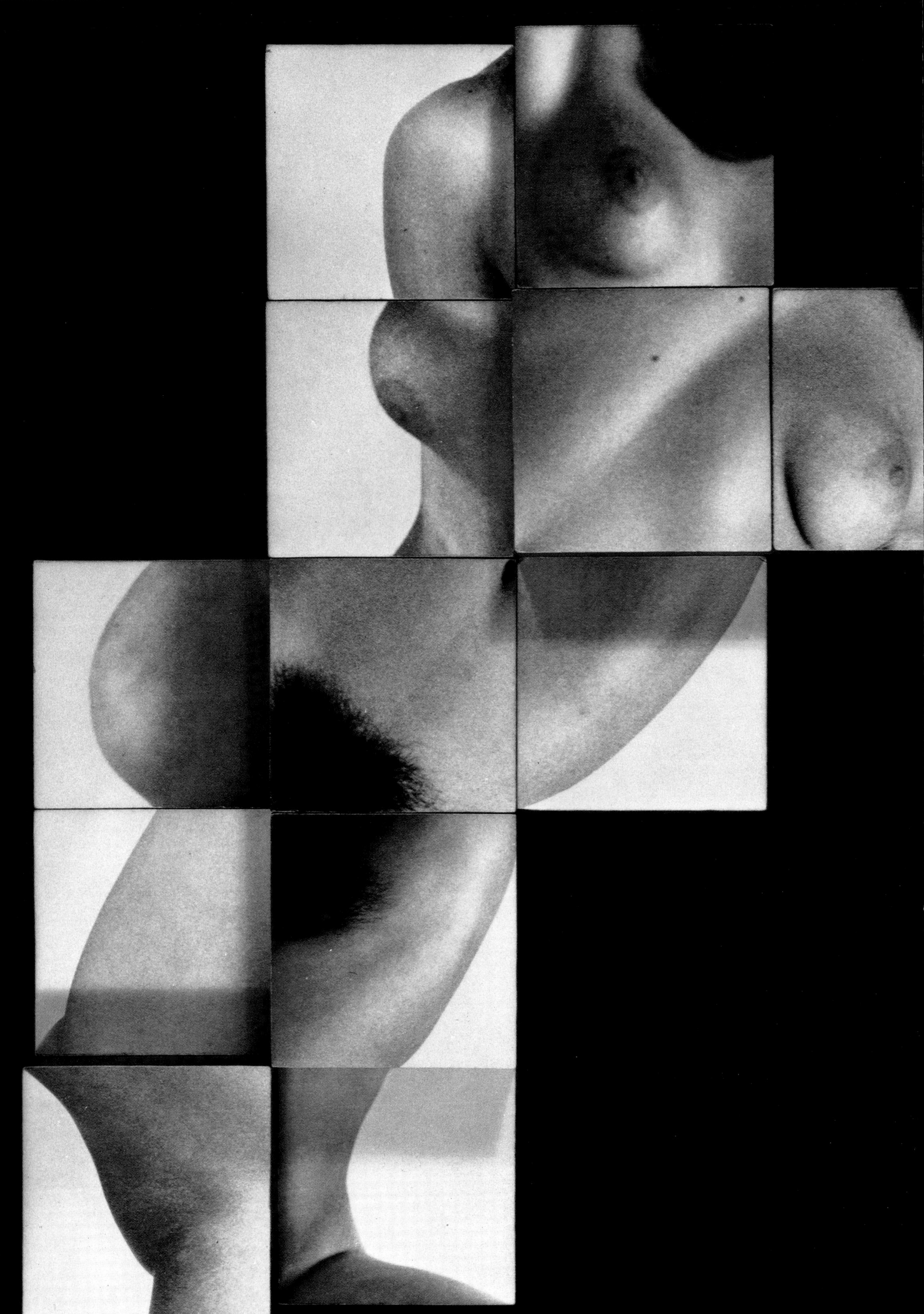

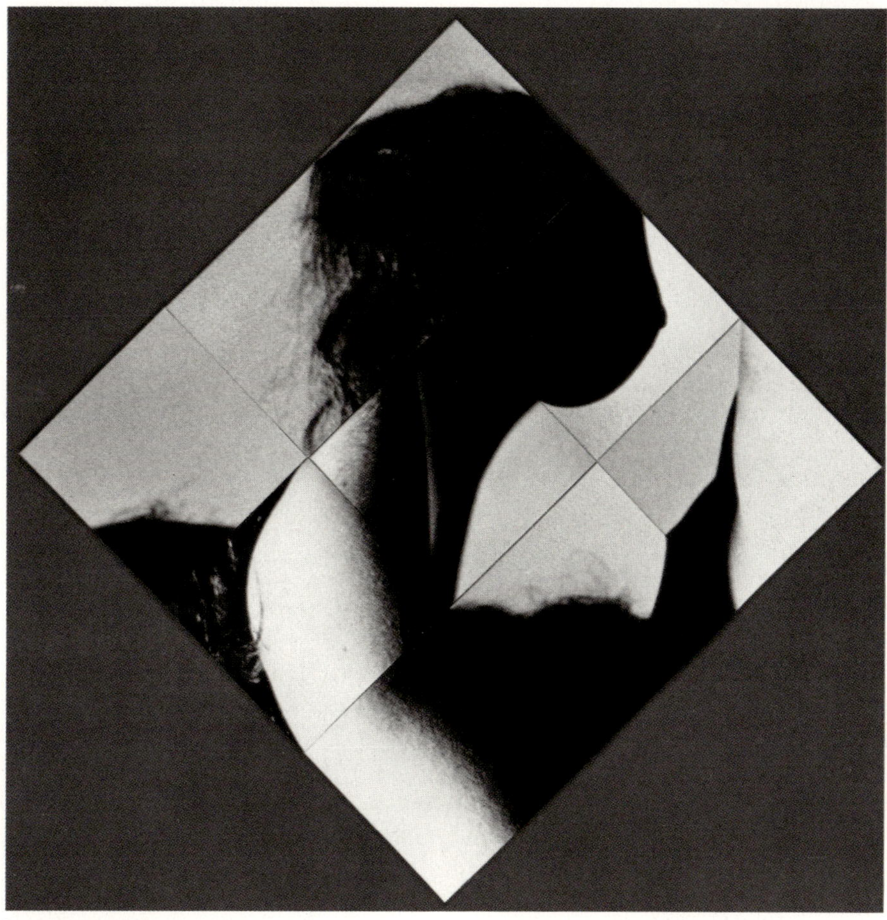

Breast Bomb, 1967

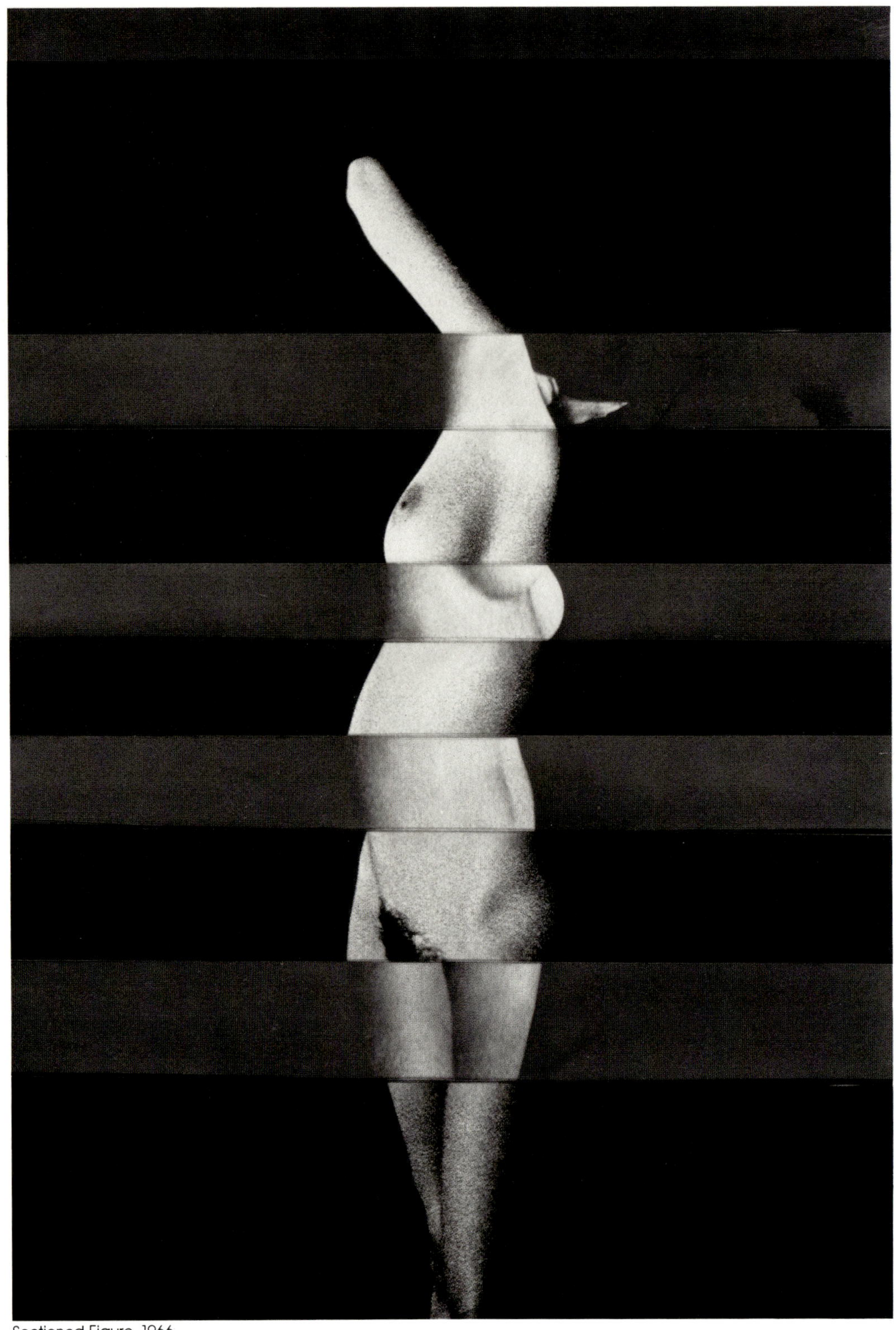

Sectioned Figure, 1966

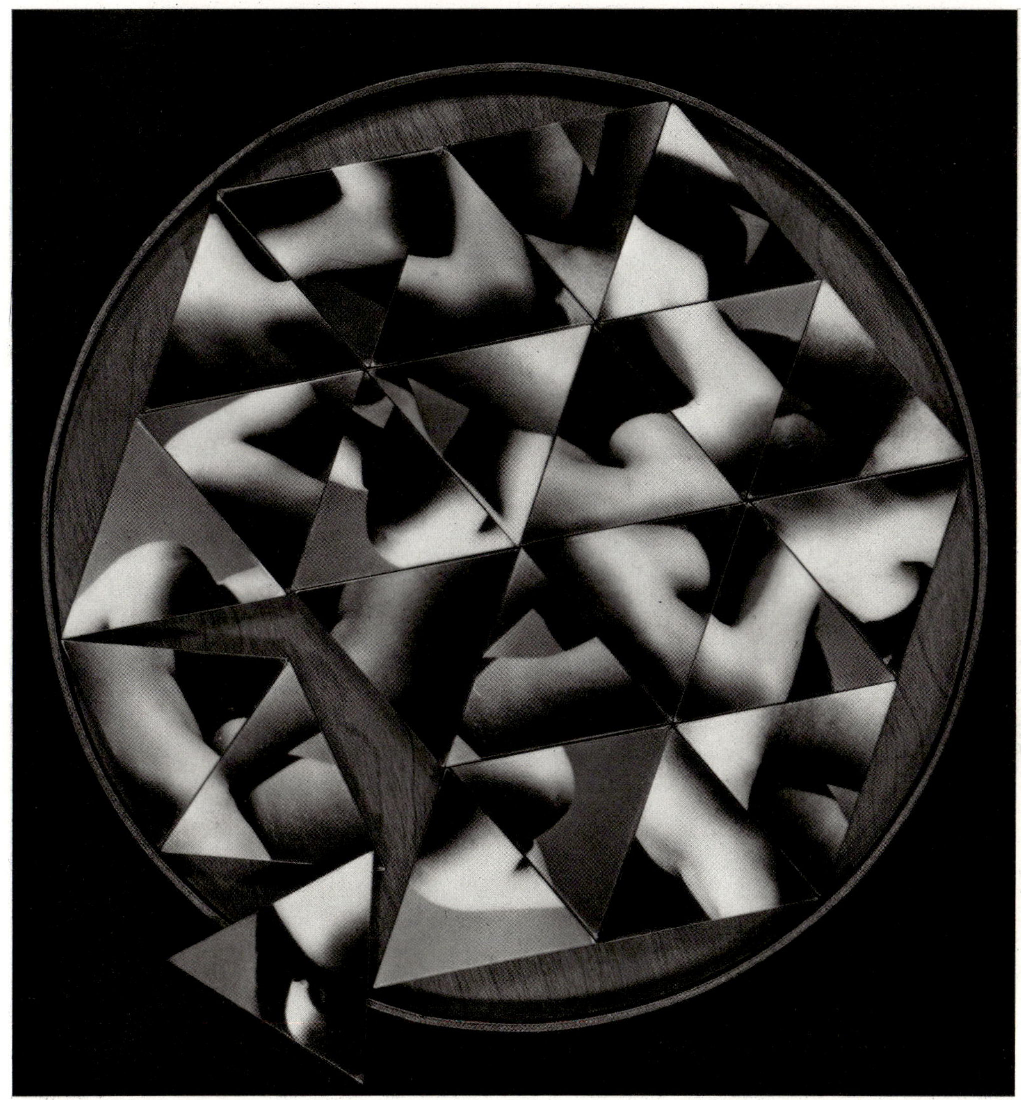

Refractive Hexagon, 1965

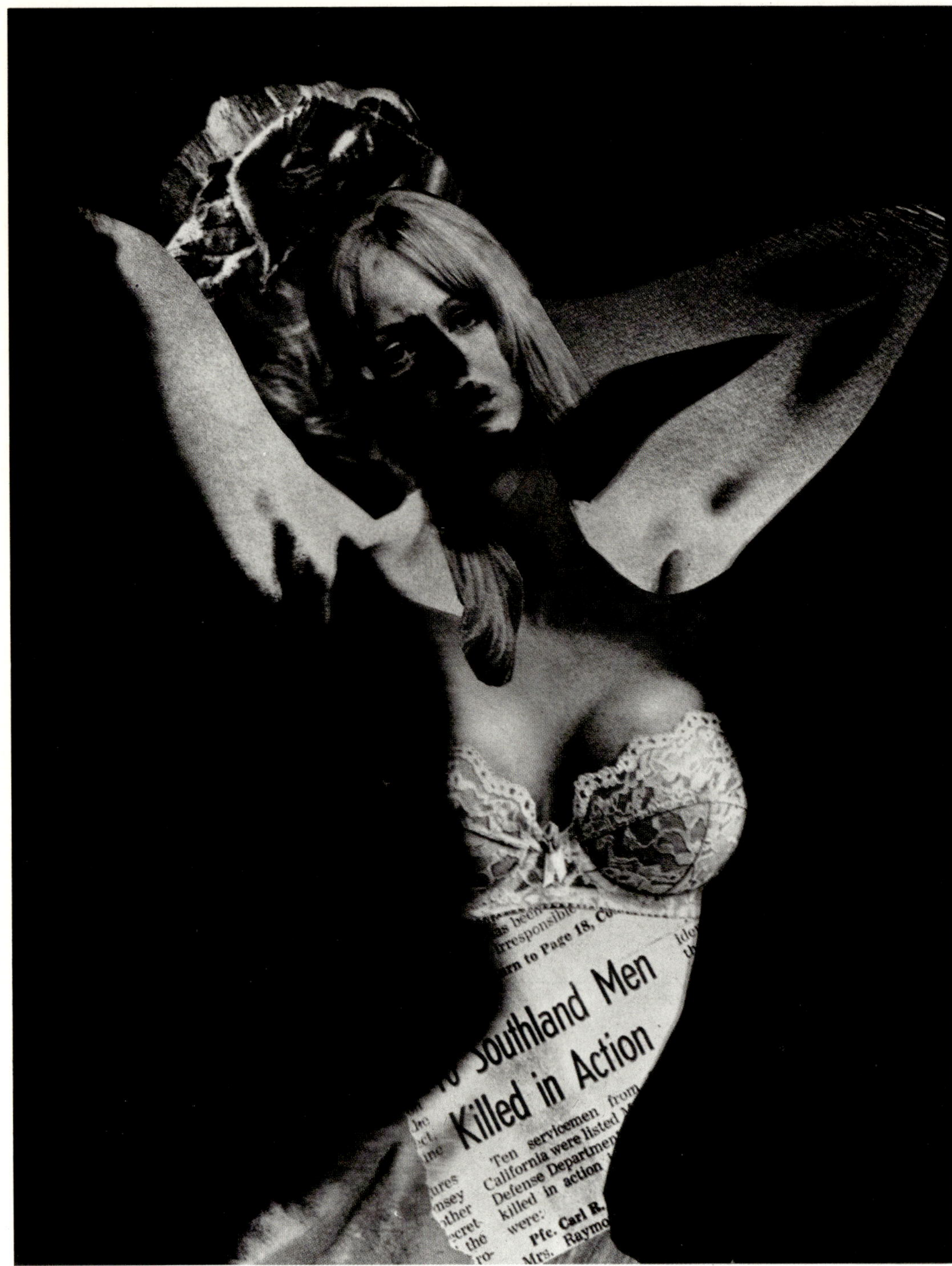

V. N. Pin Up, 1968

ROBERT HEINECKEN

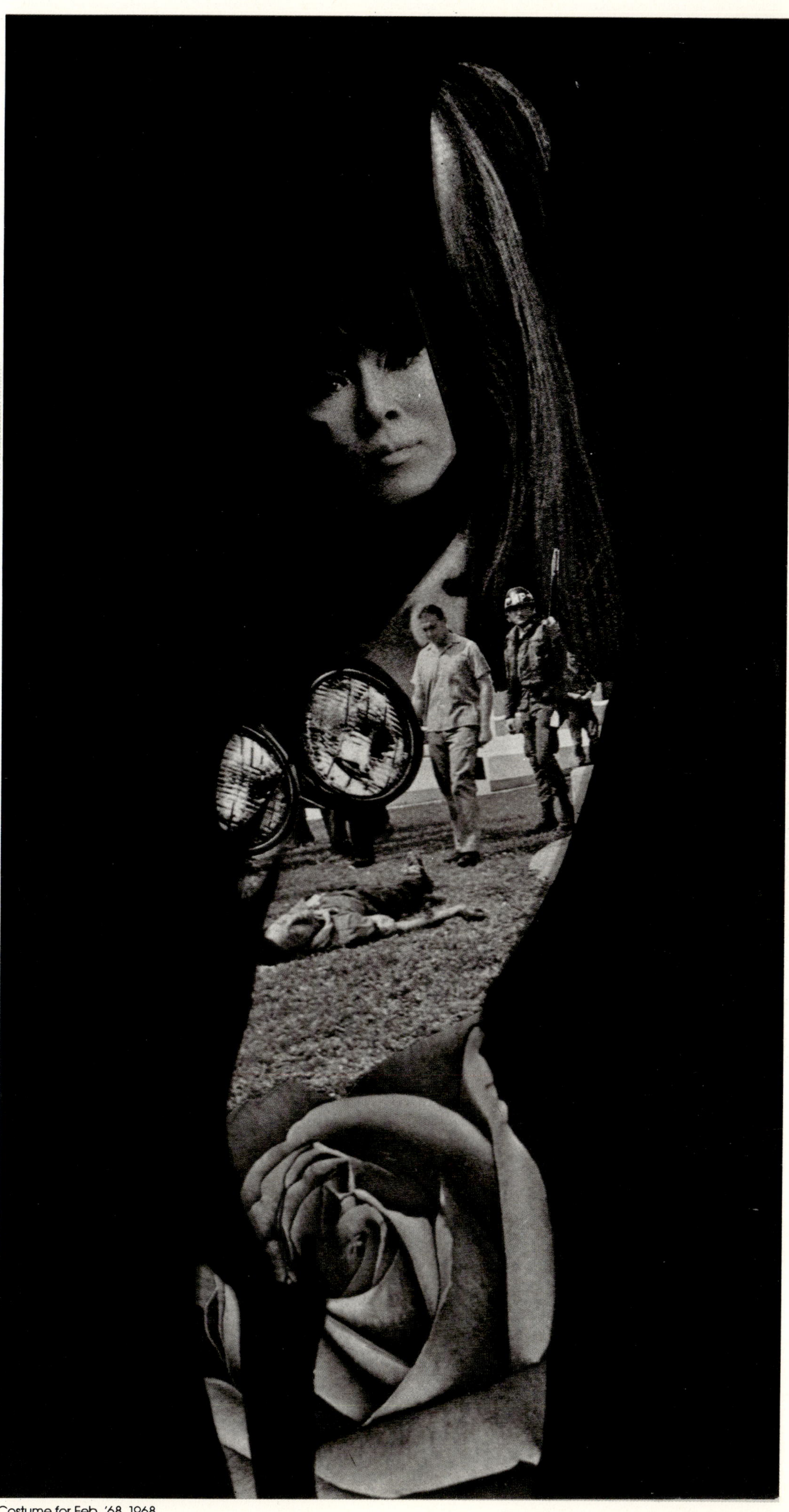

Costume for Feb. '68, 1968

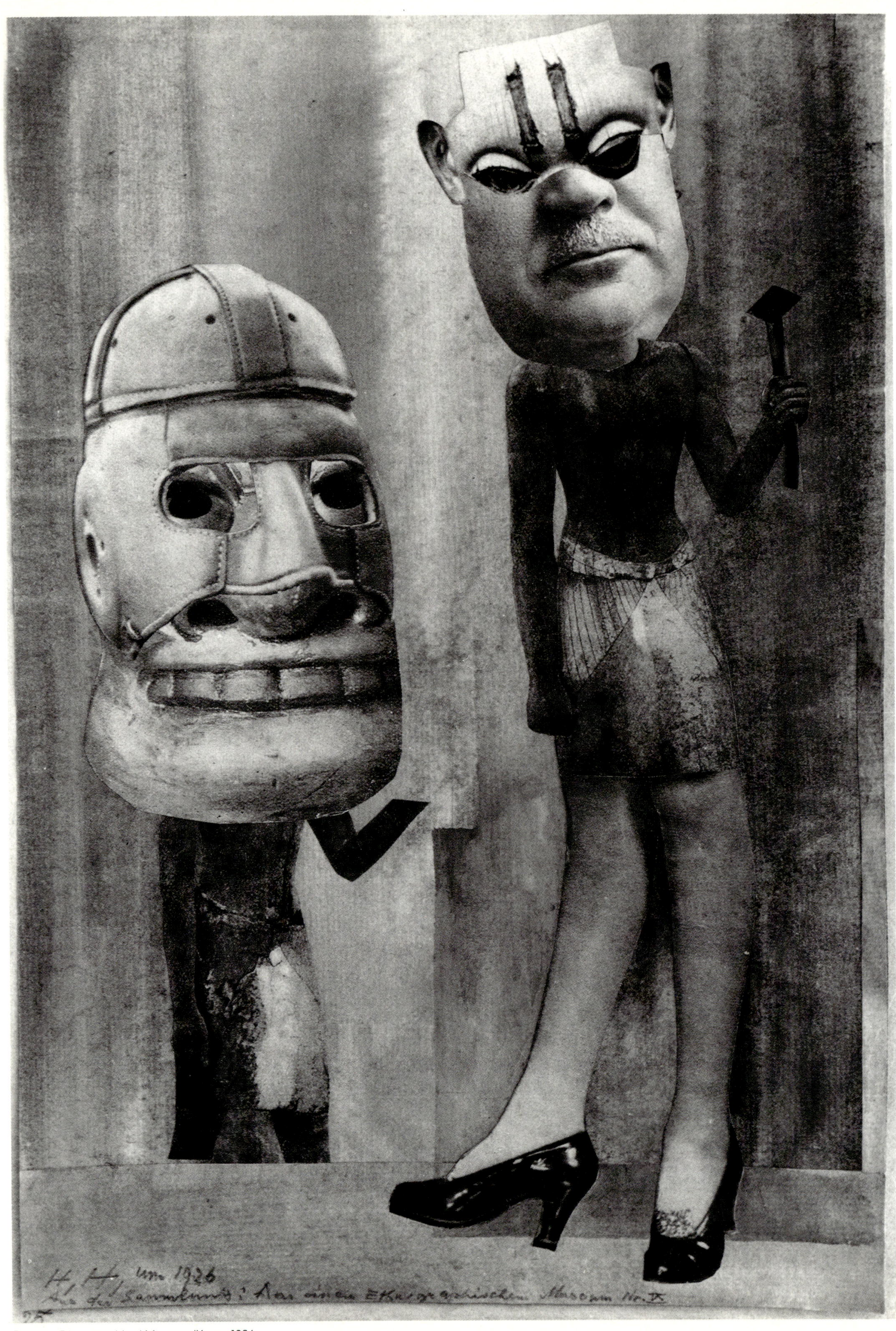

From an Ethnographical Museum IX, ca. 1926

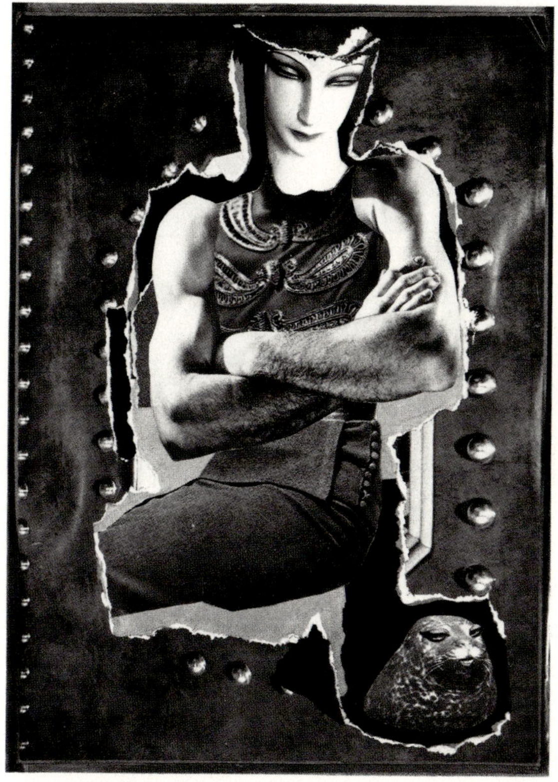

Die Dompteuse (The Animal Trainer), ca. 1930

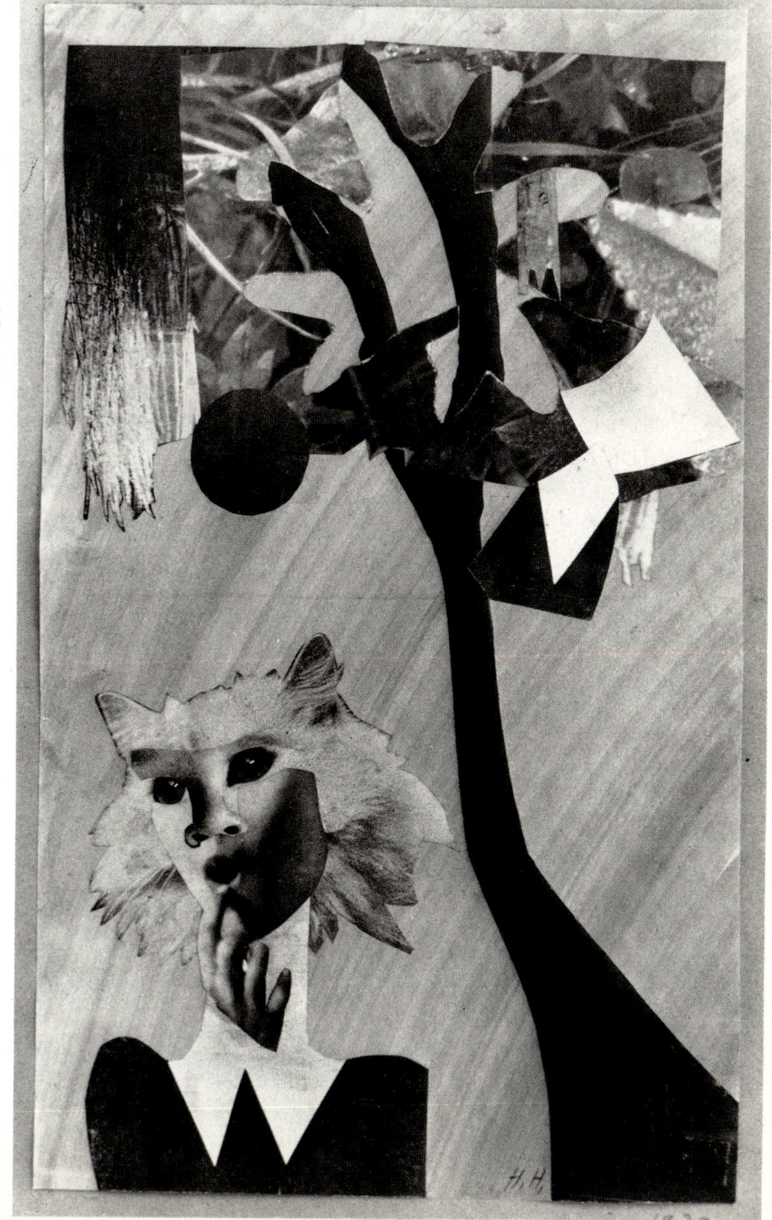

Ohhh, 1925

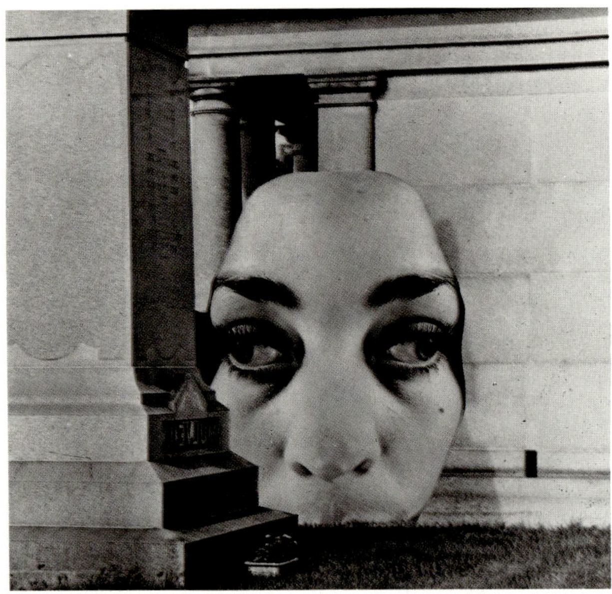

LIEVLUM, 1968

BIBLIOGRAPHY

Alvarez Bravo, Manuel. Manuel Alvarez Bravo. Pasadena, Pasadena Art Museum, 1971.
__________. Photographs 1928 – 1968. Mexico City, Comité Organizador de los Juegos de la XIX Olimpiada, 1968.
Arbus, Diane. Diane Arbus. Millerton, N.Y., Aperture, 1972.
Bearden, Romare. The Art of Romare Bearden: The Prevalence of Ritual. New York, Harry N. Abrams, 1972.
Berman, Miecyzslaw. Photomontages. Milan, Galeria Arturo Schwarz, 1973.
Brandt, Bill. Perspective of Nudes. New York, Amphoto, 1961.
__________. Shadow of Light. New York, Viking Press, 1966.
Brassaï. Transmutations. Paris, Galerie les Contards, 1967.
Delford Brown, Robert. First-Class Portraits. New York, First National Church of the Exquisite Panic Press, 1973.
__________. Hanging. New York, First National Church of the Exquisite Panic Press, 1967.
Dutton, Allen. The Great Stone Tit. Tempe, Ariz., Richard Dixon, 1974.
Gatewood, Charles, Sidetripping. New York, Derbibooks, 1975.
__________. with Spider Webb and Marco Vassi. X 1000. New York, R. Mutt Fine Art Publishers, 1977.
Gowin, Emmet. Photographs. New York, Alfred A. Knopf, 1976.
Heartfield, John. Leben und Werk. Dresden, Veb Verlag der Kunst, 1971.
Heinecken, Robert. Are You Rea, 1964 – 1968. Los Angeles, Privately published limited edition of 500, 1968.
Hosoe, Eikoh. Kamaitachi: A Tragic Comedy. Tokyo, Gendaishichosha, 1969.
__________. Ordeal by Roses. Tokyo, Shueisha, 1971.
Hujar, Peter. Portraits in Life and Death. New York, Da Capo Press, 1976.
Kertesz, André. Distortions. New York, Alfred A. Knopf, 1976.
Kirstel, Richard. Extended Reality. Baltimore, University of Maryland Baltimore County Library, 1976.
Krims, Leslie. The Deerslayers. Buffalo, Humpy Press, 1972.
__________. Fictcryptkrimsographs. Buffalo, Humpy Press, 1972.
__________. The Incredible Case of the Stack O' Wheats Murders. Buffalo, Humpy Press, 1972.
__________. The Little People of America. Buffalo. Humpy Press, 1972.
Kriz, Vilem. Sirague City. Berkeley, David McPhail, 1975.
Laughlin, Clarence John. Ghosts Along the Mississippi. New York, Scribner's, 1948.
__________. The Personal Eye. Millerton, N.Y., Aperture, 1975.
Martone, Michael. Dark Light. New York, Lustrum Press, 1973.
Meatyard, Ralph Eugene. The Family Album of Lucybelle Crater. Millerton, N.Y., Jargon Society, 1974.
__________. Ralph Eugene Meatyard. Lexington, Ky., Gnomon Press, 1970.
__________. Ralph Eugene Meatyard. Millerton, N.Y., Aperture, 1974.
Michals, Duane. Real Dreams. Danbury, Conn., Addison House, 1976.
__________. Sequences. Garden City, N.Y., Doubleday, 1970.
__________. Take One and See Mt. Fujiyama and Other Stories. New York, Stefan Mihal, 1976.
Mortensen, William. Monsters and Madonnas. San Francisco, Camera Craft Publishing Company, 1936.
Samaras, Lucas. Photo-Transformations. New York, E. P. Dutton, 1975.
__________. Samaras Album. New York, Whitney/Pace, 1971.
Sommer, Frederick. Portfolio: aperture, vol. 9, no. 3, 1961.
__________. Frederick Sommer; 1939–1962 Photographs. New York, Aperture, 1963.
Tress, Arthur. The Dream Collector. Richmond, Va., Westover Publishing, 1972.
__________. Shadow. New York, Avon Books, 1975.
__________. Theater of the Mind. Dobbs Ferry, N.Y., Morgan & Morgan, 1976.
Uelsmann, Jerry N. Jerry N. Uelsmann. Millerton, N.Y., Aperture, 1973.
__________. Silver Meditations. Dobbs Ferry, N.Y., Morgan & Morgan, 1976.
Waldman, Max. Waldman on Theater. Garden City, N.Y., Doubleday, 1971.
Walker, Todd. For Nothing Changes. Gainesville, Fla., Privately published, 1976.
__________. Portfolio Three. Privately published, 1969.
Weegee (Arthur Fellig). Naked City. New York, Essential Books, 1945.
__________. Weegee's Creative Camera. New York, Vista Books, 1959.
Weston, Edward. Edward Weston: Fifty Years, text by Ben Maddow. Millerton, N.Y., Aperture, 1973.

ON THE GROTESQUE
Kayser, Wolfgang. The Grotesque in Art and Literature, translated by Ulrich Weisstein. New York, McGraw-Hill/Indiana University Press, 1966.
Parton, James. Caricature and Other Comic Art in All Times and Many Lands. New York, Harper & Brothers, 1878.
Wright, Thomas. A History of Caricature and Grotesque in Literature and Art. London, 1865; reprinted New York, Frederick Ungar, 1968.